Library of
Davidson College

VOID

Landscape and Power in Vienna

Landscape and Power in Vienna

Robert Rotenberg

The Johns Hopkins University Press
Baltimore and London

Published in cooperation with the
Center for American Places,
Harrisonburg, Virginia

© 1995 The Johns Hopkins University Press
All rights reserved. Published 1995
Printed in the United States of America on acid-free paper
04 03 02 01 00 99 98 97 96 95   5 4 3 2 1

Design: Christine Taylor
Composition: Wilsted & Taylor Publishing Services

The Johns Hopkins University Press
2715 North Charles Street
Baltimore, Maryland 21218-4319
The Johns Hopkins Press Ltd., London

Library of Congress Cataloging-in-Publication Data
will be found at the end of this book.

A catalog record for this book is available from the British Library.

ISBN 0-8018-4961-6

For Ariela

Contents

List of Illustrations ix
Preface and Acknowledgments xi
Notes on the Text xvii
INTRODUCTION ❧ The Cultural Meaning of Landscape *1*
1 ❧ The Making of the Viennese Landscape *23*
2 ❧ Gardens of Order *47*
3 ❧ Gardens of Liberty *66*
4 ❧ Gardens of Domesticity *88*
5 ❧ Gardens of Pleasure *111*
6 ❧ Gardens of Reform *148*
7 ❧ Gardens of Reaction *188*
8 ❧ Gardens of Refuge *218*
9 ❧ Gardens of Renewal *249*
10 ❧ Gardens of Discovery *289*
CONCLUSION ❧ Landscape and Metropolitan Knowledge *316*
Notes 327
References 363
Permissions 377
Index 379

List of Illustrations

FIGURES

1. Changes in the Viennese city boundaries, 1850–1954 *40*
2. Neugebäude Palace of Maximilian I (1649) *52*
3. Garden of the Belvedere Palace as seen from one of the palace windows *54*
4. Prince's side garden of the Schönbrunn Summer Palace of Maria Theresa (1705–1706) *56*
5. Detail from the Josephinische Landesaufnahme (1773–1781) *59*
6. "Plan of Vienna," showing a portion of the Wieden district, by Josef Nagel (1770–1771) *61*
7. Plan of the estate of the Russian ambassador Rasumofsky, by Konrad Rosenthal *76*
8. Pötzleinsdorfer Park as it stood in 1850, ground plan by J. V. Reim *77*
9. Gesselschafts-Platz, by Josef Gurk *97*
10. Kleines Parterre, by Josef Gurk *98*
11. Ansicht des Thurms, by Josef Gurk *99*

List of Illustrations

x

12. Flora Parthie, by Josef Gurk *100*
13. Neo-romantic villas at the end of the nineteenth century, ground plans by Hampel (1902) *119*
14. Peacocks Island (Pfaueninsel) at the Sanssouci Palace in Potsdam, plan by Lenné (1829) *121*
15. Map of Vienna showing the fortifications and the Glacis as they were in 1857 *132*
16. Central city of Vienna after redevelopment (1887) *134*
17. Plan of the Stadtpark in 1905 *136*
18. Ground plan of the Zentralfriedhof (1905) *143*
19. Design for a Jugendstil garden *160*
20. Plan of the Türkanschanzpark (1905) *177*
21. Blick von Gipfel, or view from the summit *200*
22. Expansion of the metropolitan area in the 1920s *207*
23. First Schrebergarten in the Viennese region *213*
24. Squatter cabin, Wienerwald (1919) *220*
25. Classic Nutzgarten (1988) *226*
26. Streetscape of Rosenhügel in the 1930s *242*
27. Lawn of a Viennese bungalow row *254*
28. Garden designed for Roland Weber, by Harbers *264*
29. Allinger's design for a house garden in the Ruhr district (1953) *265*
30. Distribution of household incomes (1974) *274*
31. Initial costs for alternate forms of gardens, as a percentage of total income (1980) *275*
32. Wildgarten *295*
33. Biotop *313*

MAPS

1. District boundaries of the city of Vienna *24*
2. Baroque landscapes of the early eighteenth century *58*
3. Romantic parkscapes of the late eighteenth century *80*
4. Biedermeier gardens of the early nineteenth century *105*
5. Neo-romantic gardens of the mid nineteenth century *127*
6. Reform landscapes of the late nineteenth century and the Wald und Wiesengürtel *175*
7. Small garden development through the twentieth century *267*

Preface and Acknowledgments

This book is the second in a series of metropolitan ethnographies to focus on the experience of the Viennese. Metropolitan ethnography documents how conditions found only in very large cities affect the lives of people who live there. The goal of this work is to show that metropolitans share ideas about landscape, and through landscape, ideas about the relationship between citizen and metropolis. This sharing comes about in spite of the lack of opportunity for frequent face-to-face interaction or formal teaching. It does so because landscape itself is a language communicable to large numbers of people if they have been socialized to receive its messages. People learn the meanings of landscape in a city from long exposure to the contrasts within it. In this work I hope to convey to non-Viennese what it is that only the Viennese understand about their landscape.

A conversation I had with Andrew Lass in the mid 1970s kindled my original interest in looking at gardens as critical systems of cultural knowledge. I was fortunate in having two DePaul colleagues in art history, Sally Chappell Kitt and Simone Zurawski, who encouraged me to cross disciplinary boundaries to solve this particular puzzle. In the context of leading a student study tour of the city in De-

Preface and Acknowledgments

cember 1986, we three had the opportunity to discuss the features of the landscape while we stood in some of the gardens I will present here. Their enthusiasm for the perspective I was developing on these gardens kept me working in the early stages.

This research was made possible initially by a four-month paid research leave and a substantial grant-in-aid from DePaul University in 1988. In 1990 I was supported by a Fulbright Research Fellowship for Austria, an Austrian Ministry of Science and Technology Visiting Professor Fellowship, and a second grant-in-aid from the DePaul Faculty Research Council.

Ethnographers are only as effective as the network of people they come to know in the communities they study. After almost twenty years of research in Vienna, I have come to know a lot of people, all of whom contributed to this work in some way. Here I have space to thank only a few. When I began this project in 1985, I did not know many people with gardens. Without the help of the following individuals I never could have developed this book. Doris Langeder put me in touch with three networks of people who proved to be especially helpful in the research. One of them was instrumental in bringing me to the Gemeinnütziger Siedlungs-Genossenschaft Altmannsdorf und Hetzendorf and its friendly members. Doris believed in the project from the beginning, and I am very grateful for her assistance. Paul Asenbaum was also an early supporter of my research. Through his acquaintances among the city's architects, historians, and curators I gained much valuable information. Maria Auböck is not only the author of a path-blazing work on the history of the Viennese landscape, she was also an unselfish supporter of this research. Knowing the terrain as well as she does, she gave me highly detailed maps of the institutions I would have to see and lists of the people to meet in order to proceed successfully. Especially important was the introduction she provided for me to Ralph Gälzer, the director of the Institute for Regional Planning and Garden Design at the Technical University of Vienna. This generous man granted me access to what may be the best library on garden design and garden history in German in the world. He also gave me the invaluable opportunity of teaching his students. In this seminar on the history of the Viennese domestic garden in the twentieth century, I was able to develop much of the analytical framework for the second half of this work. Having benefited from a Fulbright to Harvard himself early in his career, Professor Gälzer knew the importance of this experience for me and made it possible for me to work at peak efficiency. I will always be grateful for his hospitality. In the institute, I also had a chance to try out my ideas on two of his assistants; Brigitta Mang was always a willing interlocutor and friend, and Eva Berger provided me with the rare expertise of an accomplished historian of Austrian landscape. She could be counted on to tell me when I was finally at the edge of what was known and what was unknown.

Long-distance research is possible only with the help of people who are willing to run errands, make connections, and help prepare the way for a research visit. Chief among my collaborators in these regards was my recently deceased father-in-law, Hans Zalud. He placed the phone calls, found the government publications, mailed the maps and books, and otherwise maintained my research effort while I taught in Chicago. Heinz Tomek and Eva Gründl found me an apartment, lent the hands of friends, asked the hard questions, and introduced me to their knowledgeable colleagues. I am grateful for the support of Heinz Altschul in all of those things, small and large, which friends do for each other. Suzana Bock helped with translations, including the text of a talk I gave at the institute, and helped me understand the metaphorical extensions of the phrases I was hearing. Wolfgang Bock helped me make informative contacts at Steinhof. I thank Thea Scholl, Maria Ferber, Walter and Karen Czerny, Martin Engelberg, and Robert and Suzanne Schwartz for acquainting me with their respective circles of friends and relations.

I am very thankful for the collegial manner in which I was received in all of the offices of the Viennese government and especially by the planners in Magistratsabteilung 22. Even offhand remarks by these people became important clues for me to track. At important moments in developing this research, I had conversations with two of Vienna's most accomplished architects, Roland Rainer and Margaret Schütte-Lihotsky, who redirected my efforts at critical junctures. In 1988 I was very fortunate in having the active assistance of Erich König, then president of the Gemeinnütziger Siedlungs-Genossenschaft Altmannsdorf und Hetzendorf, and the headmen of the cooperative's settlements: Otto Göd of Hoffingergasse, Franz Kolbinger of Rosenhügel and Künstlersiedlung, Peter Havilcek of Glanzing, and Rudolph Roder of Lainz-Speising. Their hospitality and openness to discuss their own gardens were most valuable to me.

Preface and Acknowledgments

In the final stages of the research, I acknowledge gratefully the assistance of Ruth Wodak, the director of the Institute for Applied Linguistics, for help in assessing the quality of the interview data, and Rainer Prandtstetten, of the Federal Monuments Office, for advice in preparing the illustrations. I am also grateful for the support of Johann Marte, general director of the Austrian National Library, and the assistance of Edwin Hofbauer of the library's picture and portrait collection.

Anyone tackling a cross-disciplinary problem in a foreign language must depend on the work of native scholars. I was very lucky to have colleagues involved in Central European landscape history before I arrived, whose works were of seminal insight and quality: Peter Althöfer on the Biedermeier; Dieter Hennebo on almost every aspect of the Central European landscape; Friedrich Fischer on the Viennese landscape before 1914; Kurt Mollik, Hermann Reining, and Rudolf Wurzer on the Ringstrasse landscape; Wilfried Posch on the Viennese experience with the garden city movement; Gert Gröning and Joachim Wolschke-Bulmahn on the origins of the Landespflege movement and gardens of reaction; Géza Hajós on Enlightenment gardens; and Maria Auböck on Viennese garden history. Hopefully, as a result of the discussion of their work here, they will become better known to Anglophone garden historians.

This work also benefited from conversations with colleagues in the United States. At DePaul University, Charles Suchar encouraged my efforts at documentary photography. During two marathon sessions in his basement darkroom, he and I produced the prints for this book. Larry Bennett and Fassil Demissie read drafts of chapters and made helpful suggestions. Fassil put into my hands the Foucault essay that frames the work. Larry and I had the chance to discuss the Viennese landscape together in Vienna in 1991. I am grateful to James Block for productive discussions of European culture and history and to various classes of students over the past few years who have listened to these ideas and posed those simple queries that I struggled to answer. I will always be grateful to Richard Meister and Michael Mezey for extending the support of the College of Liberal Arts and Sciences when it mattered most.

While I was writing this book I was fortunate to be part of an international network of anthropologists concerned about issues of space and place. Through their prodding I wrote papers and published articles that enabled me to try out the analysis of some parts of the work. One could not ask for a more supportive group of colleagues, and I am grateful to each of them: Gary McDonogh, Setha Low, Margaret Rodman, Matthew Cooper, Denise Lawrence, Tim Sieber, Deborah Pellow, and Ted Bestor. Constance de Roche served as my chief skeptic on the validity of the metropolitan knowledge concept and in doing so has forced me to develop ever more precise ways of describing it. Ellen Pader and Patricia Gibson read early versions of the chapters. Senior colleagues encouraged me and kept me going on this project in spite of my teaching and administrative commitments. I especially want to thank Eric Wolf for Wildgans's poetry, Jack Goody for the culture of flowers, and James Fernandez for reading the manuscript.

This work involved the technical assistance of well-placed specialists. Jola Zalud checked my translations. Frau Landwehr and her crew did careful and patient transcriptions of the one hundred hours of taped interviews. Digitek Engineering in Columbus, Ohio, scanned the location maps. Don Dewey at DePaul helped me learn the map program and figured out how to match the dots file to the program. Without his help, the maps would never have been drawn.

Sonja Rotenberg lived this project with me, packing up and moving into strange Viennese apartments on three occasions, taking up the slack with housekeeping chores and parenting responsibilities as research and writing took up so much of our household time. This work simply would not exist without her belief in and support of me. The person who paid the greatest price for this effort is my daughter, Ariela, who spent the first five years of her life sharing her father with a word processor. It is more than fitting that this work be dedicated to her.

Notes on the Text

Because this work is concerned with the language of gardens, there is a substantial amount of standard German and Viennese dialect in the text. When German terms are used in the plural, they are written as German plurals. If they are subjects of verbs in English, those English verbs agree with the German subject in number. All other applicable case endings (genative, dative, etc.) have been dropped. In German, substantives are capitalized; adjectivals are not. Only the first use of the German word is italicized. The Viennese dialect has been written with standard German vowels. In general, German umlauts have been retained. The only exception is the maps, where the alternate spellings *ae*, *oe*, and *ue* were the only options available.

Citations in Viennese dialect often contain spellings and grammatical constructions that deviate from standard German. These citations were transcribed by native Viennese professional transcribers and reflect the transcriber's best approximation of the correct rendering of the speech in literary form. Question marks in parentheses indicate that the the transcriber could not guarantee the accuracy of the transcription because of garbled or unrecognizable speech. I have

Notes on the Text

tried to use as few of these passages as possible. Transcribed speech is often difficult to read because of pauses, repairs, and the absence of voice tone. All translations are my own. In translating the more difficult passages, I ignored the imperfections in the actual utterances and translated the sense of the person's remarks.

Landscape

and

Power

in

Vienna

INTRODUCTION

The Cultural Meaning of Landscape

During the 1974–75 academic year, the Leopoldstadt district office of the Vienna metropolitan school system held an essay contest for elementary school pupils. The theme of the contest was the meaning of green space in the city. Up until then, children had not been allowed to play on any of the lawns in this particular district. To publicize the change in policy, the district commissioner organized an essay contest. He hoped that writing about the meaning of green space would fix in young people's minds the importance of treating collective property responsibly in exchange for the health and recreational benefits they would derive from playing there. More than three thousand students took part in the contest. The district council published the results in a small booklet, which I came across in the Austrian National Library. As I read through the essays that the jury considered worthy of first prizes in the different grades I began to understand the high regard shared among the Viennese for metropolitan park space. Here is one of the twelve winning essays.

> Vienna, one of the largest metropolises in the world, always attracts more visitors. They do not look only at the city with its worthwhile sites, but

A whole history remains to be written of spaces—*which would at the same time be the history of* powers—*from the great strategies of geopolitics to the little tactics of the habitat.*
Michel Foucault, 1980

Landscape and Power in Vienna

♪

2

they also visit the public gardens, parks, and green spaces, which is probably why the city administration regards the parks as such a meaningful resource. Green spaces are not only the breathing organs of the city, they also help the metropolitans to discover nature within the city. One accuses the cities of having single-handedly driven out nature. For that reason, we humans should think about and teach about the protection of nature from all of its enemies. That is why city folks try to retrieve nature in all of its variety within the city. One sees this in the front yard, backyard, and courtyard gardens, the green spaces, the parks, and the recreation centers.

The green space takes care of the ridding of poisons from the atmosphere as well as watering the soil. Vienna possesses beautiful green spaces in numbers like no other metropolis in the world. This provides a good example of how a city like Vienna need not stand outside nature. (Student Hoffinger, fourth year, Karl Marx Hauptschule; cited in Ernst 1975:7)

Many of the other essays took a similar point of view but were less extensive in the number of topics they raised. This fifteen-year-old author managed to pack into her hundred-word essay two hundred years of thought on the relationship between nature and culture in the city. What made it a prize-winning essay was that it touched all of the issues that the Viennese consider fundamental in their understanding of green space. These are the features that permit them to identify what it is about green space that is extraordinary, separating it from the places of ordinary urban life.

What I find compelling in this essay is the symbolic richness of the landscape language contained in it. The student defined the elements through which the Viennese recognize their position among other metropolises in the world, identified green space as public resource, and recognized the opposition of nature and city, describing a power relationship between the two which favors the city. She discovered a moral responsibility for custodianship through this relationship, named the specific formal devices through which this custodianship is enacted, and described a reciprocal benefit that justifies the custodianship. Her argument went on to use phrases that are meaningful to urbanized Central Europeans and, in two cases, specifically to the Viennese. In reading the essay, non-Viennese tend to miss many of the important points. This is not a question of effective translation. There are expressions in the essay which are landscape clichés.

One must hear them in context throughout a lifetime to understand how much of a specifically Viennese experience is contained in this short passage. If this were an Alpine village of four hundred people, we would not even pause at the remarkable degree of shared meaning that these verbal formulas carry. This, however, is a metropolis of more than 1.2 million people. In the district of Leopoldstadt, where the student went to school, the population was more than 106,000 people, with more than ten thousand school-aged children, most of whom had been born in that district (Magistratsabteilung 66 1980:22–23). The judges of the essays may have come from any of the twenty-three districts of Vienna. How then was such a coincidence of values possible between the students and the judges? How did the judges know a prize-winning essay when they read one?

These questions are part of a larger problem that goes to the heart of reasoned inquiry into the urban experience. Is there an integration of cultural experience within large urban populations, and, if so, what are its dynamics? For convenience, I will refer to this as the problem of metropolitan knowledge, the understandings of life which people gain only through life experiences in cities. Another way of thinking about this is to see the urban experience as a life-defining one. What difference does it make in people's lives that they live in large and dense settlements rather than somewhere else? Participation in ongoing explorations of meaning, such as the one described here for landscape, or ongoing searches for strategies to cope with institutional demands, such as I described in another study of Vienna (Rotenberg 1992b), are the areas in which the overlap in the experience of metropolitans is the clearest. This overlap in experience permits me to describe what understandings the Viennese share with one another. A careful and detailed reading of the unfolding of the experiences that generate these understandings yields the processes through which this knowledge forms, the channels through which it becomes distributed through the population, the impetus for including it in the socialization of children, and its appeal as a defining feature of Viennese identity.

DISCOURSE AND CULTURE

Because space enters all considerations of meaning, like time, identity, and event, it becomes a dominating site of symbolic production

Landscape and Power in Vienna

4

(Sahlins 1976:211). The forms that people impose upon their environment represent their social selves. Because they can build on a monumental scale, institutional leaders produce elaborate and complete representations of their vision of the metropolis. As groups of institutional leaders succeed each other in power, they appropriate a specific set of public landscape design possibilities to represent their vision. The previous group's forms continue to exist along with the new landscapes. The newer forms borrow design ideas from the old, sometimes in polite emulation of them, sometimes to invert and transform them. To accomplish this, designers and institutional patrons must develop a common language of design. This language connects the landscape forms with the vision of metropolitan life which the landscape will represent. There are as many voices of design as there are visions of what urban life can be, and together these voices produce an enduring conversation through which the metropolis is represented by its public landscape. I refer to this conversation as the discourse on landscape.

As people learn about the places of their metropolis, they discover an understanding of these forms. Specific public gardens visited and experienced in childhood stand for the period in which a particular metropolitan vision dominated public investment. Almost every Viennese I talked to identified a particular garden, the Belvedere, as the icon of the class of ornamental gardens associated with the noble garden palaces of the Absolutist Era (1683–1848). In this era, a few noble families held complete power over civic affairs in the city. Bureaucratic involvement in private lives increased. The authorities promulgated rules for all kinds of public behavior. Even though this political culture lost its hold on civic affairs more than a century ago, almost every person I spoke with in the mid 1980s defined that garden by its rules—a park in which one could not walk on the grass. Other public places were defined by different possibilities for behavior, some of which were more permissive. Few were more restrictive. Knowing the Viennese landscape means knowing what each public place permits. In this way, the metropolitan landscape provides a mirror for social relations. It is the source of all evaluations of the fundamental worth and meaning of places as arenas for social interaction.

The discourse on landscape is an example of what Habermas calls the communication system of a society, the mechanism through which implicit agreement is reached on the values necessary to hold large societies together (1979). Large societies do not have recourse to the face-to-face processes of socialization and social control so often observed in families and smaller scale communities. Instead, they must rely on more indirect systems of rewarding conformity and disapproving dissent. Of particular importance in this effort are the media through which meanings of time, space, person, and event are understood.

Hannerz has written on the mechanisms that shape the distribution of knowledge in the metropolis. He cautions that the characterization of knowledge as shared is imprecise. If sharing implies that everyone knows everything that I am about to describe about landscape in Vienna, then sharing is not what I mean. Knowledge is hardly ever evenly distributed in population, even the very small ones. Some people have more opportunity to acquire it than others do, by way of license, education, inclination, practice, or chance. This is true of Viennese landscape. Much of what I learned about it came from expert gardeners and landscape architects. Nevertheless, landscape has been a primary focus of the management and meaning of what it is to be a metropolitan Viennese. As the interactions among the state, the market, the media, and the operations of everyday life unfolded to shape people's knowledge, landscape was a key locus for giving physicality to abstract notions of ideology and thereby shaping mass culture. The critical mass of metropolitan proportions in the city provided the intellectual and emotional support for the dedication of precious real estate to purely noneconomic ends. It will soon become clear that this was a contested process. Not everyone agreed that a particular park, garden district, or municipal landscape was worthwhile, appropriate, or beautiful. Because the arguments were publicly distributed through various media, not the least of which was the medium of the landscape itself, the greater numbers of citizens came to a critical understanding of landscape than might otherwise have been the case.

Landscape acquires meaning through its design elements. Should a tree be cut into a three-dimensional geometric shape or allowed to grow freely? Should a lawn be completely free of all other plants except grass, or should flowers be planted in it randomly? Should flower beds be geometrically shaped or have a more organic line? Should a garden be open to the surroundings and incorporate their features or fenced and self-contained? The selections made from these alternatives produce gardens with distinct historical resonances. The relationships among the garden elements speak about the time when a particular landscape voice was first developed, the tastes and fashions of that time, and also of the style in social interactions, political and religious attitudes, and the way status was displayed.

FORM AND FUNCTION

Here is where this work departs from standard garden history books. As Mosser and Teyssot, editors of a tome on the architecture of Western gardens, stated in their introduction, "the garden has always had two roles, and it is as inseparable from its utilitarian function as it is from its aesthetic or ideal function. The garden is an external expression of an interior world, a setting for meditation under an open sky and for the revelation of secrets to those worthy of hearing them" (1990:11). With very few exceptions,[1] the articles in the book present the paradigm for connoisseurship studies of landscape. My work diverges from that tradition by attempting to deal with the social meaning of form—that is, the way in which landscape forms constitute a system of socially recognized signs that enter into people's conversations about their understanding of nature, the city, social power, and their experiences with these realities. In this book, a garden's utilitarian and aesthetic functions are contextualized through the particular configuration of social power in Vienna at a specific time. These functions have no universal meaning. They are not a substitute for aesthetic analysis. Further on, Mosser and Teyssot declared, "Gardens, whether they are intended for ruling princes or the general public, for philosophers, scholars or poets, or as the adornment of a suburban villa, whatever the economic or social status of their owner, whatever their situation—the city or the country, an aristocratic residence or a working farm—their purpose is always the same: to provide ['a place of sanctuary in an ancient Arcady or in the Paradise inhabited by early man, a Hermitage, a haven of solitude, a setting for theater and display']" (ibid.:17). As this work will make clear, this statement could only have been made by scholars who chose not to focus on the lived experience of people with the gardens they analyze.

Landscape forms can sustain a variety of purposes, which means that no specific form best fulfills a given function. Vegetables will grow in any shaped bed. Parties can happen in settings of any historical style. Even children's playgrounds can encompass a multitude of designs, once dangerous minor elements such as water features are removed. Form follows function in garden design only when the form and function are part of a restrictive set of class-based behavior expectations.

DESIGN AND CHANGE

Changes in the design of planted space can take two forms. The first resembles paradigm shifts in scientific research. At some moment, an established way of doing things seems antiquated, and a new practice appears exciting. The shift from the old to the new augments and transforms the design principles in ways that satisfy the new conditions, but never entirely. Elements of the earlier designs are carried forward both by the people for whom those elements have never ceased to be important and by those who are looking for a new synthesis that will redefine old elements to suit new purposes. The coexistence of the ancient, the traditional, and the modern means that at all times all of the elements employed to make planted space meaningful are available for use.

An example of this sort of change is evident in the design use of the *Juniperus sabina*, known in German as the *Wachholder* and in English as the juniper.[2] Frankish culture in the Middle Ages held the *savina* [OF] to be a highly potent plant. It was the primary herb used in abortions. Through metaphoric extension, people came to believe that the plant had ritual powers to mediate between life and death (Fuchs 1909:228). At funerals the branches were burned to honor the dead (Schweizer 1956:70). The smoke of burning juniper was also believed to ward off the spirits of the dead in the late autumn rituals (Marzell 1951:6, 19). People felt secure when they had juniper bushes around their house. In its early history in Germanic Europe, Christianity appropriated the juniper as a symbolic mediator, and it became the branch of choice to be burned on Palm Sunday. Because of its superficial resemblance to the juniper, the yew tree was sometimes substituted for it. In the medieval cloister garden of the monastery of St. Gall, a juniper bush grew in the center of the crossed paths, the *axis mundi* through which heaven and earth connected (Hennebo 1962:32). Thus, in the most important garden of a monastery designed to reflect St. Augustine's City of God, the point at which this world and the next met was marked by a bush whose symbolic resonances belonged to the pagan past.

The later history of the juniper bush is better known among garden historians. In the courtly gardens of Renaissance palaces north of the Alps, the juniper was the foliage connecting the statuary and architecture of the garden to the ground. A century or two later, in the age of absolutism, the juniper's wild growth was checked and cut into topiary shapes, which made it part of the garden architecture. Enlightenment gardeners had little use for the plant, since by then it had become so firmly associated with human design that it had no place in a garden supposedly fashioned by the hands of nature. In the domestic gardens of the early nineteenth century, the bush neatly filled the corners of the band of shrubbery that bounded the garden and provided greater intimacy and privacy. In the second half of the century, the use of the shrub as a connector between architecture and ground was rediscovered. By the mid twentieth century, gardeners again esteemed the decorative value of the plant and used it to surround houses; it thereby served the same function that it had two thousand years previously.

The juniper is just one plant traced through some of the shifts in its social meaning. Every other plant, every ground plan, every water element has a history of similar depth and complexity, and as the meaning of an element is augmented and transformed, it still retains something of its early usages. Do the owners of a ranch house in a suburban subdivision of southern California know that the junipers surrounding their front door were originally placed there to ward off evil spirits? Probably not, but what is knowable about the juniper without having to study its history is that it is commonly used around houses, that visually it helps to connect the house to its ground, and that the berries are inedible. Each of these offers some echo of the earlier meanings of the juniper. We can know these things because those pieces of information are part of our experience with the plant. The social meaning of the plant follows it across the generations. The meanings of the various plants therefore contribute to the meaning of the places in which the plants are appropriate. We only seem to be free to use the juniper within the range provided by these meanings.

DESIGN AND POWER

A second factor influencing the design regime for planted space is the conflict engendered by competing power centers. Groups choose icons of landscape designs for themselves which are juxtaposed to those of their rivals to concretize more fully the oppositional, irreconcilable nature of the competition. As these groups win control over municipal resources, they impose their landscape iconography on public space, distorting the slow, paradigmatic shifts we discovered for the juniper bush. One sign that this more rapid, oppositional change is at work in a city is that metropolitans pay more attention to the politicized qualities of the landscape. I contend that in Vienna a heightened consensus on the value of certain elements of landscape exists because of the persistence of an unresolvable opposition between the symbols of order and the symbols of liberty. This opposition first took shape in the second half of the eighteenth century and remains the wellspring to which all proponents of new landscapes return when they forge their synthesis. The geometrically ruled elements that are identified with the symbols of order and the verdant, unrestrained growth associated with the symbols of liberty recur in different eras and under different regimes. Only by exploring the fate of these symbols through time can we begin to sort out the fundamental understandings that constitute the Viennese knowledge of landscape. That is what I will attempt to do in this book.

PRIVATE AND PUBLIC

What is debatable about this perspective is its ability to make explicit the implicit meaning of specific landscape designs. It is always difficult to fathom the actual experience of agreement and consensus. Most people rarely have the opportunity to articulate their understandings of their immediate landscape. They have even fewer opportunities to experience the building of a public consensus on a landscape design issue. For these reasons, evidence of the direct impact of discourse on public landscape actions is difficult to come by. By looking at the historical debate over various kinds of publicly accessible landscapes, we can discover the values around which consensus was built.

Agreement on value is more than the building of a workable consensus on the design of public landscapes. Conceivably, a community can be browbeaten into accepting a park that is quite alien to its values. To discover the values that do operate within people's everyday lives, we must look to where they live, to the environments they themselves control, and to the meanings they give to those environments. By exploring many different kinds of domestic gardens with their owners and by probing the language these gardeners use to describe what they experience in their gardens, we can observe whether there are common meanings to the experience or not. The private landscape becomes the repository of design ideas that people find most useful in representing their relationship to society, unmediated by public, political icons and design principles. It is in the elucidation of the meanings of this middle landscape that the ethnographer can make a useful contribution to the study of landscape design.

THE CONDUCT OF THE STUDY

The essence of good ethnography is the familiarity of the researcher with the group being studied. In that sense this project began in 1975, when I first set out to live in Vienna and discover what it meant to be a Viennese. In all, I have lived in the city for periods of weeks and months which total four years of the previous seventeen. I have lived in all but three districts of the city. My networks of acquaintances gave me access to metropolitans of almost every socioeconomic stripe. I speak, read, and understand standard German, and I can read and understand the main dialect of Vienna. Ethnographic research requires a long-term commitment of time and effort. I believe that no fieldworker, no matter how broadly experienced, could acquire sufficient awareness of the meaningful contexts of social life in a short time and generate worthwhile analyses. Contextualized understanding of the social experiences of the city is necessary. By saying this, I do not mean that only I could have done this study. I do mean that ethnography is not a data-gathering method that one can mount with the detachment and speed of other social science techniques. The virtue of ethnographic data is that they derive from the commitment of the researcher to the site. Therein lies their power as well as the reason for their rare appearance in the design research literature.

More directly, the information in this book is the product of a series of visits between 1986 and 1991 during which I researched the issue of landscape meanings through archives and libraries and through conversations with Viennese who were directly involved in the ongoing creation of landscape, as gardeners, designers, and park visitors. A short period of preliminary research in which I tried to discover how difficult it would be to get access to written materials and engage people in conversation convinced me that the project was not only doable but that it generated a surprising amount of interest among my acquaintances in the city. My strategy was to begin with the archival materials. I wanted to teach myself the language of landscape. While reading in the archives, I discovered verbal formulas that kept recurring in the texts. As I worked backward in time, I saw the contexts for these formulas change. I intended to shape a certain portion of my conversations with contemporary gardeners through a formal questionnaire in which I would specifically ask them about the relevance of certain verbal formulas to their understanding of gardens. By the time I was finished I had generated twenty phrases. In the end, some of these turned out to be far more salient than others, and I discovered two or three more in the process. These provided the formal links between my conversations with different people and in the end permitted me to specify the enduring contents of Viennese metropolitan knowledge about landscape. In the descriptive chapters that follow, exemplary responses from my interviews serve to describe and define the characteristics of different kinds of garden images within the discourse.

I structured the interviews to unfold in the same manner for each respondent. I opened the interviews by asking the subjects to relate the history of their family's involvement with the garden. I followed up with questions on family background, on previous housing and garden experiences, on the garden's form and plants, and on the sequence of gardening activities through the year. This initial section built rapport by permitting the respondents to do all of the talking while I listened intently. In a second section of the interview I then explored the social use of the garden. I asked questions about the family's involvement with garden work, visiting patterns, relations with neighbors, and social activities in the garden. As these questions were a bit more private than those in the first section, they permitted me to gauge the degree of rapport which was developing between the respondents and myself. The third interview section concerned the verbal formulas. I prefaced this section by asking the respondents

Landscape and Power in Vienna

to relate why they had committed so much time to their gardens and why they had chosen to have a garden when there were alternative ways of experiencing nature in the city. I posed the verbal formulas in the form of a declarative sentence such as "My garden is a utility garden," or "In my garden, I feel secure." I asked the respondents to specify their agreement or disagreement with the statement and then to elaborate on the answer. I would prompt them to define the statement as they understood it, if they did not do so themselves. I concluded the interview with a fifth section in which I asked about contemporary political issues facing Viennese gardeners. These questions permitted me to judge the extent to which the local political problems affected various kinds of gardeners.

In 1988, I was able to spend six consecutive months in Vienna with the support of my home institution and a visiting scholar's stipend from the Austrian Federal Ministry for Science and Research. During this period, I tapped acquaintances in my networks for referrals to people who had gardens. When I contacted these referrals, all but one person agreed to speak with me. I ended up with a group of forty-five gardeners, portraying several housing situations and many garden design complexes. Following the standard ethical practices of ethnographers, I have used pseudonyms for all of my interview partners, unless they were public officials speaking within their official capacities. There is probably nothing in what they said to me which could cause them any harm, and all of them signed releases for publication of the photographs I took of them in their gardens; nevertheless, I am using pseudonyms to protect against the possibility of some unexpected use of information provided in good faith once that material is made public.

The interviews took place in the respondents' gardens, their homes, and in other private settings. We took care to eliminate as many distractions as possible to permit the conversation to concentrate on its purpose. The interviews lasted between one and two hours. I taped the conversations and made continuous notes. Soon after the end of each interview I recorded my impressions of the atmosphere surrounding the interview. After some frustrating and error-ridden attempts at transcribing the tapes onto paper and diskette, I found a translation service that was willing to do it for me. I then reviewed the transcriptions versus the tapes to ensure that the transcriber had rendered everything accurately. The transcribers were native Viennese, fully conversant in the dialect, and, as I discovered after the fact, with some of the gardeners as well. In Vienna, people seem to be linked to each other by fewer degrees of separation than in North American cities.

At the conclusion of the interviews, I asked the respondents to permit me to photograph them in their gardens. In fifteen cases, the interview occurred so late in the autumn that the photographs would not have depicted the gardens' forms accurately. In those cases, I returned the following summer to complete the photographic record. I asked the respondents to decide where in their gardens they wanted me to point the camera to provide the best view of them. In this way, the direction of the camera was determined by the gardeners and not by me. When I returned in summer 1989, I brought prints of the gardens as gifts for the respondents. I tried to use the prints as elicitation frames, asking the gardeners to tell me what they saw in the photographs. This procedure has worked well for visual sociology in the United States, but I found that it only confused my respondents. If they answered at all, they focused on the most obvious elements and began to relate the history again. In comparison with the self-confidence and nuance that characterized the original interview narrative, the photographs yielded impoverished and abbreviated responses. Nevertheless, the photographic record provides a valuable documentation of the variety of design complexes discussed in the work. For that reason, I have included as many examples as possible.

In 1990, I was able to spend four months in the city with support from a Fulbright Research Fellowship and a visiting professorship at the Technical University of Vienna. I was fortunate to be affiliated with the Institute for Landscape Planning and Garden Design, which is part of the School of Architecture at that university. With the photographs and interviews from 1988 in hand, I spent my time testing ideas against this extensive literature. My colleagues at the institute included landscape historians and planners who were more than willing to confirm my understandings of technical material and gaps in the historical record. Professor Ralph Gälzer, then the director of the institute, challenged me to present my ideas to the architecture students through my own seminar and to colleagues in a public lecture on the Viennese landscape. Both of these experiences forced me to work quickly and efficiently in assimilating the copious materials available at the institute. I arrived at my decision to structure this book as a historical narrative in the course of that challenge.

During this period, I consulted Professor Ruth Wodak, a sociolinguist at the University of Vienna's Institute for Applied Linguistics, and asked her to read and comment on the interview materials. For you to evaluate these materials properly, I must disclose her assessment that many of the interview subjects were responding to my status as a professor rather than to my questions. In doing so, some used unusual, "highfalutin" phrases that one would never hear in everyday Viennese speech. Wodak explained that social status is often communicated through language and is an important part of the Viennese sense of self. In these circumstances it prevailed over some people's ordinary ways of talking about gardens. Since my argument here depends on a high level of confidence that people are speaking truly and accurately about their gardens, Wodak's assessment concerned me. I have gone over the data included here with a native Viennese, who also happens to be a skilled German translator. After doing so, I saw that the statements in question were few and did not contradict the argument. Sometimes within the same response, some statements would be pretentious and others not. What is more important is that for every respondent who inflated his or her remarks, there were others who did not. The questionable phrases seemed to cluster around individuals with some technical postsecondary education but were absent among the less educated and those with university degrees. Whenever I have included in a note a respondent's original German response to support my translation in the text, I have italicized the verbose phrases.

THE PLAN OF THE BOOK

The meaning of landscape in Vienna developed by way of a three-hundred-year-old discourse on how best to symbolize the relationship between culture and nature in the city. More specifically, the discourse is about the proper depiction of the relationship between the citizen and metropolis. Over the last three hundred years, as different groups came to power in the city, they used the landscape as a canvas on which to paint their social theories. In the eighteenth century, these theories ranged from the overtly hierarchical models of the Absolute monarchists to the libertarian models of the Republicans.

They were portrayed in the landscape by the antithetical styles of the French and the English. In the nineteenth century, the need for some form of individual freedoms collided with the serious social problems of the Industrial Revolution. In the landscape, these conflicts produced vernacular forms such as the Biedermeier, regional forms like the German neo-romantic, and international forms, for example, functionalism. In the twentieth century, a radicalization of social life ensued from the inability of the city to solve its social problems. Fascist, socialist, and consumerist landscape forms predominate. The formal design elements have become so intimately associated with the social condition of their production that one can read the various worldviews of contemporary gardeners from their gardens.

The Viennese believe that gardens are extraordinary places. They may not say so in words, but they act toward gardens as though they are delicate and rare. There ought to be a formal method of differentiating between the ordinary and the extraordinary places. Such a method would provide a necessary level of consistency as the discussion continues from epoch to epoch. In the clash of group interests in the last two hundred years, successive groups attempted to define themselves as entirely different from those who came before, thereby legitimating their solutions as more modern. Left to their own rhetorical devices, these groups would generate incomparable oranges to a previous group's apples. We need some guideline that permits ideas about gardens to be contrasted through time. In the concluding section of each chapter, I examine the landscape ideas and the gardens they produced through six features that Michel Foucault once offered as the defining criteria for separating an extraordinary place from an ordinary one. These include how the spaces interpret nature; how they express the fulfillment of some utopian ideal; how they refer to unresolved issues; how they transform time; how they are bounded from the ordinary; and how they close out, camouflage, or mystify everyday experience.

Foucault provided these criteria in a lecture he gave in 1967 called "Of Other Spaces" (1986).³ He called these extraordinary places *heterotopias*, other-places, to distinguish them from the *utopias*, no-places, and defined them as "real places—places that do exist and that are formed at the very founding of society—which are something like counter-sites, a kind of effectively enacted utopia in which real sites, all the other real sites that can be found within cultures, are simultaneously represented, contested, and inverted." The name *heterotopia* requires that these sites be absolutely different from all of the sites that they reflect and about which they speak. This contradiction between the need to be different and the need to be linked gives heterotopias their special status.

Two dimensions of space are involved in distinguishing heterotopias as real spaces. The first differentiates utopic sites from the abstract, technological space of planners. Both are fantasies of power, but the latter is formulated with the express intention to act, whereas the former is didactic. Heterotopic sites have this didactic quality as well, but they are neither utopic nor abstract. The second dimension differentiates between the sites of ordinary, everyday experience and the heterotopic sites that reflect the everyday sites in some concentrated fashion. Ordinary sites have minimal specification and demarcation. We know where we are, but where we are is not particularly special. It might be the street, a shopping strip, or a parking lot. Ordinary sites might include the workplace, the home, or the local pub. These are middle-range sites because they retain their ordinariness but include important personal and social meanings that cannot be ignored. They are nevertheless ordinary compared with these other-places. The heterotopic sites attempt to reflect the everyday experience, but they do so in a way that is highly selective of activities or ideas. Heterotopias are different from the geographies of everyday experience and thus are irreducibly linked to the ordinary geography. Without the ordinary, the extraordinary has no meaning.

Foucault named six specific characteristics for identifying heterotopic places. The first is a quality of universality within the scale of the society. The site is a common place, in spite of its special qualities. Unique or temporary sites cannot qualify. Foucault specified two types of universality: places of crisis, such as seclusion huts or funeral homes, and places of deviation, such as asylums and hospitals. We could probably delineate a number of additional types. It is characteristic of Foucault's lecture that important ideas, such as how one generates the universal criterion under differing social contexts, are undeveloped. This has left me room to define how the universality criterion applies to Vienna. With it I generated two broad classes of heterotopias: places of power and places of control. Places of power are public spaces in which those who control the agenda for metropolitan planning use landscape to enshrine their model of the relationship of the person to the state. Places of control are domestic gardens in which individuals use landscape to display their model of the relationship of the person to nature. These are neither unique nor ordinary. Their universality derives from the structure of urban society with its hierarchical distribution of social power and the virtual sanctuary of domestic space.

The second criterion is the necessity for such sites to have identifiable functions. Foucault suggested that in Western societies this characteristic is best illustrated by the cemetery. In periods of strong religious belief this site is centrally located, and concern for the integrity of the physical remains is absent. The cemetery is small and internally undifferentiated. Under conditions of weak religious belief, the concern for the integrity of the individual remains requires larger areas, systems of streets, and hierarchies of neighborhoods. In Vienna, the criterion of function is best imagined as an artifact of the conditions of social production which produce heterotopias. The word *function* is itself embedded in a social science discourse that privileges the explanatory power of certain models of causal contingency. One way to avoid entering this narrow understanding of *function* is to place the emphasis of this criterion on the view of extraordinary places as containers for permissible actions. Henri Lefebvre called this "the social order function of spatial practice" (Gottdeiner 1985:123). By emphasizing the broader vision of permissible activities rather than the narrower and more abstract issue of causal contingency, Foucault's criterion of function in extraordinary sites can provide a connection among the formal elements, the meaningful content (what the space contains), and the planned function (what the space permits). This division mirrors Lefebvre's three phases in the production of social space: the perceived (spatial design practice), the conceived (representations of space), and the lived (representational space (1991:38–39). In Vienna, planned functions are often ignored or transformed by people in public gardens, and private gardens have layers of permissible activities, many of which have little to do with what gardening families do in their garden.

Third, extraordinary sites cannot be reduced to a single meaning. They are multivocal symbolic artifacts that mean different things to different people. Foucault offered the example of the Persian garden reduced to a design on a carpet that can be carried to the mosque for prayer but still exemplifes the geography of heaven. The carpet is simultaneously a carpet, a model of a garden, the garden itself, a model of heaven, and heaven itself. In the same way, Viennese gardens are designs that model social relationships in society. Unlike the Persian carpet, the gardens do not move. Instead, the citizen moves from garden to garden, meditating on the variety of models displayed.

Fourth, the sites are heterochronic. They constitute a break with the continuity of time as well as that of space. The temporal break can be achieved through the accumulation of meanings over time. The contemporary meaning of the place and the aggregate of its past meanings are indistinguishable. The museum or memorial square operates this way. The temporal break can also be achieved by creating a feeling of the fleeting, the transitory, or the precarious. An example of this is the circus that appears overnight in an open field and disappears a few days later. In Viennese gardens this heterochrony is served by the contrast between the annual life cycle of botanicals and the conventional structure of metropolitan time schedules. Even so, different emphases are constructed around this contrast to suit the linkage to everyday life in every epoch.

The fifth characteristic is a clearly identifiable system of opening and closing. Such sites are neither completely inaccessible nor completely open. Instead, entry is either compulsory, as with the army barracks or the prison, or it is available only through permission from some authority. Sites of purification, such as the Moslem hammam, the Jewish mikva, or the Finnish sauna, qualify here, along with sites of familial intimacy, rooms marked "Authorized Personnel Only," and drug houses. Every garden form in Vienna has a boundary. Some are abstract, like the differences in zoned use, and others are masonry walls. *Opening* can refer to sight as well as site. Some gardens were intended to be viewed from the inside outward; others were open to viewing by passers-by.

The final characteristic is that all heterotopic sites share some linkage to all of the remaining places in society. The nature of the linkage can be as complex and multivocal as the sites themselves. The linkage can reflect on the total space, creating an illusion that the remaining spaces are not what they appear to be. Foucault suggested the brothel as a "heterotopia of illusion." Archetypal brothels, like Jean Genet's "The Balcony," certainly qualify here. The linkage can reflect the heterotopic sites, creating a feeling of order as perfect and meticulous as the remaining spaces are clumsy and jumbled. Foucault saw such "heterotopias of compensation" in the efforts by early seventeenth-century colonists to create extraordinary communities in Puritan North America or Jesuit Paraguay. As with the criterion of universality, Foucault left this important idea underdeveloped in his essay. I have concluded from his brief discussion that the notion of *linkage* refers to those aspects of everyday experience which are closed off, shut out, mystified, or camouflaged by the extraordinary space. To be effective didactic fantasies, public gardens had to ignore the inevitable realities that contradicted the abstract and idealized view of society they put forward. Visitors to such gardens could choose to accept the program, agreeing to suspend disbelief in exchange for a satisfying ordered presentation of "nature," or they could meditate on the radicalizing juxtaposition of the ideal garden with the real city. Either way, the linkage remains self-evident and an integral part of the characteristics of an extraordinary site.

Places that can sustain this weighty apparatus are all around cities. We have not classed them as belonging to such an extraordinary genre before because their meaning is elusive, and the sites themselves display a variety of tropes. Green space in cities fulfills all of the criteria of Foucault's heterotopias. These extraordinary spaces are ancient and found in most cities. They were defined at the founding of urban society in West Asia and the Mediterranean littoral, even if we place that moment far back in the early Neolithic.[4] The evidence for this is linguistic as well as archeological. The earliest meaning of the Indo-European root for garden, **gher*, refers to a specialized, enclosed space.[5] Plants and plantings originally were necessarily not part of this special place.[6] That came later and points to an extension of the meaning of the garden to the growing of food plants or the growing of plants that are specifically nonfood. Originally, gardens were circumscribed areas of symbolic import. They were linked to the circumscriptions that identified and controlled food resources, the fundamental social action that differentiated the Neolithic from the Mesolithic. Pastures, woods, grasslands, and streams were the everyday experience. The **gher* was the heterotopic site. It too was an enclosed green space, but its enclosure was higher, its separation was complete, and its meaning was more ambiguous. Entrance was either compulsory or permissible. Inside, the function of the place related to the ordinary activity of life in some manner. Actions involved heavy amounts of ritual as well as quotidian behaviors. Such places were sacred not only because of their spatial otherness, but also because they were heterochronic; generation after generation used the same ground as the site for an evolving urban tradition. When the first urban societies began to form, the emerging pattern of sociospatial differentiation between the elite, sacred sites and the common, profane sites easily incorporated the specialized enclosure. By the time the Bronze Age cities evolved, the enclosure was a high earthen wall. Inside the sacred wall, the buildings of the elite and the plant beds were mixed together. The plants were a reminder of the original botanical construction of the enclosure. Outside the wall, the architecture of everyday life, profane and ordinary, dominated. The plants were thus accidental to the final design that we designate as *garden!* (Hennebo 1970:11–24). From this point onward, planted spaces in cities signaled the intentional demarcation of heterotopic space.

The universality of the city garden as heterotopia lies instead in the ancient association of green enclosures with the sacred. In the broadest sense, they are sites of environmental deviation. Green space is alien to the city and must be tended carefully. The pliability of the site designs reflects the diversity of the worldviews of their designers. Green space is resplendent with symbolic elaboration and layers of meaning. Green space is heterochronic because it can be sustained across a number of generations. In Vienna many palace gardens and parks date from the eighteenth century. Today, the consciousness of landscape preservation is increasing both within the government and the population. The green sites in cities stand apart from the buildings that surround and shadow them. The conditions of the boundaries include all of the exclusions and inclusions observed in heterotopic sites. The nature of these boundaries changes over time. Parks that were the exclusive domain of a single family or class can become publicly accessible. Public parks can be sold to private interests, or their hours of operation can be restricted. Finally, green space is linked to the nongreen spaces that surround them. They are simultaneously illusory and ordering—illusory because they present an icon of nature which stands apart from the surrounding artifice of human society; ordering because the formal arrangement of the plants by the designer is a comment on the relationship between people and nature, the individual and society, and the powerless and the powerful. Both the illusion and the order are meaningless without a knowledge of the ordinary experience of the daily lives of the people who possess the site. It is the linkage between the ordinary and the extraordinary that is important.

This book is an effort to describe the cultural meaning of space in a metropolis by focusing on the green heterotopias created by the people who live there. It involves an exploration of heterotopic sites in the urban environment, of the language people use to describe these sites, and of the meanings that this language reveals. These sites may be the product of the metropolis acting as a whole through its organs of government. In this case, the heterotopias are publicly accessible green space, such as parks and forest preserves, or they may be private gardens created by individual households. The language reveals the tropes that I use to separate the meaning of gardens into themes, each theme a separate chapter. This is the "sight" of the garden, the instantaneous interpretation that the enculturated mind imposes upon sense impressions.

In language, there is a relationship among the formal elements, the experience of the gardeners, and what the landscape means to them and their fellow metropolitans. The dual approach to the meaning of the urban landscape through history and ethnography permits me to describe how the content of the shared ideas about landscape emerges in a city. The following chapter summarizes the geographic, political, and social forces that shaped the cityscape before and during the period under discussion. The remaining chapters describe the meaning of garden designs produced in various eras: gardens of order, of liberty, of domesticity, of pleasure, of reform, of reaction, of refuge, of recreation, and of discovery. A concluding chapter discusses the meaning of landscape in Viennese metropolitan culture in these terms. The chapter titles do not refer to the gardens themselves. Actual gardens can be described by all or some of the themes I am analyzing. Rather, the chapter titles refer to the meaningful fragments that Viennese may read from the gardens around them. For the ease of the reader I have arranged the garden themes in the historical order in which they emerged. Many tropes are involved in this study, and keeping track of them will be difficult enough without a historical framework in which to place them. This history is a mere convention in this study. There are no inclusive dates to provide a summary table of the "evolution of the Viennese garden." There may be beginning points, but there are no ending ones; even the beginning points are arguable. These gardens twist to their own purposes that flow of time which ordinarily helps us locate other kinds of events or persons in history.

In the introductory section of each of these descriptive chapters, contemporary Viennese contribute in their own words their understanding of the forms. The testimony supports the contention that these distinctions have relevance for the residents and are not merely the reflective musings of the author. In each chapter, two expository sections then follow. The first describes the emergence of the ideas about landscape in the discourse, focusing on the words and works of the designers most closely associated with the form. Many of these designers were not Viennese, but their work influenced urban landscape design far from the European cities in which they worked. Historical citations explain how these ideas came to Vienna and why they found fertile ground there. Although German scholars have researched much of this material, very little of it has appeared previously in English. The second expository section concerns the social conditions in Vienna which encouraged the building of public and private gardens during the period when these ideas dominated public landscape investment. This section particularly concerns why gardens are built where they are and who is intended to use them. By situating landscape forms in a political economy that was trading off the social value of place and the economic value of space, landscape was integrated into other forces shaping urban life.

By reconstructing the development of these heterotopias, exploring the ideas that gave them shape, and hearing the language used by Viennese today to describe these sites, we can grasp a greater portion of the lived experience of the city than is available through any of the mainstream models.

The Making of the Viennese Landscape

The forms that people impose upon their environment represent their social selves. Individual Viennese residents represent their class affiliation in their gardens. By *class*, I mean something quite specific to the historical experience of Central European cities over the last three hundred years, namely, the coming to power in municipalities of successive groups defined by their control over taxable property. The evolution of the states in which these cities are embedded forced each class to surrender power to the next. No single class succeeded in imposing its interests on the city for more than a few generations.

The classes that I observe acting in this history bear a relationship to Marx's notion of class as a force in history. Marx was, after all, a Central European. The people who made up these classes became aware of their mutual interests and bonded themselves into organizations that could exert political force under oppressive conditions. Once in power, they oppressed others as they oriented social resources toward fulfilling their narrower class interests. This engendered such resentment and ill will that the power of the ruling class was eventually deposed and replaced by an emergent class, which then repeated the pattern. If this is only true of the history of Central

Social space is never neutral, never homogeneous. Some sites have more power and significance than others, and these qualities need no fixed relationship to a physical, empirical dimension.
Hilda Kuper, 1972

Garden design is a class prerogative.
Leberecht Migge, 1913

Landscape and Power in Vienna

24

MAP 1. *District boundaries of the city of Vienna.* 1, *inner city;* 2, *Leopoldstadt;* 3, *Landstrasse;* 4, *Wieden;* 5, *Margareten;* 6, *Mariahilf;* 7, *Neubau;* 8, *Josefstadt;* 9, *Alsergrund;* 10, *Favoriten;* 11, *Simmering;* 12, *Meidling;* 13, *Heitzing;* 14, *Penzing;* 15, *Rudolfsheim-Fünfhaus;* 16, *Ottakring;* 17, *Hernals;* 18, *Währing;* 19, *Döbling;* 20, *Brigittenau;* 21, *Floridsdorf;* 22, *Donaustadt;* 23, *Liesing.*

Europe and of nowhere else in the world, then so be it. In seeking to understand how the culture of a particular group takes the shape it does, one has to accept and work with the extant historical record. This succession of class-based power groups has shaped the way in which the Viennese, as metropolitans, view their city. This history, then, produced more than a series of governments, party platforms, and personalities; it produced a detailed and richly layered metropolitan culture. This work is an effort to describe that culture as it is reflected in the landscape of the city.

In nineteenth-century Central Europe, class was a jural reality. Membership in a class was defined through the control of income-producing property and the political rights the property ensured. Throughout the last two centuries, the way in which property rights conferred political rights changed periodically. Each change immediately enfranchised a new majority group. I refer to this experience of shared political involvement in a group defined by property and taxation as the experience of class identity. This identity included more than political orientation. Before classes came to power, they were viewed by the classes in power as adversaries and were oppressed by them. In their state of oppression, these powerless classes developed a structure of meanings which permitted them to resist this oppression and forge a new model of the relation of the person to society. As each class came to power, it appropriated a specific set of landscape design possibilities as its language for representing this model.

Because it was politicized by historical experience, people's talk about landscape is more precise, more nuanced, and more engaged than the talk I am accustomed to hearing in North American cities. The same categories need not have saliency for all metropolitans everywhere in the world. Landscape is conspicuous for the Viennese and for other European metropolitans who have experienced the same degree of politicization of urban space. From them we learn how people apply meaning to their environment and how metropolitans forge shared values in spite of their population size and ethnic complexity.

All Viennese participate in this discourse to some extent as they speak about the places in the cityscape which are important to them. Ask park visitors what they think of the current state of the urban landscape, and, according to Gälzer, you are likely to receive one of two possible responses. The person will either lament that the city has destroyed those wild areas they used to play in as children and replaced them with monotonous plantings, or the person will grumble that the beautiful parks are no longer tended properly, that they are being slowly allowed to grow wild, while the lawns are developing footpaths and weeds, and that the taxpayers are being let down (1987b:82). Both complaints reflect ideas about what the urban landscape should be like. Both are filled with echoes of a rich knowledge that metropolitans possess about their landscape and the variety of meanings it can hold for them. Of necessity, the knowledge is local in the sense that it refers to specific places in the person's experience. Simultaneously, all metropolitans produce similar opinions about their landscape. Ideas about landscape are truly a domain of metropolitan knowledge, ideas that are learned and shared by people who live in a common urban space.

THE LANGUAGE OF SPACE

This study is as much about the language of space as it is about space itself. As Viennese talk about landscape, they use the same formulas and phrases that one hears throughout the city or reads in the popular media. The Viennese have separated this language into at least two codes. The most commonly heard code is a vernacular of gardeners. Words and phrases in this vernacular are concrete and often place specific. The following chapters are filled with the speech of gardeners. A second code belongs to the jargon of professional planners. Words and phrases in this jargon are abstract and generalized. Professionals use this language with precision and reflection. Professionals can also employ the international language of style. This code is best suited for describing the Viennese landscape in general.

The term for the features that surround the city's built environment is called *die Landschaft,* landscape. This is divided into at least three subtypes: private landscape, public landscape, and open landscape. The *Privatlandschaft*, or as it is called in the planning literature, *Baufäche mit umgebenden bzw. eingeschlossenen Grünanlagen* (green areas surrounding or enclosed by buildings), includes all of those areas that are accessible only through the invitation or permission of the owner, lessor, or renter. These are primarily house gardens, lawns, courtyards, or balconies that are attached to housing, but green areas associated with commercial, government, religious, social, cultural, or medical buildings are also included. In Vienna, fewer houses than one might expect have been built with gardens, and certainly fewer than the Viennese want. The total amount of green space surrounding or enclosed by buildings is 7,500 hectares, or 27 percent of the total green space (Magistratsabteilung 66 1983:25). This translates to a mere five square meters of private green space for every inhabitant. The house gardens that do exist provide possibilities for enjoyment which are distinct and rare in the city. Possessing a house with garden is the dream of most young families. Another common form of the private landscape in Vienna is the *Kleingärten*. This is a parcel of one hundred to three hundred square meters allotted to a person for gardening purposes by a leaseholding association. These associations can be large, allocating hundreds of parcels per year. There are more than twenty thousand Kleingärten in Vienna, adding 1,230 hectares of private space, or 6 percent of the total green space in the city (ibid.:293). This gives the leaseholding associations substantial political weight in green space zoning issues and open space policies.

The public and the open landscape together comprise *die Freifläche*, the open spaces. Within the city boundaries are 20,710 hectares of open space, or 56.3 percent of the total area. Open spaces include water surfaces, parks, forests, commercial land, open fields, sports facilities, swimming places, camping areas, public nurseries, and cemeteries. Within this open portion, *die Grünfläche*, green space, refers to those lands covered with noncommercial plant growth. For a European city, Vienna has a relatively large amount of open space but only an average amount of green space. For a city of its population size, Vienna has an above average amount of open and green space per inhabitant. The proportion of open space taken up by commercial production is relatively high for a European city of more than one million inhabitants. The eastern rim of the city is still farmed for grain and hay,[1] and there are dairy farms within the city limits, especially in the northern section. The western and southwestern hills are famous for their vineyards.

The *öffentlich zugänglichen Anlagen*, publicly accessible spaces, comprise 854 hectares, or 6 percent of the total area. These include parks, sports facilities, swimming places, camping areas, and cemeteries. Vienna has a less than average amount of space devoted to these public uses; given its population, it could easily support twice the area it currently has. However, forests are also publicly accessible green space, and the Viennese use their forest, the Wienerwald, quite extensively. Vienna ranks first among European cities of more than one million people in the percentage of metropolitan area devoted to protected forest land and second in the amount of forest land per inhabitant (Table 1).

Park and recreation land are not evenly distributed. Eight large, outlying parks—the Prater, the Augarten, the palace gardens at Schönbrunn, the Lainzer Tiergarten, the Laarberg recreation center, the Oberlaa sanitarium, Pötzleinsdorf Park, and the Donauinsel—account for one fifth of all park space. The green space in the Ringstrasse zone surrounding the central district accounts for 34 percent. The remaining park spaces are palace and villa gardens, *Besserlparks* (vest-pocket parks), smaller parks converted from former cemeteries, sport facilities, and playgrounds. The small size of the metro-

TABLE 1

Allocation of Open Space in Seven Metropolises with More Than One Million Inhabitants

	Total Open Space	Rank	Commercial Land	Rank	Forest Preserves	Rank	Kleingärten	Rank	Parks, Playgrounds, etc.	Rank
Vienna (1,531,346)										
m²/person	56.30%	1	25.90%	2	17.30%	1	3.40%	2	6%	6
% of total area	150	3	69.1	3	46	2	9	3	16.1	6
Berlin (1,879,032)										
m²/person	38.50%	7	2.60%	7	17.10%	2	2.40%	4	11%	3
% of total area	97.6	6	6.50%	6	43.2	3	3.9	5	30.8	4
Budapest (2,081,969)										
m²/person	49.50%	4	25.60%	3	10.90%	4	5.70%	1	5%	7
% of total area	121.5	4	62.9	4	26.7	4	13.9	1	9.9	7
Hamburg (1,630,367)										
m²/person	52.70%	3	27.50%	1	5.50%	5	2.60%	3	10%	4
% of total area	238.8	2	124.9	2	24.9	5	11.6	2	45.6	3
Lyon (1,156,387)										
m²/person	54.70%	2	25.10%	4	16.30%	3	0	6	10%	5
% of total area	337	1	154.6	1	100.1	1	0	6	55.4	1
Milan (1,684,000)										
m²/person	45.20%	5	21.60%	5	0	7	0	6	23%	1
% of total area	49	7	23.4	6	0	7	0	6	25.2	5
Munich (1,288,213)										
m²/person	43.60%	6	14.7	7	5.3	7	1.70%	5	21%	2
% of total area	104.5	5	32.2	5	12.7	6	4.1	4	50.1	2

Source: Gälzer 1987:75–81.

politan area devoted to recreational land outside the forest is the product of city-planning principles that give priority to commercial property development. Some districts are well served by the park system. Others, especially the new, outlying residential districts, are served only by the larger parks. These lack local facilities altogether or lack maintenance of existing facilities.[2]

THE HISTORY OF THE SETTLEMENT

The historical references in the chapters that follow pertain primarily to landscape-transforming events of the last two hundred years. The settlement itself is two thousand years old. Many of the features of the previous eighteen hundred years have been lost to time. The meaning and importance of some elements were only partially transformed by more recent changes. Since my purpose is to understand the meaning of the contemporary landscape, it is inappropriate to try to describe the events and personalities of the distant past in too much detail. All cultural formations have precedents, however, and in the sections that follow I will sketch the forces that shaped premodern Vienna. Since most readers will not be familiar with the details of Viennese urban history, this sketch provides a temporal framework in which to place the social and political changes discussed in the subsequent chapters.[3]

The settlement that eventually became Vienna developed on the terraces on the southwest side of the Danube River as it enters the extreme northwest corner of the Pannonian Basin. The river flows from northwest to southeast through the urban area. The river divides into a series of channels and blind arms creating a broad fluvial plain. The terraces and the surrounding hills form the boundaries of a small basin on the southwest side of the river. The hills connect southward to the Eastern Alps. The northeast side of the plain is open to the vast grasslands of the northwestern portion of the Pannonian Basin. Preurban vegetation included at least three zones: a mixed hardwood forest in the Wienerwald, the hills and terraces above the river; the Auwald, a wetland forest zone along the river; and the Marchfeld, the Pannonian grassland zone on the north side of the river.

The availability of foods throughout the year from forest, field, and river suggests a probable Mesolithic occupation at the end of the last Ice Age. Archeologists have certain evidence of human occupation on the terraces beginning with the coming of agriculture in the fifth millennium B.C. Although trading centers developed along the Danube farther to the east, there is no evidence of urban development in Vienna before the coming of the Romans. The Romans built the fortress Vindobona on the lowest terrace overlooking the fluvial plain of the Danube sometime between 15 and 100 A.D. The importance of this first permanent settlement came from its strategic location in the wars between the Romans and the Germanae. The fortress was located on the westernmost spur of the river as it cut into the first of the terraces. The Danube formed a natural moat on the northern side. Two smaller riverbeds, the Vienna River on the south and east sides of the fortress, and the Ottakringer Brook on the west side, provided additional defense. The fortress was typical of Danube and Rhine fortifications: a square enclosure, surrounded by a moat, with gates in the middle of the east, west, and south walls. From the walls, one could survey the activities of the Germanae in the ten-kilometer expanse of the Danube's flood plain.[4] A civilian village developed on the east side of the fortress beyond the banks of the Vienna River. Who these civilians were, what languages they may have spoken, and what the ratio of locals to immigrants among these first Viennese may have been are not known. After the fall of Rome, the fortress and the village fell into ruins. The inhabitants appear to have dispersed or returned to Italy.

The fortress walls remained intact, and the site was used as a refuge for people dislocated by the migrations of the period from 500 through 800 A.D. During most of this time, the region was under the control of the Avars. Under their protection, Slavic speakers settled throughout the region after 600 A.D. The site was probably incorporated into the Great Moravian Empire under Samo, but there is no specific evidence of this. Maps of the Great Moravian Empire include the entire northern section of the Pannonian Basin. The area, now renamed the Provincia Avarorum, was integrated into the empire of the Franks under Charlemagne after his victory over the Avars. Barely eighty years later (907), the Magyar invasions temporarily ended Frankish control. Otto I, the Bavarian founder of the Babenberger dynasty, conquered the Magyars at Lechfeld in 955, reestablishing Christian dominance of the region.[5] The region was renamed the Ostmark and later, the Ostreich. It is the Latinized version of this name, Austria, which is used in English. Administrative and taxation rights to the region were vested in a vassal called a *Markgraf*.[6]

The Medieval Civitas

Succeeding Babenberger Markgrafen extended their control eastward, liberating Vienna in 1030, and establishing the borders with Bohemia and Hungary. As they did so, they moved their residence eastward, finally establishing Vienna as the seat of their duchy in 1156. In 1137, Leopold IV secured permission from the bishop of Passau to build a cathedral in the *civitas* Vienna. This was the first written reference to Vienna as a city. The building of St. Stephen's cathedral ensured its importance in the political and economic system of the region, as well as in the church hierarchy. By 1172 it was described as a *civitas metropolitana* in documents.

The Babenberger city thrived on Danubian trade. The fortifications were enlarged and improved. The population increased. The prosperity was regional, and a number of agricultural villages developed around the city.[7] The citizens living within the walls enjoyed some degree of legal autonomy. Noble families, the so-called *Erbbürger*, could elect a *Stadtherr*, an early type of mayor, among themselves. The cathedral itself was built on the east side of the city, outside the defense wall. The building took hundreds of years, during which a large settlement of craftsmen and artisans grew up around it. Each craft and trade was concentrated on a separate street, such as Bakers' street, Butchers' street, and so on. The first guild, the shoemakers, organized itself in 1310.

In 1211, the first city institution built outside the defense perimeter, the Holy Ghost Hospital, began a small building boom on the south side of the fortress. A number of churches followed, and clusters of residences were soon built around these. This is the beginning of the many suburban clusters that developed as settlements wholly dependent on the central city for defense and livelihood. Today these suburbs survive in name only.

Control over the city passed to the Habsburg family in 1276 and remained in their hands until 1914. They doubled the area within the fortifications to include the cathedral district and the area beyond the southern moat. This former moat area, the *Graben*, became the main food market for the city. The Habsburgs built a new palace on the far southern edge beyond the Graben. In 1284, the first building ordinance allowed no more than two stories to a house. In 1316, Friedrich I gave the Viennese their city hall, the palace of a former lord who had fallen into debt to the duke. In 1331, the city was divided in four sections, each with its district administrator, the *Viertelmeister*. Each quarter had a bell for people to ring in case of fire, crime, or other emergency.

The *Silva Viennensis*, the Wienerwald, was first mentioned in documents in 1324, indicating the growing importance of the surrounding region to the city. The hills offered lumber resources, wild foods, and the increasingly valuable harvest of grapes. Wine production in the Wienerwald villages of Nussdorf, Sievering, Grinzing, and Neustift had begun already in the eleventh century.[8] In 1476, Friedrich III issued an order that closed the forest to further settlement. In 1493 Maximilian I renewed the ban on settlement.

The first mention of the royal hunting park in the section of the flood plain known as the Prater comes from a 1403 document, although there is evidence that the Babenberger dukes used the area for hunting as early as the eleventh century. Ferdinand I laid out the main alley of the hunting park in the 1520s. Hunting was such an important social event for the higher nobility that one hunting park was not enough. During his brief conquest of the city in the mid fifteenth century, Matthias Corvinius enclosed two additional areas as hunting reserves: the Katterburg, which later became the grounds of the Schönbrunn Palace, and the Alten Favorita, which in 1655 became the grounds of the Augarten Palace.

The years 1338–49 began a long economic decline for Vienna following a storm of locusts, the Black Plague, a remarkably strong earthquake, and two destructive floods. Many of the regional villages were depopulated. In spite of the decline in living standards, in the late Middle Ages Vienna was a relatively luxurious place to live. Garbage was collected regularly. The water was clean. Market inspectors guaranteed clean, fresh food. A destructive fire in 1562 created the opportunity to rebuild the city's water system completely. Throughout the fifteenth century, the fortifications were systematically heightened and thickened, with six fortified gates and nineteen towers.

*Transitional Period from Gothic Bürgerstadt
to Baroque Imperial Residence*

This period between 1529 and 1683 is defined by the two separate Turkish sieges of the fortified city. Before the 1500s, Vienna was a relatively autonomous *bürgerlich* commune. In 1522, after an attempt to defend the autonomy of the city council, the mayor and the more important councilors were arrested, imprisoned in the southern town of Wiener Neustadt, and beheaded. Emperor Ferdinand I withdrew the legal autonomy of the city, setting in motion a series of events which promoted Vienna's importance as the residence of powerful aristocracy and ambassadors from all over Europe. It also guaranteed that the subsequent development of this city would follow the needs and prerequisites of the imperial house rather than those of trade and commerce.

There were four important effects on the landscape of this special role as imperial residence. First, the ownership of ground within and around the city began to shift from bürgerlich to noble families and religious brotherhoods.

Second, the built forms began to serve the ceremonial needs of the imperial house, the nobility, and the powerful church institutions, primarily the brotherhoods, rather than the utilitarian needs of the *Bürgertum*. Ceremonies required increasing the power of a site through all of the features of the heterotopia. This meant larger buildings, occupying greater amounts of space.

Third, the stylistic taste in the buildings and layout of the gardens changed from North European gothic to South European baroque. These different styles demanded a dramatically different relationship between the house and the land. Gothic houses fronted the street, and gardens were built behind or beside the houses. Baroque buildings sat within the parcels, employed setbacks from the street, and enclosed a garden or courtyard on all four sides. In practice, this meant that the long, thin, "gable" houses of the Bürgers slowly began to disappear and were replaced by the square houses of the nobility. These square houses required lots of a different shape. New building zones, especially those outside the wall, were subdivided into quite different forms as a result.

The final effect concerned the importance of the fortifications. As the residence of the dominant political and military power in Central Europe, the city was the target of sieges by the chief rivals to Christian Europe, the Osmanen Turks. Before the 1500s, the fortifications were low thick walls surrounded by a moat. As the Turkish threat increased, so too did the height and complexity of the fortifications. Over the sixteenth century, the size of the *Glacis*, the free-fire zone immediately in front of the fortification, was extended from one hundred to three hundred meters.

By 1500, Vienna had approximately fifty thousand inhabitants within the walls and an additional ten thousand outside. This was the beginning of the social, economic, and architectural division of the settlement into the *Altstadt*, old city, and the *Neustadt*, new city. The Altstadt was the commercial center and residential quarter for the nobility and patricians. It contained the tallest buildings, with most houses raised to three stories. At the same time, the old city was the densest residential area within the settlement. Inside its walls there were no stables, smoky workshops, warehouses, or commercial gardens to be found. All of these features, together with the one- or two-story homes of the handworkers, were found outside the walls in the Neustadt (Lichtenberger 1977:95). A 1547 city map by Wolmuet shows 150 grass and tree gardens inside the walls of the city. By the end of the century, all of these had disappeared, pushed out by the increasing land rents and population boom.

In a description from 1559, Conrad Gesner divided the gardens of Vienna into six kinds: vegetable gardens for provisions; herb gardens for healing; botanical gardens of rare species for the scholars; decorative gardens for patricians and the cloisters; magnificent gardens for exalting the nobility; and hunting gardens for the rich (cited in Auböck 1975). Each type of garden had its separate influence on the contemporary landscape.

There were two kinds of vegetable gardens in the city: the small kitchen garden behind the private homes, which supplied the roots and herbs for the daily soup, and the commercial vegetable garden, which supplied greens for the thousands of renters and those who did not have kitchen gardens. The small kitchen gardens had always existed but were not observable to anyone but their owners. Aeneas Sylvius Piccolomini, the future Pope Pius II, provided one of the earliest descriptions of the Viennese landscape. In 1477 he wrote, "Vienna's entire area is a giant handsome garden covered with beautiful vine-crowned hills and orchards" (cited in Auböck 1975). The truck gardens that appeared numerous and robust in the sixteenth century lost ground in the ensuing periods. The vegetable and fruit gardens then were situated in the Neustadt area and in the farming villages on the slopes of the Wienerwald. The Guild of Viennese Kitchen Herb Gardeners was founded in 1626. The two Turkish sieges of the city in 1529 and 1683 destroyed people, farms, and villages, creating discontinuities in the development of a stable truck farm economy. The industry was again severely disadvantaged in 1704 by the construction of the outer defense wall and the imposition of a head tax for all those who wished to enter the city to sell goods. Already in the eighteenth century, the farms in the immediate area were few and played a smaller role in provisioning the city compared with farms in the villages farther to the east and the south. Only in the aftermath of war, when access to more distant commercial farms became difficult, did Viennese commercial gardens thrive (Greif 1966:5–6).

The herbal gardens were extremely important for the contemporary medical system. Every practicing physician had his own medicinal garden. These pharmaceutically active plants were among the most effective therapeutic techniques available. Botanical gardens were an important part of the competition for the accumulation of treasures which pervaded the world of the elite.

Along with a collection of the best musicians, the best artists, the best scientists, and the best architects, the truly accomplished Renaissance monarch had to have the best botanical gardens full of rare and distinctive species. Botanists capable of collecting and sustaining such gardens were expensive and hard to find. The tulip, lily, and daffodil—all imports from Asia—could have first been adapted to European soil and climate in Vienna.[9] Maximilian II managed to attract the French botanist Carolus Clusius to a professorship at the University of Vienna in 1573. In 1576, Clusius successfully transplanted the horse chestnut (*Rosskastanie*) tree and in 1588, the potato, to Vienna. The horse chestnut, together with the poplar, would become among the most often planted street trees. The botanical craze had much the same popular appeal as the other royal pursuits, and soon lesser lords, cloister abbots, and wealthy Bürgers were building gardens in the Neustadt to breed new plants. The district northwest of the city along the Danube canal, the Rossau, was especially favored by these gardeners. In 1628, Emperor Ferdinand II founded the

Brotherhood of Pleasure- and Ornamental-Gardeners, whose purpose was to educate aristocratic gardeners and to recognize the accomplishments of its members.

In early descriptions of life in the city, there are indications of an ornamental garden experience very similar to that of other European cities. A 1370 document speaks of a *Paradiesgarten*, paradise garden, near the mouth of the Vienna River.[10] A 1373 document placed another paradise garden about a half-kilometer upstream on the Vienna River in Wieden. Emperor Albrecht II planted a Paradiesgarten near the Habsburg Palace in 1385. The garden was still in existence in its medieval form in the late 1490s when Emperor Maximilian I featured its beauty in his treatise on gardening. It was destroyed by the first Turkish siege and rebuilt by Ferdinand I in a different style (Neubauer 1975:7). In 1755, during the building of new wings to the palace, the imperial pleasure garden was moved to a spot between the Palace and Lions Bastion. Today, this is the site of the Volksgarten.

In 1569, Maximilian II began building the most impressive of all Renaissance ornamental gardens north of the Alps, the Neugebäude.[11] It was completed by his successor, Rudolf II. The palace was built on a terrace overlooking the Danube south of the city, on the exact spot where the Sultan Suleiman I had put his tent in the first Turkish siege of Vienna in 1529. Important for introducing to Vienna Italian ideas about garden design, including terracing, water elements, scenic views, and large-scale geometric layouts, the palace was destroyed during the second Turkish siege in 1683, and its marble pieces were incorporated into other gardens in the eighteenth century.[12]

The Baroque City

In 1700, the population of Vienna had reached eighty thousand. The eighteenth century saw a great deal of garden palace building in the Neustadt. A new outer defense line, the Linien Wall, was built in 1704. It defined the outer boundaries of the Neustadt. Today, that line is the second ring boulevard, the Gürtel, built in 1873. The effect of the new wall was to transfer to the outlying villages the same roles played by the Neustadt suburbs in the sixteenth century: warehousing, truck gardening, locations for workshops, and housing for the lower classes. Control over large sections of the Neustadt which had been in the hands of religious brotherhoods and noble families passed to the imperial committee that ran the city's affairs.[13] The parcels were then subdivided and sold for development. The Neustadt became the site of a building boom featuring magnificent baroque palaces and gardens, cloisters, and patrician estates. A new building ordinance in 1704 required new structures to be covered in brick and to conform to the style of the existing buildings. The city's aristocratic governors seemed intent on imposing a single style on the imperial capital.

By the end of this period, around 1770, the population had doubled to 160,000. These ninety years delineated the second greatest period of building in the city's history. Thousands of rental apartments, palaces, churches, and cloisters were built. The increased sense of security produced by the disappearance of any further Turkish threat prompted much denser building in the Neustadt, tripling there during this period. Perhaps the greatest development in this time frame was the emergence of a clear social hierarchy. At the peak of the hierarchy was the walled city. It was typified by the imperial house and the organs of the centralized absolutist state. In the districts surrounding the city were the palaces of the nobles and the few wealthy Bürgers. Beyond this ring of palaces were the houses of the artisans, whose work served the building and ceremonial needs of the wealthy. The implications of this building boom on the urban landscape are discussed in detail in the next chapter.

The Manufacturing City

Historians ascribe the boundary line between the high baroque and the beginning of the decay of absolutism in the face of the Industrial Revolution to the ascension to the throne of Joseph II, the most enlightened of the absolutist emperors. The period lasted from 1770 to 1848. During this time, the population grew from 160,000 to 440,000. Most of the increase stemmed from the migration of skilled industrial workers to the city. They were housed beyond the Linien Wall. The period saw the emergence of the *Grossbürgertum*, the new class of industrial property owners, and the retreat from cultural prominence of the nobility, the class of nobles who had held sway in the city since the sixteenth century. In architecture, the major features of the period were the specialization of rooms within the house, the increasing importance of privacy, and the integration of the garden with the house interiors.[14] Public parks were opened for the first time.

In seventeenth-century Central Europe as absolutist regimes increased to implement the Counter Reformation and to bring the independent urban economies back under control of the leading regional military powers, the formerly independent urban communes such as Vienna found their internal affairs increasingly in the hands of militarized, Catholic nobles appointed by the imperial house. This process was complete by the end of the second Turkish siege of Vienna. This class of primarily urban aristocrats served their emperor and church with unquestioned loyalty. They held power in the city government until the 1848 Revolution.

This class was not always unified in its political strategy. In the last quarter of the eighteenth century, younger members of the most powerful families (including Emperor Joseph II) endorsed the Rousseauian principles of the liberal state and sought ways of reforming the absolutist state (through absolutist political strategies) to incorporate a platform of universal, secular rights. This group, which I will refer to as the Enlightenment nobles, strongly influenced politics at a local and imperial level while Joseph II was on the throne. Their republicanism so threatened the nobility, especially after the French Revolution, that many of the reforms were repealed after the death of Joseph, and the city and empire experienced a protracted period of conservative reaction in culture and politics leading to the 1848 Revolution.

The brief period of Enlightenment in Vienna brought many rich commercial barons to prominence. Because of their resources, they were able to underwrite many of the projects of the Enlightenment nobles. Their political influence and their honorary baronets continued through the period of reaction. This group, which the Viennese call the Grossbürgertum, was initially composed of families who had made fortunes in urban-based, non–guild labor-dependent commercial operations, such as banking and watchmaking.[15] I will use this term to refer to this class, rather than the French *haute bourgeoisie*, throughout this work. During the first half of the nineteenth century, the ranks of this class were swelled by rich provincial manufacturing families who migrated to the capital to influence the empire's economic politics and to display their new wealth and titles. These

Grossbürger families built palaces that emulated those of the Enlightenment nobles who had sponsored their rise to power. Under the system of reaction associated so personally with the political management of Prince Metternich, republicanism was so feared that there was no possibility for these potentially powerful families to act in concert to form a political alternative.

All of this changed with the 1848 Revolution and the neo-corporatist political model instituted in Vienna. Having substantial property in the city, the Grossbürger families were subject to levels of taxes which guaranteed their voting rights for the *Bürgermeister* and *Gemeindeausschuss* (community council). The boundaries of the city expanded until the Gemeindeausschuss controlled all of the territory within the Linien Wall. Based on the twin values of *Besitz* (property) and *Intelligenz* (intellectual leadership), a Bürger consciousness quickly began to form, which attempted to unite the highest ranks of the Grossbürgertum, the new industrialists, and the smaller artisans and shopkeepers of settlements outside the walls of the city (Boyer 1981:10–12). The impact of this period on the Viennese landscape is discussed in detail in Chapters 4 and 5.

The Grunderzeit Metropolis

This name for this period, which translates as *foundation period*, refers to the most intense period of building in the city's history. It began in 1840 and lasted until the end of World War I. At the beginning of the period the Grossbürgertum were under the political banner of liberalism, forcing changes in the economic policies of the region to open up the city to railroads and industry. During this time, the population grew from 440,000 to more than two million. The increase was due almost entirely to the migration of industrial workers from the provinces. Thirteen additional districts were incorporated into the city administration, tripling the size of the city (Figure 1). In this seventy-year period, three quarters of the city's area was rebuilt, destroying all vestiges of the premodern city and much of the building of the previous three modern periods. The rapid building and the intense demand for housing in the rapidly expanding city set in motion waves of land speculation markets, which, in turn, increased further the building density and land speculation. The municipality responded with a new series of building codes, transforming the practice of architecture and city planning into professions requiring ex-

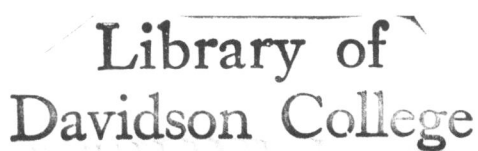

Landscape and Power in Vienna

40

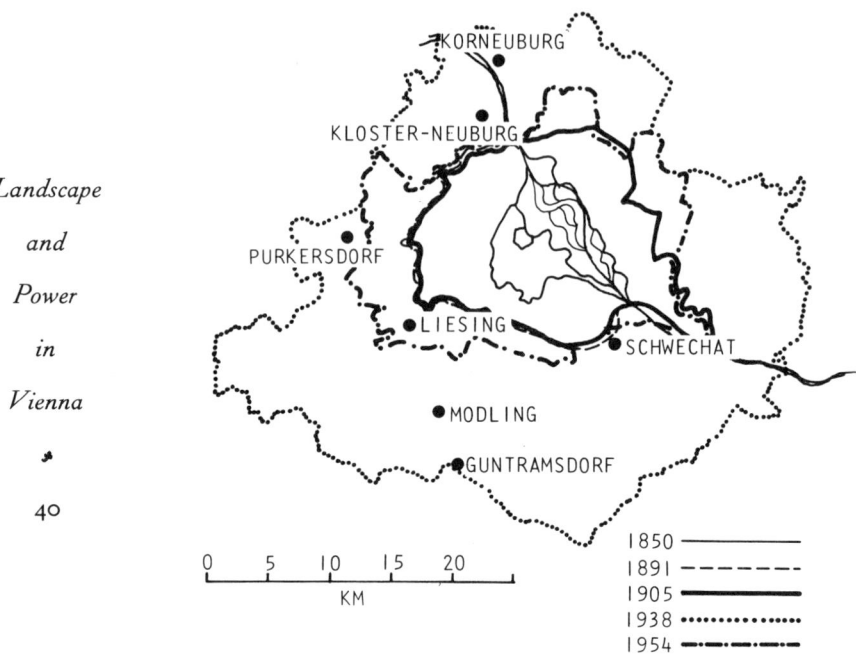

FIGURE 1. *Changes in the Viennese city boundaries, 1850–1954.*

tensive engineering training to ensure that buildings would meet the specifications of the codes. One of the major projects of the period was the razing of the fortifications and Glacis. In their place, the city erected the complex known as the Ringstrasse. This project created an enlarged city center, expanding the size and importance of administrative and cultural buildings. Housing development shifted from the overbuilt south and west sides of the metropolis to the north side of the Danube, northeast of the city. The period concluded with the dismantling of the bürgerlich monopoly on urban development politics and the extension of voting rights to the working class. There was a net decline in area of public parks, but initiatives taken toward the end of the period established for the first time protection from economic development in the Wienerwald.

The Ringstrasse project was the most far-reaching alteration of the city geography since the expansion of the city fortifications in the early sixteenth century. The key to the project was the tearing down of the fortifications and the development of the space occupied by the walls, the moat, and the Glacis. City council efforts to secure permission to expand the inner city dated back to the time of Joseph II. Various proposals in the 1840s were effectively suspended by the civil unrest of 1848. By the end of the 1850s, the demands for housing and commercial building had become so shrill that the emperor was again willing to consider razing the walls. At this time, Vienna was the last major walled city in Europe (Bernatzky 1960). On April 17, 1857, the emperor agreed to remove the walls and to enlarge the city area to include the region formerly occupied by the Glacis.

Since the time of Joseph II, the Glacis had been characterized as the most important recreational area in the city. Destroying the walls pushed the ownership of Glacis ground rights, rather than the recreational needs of the population, into the foreground of political debate. Parks were established grudgingly and only after pressure from the emperor and the electorate. In the final ground plan, the development commission agreed to provide park lands for "fresh air, water areas, and generously measured green areas immediately next to residences and workplaces." Of the former Glacis, 48.4 percent became streets; 32.8 percent became buildings; and 17.4 percent became parks, green strips, and tree rows (Fischer 1971:71). By this reckoning, the Ringstrasse project caused an 80 percent reduction in the green space in the center of the city.

In the period of building which began after the redesign of the Ringstrasse zone, a high-gravity water system was installed, a city railroad system was established, and the Danube and Vienna Rivers were regulated. In 1871, the first district on the other side of the Linien Wall, Favoriten, was incorporated. By 1890, Vienna's area increased from 55 to 178 square kilometers. During these last decades of the Grunderzeit, the city municipalized the gas and electric systems, built two new electric generating stations and a gas production station, took over the private streetcar lines, built the Gürtel over the Vienna River, and erected a second high-gravity water system.

In 1890, a second city expansion project was launched. It also entailed an international competition to develop a long-range plan for traffic, new housing, and industrial areas. It required for the first time the development of a general zoning plan for the entire city. The city council stipulated that the design should develop the western edge of the city for housing and the southeastern edge, up to the Danube, for industry. The project designers were also admonished not to change the character of existing green space, whether it be the Ringstrasse parks or the forested hills. This last is the first indication of the city's concern with protecting its open space and foreshadows the political actions fifteen years later to establish a greenbelt preserve. Finally, the project designers were required to reserve 652 square meters of green space for every 1,000 square meters of built space, a ratio of 1:0.6. This was the inverse of the built-to-open-space ratio in Stache's Ringstrasse plan.

The competition produced fifteen prize-winning projects. The two first prizes were won by Viennese architect Otto Wagner and Kölner architect Josef Stübben, who were among the top five architects in the German-speaking world.[16] Wagner saw the parks of the inner districts as hindrances to development and recommended tearing them up. He believed that green space was essential to the city's sanitation and wanted to distribute the space more evenly throughout the city, instead of massing it in park areas. He envisioned a high frequency of playgrounds, ice skating rinks, and public baths and wanted to line every street, no matter how small, with trees. Stübben wanted to add twenty-five more parks to the outer districts, seeing these as primarily aesthetic, softening the cityscape, and "providing rich and poor alike with the conveniences of residing in and visiting Vienna" (Fischer 1971:40). He saw no need to mention the existing city parks, as if their protection were self-evident. None of the plans had the galvanizing effect of Stache's in the first competition. Each plan contained elements of the late Grunderzeit development, but no one concept dominated. The one exception was Eugen Fassbinder's plan for a 750-square-meter-wide belt of *grünen Ankers*, village greens, on the outer edge of the districts beyond the Gürtel, including a concrete plan for a protected greenbelt. Another influential suggestion from the competition was to close the cemeteries around the Gürtel for sanitation reasons, redesign the spaces as parks, and centralize the cemetery function in a large development in the southern section of the city. This was carried out. It not only led to the creation of a number of parks near where Stübben would have placed them, but also inaugurated the development of the Zentralfriedhof, the huge central cemetery in Kaiser Ebersdorf. In general, the actions of the second city expansion program increased the number of parks dramatically, but the rapidly increasing population held the area of green space per inhabitant essentially constant (Fischer 1971:71).

This unified Bürgertum that had been the dream of the Liberal Party failed to hold together. The system enacted by the city council in 1849 excluded the lower taxpayers, what the Viennese call the *Kleinbürgertum*. As before, I will use this term instead of the more common French *petite bourgeoisie*. This so-called curial system divided voters into three separate categories based on very complicated tax and education criteria, consigning the small shopkeepers and artisans to the least powerful Third Curia, the intellectuals and smaller property owners to the Second Curia, and the highest taxed to the most powerful First Curia. The First Curia included the traditional Grossbürgertum and also a second group of property owners with quite different credentials. The real estate tax system allowed landlords to credit their tenants' rent tax as their own personal income tax, greatly inflating the income tax of this latter group. This middle class was composed primarily of the wealthiest shopkeepers and artisans. They, rather than the Grossbürgertum, formed the nucleus of the Liberal Party. The system excluded people who paid less than ten florins in taxes, thereby relegating a large number of shopkeepers and artisans to the disenfranchised category even though they were property owners. This situation created the historical conditions for the Kleinbürgertum to emerge as a political force at the end of the century when the election laws were reformed to include all taxpayers (Boyer 1981:15–17). The party of the Kleinbürger which developed to oppose the Liberal Party was that of the Christian Socialists. It was led by Karl Lueger, the charismatic Bürgermeister from 1896 through 1914, who brought the party into political maturity. This party held the majority of seats on the community council for some years before and then throughout his term in office.

Red Vienna and Brown Vienna

These descriptions refer to the shift in political control between the extreme left (red) and right (brown) parties as they struggled to control the direction of the city after the dismantling of the Habsburg empire. The unity of the Bürgertum was defined in opposition to the great propertyless workers who, throughout the nineteenth century, first as a trickle and later as a tidal wave, had taken up residence in the suburbs outside the second defense line. Since I am employing the German words for the other classes, I will refer to this class as the *Arbeiter*. They had already shown their animosity toward property in the 1848 Revolution, when, while the intellectuals and small shopkeepers were battling within the city for the return of political rights, they as workers were storming the factories and destroying machines in the suburbs in the hopes of restoring their rights to control the tools of production (Häusler 1980). This group was systematically excluded from voting, even after the reforms that enfranchised all taxpayers. They paid no property or income tax, and the rent taxes they paid were still included in the taxes of their landlords. Since they contributed no financial resources to the city, the argument went, they should have no voice in municipal affairs. This situation changed with the end of World War I, the creation of the First Republic of Austria, and the extension of universal suffrage. The political development of this class parallels that of the Kleinbürger. Excluded from political participation, they evolved a number of socialist parties in the late nineteenth century. Under universal suffrage, the party most closely associated with the trade union movement, the Social Democratic Party, won a majority of seats in the community council.

Socialist control over the city council lasted barely nine years before repercussions of the perceived oppression among the Bürgertum destroyed the political stability of the First Republic. Civil war erupted between Bürgertum and Arbeiter after a series of isolated incidents in 1928 and lasted for four years. After pitched gun battles between the army of the state and the home guard of various socialist organizations, socialist hegemony gave way to fascist reaction in 1933 and in the 1938 Anschluss with the German Reich. The defeat of the fascists in World War II and the occupation of Vienna by the four powers restabilized the city.

This complex period between the end of World War I and the end of World War II saw a decline in population through war deaths and outmigration, but this decline was insufficient to offset the severe housing shortages of the preceding liberal era. After unemployment, the housing crisis was the most important problem of this twenty-five-year period. Precipitating the crisis was the rent control ordinance of 1922, which froze the rental market. The municipal government created a public sector housing initiative that completely altered the face of housing in the city. Public parks increased. After incorporation into the German Reich in 1938, the city was expanded to include most of the Vienna Basin, a land form that extends sixty miles south of the city to Wiener Neustadt. After the war, the boundaries of the city administration were reduced again to approximately their prewar size.

The Postwar City

This last period in the city's development began with the end of World War II. By 1955, sovereignty had returned to the Second Republic of Austria. Nationally, socialist and liberal conservatives ruled in coalition for decades, but locally, the socialists retook control of the Bürgermeister office and the city council and continue to hold those positions today. The population declined to the one million mark. In this period, war damage and the aging of existing housing forced the city to step up its building program. By the 1970s, the city had built more than 75 percent of the housing that stands today. Two new districts were added. Extensive bombing damage had opened up small parks between structures. Decisions of whether to tear down, restore, or reconstruct older buildings also forced planning choices in the area of increasing open space. The environmental inheritance of one hundred years of industrialization, together with the heightened insecurity of the Cold War superpower rivalry, combined to increase Viennese awareness of the quality of their surroundings. In the final years of this period, preservation considerations limited the economic development of open areas. This conflict defines many of the landscape policies at present and will continue to influence them in the near future.

These class experiences of the last two hundred years seem to be the product of the systematic disenfranchisement of groups of people from political participation. The social process that produced these dislocations in the urban experience is far from over. At the present time a new class seems to be evolving for whom the disenfranchisement concerns environmental policy. Represented politically by the *Grünen* (Greens), this class is still in formation. Consciousness that environmental problems are out of control is widespread. People from across the old class lines are dissatisfied with the solutions offered by the mainstream parties. Even the Green Party itself is viewed as insufficient for dealing with many of these problems. What makes this new class struggle similar to the older ones is that the reaction to disenfranchisement involves the development of a landscape style in which the language of dissent can find a privileged site.

The history of succession of landscape vernaculars, at least since the end of the seventeenth century, is the history of the succession of class interests in the arena of social power. Wolf said that there are four ways of understanding social power: as an attribute of persons involving potency or capability, as the ability of one person to impose his or her will on another in interpersonal relations, as the control over the settings in which people may show forth their potentialities and interact with others, and as the organization and orchestration of the universe of settings through the distribution and direction of energy flows (1990:586). Class involvement with space involves this last aspect of social power. The urban landscape is a universe of settings through which dominant power groups direct and distribute energy. Such groups arrange this landscape to suit their purpose, in terms of energy necessary to produce space as well as the symbolic forms through which that space is identified.

Gardens of Order

Places that offer a heightened experience of order are among the most frequently visited gardens in the city and include the palace grounds of the Belvedere, Schönbrunn, and Augarten estates. The design of these gardens includes elements that are as old as the most ancient royal gardens in Persia. Certainly the mannerist designs of the aristocratic town gardens of the Italian Renaissance are at the core of the geometric ground plan of these landscapes. However, it is the association of this landscape style with the Bourbon Louis XIV and the birth of absolutism in the late seventeenth century, as enshrined in the gardens Le Nôtre designed at Versailles, which results in the design being labeled the *French style* by historians. School trips enable almost every school child to visit these gardens. The scale and balance of these landscapes, however, are not the most enduring memory of these early experiences; rather, it is the political will that designed these gardens as monuments of absolutism which still haunts the grounds. It is this spirit of control that most ordinary Viennese relate to when they describe these gardens.

The language of styles and design elements need not have any relationship to the popular meaning of a landscape. In the case of the

French style, historians and architects see one kind of place, and ordinary Viennese see another. In everyday language, French gardens are known as ornamental gardens (*Ziergärten*). The stylistic nuances that fascinate the experts will be discussed later in this chapter. The more widely distributed meanings are those of the residents. These include a range of ideas with no single interview partner expressing the totality of images.

Four general themes emerge as the Viennese talk about their understandings of these gardens of order. The first is that ornamental gardens are for viewing only:

> In my opinion, an ornamental garden is only for looking at and not for stepping on. That is more pure ornamentation. I can imagine a comparison with the botanical garden or with the garden palace Schönbrunn, which are tended and trimmed by gardeners, but only for the eye of the visitors, but not for their use.

> I call a garden ornamental if it has such an architectonic order that this can only stand there. This must be cut so that it is never higher than this level. The lawn must be cut in stripes. The stalks must stand straight. And the borders must be marked out and lined with little stones. That is an ornamental garden for you.[1]

One is not permitted to step into these gardens. One cannot use them in any informal way. This is extraordinary because most planted spaces encourage people to interact with the space and change it in some significant way. It is this interaction in particular which is banished from the ornamental garden.

The second theme is the strong architectonic, symmetric, geometric, and unnatural ordering of elements in the garden. "An ornamental garden is laid out with precision and symmetry."[2] What makes it so sightworthy is the juxtaposition of originally natural elements to human order. What was once the produce of random germination is now the self-evident product of the gardener. Straight lines dominate. Heights and widths never falter. Bushes take on the shapes of balls and Turkish war helmets. Trees sport perfectly cut upside-down cones instead of crowns of branches. Lawns are square.

The third theme is the purity of the planting. Ordinary growth is mixed and complex with different grasses and perennials competing with and succeeding each other. "An ornamental garden is a garden which is only for decoration, which is beautiful to look at, which is beautifully looked after, where nothing is left lying around . . . where there are no weeds! [*laughs*]."³ In the ornamental garden, each plant mixes with its own kind and only with its own kind. Flowers bloom out of season. The effort is highly labor intensive. Someone must weed those endless lawns that provide the ground against which the flower beds and walls of bushes and trees provide the figure.

The fourth theme is that all of this work is intended for others to consume. There is nothing personal in the garden beyond the obvious show of horticultural, hence social, power.

> An ornamental garden . . . one is not allowed to walk on it, only to look at it. And it is too trimmed.
>
> [Mrs.:] Y' know, where everything is neat and clean, right. I'm a real person. I'm not sloppy, but I'm also no pedant. I hang laundry in my garden and that's important to me. [Mr.:] And not to be a slave of a garden but it has to be looked after.⁴

Unless others are impressed, the effort bears little fruit. Missing here is the sense in which effort is followed by the contemplation of the product. The garden is barren. Its fruits are artificial. It proclaims the power of its patron to rule others in the same absolute fashion that he rules nature in this extraordinary place.

The design principles are neither technical nor historical abstractions. These gardens enter into the common discourse on the meaning of extraordinary and ordinary places for those Viennese who visit them. These principles are found in public parks financed by the municipal government for popular use. They are to be found in serious models for domestic gardens in the popular press. Most importantly, one can find the attempt to create such gardens of order domestically.⁵ This means that within the field of meanings that constitute the contents of the metropolitan cultural domain for landscape, the garden of order is active and productive.

DISCOURSE ON GARDENS OF ORDER

In the early modern period, the developments in garden design lagged behind the Italian. The German nobility never lost its close connection to the land. This class, which in Italy played an important role as patrons of garden architecture, was content with their small Paradiesgarten and Lustgarten forms.⁶ Since agriculture played so important a role in their wealth, fields given over to the growing of decorative flowers, grasses, and shrubs provided a convenient symbol for wealth.⁷ In contrast, the newly prominent urban Bürgertum had no connection to the land. They, too, sought to symbolize their emerging class aspirations through the design of gardens. The result was a rational but sentimental search for nature—naturalism. This early form of the worldview that would become the central tenet of the eighteenth-century Enlightenment involved a rejection of the diety as separate from nature, substituting the search for the divine within nature. Fueled by literacy and the increasing availability of protoscientific findings, primarily in astronomy, the people of the new class saw the regularities of nature as an alternative model of universal power to the figures of the Holy Trinity and Mary. For the early modern Bürger, to be surrounded by nature was to be devout.

Already in 1500 the bürgerlich ideal of the garden was perceived by Geiler von Kaiserberg, who observed his fellow citizens deserting the city on Sunday for the rural serenity of nearby villages.⁸ In the paintings, city maps, and house plans of these sixteenth- and seventeenth-century Germans Hennebo saw a strong wish "to have a bit of property, a garden outside the door, in which to enjoy nature in an orderly form and to produce something for the kitchen" (1962:167). These were revealed in an increase in the number of *Hofanlage*—a term, like the medieval *villa urbana*, that implies the existence of a courtyard in the center of the Roman house. Most of these gardens were next to the house. Like the old Lustgarten, the Hofanlage was separated into clearly defined sections for each of its three dominant functions: to produce fruits and vegetables for family consumption, to satisfy the botanical inclinations of its increasingly literate owners, and to appeal to naturalist ornamental aesthetics. Each function was served by its own geometric shape. The ornamental bed was composed within a square or round. The producing orchard was a regular spacing of trees within a rectangle. The vegetable and scientific beds were parallel lines of plants with paths dividing groups of lines into elongated rectangles. The beds had clearly defined edges but lacked distinct centers. The visitor's eye was drawn outward to the edge of the bed. Nature was to be observed but only under the conditions of order.

By the end of the sixteenth century, the influence of the Italian style was already becoming apparent in the lack of a clear ordering among the parts. In contrast to the Bürger gardens, the Italian Renaissance gardens were more like Charlemagne's paradise gardens—expansive, expensive estates built on stacks of terraces and organized to emphasize the social importance of the owner. The highest terrace was crowned by the house itself. One descended the terraces on stairs. Streams of water often flowed over artificial falls. On the terraces, the productive and recreational functions were often mixed together. Paintings of these gardens show shrubs and trees arranged to bind the architectural elements, such as stairs, waterfalls, terrace walls, and statue niches, to the open lawns of the terraces. The larger plants had natural growth patterns rather than sculpted ones. These plants also provided screens that permitted statues or scenic vistas to surprise the visitor walking through the garden.

In Vienna, the most important of these Italian pleasure grounds was Maximilian's Neugebäude (Figure 2). The palace was built on terraces in the smooth flood plain of the Danube below Vienna. On the highest terrace was a hunting preserve, a walled square with turrets in the four corners. Inside the preserve on the same level was another square that held an open lawn, and in the middle of this lawn lay an ornamental flower bed with a marble fountain in the geometric center of the nested squares. A covered arcade of marble columns and copper roof surrounded the ornamental bed and separated it from the lawn. The palace itself sat on the northern edge of the highest terrace. A grand staircase led from the garden terrace to the palace, which overlooked three more terrace gardens descending into the shallow basin of the Danube. In all of the ornamental beds, the square pattern repeated itself by dividing the beds into smaller and smaller squares with cross-cutting walks. This nesting of shapes pulled the viewer's eye inward toward the center of the bed. Beginning at the river or the hunting preserve, the visitor would encounter enclosed but disordered plantings, which became increasingly ordered and geometric as he approached the palace. The design was a worldview: the bridge between God's works and the works of man was the garden.

Unlike the bürgerlich naturalism, in which the scenic orientation would be outward, away from the house, and toward the ensemble of nature, the Italian style gardens of the German nobility in the seventeenth century were oriented inward, toward the house. The difference between the classes is clear in a series of architectural drawings by Furttenbach from 1640.[9] His bürgerlich houses had

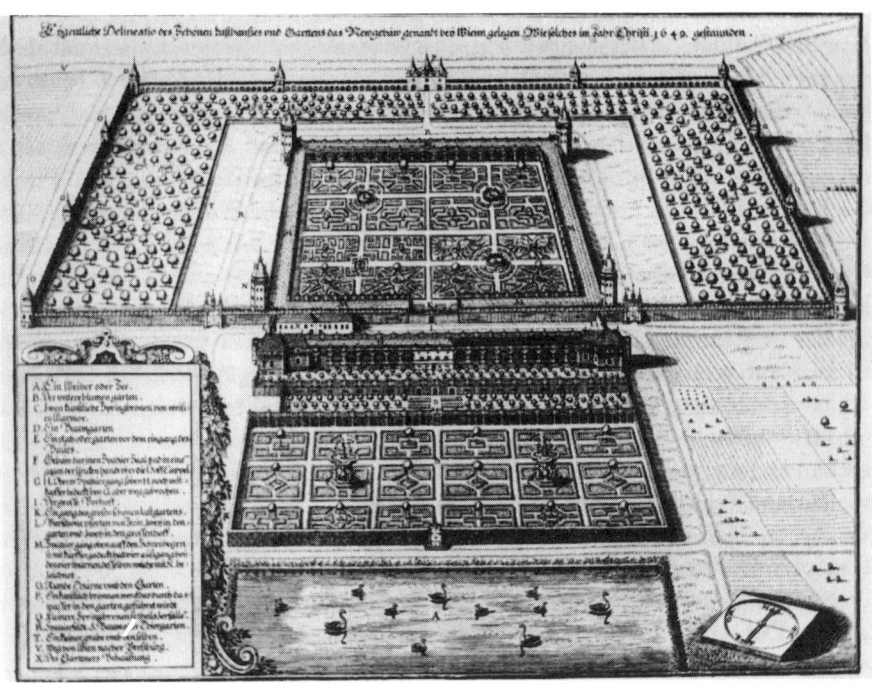

FIGURE 2. *The Neugebäude Palace of Maximilian I (1649), by Matthäus Merian, lithograph. The palace was located on the Danube below Vienna. This most important of Renaissance palace gardens north of the Alps had sixteen mazes, a hunting preserve, orchards, and twenty-four formal gardens.*
Bavarian State Library, Munich

Lustgärten behind them and no terracing, whereas the noble palaces had terraced pleasure gardens on all four sides of the house (1640: plans 2, 9, and 24). In the bürgerlich estate, ornamental beds, orchards, and vegetable beds shared the garden space evenly. The beds themselves were separated from each other by placement and simple geometric shaping with no nesting. In the noble estates, the ornamental beds dominated. Orchard and vegetable beds were of irregular shape and were relegated to a small section behind the kitchen area. These were among the first garden designs north of the Alps to build in class distinctions self-consciously.

Furttenbach showed that he could design for the sensibilities of both classes even as the bürgerlich and nobles were growing farther and farther apart. They would become even more distant in the next

150 years as the Catholic nobility of Austria seized control of the institutions of the empire and fashioned the Counter Reformation's ideological uniformity in political guise: the absolutist state.

When the second Turkish siege ended in 1683, Vienna experienced a building boom, as foreign ambassadors and nobility found increasingly strong reasons to live in the capital all year. Previously, the winter palaces within the city walls had provided sufficient housing for nobles involved in the affairs at court. But with the growth of the absolutist state, the crown demanded ever more involvement by the nobility in government affairs, and less time was available for the nobles to live at their country palaces. In the summer, the city could be quite unpleasant, especially inside the walls, and so the nobles began to construct large airy estates for themselves on the gently rising slope of the Neustadt.[10] Their palaces always faced the walled city, and their gardens lay before the palace. As seen from the palace windows, the city appeared to be another element in the composition of the garden scene (see Figure 3). The vocabulary of this garden formed a coherent corpus that was applied repeatedly in hundreds of variations to nobles' estates throughout Europe, but especially in the absolutist capitals. The baroque garden became synonymous with elite power.

The dominant stylistic influence in gardens at this time was that of the French. Le Nôtre built the gardens at Versailles in the early 1660s and in so doing, advanced three new design principles, as interpreted by the Viennese garden historian Erika Neubauer. First, every garden required a strict ground plan in which the human transformation of natural forms was complete. The plan featured a flat garden plane organized around a strong central axis. The garden was further subdivided by radial axes that cross-cut each other at regular intervals and created rectangular, triangular, and round beds. In most gardens, at least one intersection formed a cross. At first this element was merely symbolic, but over time it became the most often used motif in city planning and garden design. The subdivisions formed rooms, some large and open (*parterres*), some small and enclosed by finely groomed hedge walls (*bosquets*), and some sunken below the level of walks (*boulingrins*). Exhibitions of every kind, theatrical performances, ballet, and waterworks, as well as parties for the highest levels of society, took place in these outside rooms.

A second postulate was the design for eternity. This meant that

FIGURE 3. *Garden of the Belvedere Palace as seen from one of the palace windows. The city of Vienna appears to be part of the composition. Located on a hill overlooking the city, the palace was built by Prince Eugene of Savoy as a residence and reception palace for foreign ambassadors. It is this garden that most Viennese name when they are describing gardens of order.*

evergreen plants were most often employed, first to ensure that the garden was green in every season and second to permit the geometric cuttings that transformed their natural growth patterns. No plant was allowed to keep its natural shape. All conformed to the forms of the intellect as coded in geometry and the conventions of antique sculpture. At his palace, the Belvedere, Prince Eugene of Savoy had one yew tree cut into the shape of the Turkish helmet to commemorate his role in the defeat of the Turks during the second siege.[11] Through this imposition of control, the aristocrat proclaimed his limitless power.

Finally, the unexpected was banned. From entry to exit visitors responded passively to the impressions evoked by the garden's construction. This intense control over how the garden was to be experienced mirrored the ideal of absolutism in which the citizen was led passively by the nobility to effective economic and political participation (Neubauer 1980:9–15).

The main axis began at the façade of the house (middle tract) and led the visitors from the house interior to the exterior garden rooms, which were continuations of the interiors and served as ornamental showcases reflecting the magnificence of the lord. Here the guests could walk or ride horses or coaches through the architecture. When they left the palace, the visitors would be immersed in the shadow of the main building, where the garden appeared cool and airy. Once out of the shadow, the visitors were in the parterre, the main room of the garden, with its symmetric beds lying along the main axis. These were sometimes called carpet parterres because of the complicated patterning of greens and flowers, as in a woven rug. The patterns followed formal rules derived from pattern books dating back to the sixteenth century. These carpet gardens were among the proudest possessions of the lord, and complex well-embroidered beds were famous throughout Europe.

A garden that typifies the French style in Vienna is the garden palace Schönbrunn. A portion of this garden can be seen in Figure 4. The grounds of this palace have remained relatively intact since its initial design by the French garden architect Jean Trehet in the years 1705–6.[12] The stylistic elements of the gardens were enhanced and refined by two later garden directors, Adrian van Steckhofen in 1753 and Johann Ferdinand Hetzendorf von Hohenberg in 1772 (Neubauer and Auböck 1980).

The garden was first opened to the public in the 1820s. For generations of Viennese the magnificence of these grounds has served as the most exquisite example of this style and represents the most humanized of the gardens of order. Perhaps because the original designers took Maria Theresa's young princes and princesses into account, Viennese children have always enjoyed playing in Schönbrunn. The little paths through the bosquets, the secret "rooms," the ducks swimming in the fountains at the intersections of paths, the small zoo, the huge statuary, and the intimacy of the flower gardens have engaged the imaginations of children for generations.

The huge main parterre begins immediately behind and on the same plane as the palace. There are two long lawn beds on either side of the main axis, which itself is a gravel walk as wide as the lawn beds.

FIGURE 4. *Prince's side garden of the Schönbrunn Summer Palace of Maria Theresa (1705–1706). The principles employed by Jean Trehet for the entire palace grounds are evident in detail in this small garden: a strict adherence to geometric symmetry, the use of evergreens to keep the garden attractive in every season, and a high level of predictability in line and mass.*

The lawns were originally cut into carpet patterns. Today, the patterns are created with plantings of different colored flowers. The main parterre was enclosed on the sides by high walls of yew trees. At the far end, facing the back of the palace, is a steep hill, at the base of which are a large pool and a collection of statues in the Greek Antique style depicting Neptune and his court (installed in 1780). Towering above the parterre on the crest of the hill is the Gloriette (installed in 1775), a treillage arcade whose columns were taken from the Neugebäude. On either side of the main parterre are two large areas of bosquets, boulingrins, and labyrinths. The cross-cutting paths are many. Trehet brought a thousand taxus trees with him from France for the bosquets and hedge walls. Wherever eight paths intersect, a round fountain is placed in the center. Two formal gardens extend on either side of palace, each with its own chain of bosquets with the central axis cutting through the middle. On the sides of the hill with the Gloriette are forests. The left side is cut through with paths but is otherwise undeveloped. The right side is more interesting since it includes two gardens designed by members of the royal house: an alpine garden laid out by the Archduke Johann in the English style (1800) on the north slope,[13] and a Swiss garden designed by Maximilian I of Mexico on the west slope (1850, today Maxingpark).[14] At the base of the hill below the Swiss garden is the Dutch style botanical garden (1848).[15] At the base of the alpine garden is a zoo, first built in 1752 by Franz I, the most horticulturally accomplished of all Habsburg royals. In the later half of the eighteenth century, a period art historians call the rococo, von Hohenberg placed a number of curiosities at strategic points in the garden to surprise and delight visitors. These include the Gloriette and Neptune fountain and also a Roman ruin (1778), a cascade with an Egyptian obelisk (1777), and stone sculptures of mythic figures by Wilhelm Beyer (1781). In 1882, the largest glass house in Europe, the House of Palms, was built near the zoo to hold the collection of palm and cactus plants accumulated by Habsburgs from their sponsorship of various voyages of discovery. The Schönbrunn gardens were sumptuous, rich in visual interest, and overwhelming in size and variety. More importantly for the present discussion, they were magnificent portrayals of royal power.

To be effective, the absolutist values of the French style required clear views of the design elements that communicated power. Two additional qualities of these gardens are their transparency (*Durchsicht*) and scenic views (*Fernblicke*). As one walks inside the gardens there is a constant change in points of interest. One can see through from bosquet to bosquet, often through treillage arches. There is always something to catch the eye—a statue, a bush cut into a bizarre shape, a chapel, a bird cage, or a fountain. One can stand a few yards behind the palace and look down eight different alleys, each with something at the end of it. The powers of these devices diminish if they are not immediately accessible to the eye. As one climbs to the Gloriette, the axes and alleys are seen extending beyond the limits of the palace grounds. They cut through the entire city, drawing the eye to faraway churches, other palaces, or sites of importance to the history of royal power. These are the so-called *points de vu*. In Schönbrunn, the alleys were laid out in such a way that the palace was always visible at one end and some important landmark at the other.

MAP 2. *Baroque landscapes of the early eighteenth century.* Shaded areas indicate districts that experienced a building boom in garden palaces among the nobility. The locations of the four major sites discussed in the text are indicated.

The landmark could be quite far from the park. If these distant places were visible from the Gloriette, then the Gloriette was visible from them, as well. This was the hallmark of the absolutist garden: a clearly defined center to which everything else, even nature, bowed.

SOCIAL PRODUCTION OF GARDENS OF ORDER

Originally, housing in the city lay inside the walled fortress. It was inevitable that population growth would first consume all free space within these confines. Beyond the Glacis, individual noble families or church organizations developed a series of tracts for housing, provisioning, and other services for the central city. At the far end of these tracts independent agricultural and craft villages stretched up the low hills of the Wienerwald. Each of these zones included a different type of Viennese house and garden (Map 2).

The earliest plan of the city to specify garden space was that of Wolmuet from 1547. His map had green-colored areas to specify the gardens behind, within, and sometimes in front of the houses inside the city walls. The gardens were not evenly distributed; most of the

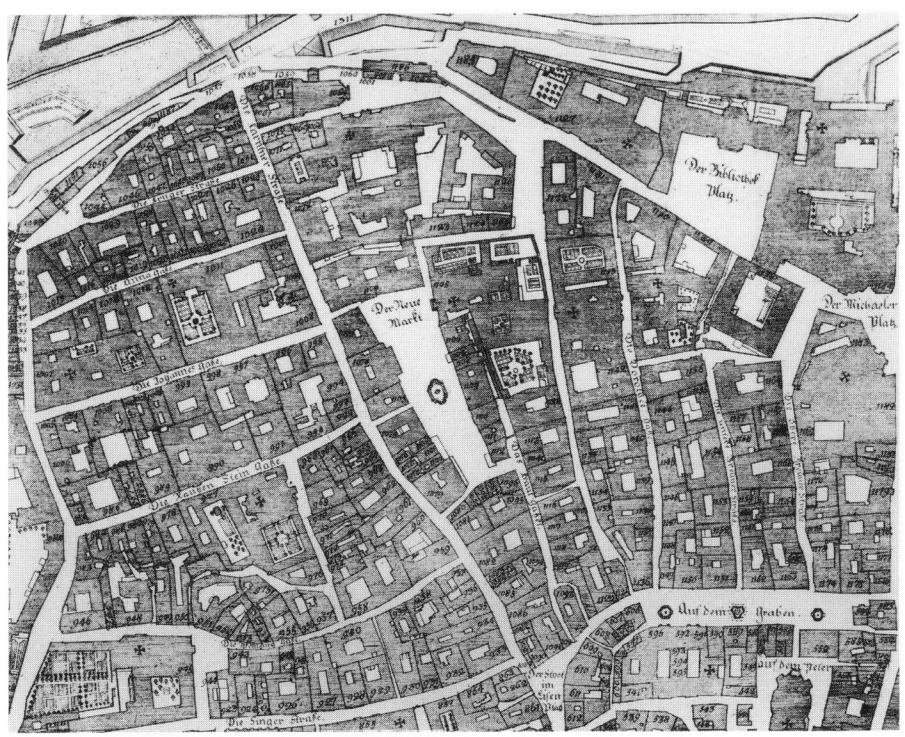

FIGURE 5. *Detail from the Josephinische Landesaufnahme (1773–1781). This figure illustrates the density of the built space inside the walled city in the late eighteenth century.*
Austrian National Library

city had already built over its garden space (see Figure 5). Only the newest residential quarter of the city, the streets south of Kärntnerstrasse, still retained their private gardens. There were also still large convents and cloisters within the city, and these possessed the largest gardens. Visitors to Vienna in the sixteenth century were impressed by the care people took in their gardens. However, we know that gardens had been completely crowded from view within the confines of the walled city by the end of that century. The houses there were two- and three-story structures on the Italian model: a square building surrounding an open courtyard. This courtyard once housed the garden. But as ground rents rose, the courtyard became smaller and smaller until its equestrian and storage functions alone remained. What the visitors were remarking about were the new so-called garden developments in the tracts just beyond the Glacis. Here the nobility built their summer palaces and the religious orders their cloisters. These buildings, influenced by Renaissance and later baroque models from Italy and France, included the garden as an exterior room.[16] Among these expensive and expansive estates were smaller patrician houses illustrating the kind of housing that may have existed within the city walls before the sixteenth century. These were rectangular plots of 600–800 square meters, with a house on the street and a walled garden behind. These are completely obliterated today but can be seen clearly on earlier lithographic cataster maps. In the nearby villages, the housing was the same as that found throughout this eastern section of Lower Austria: courtyards closed to the street by a wall, with the house surrounding the courtyard on one, two, or (rarely) three sides. The courtyard was large enough to include a garden. These villages formed the core around which factories and workers' barracks were built (see Figure 6).

The eighteenth-century maps show the result of the building boom that began after the lifting of the Turkish siege in 1683. The noble estates were built closer to the city walls. In 1720, the numbers of noble houses with gardens were as follows: in Leopoldstadt, 200; in Weissgrund, 110; in Wieden, 58; in Lerchenfeld, 137; in Josefstadt, 119; in Alsergrund, 58; in Rossau, 86 (Bermann 1881:392ff.). Before the war, these districts had contained a mix of patrician houses and small trade and commercial establishments. These numbers demonstrate two aspects of the building boom in this period. First, it was politically necessary for nobles to have larger-scale domiciles in the capital, as the aristocrats were spending more time there. Second, the ostentatious displays that larger-scale estates permitted had become an important element in class behavior. The estate building pushed civilian functions farther away from the Glacis. Small trades, transport and warehousing, and commercial farms were no longer within a short walking distance of the city. In this way, the size of the activity area for urban economy increased dramatically and with it the volume of carriage traffic.

In this building boom the relationship of public and private investment was skewed. Many of the noble estates were built with money provided by the imperial house in gratitude for military services rendered during the Turkish siege. The most famous of these endowments was the Belvedere of Prince Eugene. The land for this

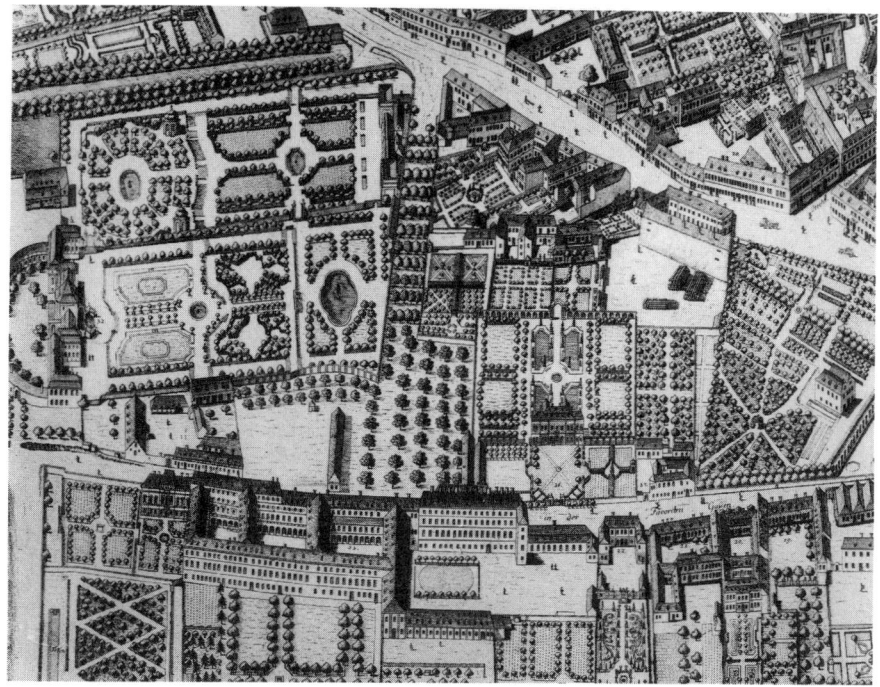

FIGURE 6. *Josef Nagel's lithograph "Plan of Vienna" from 1770–1771 showing a portion of the Wieden district. This district was rebuilt with aristocratic palaces in the early eighteenth century. The large palace and French gardens in the* upper right *are those of the Schönborn family. Also visible are smaller gardens, including four paradise gardens (paths in the shape of a cross), orchard gardens, and small Renaissance gardens (*center*).*

estate and much of the building costs were direct gifts from a grateful emperor. Large tracts in the most desirable districts belonged to religious orders. Over time, these estates were either bought by the crown, exchanged by the crown for estates farther from the desirable building ground, or, with the permission of the crown, sold as sections by the orders directly to aristocratic clients. In this way, the crown also controlled the availability of building land near the city. The rebuilding of the civilian sector, on the other hand, was entirely a private affair. With the exception of a few wealthy Bürgers, most civilian investment went to the less visible outlying sections of the inner districts. The massive costs of building the aristocratic estates did remain in the Viennese economy, and these funds trickled down through the commercial outlets, permitting civilian building to continue at a steady rate. By 1720, thirty-seven years after the lifting of the siege, the city had doubled in size.[17]

The strong ornamentality of the Dutch and French styles continued as the dominant garden style among those Bürgers who built their estates in the early nineteenth century. The style turned up in otherwise modest gardens in the lithographic maps in the 1830s. The garden style provided a simple way of declaring one's identification with aristocratic interests and served the social needs of businessmen who frequently entertained nobility. Alternative styles were available to these Bürgers, as the next two chapters will demonstrate. Thus, the businessman's willingness to build a garden of order, though couched in the language of taste and distinction, was a political signal and a symbol of class-based interests.

THE HETEROTOPIA OF ORDER

The period of absolutist ascendance produced gardens that were extraordinary places. Each was systematically designed to extol the glories of the aristocratic state. The icon of these gardens was the geometrically straight line. Nothing is less natural than an uncompromising file. By successfully imposing the line upon its antithesis, the antigeometry of plant growth, the garden patron explored the limits of absolute rule. From conception to daily maintenance, the baroque garden was the product of command decision making. It evoked the image of security and harmony which emerged out of aristocratically imposed order. In the climate of today's democratic municipality, the effect of these gardens, preserved in their baroque arrangements, is more sublime than beautiful.

This exercise of power was worthless unless it was observed and understood by the subjects of the aristocrat. This required that the space be large enough to attract attention, a theatrical landscape in which chamber-sized versions of the absolutist drama could be played out as entertainment. These landscapes had to evoke the same fear and pity among those who visited them as that evoked by the *Trauerspiele* played on the real stages of the seventeenth and eighteenth centuries (Benjamin 1977). The baroque landscape in Vienna dwarfed the individuals, reducing their wills and desires to insignificance and proclaiming the glory of the men who would build and maintain such places.[18] Ironically, the very people who the Viennese gardens were ostensibly meant to impress, the urban craftsmen and local commercial barons, were specifically excluded from visiting the gardens until the end of the eighteenth century. By then, aristocratic confidence was on the wane and turning reactionary. Mere landscapes of control were no longer enough.

The baroque landscape is a fantasy palace. It is a building made entirely of landscape materials and plants, but it is roofless. In this palace, men have consecrated the divine recognition of their election to greatness by living in a house that rules nature the way a carpenter rules wood, or a mason brick and mortar. Thus, on one level, these landscapes are metaphors of construction. To accomplish this imposition of geometry, all of the quirks of nature must be smoothed away. The process is unrelenting. The materials are alive and growing in disorderly and anarchic directions. Their movement toward light and water must be constantly monitored, snipped, redirected, and disciplined. In this sense, the landscapes are metaphors for destruction. The radical rule of geometry betrays the unruly power of nature.

The temporal quality of the baroque landscape today is that of an anachronism, a museum to a political discourse that is no longer relevant to Vienna. When first designed, it distinguished its special feeling for time by moving to its own rhythm and not the rhythm of nature which governed other gardens. The orange trees that formed the walls of a bosquet near the lower palace of the Belvedere were moved inside to a special glass-walled Orangerie and continued to bloom through the Viennese winter. Plants whose flowering was forced by special techniques in greenhouses were then moved outdoors in early spring far ahead of blooms deprived of such special treatment. Summer flowers continued to bloom through the autumn, as more plants whose flowering was artificially held back in glass houses replaced those in the flower parterres whose bloom was finished.

Contemporary baroque landscapes exhibit a different break with ordinary social time. They are museumlike accumulations of indefinite time, relics of earlier epochs preserved to serve as models for a past social order. In these gardens, time never stops accumulating. The act of preservation, of valuing the past precisely because of its distance from the present, is the quintessential project of modernity.

For the late twentieth-century Viennese, the baroque garden was an object lesson in why the past had no social relevance to the present. It became a museum of landscape, as prized for its historical reference as the palaces within it.

Baroque landscapes are simultaneously open from the inside and closed from the outside. They are positioned in the topography to take advantage of *points de vu* over the dominion of the aristocrat. When one is standing at the appropriate spot, the view from inside the garden extends to the horizon. At the same time, the high walls around the entire estate ensured that there could be no mixing of the social classes in the garden. There were no lookout points for the powerless to stare inside at the gardens of the rich. These boundaries derived from the confident belief that the separation of different orders of beings into their distinct realms was dictated by the natural order of things. These walls protected the garden and this aging philosophy from unruly affronts to their integrity. The garden was constructed as if the audience for its design needed to be reminded of the patron's power. Given the narrow range of Viennese who would have visited these gardens in the eighteenth century, the reminder could only have been intended for the patron himself and members of his class. The garden represented social power to the members of the class that possessed it.

The meaning of the baroque landscape was to offer in space a perfect and meticulous tribute to the glories of the rule by absolutist aristocrat and to set this off against the jumble and disorder of the ordinary landscape. This was true at the time of its design, when civil unrest, plague, and wars were the norm of city life. It is also true of the landscape today, when the fastidious lines of the gardens evoke feelings of coldness, artificiality, and constraint. Analyzing the gardens of order is no mere historical exercise. The struggle in the metropolis to dichotomize the landscape into the sacred and the profane, the intimate and the foreign, the ordered and the disordered is as important today as it was in 1700. The battle is taking place simultaneously in the newly created public spaces and in the gardens of private homes. In this contest, the icons of the gardens of order continue to mark the ground that has been recaptured from chaos. Gardens of order are linked to those other gardens in which nature reigns and in which the work of the human hand is unseen. These natural gardens, these gardens of liberty, are the next form to evolve in the Viennese landscape. Without the prior existence of the gardens of order they would lack any significance. Because the gardens of order came before them, these gardens of liberty defiantly reminded the forces of control that order is fleeting, and chaos is the rule of the universe.

Gardens of Order

Gardens
of
Liberty

The eighteenth century saw a clash of political culture in Central Europe at least as profound as the conflict between bureaucratic socialist and liberal capitalist states in the twentieth century. The competing ideologies were absolutism, which vested political power in a dynastic monarchy, and enlightened republicanism, which vested power in a broad base of powerful economic interests. Both forms could be progressive or conservative. All of the Habsburg emperors endorsed absolutism. Some were reformist and progressive, like Maria Theresa and her son Joseph II. Others were conservative, like Franz I and Franz Josef. Republican elements were popular among young Viennese aristocrats and merchants before the French Revolution. These men read Rousseau and discussed Tom Paine. All were classic liberals in the sense that they wanted to free capitalist development from the constraints of governmental restrictions and to free civic affairs from government censorship.

Following the death of Joseph II in 1793 and the subsequent reversal of his reforms by aristocratic politicians, and especially after the Congress of Vienna (1812–14), republicanism was severely persecuted. Under these repressive circumstances, the only kind of middle-class public life permitted was one that mimicked the conservative social ideologies of the aristocracy. The harassment of anything that suggested liberalism or republicanism was achieved overtly by hostile editorials in newspapers and covertly by an effective secret police operation under the control of the chief minister of state, Prince Metternich. This persecution persisted for three and a half decades. Metternich was finally ousted from power by the widescale uprisings known as the 1848 Revolution. These riots had middle-class nationalists revolting against aristocrats, foreign-born fighting local Viennese, workers burning factories in the suburbs, and tradesmen and small property owners attacking the government offices that regulated their businesses. Assaulted on so many different fronts, the military suffered an embarrassing stalemate, and the absolutist state crumbled. The emperor was forced to negotiate with liberal politicians, eventually permitting them to form a government, first in the city of Vienna and later in the councils of the empire. The liberal political platforms that emerged after the 1848 Revolution emphasized economic freedoms over broad-based social and political empowerment. A liberal platform that benefits only the rich is a conservative republicanism.

Absolutism made its statements about culture and nature, person and state, through the ideas enshrined in the gardens of order. The Enlightenment carried on its images of these issues in a form I call the gardens of liberty. These landscapes were symbolic calls to revolution in the late eighteenth century, and only aristocrats whose loyalties were beyond reproach could politically afford to install the first ones. The free development of the landscape, like the development of civil society, was emblematic of the liberal movement. Within a few decades this style grew in popularity as greater numbers of wealthy Bürgers endorsed it. The style evolved into a canon of landscape design which held sway until the late nineteenth century.

What the Viennese call English style is actually a class of landscapes designed to avoid as scrupulously as possible any hint of the hand of human design. The randomness and chaos of nature are imitated or, at the very least, alluded to. No geometry, symmetry, or artifice is permitted. In its purest form, the English style is identical with the undeveloped environment. In this formulation, the French and the English styles are as opposite a set of styles for design of places as one could imagine.[1] The French gardens are easily recognized by their strangeness. The English are so comfortable to the eye that they are unremarkable. Only when the English and the French styles are juxtaposed with each other in the same estate does the English stand out.

The juxtaposition of human order with the order of nature is not as simple as it first appears. Nature's order is represented in different ways, and during the period in question, one or another of these dominated the gardens of liberty. Longinus, the first-century A.D. Roman, described the approaches to nature's order as the beautiful, the sublime, and the picturesque (1987). Briefly put, nature is beautiful when it reveals qualities that we can identify as human. It is sublime when its awesome power and inhuman enormity overwhelm us. It is picturesque when it reveals itself as playful, childlike, and harmless. Aspects of the earliest gardens of liberty around Vienna toyed with incorporating the sublime, especially if a view of the high Eastern Alps (fifty miles south of the city) was available. For the most part, however, the local experience with these gardens emphasized the beautiful and the picturesque. The concept of nature remained within the Enlightenment mind set as a force made acceptable and benign through rational understanding. Nature had become a good neighbor. The human qualities projected onto nature were the dark, romantic yearnings for the transcendence of human problems, especially death, but also the friendly playground of eternal childhood. Depending on the social standing of the patron, one of these themes might dominate the other. Gardens of enlightened republican-leaning aristocrats, like Field Marshall Lacy's park at Neuwaldegg, were consistently dark and ominous with memorials of various kinds scattered through shadowy woodlands, waiting to be discovered by the pensive wanderer. Others, like the park built by the liberal banking family Geymüller at Pötzleinsdorf, were open and airy, with heroic statuary scattered among the trees.

Because of the commonplace, unbounded quality of the English parkscape, there is no single word that describes gardens of liberty in contemporary Viennese parlance, as Ziergarten was for gardens of order. The closest is *Naturgarten*, nature garden. Twentieth-century experiences have added connotations to this term which make it less precise as a label for the late eighteenth- and early nineteenth-century landscapes. Like gardens of order, gardens of liberty exist today primarily as symbolic echoes within the complex urban landscape. One rarely finds their principles fully developed in actual gardens. Thus, although Neuwaldegg and Pötzleinsdorf still exist and are publicly accessible, their design has been altered to serve the needs of a modern park administration. Today, one sees the gardens of liberty design principles expressed in combination with later ideas, as evidenced by how the Viennese describe their gardens.

Three themes emerge from these descriptions. Like gardens of order, gardens of liberty have a specific visual component: an absence of humanly imposed order, a lack of symmetry. The formula for referring to these gardens always includes the phrase *seeing green* or *living in green*, as in the following statements: "We wanted a little bit of green and peace and quiet, so that we could work in the studio and feel the connection between life and nature."[2] "It is simply beautiful when you see the green that you plant and watch it grow."[3] This connection between life and nature is one of the original elements in the Central European interpretation of the English canon. The connection is visual. One plants, and then one watches. From this meditation one realizes beauty. What exactly constitutes the aesthetic of nature can be discovered in the garden of liberty more easily than in the garden of order.

A second theme is that of free and unrestricted growth. The formula phrase for this theme is, "Everything that will grow, grows as it will." This means that the less intervention in the development of the garden the better. This formula has many variations, but the underlying meaning is always clear:

> Everything that grows and that grows in the wild, grows wild here. There is not much cutting. Everything comes from Nature. I do nothing to it, like cut the trees in a form or cut them shorter, or I don't know what else. Everything should grow as it grows.[4]

The advantage of giving the garden over to the processes of nature is the realization of the secrets that lie hidden in nature's fecundity. These secrets speak not only to the hidden processes but also to the spirit of the place:

> For example, it pleases me to enjoy seeing the history of this settlement, the history of my garden in the course of the year. Things grow there that

are unbelievable. In winter, one cannot see what sorts of bizarre bushes are there. And suddenly in spring one sees rare Japanese lanterns that must have been planted here years ago because they grow so slowly.[5]

This last garden happened to be seventy years old. Other people with whom I spoke had created gardens of liberty from scratch. These gardens contained species that had blown in with the wind and were allowed to take root and grow. Some of the modern gardeners of liberty add a *Biotop*, an open pond intended to attract algae, water plants, amphibians, and the like. These extreme experiments in biological freedom are known as nature gardens. As mentioned above, they have characteristics belonging to the experience of the twentieth century, such as the native plants movement and the organic gardening movement. They will be discussed more fully as gardens of reaction and gardens of discovery.

The eighteenth-century conflict between gardens of order and gardens of liberty has never ceased. The nature of the contradiction has moved from radical understandings of the relation of people and the state to radical understandings of the nature of neighborliness in garden maintenance. Unrestricted growth gardens are not compatible with neighboring weedfree lawns. Garden settlements and garden associations have strict rules against unrestricted growth. The municipal parks department has the authority to order pesticide spraying and can even take control of any garden on municipal land which is considered to be a biological hazard to its neighbors. On privately owned lands such intervention requires court action. The few gardens of liberty I observed were all on privately owned land or in the courtyards of small apartment buildings where the renters and owners were all in agreement on their preference of this garden form.

The final theme expressed in the image of the garden of liberty is the flexibility to express one's own will. At the domestic level, such gardens are often remarkable for the way they sustain idiosyncrasy in ground plan and plants.

> We have planned the garden more or less to realize all the wishes that we wanted for our garden and our home. We have a certain amount of privacy, a certain amount of free space. There are also cozy corners where, as they say so beautifully, one has a home away from home. There is enough free room for the possibility to use the space optimally as both a recreational garden and a vegetable garden.[6]

The formula that expresses this theme involves the declaration of one's wishes or desires in the garden, or the pleasure found in a garden that mirrors one's personal taste.

> We planted everything. In that sense, it actually mirrors our wishes. We weren't influenced by others' opinions. Only our own wishes. We said we wanted certain plants here. We wanted thin conifers there. We wanted skyrockets, we have skyrockets.... When we look at it we see our decisions mirrored back to us.[7]

The idea that some places are extraordinary because in them people can express themselves through the garden form is only possible if this self-expression is seldom realized elsewhere. Much of the appeal of domestic gardens is this provision.

These design principles are not merely technical features or historical abstractions; rather the elements enter into the common discourse on the meaning of extraordinary and ordinary places for the Viennese who plant and cultivate gardens. These principles are found in the public parks financed by the municipal government for popular use. More importantly, the popularly understood principles that make such places extraordinary are frequently cited as people describe the garden forms that give them the greatest comfort. This means that within the metropolitan discourse on landscape, the garden of liberty is a powerful and productive image.

DISCOURSE ON GARDENS OF LIBERTY

Landscape is a way of seeing the products of human activity in the environment. Landscape is based not so much on how things are but on how they should be. A *natural landscape* is a contradiction in terms: it refers to an environment in which human activity is invisible. One expects to see an unsullied and chaste countryside. In the eighteenth century, these natural-looking parkscapes became very popular in England and the Netherlands. These English gardens, as they were called, originated in the 1720s when an architect named William Kent incorporated the features of the surrounding countryside into the grounds of a country house.[8] Kent was a trained theatrical designer-turned-garden architect whose designs responded to the topography, botanical variety, plant density, interplay of sunlight and shade, and water features of a particular place. Kent celebrated nature as beautiful in itself and worthy of imitation. He was a self-conscious garden designer who was concerned that visitors to gardens become actors in a drama. To this end, he designed gardens to be read like texts and divided into scenes. The text often concerned the history of garden design as a narrative of human civilization. The margins of his drawings frequently included texts culled from classical authors and poets (Hunt 1990:233). His stance was that of the picturesque—the playful elements in nature, stripped of their awe and their danger.

Seeing nature in this way contrasts sharply with the Italian and French views of nature as a realm of chaos which must be subjugated and ordered, just as the chaotic tendencies of society were rectified by the strong rule of the Christian monarch. A number of English scholars have suggested that the new style coincided with the rise of a new power elite in England, the gentry, who had profited from the enclosures and the rationalization of capitalist agriculture (Hunt 1986; Pugh 1988; Williams 1973). In part to differentiate themselves from the older feudal families and in part to reach back into an older language of exterior space, the English gentry restyled existing estates or laid out new ones in the new style of gardening. In most cases, the houses imitated on small parcels of land the country homes of the old aristocracy. The genius of gardeners like Kent, and later Capability Brown, was to create sweeping vistas of seamless countryside in which the geometric fields of rationalized agriculture and the smokestacks of nascent industry would disappear. Another view is that the constitutional monarchy of eighteenth-century England was looking to distance itself from the past trappings of absolutist power, itself best accomplished by the French style (Pugh 1988). This helps to explain why even older English aristocratic families had built natural gardens on their estates by the 1760s. By 1780, the English garden type had begun to establish itself in the surroundings of Vienna. Within thirty years, numerous estates were created or redesigned to incorporate the new principles.

According to Hennebo, Vienna was not far behind other German cities in adopting the form and rhetoric of the English style in noble estates. He placed their first appearance in northern German estates around 1760 (Hennebo 1980:15). Even so, the aristocracy had begun to turn away from the French style as early as 1710. This was as political a decision in Germany as it was in Vienna, involving a moving away from the architectonic garden as symbol and image of the hierarchical world and social orders.

This relatively late acceptance of the style can be attributed to the conservatism of the potential patrons. State Chancellor Kaunitz, who often supported French Enlightenment political philosophies, defended his baroque palace gardens in the 1780s as the more rational design in comparison with the disorder and melancholy of the English garden. The imperial family itself also favored French baroque gardens at its residences and maintained these even into the twentieth century. Joseph II knew that most of his aristocracy would tolerate reforms, such as universal education, free movement of agricultural workers, a centralized tax administration, a single language of administration, and the partial demilitarization of the city of Vienna, but not English constitutionalism or English parkscapes. A smaller number of nobles held more radical ideas and became the patrons of English parkscapes in their Vienna residences.[9]

The English parkscape presented a new way of seeing nature, especially the nature that is found in the "in-between" places that one passed through on the way to various aristocratic country houses. In the baroque, nature was understood as both beautiful and useful, as a possession that is both sensuously desirable and economically profitable, as is evident in this 1730 passage from the writings of Johann Küchelbecker:

> The surroundings of the city begin below Klosterneuburg on the Danube with the heavily forested hill named the Kahlenberg. From there, one proceeds westward to the Vienna Woods, which gives the appearance of unlimited pleasures, especially in Spring and Summer when everything is green. Still further on, the eyes are charmed by convenient wine villages on the merry, fruitful, and semicircle-shaped hills that surround the city, from which an overflow of quite good wine is produced. The broad arms of the Danube itself bestow upon the City the pleasant feature of many wooded islands, a property that cannot be found in any other German city. To the South, many fields, hillside vineyards, and beautiful pleasure gardens surround the hills.[10]

Küchelbecker's passage is an inventory of possessions. His highest pleasure was the view of a hillside vineyard.

By 1766, the perspective on nature changed. In a chapter entitled "On the beauty of the site of the City of Vienna and the surrounding district...," Fuhrmann used Küchelbecker's passage as a model to develop his own portrait of the Vienna surroundings. In his account, there was a change in viewpoint. Fuhrmann saw nature as not only beautiful, but also generous; it was the creator of lush visual sensations.

> What can one report of the beautiful site and pleasant rural surroundings of Vienna, which is certainly the most desirable of all German cities. Those who have climbed the Leopoldsberg, or Josephsberg on a bright day, two hills not far from the Kahlenberg, and have taken in the rich scenery from there, agree. Oh, what a beautiful district is revealed! Certainly the most beautiful landscapes in the entire world unfold before the eyes. Were one to view the entire city with the suburbs to the south, to the east, and to the north, width and breadth, the many miles of trails running out to fertile fields, interspersed with frequent villages; to the west, and on the side of the Kahlenberg, this side and beyond the Danube to the Bisamberg, and far around, one sees the uncountable vineyard hills, green undergrowth, and the plethora of meadows, islets, and Danube islands. One seldom finds elsewhere such a feast for the eyes as is revealed there. (1766:231)

In Fuhrmann's hymn of praise to the Viennese district, the view from the top of the mountain replaced Küchelbecker's bird's-eye view. These writings are an effusive and purely aesthetic estimation of the landscape as seen from a specific viewing point. Atop the mountain, one no longer needs the transparent geometry of the baroque to see what is valued. The eyes are permitted to wander through the boundlessness of the countryside. After hiking and climbing to the mountaintop, one attains a sacred place, from which nature—heretofore perceived as disordered—transforms itself in a coherent ensemble (Hajós 1989:24–25).

That new way of seeing was the growing appreciation for looking upon and contemplating the *Gegenden*, the district surrounding the city of Vienna. The reinvention of nature in the Viennese surroundings began with the acknowledgment of the freedom of nature. By incorporating this freedom into garden design, parkscapes became leisure time attractions to the urban population and objects of worship which satisfied the new secularism favored by those antagonistic to the aristocracy and its church. Freemasonry, classical humanism, and ultimately nature sciences, especially botany, ecology, and geology, were the denominations within this romantic nature religion.

By the end of the eighteenth century, the English style had diffused from the Enlightenment aristocracy to the landowning bourgeoisie. The increasing popularity of parkscapes produced a profusion of guidebooks for hiking through the Vienna surroundings. These began to appear after 1790 (Gaheis 1794; Oehler 1807; Pezzl 1807; Widemann 1805). The guides prompted the Bürger to take his family on long walks in the countryside on weekends, to find those blessed places, the culmination points, from which the view was breathtaking. The newly designed parkscape gardens of the Enlightenment aristocrats were irresistible attractions to the wandering Bürgers, symbolizing the ideal view of nature in the Vienna district. Park sites were chosen for their outlooks of the surrounding landscape or the city itself.

The earliest of these gardens was Neuwaldegg (1779), the garden of Field Marshall Moritz Duke of Lacy. It lay an hour's carriage ride west of the city in the Wienerwald. The original estate purchased by Lacy in 1766 was a French style country villa with a small formal garden. To reach it, carriage paths had been cut through the surrounding forest. Out of gratitude for his military service and his close friendship with Joseph II, Empress Maria Theresa exempted Lacy from securing permits to remove trees on his estate and thereby enabled his gardeners to transform the forest land into a parkscape. When Rousseau died, Lacy planted a tree group in his memory. As Lacy grew older he seldom left his estate and eventually became known as the hermit of Neuwaldegg. The duke had philosophical ambitions, read all of the French philosophers, and belonged to a salon whose members included progressive aristocrats, many of whom would eventually establish English parks in their estates. The gardens of Rasumofsky, the Russian ambassador to the Habsburg court after 1793, were built under the direction of the most famous gardener of the time, Konrad Rosenthal (Figure 7). The garden was a favorite gathering spot for the lower aristocracy and the bourgeoisie at the time of the Congress of Vienna (1814).[11]

The new English gardens differed from their French predecessors in the way that they relied on visual perspective. Instead of an absolute center defined by a clear geometry, the new type of garden offered artistic and spiritual culmination points arrived at through the freedom of fantasy. These culmination points included outlooks and views of the countryside, but also *fabriques*: Gothic ruins, Palladian

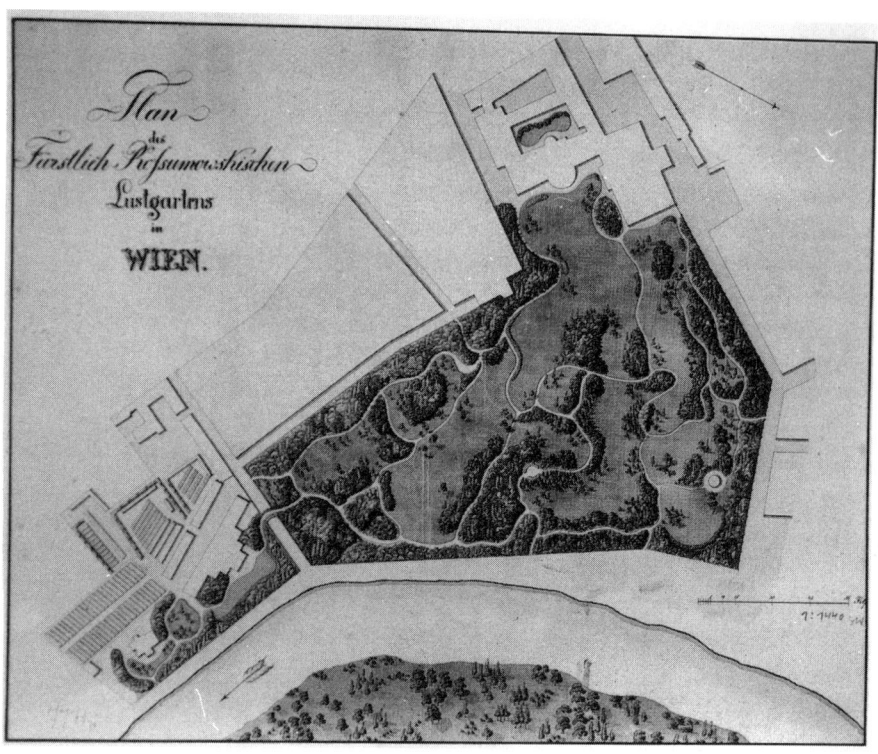

FIGURE 7. *The plan of the estate of the Russian ambassador Rasumofsky. The plan was executed by Konrad Rosenthal, who also contributed to Lacy's Neuwaldegg and many other romantic gardens of the early nineteenth century. Note the use of denser growth to create the park boundaries and the free-curve carriage paths cutting along the edges of the meadows.*

temples, Chinese bridges and temples, grottos, fishing huts, log cabins, mausoleums, monuments, and memorials. The park designed for the Geymüller family by Rosenthal in 1891 (Figure 8) featured a small number of fabriques that can still be seen today. Among these were Greek style statuary, a temple, a grotto, and a pedestal urn. Mosser (1990) reviewed the extensive literature on fabriques. So popular were these constructions that entire magazines devoted to distributing the latest designs, such as LeRouge's *Les jardins anglo-chinois* (1787) and Grohmann's *Ideemagazin* (1796–1802), had very large circulations. Mosser believed that the art of garden fabriques constituted a separate branch of architecture in which "obsession may verge on mania; where the taste for concealment (and for rev-

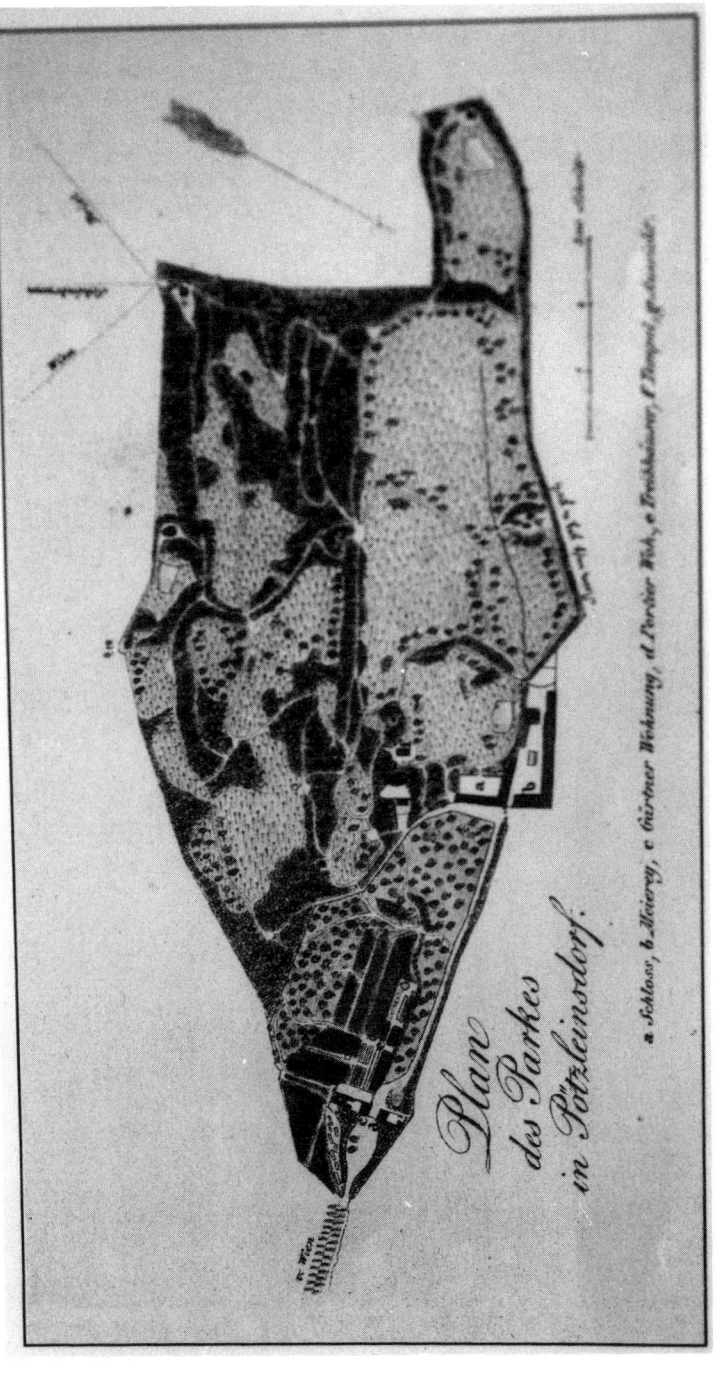

FIGURE 8. *Pötzleinsdorfer Park as it stood in 1850, ground plan by J. V. Reim. By carefully tracing the footpaths, the stroller could discover the twelve fabriques placed in the park, including statuary; a fishing hut; a vase on a pedestal; a temple; and, in the southwest corner, a lookout point.*

elation) may inspire many curious contrivances; where excess, pure and simple, is adequate proof that it was in gardens that these cherished 'visionaries' were able to realize their finest fantasies" (1990:263). Each fabrique became part of the garden's narrative. Often the connections between fabrique and text were known only to the garden owner and his circle of guests. In other cases, the objects partook of more widely recognized references.

Hajós researched the fabriques in the gardens of Vienna in this period and found a sizable number with common references (1989:73–102). The Chinese bridges, pagodas, and temples were homages to the romantic respect for the Confucian—that is, philosophical—basis of the central kingdom. This Chinese vogue began in England and spread quickly to European centers of enlightened learning. The Palladian temples were round and variously named the Temple of the Night or the Temple of Knowledge. They were linked closely to the Freemason lodges and the Illuminati networks to which many of these aristocratic and wealthy bourgeoisie belonged, and they symbolized the Temple of Solomon, the only earthly building for which God Himself was the designer. The grottos were shadowy and filled with Freemason-inspired statuary of Egyptian deities. Gothic ruins were preferred over Greek ruins because the Gothic reminded the viewer of the perfection of the spirit through the passage of time, whereas the Greek ruins illustrated the victory of the barbarians over the first enlightened European civilization. Similarly, Roman ruins were philosophically appropriate as objects of melancholic meditation on the ultimate death of all great things.

The fishing huts, log cabins, and grottos were also hermitages—retreats from the world of military, commercial, and civic affairs through which the garden patrons gained their power. The patron was no hermit, however; the hermitage was a social statement in sharp contrast to the utter worldliness of the baroque palace. The hermitage was given greater prominence in the garden design than the palace residence; its message was that the patron was a true nature lover, an enlightened man who sought a new liberal world order.

The mausoleums, monuments, and memorials were elements in the melancholia wave that accompanied the early romantic movement in the late eighteenth century. The focus on the freeing of the soul through death and on the memorializing of those so freed was expressed by memorials and gravestones in the culmination points of the gardens.[12]

The ideal naturalism of the Enlightenment required a turning away from the previous pattern of celebrating secular power. Instead, it sought a creed of precious, heroic nature beyond the human. These landscape enthusiasts sought a nature—in a humanly crafted garden—not as a socially useful object, but as a beautiful creation in itself. The parkscape style was limited because natural forms were themselves limited. One could speak of greater or lesser successes in giving nature its freedom, but otherwise there was no room for stylistic elaboration. The limits of the idea were contained in the limits of the form: namely, the abandoning of every artful shape while simplifying selected natural forms to the desired degree of size and simplicity. The executed gardens revealed that the limits of the form did not mean monotony and uniformity; if anything, the reduced forms permitted too much variation. They unfolded their charm, their fluidity, always at the same slow pace. This rhythm could hold the attention only until the observer was distracted by other things (Althöfer 1956:250).

SOCIAL PRODUCTION OF GARDENS OF LIBERTY

When the discourse on English landscapes first entered Viennese culture, it had very little immediate effect on the cityscape. Most of the people who restyled their estates in the new fashion were either aristocrats with large holdings in the Wienerwald or Bürgers with estates some distance from Vienna. It would take three generations before the English style was commonly erected on the grounds of urban villas. By this time, the terms of the discourse had changed completely. Bürgers no longer spoke of the republican revolution to come, but rather of how to preserve the liberal state they had attained. The one place within the city limits of Vienna in which the English landscape was cultivated openly in the late eighteenth century was in the closed gardens of the imperial palaces. Here, over the course of the century, gardeners had been free to experiment with landscape forms that would never have been tolerated in more publicly accessible places. The imperial hunting grounds of the Prater and the Lainzer Tiergarten had sections that were exquisite groves. The stately gardens of the Augarten Palace and the summer palace

MAP 3. *Romantic parkscapes of the late eighteenth century. Shaded areas indicate districts in which the major romantic gardens were situated. The gardens discussed in the text are indicated.*

of Schönbrunn included sections in which the grove predominated. Joseph II was raised in these gardens. Of all of his reforms, that destined to have the greatest impact on the Viennese cityscape was the opening of the imperial gardens to the public. This brought many more ordinary Viennese into contact with the English style as an alternative garden form (Map 3).

In 1770, Joseph ordered the planting of grass on the Glacis. In 1781, he had the footpaths through the Glacis paved and 2,650 trees planted to provide shade. In 1766, he opened the Prater "during all times of the year and every hour of the day for everyone without exception" (Habsburg 1766). Nobles and high imperial officers had enjoyed the use of the large hunting grounds since the end of the 1600s. Even then, the park had always closed at sundown. The increased access was an immediate success.[13] Joseph allowed innkeepers to set up shacks to sell wine, beer, and coffee. By 1780 forty-three pubs assembled in one corner of the Prater, which became the so-called *Wurstelprater*, or carnival midway.

In 1775, Joseph opened the Augarten Palace garden to the public.

This palace had been a summer residence of his family. His reasons were, for the time, scandalously republican. When asked why he had taken this momentous step of sharing his most intimate palace ground with commoners, Joseph replied, "If I only wanted to associate with people like myself, I'd have to go down into the imperial crypt." The liberalism of the emperor was tempered by the scrupulous protectiveness of the imperial bureaucracy. They fashioned strict rules of behavior for the public use of the new parks: no noise (Anonymous 1828:22), no running on the grass or stepping into the flower beds, no dogs, no writing on walls, no picking flowers, and no smoking tobacco (Sartori 1809:5, 9). Although there is much variety among the parks today, in the old imperial palace grounds people still seem to respect the spirit of the places by staying on the walks and sitting on benches instead of on the lawns.

These parks were not only a revolutionary use of space in Vienna, they were also among the earliest such uses in all of Western Europe. The most important theorist of garden design at the end of the eighteenth century, Hirschfeld, cited the Prater and the Augarten as examples of how increasingly important the *Volkspark* had become to modern city residents. He encouraged other cities to follow Vienna's example.

> These public gardens are an important necessity for the city dweller to consider. They refresh themselves not only after the exhaustion of the day with charming images and feelings, they also come away with the natural showplace that is imperceptible in the base and costly sorts of amusements, and they gradually become accustomed to the inexpensive amusement, the gentle conviviality, the communicative and friendly persons. When they come in contact with each other more often, the different classes acquire the proper demureness and modesty and the condescending friendliness of elaborate pleasantries. (1779:68)

The reality of this great social experiment in the parks did not meet the expectations Hirschfeld evoked. Although eyewitness accounts disagree, classes seem to have cautiously avoided mixing in the park. Consider the following evidence: "Here [Prater], princes and princesses, dukes and duchesses, handworkers and their wives and daughters, go in thick colorful rows behind and next to each other, without any of the usual advantages. The princely daughters themselves take account of the public by wearing only their most festive dresses" (Meiners 1794:55). The free mixing of the classes pictured here would have fulfilled Joseph's wildest dreams. Perhaps it was a feature of the newness of the experience; the nobility and the Bürgers were unaccustomed to encountering each other in public. There is evidence that this Josephine spirit carried on right up through the fateful 1840s: "All different kinds of classes belong to the wide social sphere of the [public] gardens. The legitimacy of their presence of high and low together supports the feeling of perfect equality" (Bacherer 1843:95).

Other observers saw a different kind of interaction in the parks: "The Main Allee in the Prater and Constantine's Hill have been the assembling places for the noble society in the Prater, in opposition to the Wurstelprater where the underclass would collect" (Hebenstreit 1832:130). This suggests a strong segregation between noble and Grossbürger, on the one hand, and the lower classes on the other. Being able to visit the parks at different times of the day may also have helped the classes avoid each other. Every Thursday afternoon, a selected group of noble and educated Bürgers would collect on the Lions Bastion near the Volksgarten, to walk and talk together (Pietznigg 1833:119). Musical and theatrical events in the parks required tickets whose cost was beyond the reach of most nonwealthy visitors. These productions were held during the day, and nets were used to seal off from the public the otherwise accessible grounds (Masaidek 1832:130). Because these events were often held in the best weather, the public quickly got the message that the parks were really for the nobles, the intellectuals, and the writers of travel literature.

These new parks initiated among the Viennese a habit of walking. The opportunity to parade one's finery and station was irresistible for the lower aristocracy and the Bürgertum. Walking was used to assess and display fashion as social communication; to make and arrange marriages, especially on the Wasserglacis and the Prater Hauptallee; to see and to be seen in good company as a sign of achieved status and earned deference; to forge connections in business and introduce post seekers (Anonymous 1781; Gross-Hoffinger 1833:129; Pietznigg 1833:120). Walking also provided a private time for making business deals, talking over indelicate gossip, or begging a favor (Tanzer 1982). The optimal setting for these walks was along the bastions of the city walls or on the paths of the Glacis. Under Maria Theresa, a Paradiesgärtlein was constructed behind the Lions Bastion. It provided tables and chairs for people to rest and drink something in hot weather and was still in use in the 1840s. Around it the triangle-shaped paths of the nearby bastion formed a circle, popularly known as the Oxen Mill, particularly favored by nobles for their midday promenades.

The Volksgarten was the first park designed explicitly for public use. It was built on the site of an old defense work that Napoleon's army had no difficulty breaking through in 1810. The gap in the walls was rebuilt to include a new gate. The idea to build a park inside of this gate had already been in the mind of Emperor Franz I before the Napoleonic War. Hetzendorf von Hohenberg, garden director at Schönbrunn, had drawn plans for the park in 1809, but these were never executed. The designs that were used were drawn by Ludwig von Remy. Built between 1820 and 1823, the park was officially opened on March 1, 1823, even though it had been used for more than a year at that point. The park was laid out in regular form: the axial small squares of the Rosarium tract; the semicircular free space of the fountain tract out of which a star-diagonal layout of paths flows; and the Theseus temple tract containing a series of orderly beds. This was a time when the favorite architectural style among the nobility was a neo-classic canon of geometric forms and figures. For this reason, the Volksgarten is usually cited as the only example of classic revival in garden architecture still standing in Vienna.[14] A contemporary explanation for the regularity of the layout of the Volksgarten insists that it is a departure from existing styles:

> These gardens are laid out in a regular fashion, but not in strips. English parks are depraved in the views of most people. Every possible way for executing these perfect indecencies and nuisances should be expressly denounced by the highest authorities. (Böckh 1823:148)

The *strips* in the first sentence are the parterres formed by the central axis in the baroque garden, most likely a reference to Belvedere. The central section of the Volksgarten, the Rosarium, was a regular layout, but not in the old authoritarian fashion. It was actually an ensemble of four rectangles separated by a circle. The round paths around the circle softened the straight paths that ran along the sides of the rectangle. The paths were lined on the outside with two ranks of rose bushes, grown to different heights, so that the flowers of the first rank did not obscure those of the second. The star-diagonal is reminiscent of a similar feature in the baroque Augarten. Its radiating paths were lined with trees. The temple tract beds were also enclosed with trees, but these were leaf trees allowed to develop a natural shape rather than yew trees cut to form perfect walls. This gave the beds an open, airy feeling. Playfulness and irony appeared in the layout, which was quite different from the symmetry of the palace façades of the period.

The imperial parks, the Glacis, and the Volksgarten in the first half of the nineteenth century were important civic institutions that were visited frequently and provided new opportunities for social interaction. Foreign visitors described the beauty and marvel of the public gardens "which amused the entire city and all age groups. The boys play, the adults walk around, or enjoy the comfort of table wine and music" (Realis 1848:32).[15] In the public park, the entire city population could have what the private owner was accustomed to enjoy. The provision of these amenities by the emperor was a dramatic transformation of public space. The effect was summed up thirty years later by Hügel in his opening address as president of the Gartenbaugesellschaft, the Imperial Garden Society, in 1825:

> The Chair looks upon this undertaking as a highly enjoyable development, as well as contributing to the development of the intelligence of the municipal government. For example, they realize that the covered areas that encourage movement in the open,[16] but also crowd people together in a narrow space, belong to the important public health facilities of the city. Clearly, these parks not only provide the opportunity and the means to increase the widespread enjoyments of the beauty of nature, the sum of life enjoyments. Rather they can at the same time ennoble the people and result in the improvement of morals. (Cited in Koch, 1914:88)

The municipality did learn from the example of the imperial parks. When the liberals came to power in the 1860s, they initiated one of the greatest periods of park building in the city's history. Unfortunately, it was at the cost of the almost complete destruction of the Glacis.

THE HETEROTOPIA OF LIBERTY

The period of Enlightenment produced gardens of liberty in Vienna. The icon of these gardens is the free growing, asymmetric tree. Nature is given its head and allowed to develop in whichever way it sees fit. Nature becomes the higher power to whom all earthly judgment can be appealed and the criterion for relations among people. Only by unrestrained—and thereby natural—speech, movement, thought, and legal development could government be legitimated. The Enlightenment garden was the product of wealthy, philosophically inclined aristocrats and merchants. It evoked an image of balance and harmony which can only emerge out of the order of nature.

These gardens worked by creating awe in the face of nature's power and beauty. People both comprehend this display and participate in it. Seeing oneself as part of nature's scheme immediately dwarfs the authority of the absolutist state. The emperor may claim to be acting in the name of God, but ordinary people can also claim to be part of a divine scheme that is as powerful and just as the absolutist. The appeal to higher, natural law immediately unravels the claims to special legitimacy by the state, places all people on an equal legal and social basis with each other, and radically deconstructs the absolutist state. The Enlightenment garden stands in eternal opposition to all claims of privilege.

The English landscape is a fantasy world of a wild and unrestrained nature. It is a delusion of freedom which hides the gravest inequities of the industrial transformation of capitalism. The façade is one of an eternal pastoral, a heaven on earth in which all social contradictions are resolved. The symbol system for this style was developed fully by the end of the eighteenth century. The symbolic repertoire stressed emotional place attachments. Ruins, bridges, memorials, and temples reminded the visitor of lost golden ages and brought on a melancholic reverie. The entire experience was more like a religious service than a walk in the park. The emotional messages were sought after. The parkscape designer carefully set the stimuli in visual angles that would maximize the element of surprise, thus heightening the sense of fantasy associated with these parks.

The parks preserved their own feeling of timelessness. In them, the owner could visit a presocial, pre-Christian landscape whose historical resonances denied the authority of the absolutist state. Here he could retreat from the time of his contemporaries and become a hermit. Compared with the time of lived experience in the ordinary spaces of the city, the parks suspended people in an ageless domain in which the seasonal cycle of the animals and plants reigned. The historical images were plucked from their original contexts and swirled into the landscape as if they, too, were the fruits of nature's abundance. There was no incongruity of coming across a Chinese bridge, a Palladian temple, or a log cabin in the deepest woods. They fit the scene as absolutely as the trees, the rivulets, and the rock outcroppings. In these parks, all moments of history existed simultaneously.

The boundary between the garden of liberty and the ordinary spaces of urban life was created initially through the distance required to travel to visit an early English parkscape. Later, when these forms were incorporated into the public parks, a wall of trees usually surrounded the garden. This was often reinforced by a masonry and iron fence, broken in a few places to allow access. Imperial parks and the Volksgarten entrances had gates that were shut at night. In the Glacis, the gates of the city's fortifications, which were closed at night, prevented access from the Altstadt side. On the Neustadt side, however, the Glacis was open. The walls of the suburban buildings formed a sort of boundary, at least visually. The many roads and footpaths that opened into the Glacis and its expanse gave just the opposite impression. Symbolically, the lack of boundaries on the suburban side of the Glacis reinforced the popular atmosphere of the esplanade. There was a dash of the dangerous and the unpredictable on the Glacis. The grounds were regularly patrolled by military units and were as safe as any of the other streets in the city. This exposure was inherent in the spirit of the place. In a city of locked gates, locked buildings, and closed social networks, this openness was extraordinary.

The gardens of liberty held a special position opposite the ordinary places of Vienna in the period between 1770 and 1820. Although the natural growth of the plants might superficially resemble that of vacant undeveloped land, the compositions were carefully designed and well tended. These elaborate stage sets were every bit as deliberate as the baroque gardens they annulled. In this way the gardens of liberty were different from the fields, streets, shops, and offices in which the residents worked. They were also different from the primarily agricultural landscapes in which the Viennese hiked and took their leisure. Yet all of these places were linked to the gardens of liberty through the symbol system, especially the alternation of freedom and constraint. Only the vacant undeveloped lands the gardens were trying to imitate remained conspicuously apart from the gardens of liberty. As demonstrated by the existing first growth forests, such as the one downstream from Vienna on the Danube near Hainburg, the unimproved Gegenden was so heavily forested that the gaze was restricted. Instead of noble assemblies of trees standing independent and strong, hundreds of trees crowded together with thick undergrowth that restricted movement of both the body and the eye. This is definitely not what the designers of the gardens of liberty had in mind when they attempted to unbridle nature.

The effort to set aside a place in which to celebrate the ideal of liberty is only necessary in a world where liberty is scarce. This was the case in absolutist Vienna. The same Joseph II who opened his gardens to the public, initiated enlightened governmental reforms, and secretly read Rousseau, also instigated one of the most effective secret police organizations in Europe. He meant to use it to remove from the bureaucracy saboteurs to his reforms. His successors used it to undermine bürgerlich liberalism and other threats to aristocratic control. In the hands of such masters as Prince Metternich, the absolutist state drove republicanism from the political scene in Vienna. For ordinary Viennese, there was no alternative but to look for meaning inwardly, within the domestic circle. This moment produced its gardens, too—gardens of domesticity. In form and meaning, they borrowed heavily from both the gardens of order and the gardens of liberty. But unlike these forerunners, the gardens of domesticity were uniquely a Viennese experience, a coming to grips with cultural repression.

Gardens

of

Domesticity

Two related political events gave the Viennese their opportunity to contribute to the landscape. After the death of Joseph II, a period of reaction against the reform policies set in. Conservative governments bent on reviving the strength of the absolutist policies of the early eighteenth century came to power. Napoleon's armies captured Vienna in 1805 and again in 1809. On both occasions, troops occupied the city for only a short time. The threat from the forces unleashed by the French Revolution and the spread of republicanism haunted the next two generations of Austrian aristocrats. After the Congress of Vienna redrew the map of Europe (1814–15), the tone of politics in Vienna became increasingly bitter. Imperial chancellor Prince Metternich initiated repressive state policies, hoping to preserve aristocratic rule by undermining efforts at republican political reform.

The effect was to drive the expanding and increasingly affluent middle classes into their homes. The liberal elements of the metropolis retreated to the security of their families. Economic stagnation followed. Those who had established manufacturing plants before the congress continued to make money, but at a slower rate. New concerns became difficult to establish. This political era is known as the *Vormärz*, referring to the period before the March 1848 Revolution, which ended the period of unbridled police control. The cultural products of this era, including landscape, are referred to as *Biedermeier*.[1]

The Biedermeier produced gardens of domesticity.[2] Locked inside the often tiny courtyards of the two- and three-story Bürger houses, family and friends were shielded from the snooping of the secret police. The objective of this kind of garden was not conspiracy; it was rather protection from the provocateurs in an increasingly paranoid absolutist state. In these gardens, a new domestic culture evolved which was based on a sentimentality of childhood and innocence and a rigidity of gender roles.

This was the first attention by the Viennese toward developing a sense of distinction within domestic space. The design principles evolved through the efforts of three remarkable gardeners, who opened their work to the public. Between 1820 and 1840 these gardens were popular among families, who picked up from them design ideas, especially a taste for particular kinds of blooms and bed layouts. In this way the distinctive features of the Biedermeier garden spread throughout the residential districts of the middle class. Thousands of ordinary gardens built in this style occupied a plot of fifty to two hundred square meters behind a house.

The Biedermeier was a renaissance of intimate style in the periods when the French and English gardens were dominant. It was a renewal of the paradise garden form of the Middle Ages. These gardens were linked to the traditional domestic kitchen garden. The soup herbs and leaf plants that were the ingredients of the metropolitan household menu in the Middle Ages still occupied the transitional space between the house and the garden. The garden was so closely bound to the house itself that it penetrated its very walls. In a small enclosed space the gardens synthesized the opposing features of the gardens of order and liberty. Like the gardens of order, they opened the boundary between house and garden and compressed ornamental plantings into beds. Like the gardens of liberty, they evidenced an interest in botanical curiosities, formed beds of irregular shape, provided an area for socialization, and incorporated playful fantasy within the garden.

All of my interview partners knew some feature of the Biedermeier style—most frequently the colorful and varied blooms in the same bed, an image kept fresh by the floral arrangement known as the Biedermeier bouquet, a hand-held nosegay of colorful flowers interspersed with greens. A second familiar feature is that of the frivolous in the garden—swing sets, mirror balls, wind-blown banners, and bird baths. Although few of my partners would have known this, the popular *Gartenzwerg*, a small sculpture of a red-capped dwarf pushing a wheelbarrow, originated in this era.

The verbal formulas of gardens of domesticity included the desire to have children grow up in a garden close to their home or to provide a setting for the extended family to assemble for birthdays and holidays. Socializing with close friends in the garden was another theme that suggested the turning away from civic affairs for the comfort of a closed domestic circle. All of my interview partners described their gardens as safe and secure. Most felt that they had enough privacy. When given a choice between describing their gardens as safe and secure (*Geborgen*) or as healthy and happy (*Wohlsein*), all felt that healthy and happy were more accurate adjectives for the atmosphere of their gardens. *Domesticity* is no longer defined as the refuge from civic exposure; it is rather the site where the family can gather for recreation.

The special affinity of the gardens of domesticity for children is one of the moving forces behind the great demand for owning or leasing a house with an attached garden:

> It is a playground in a variety of ways. And naturally, it is realized piece by piece. First, the garden is where a mother parks the baby cradle, the carriage, for fresh air, still close to her. She doesn't have to go to the park or drive somewhere to find green. Then later, the garden is the closed, protected playground of the child, where it does not matter if something should get destroyed, as happens with children. Still later, it is a place of learning and teaching. Growing up with nature, seeing how plants grow and what happens after that will become part of play. And when the child arrives at school age, with supervision, he begins to plant and learn from his own garden in the fresh air. And then finally, as you said, the child follows the parents [in taking possession of the garden].[3]

On the waiting lists for new members cooperative garden city settlements give priority to young couples with children. One of the families I interviewed was so committed to having a garden for their child that they bought a house with an attached garden even though they could not really afford it. The protected environment would permit the child to run and explore safely while the mother accomplished her household chores. The garden would become the child's playroom.

What gives the formula its distinctive Biedermeier flavor are the underlying values that children need protection from the world and that the orientation of family activity should be directed behind the house in the garden, rather than in front of the house, on the street. This contrasts with those values found, for example, in Mediterranean cities, where the street is the stage for family life, or Dutch cities, where the front room of the apartment is open to public view through a large window, exposing the family to public scrutiny. Before the Biedermeier, family life in Vienna most closely resembled that of Italy. The area in front of the house was used by the family for socializing and play, an *Aufenthaltsraum*. The kitchen garden was planted on the side and just behind the house. After the 1820s, the orientation changed, and the garden space expanded to incorporate the family activities.

The term *Aufenthaltsraum* itself is another indication of the domestic value of gardens. An Aufenthalt is the place where one stops. Aufenthaltsraum can be translated as either a day room or a recreation room. It is the room in the home in which the family spends its time together. When the Aufenthaltsraum is a garden, it heightens the sense of domestic privacy outside as well.

> It is a second recreation room, a large one, and one doesn't have to be dressed up. I can go out in pajamas. I can go out in a bathing suit. Right? One does that.[4]

The feeling of not having to be dressed has little to do with modesty. Any visit to swimming clubs, public baths, and the beaches on the Danube will show that contemporary Viennese tolerate some public nudity. Instead, the statement refers to the difference between the presentation of self in public as opposed to the family circle. Dress is an indicator of status, expressed through fashion, taste, and accessories; but in the garden, these trappings can be shed.

The Biedermeier was one of the first instances in which people used space to define status. To be a member of the new middle class meant that one must own or lease a house with a garden. The number of households involved was small. The rapid expansion of single-family homes did not take place until the 1870s. In the 1820s, few people had grown up with large gardens. They had no idea of how to plan them or cultivate them. A single garden firm in the city supplied most of the plants and materials. Three or four publicly accessible private gardens influenced public taste. As a result, most of the gardens looked the same. Garden form had become like fashion in clothes—it could be influenced by a few prominent individuals. At the same time, people became wary of conformity. They had to struggle to be different, to have some aspect of the design identified specifically with their family. No one wanted a garden that was exactly like the neighbor's. Even in current descriptions of gardens, this concern remains, especially in allotment garden settlements and garden city settlements, where the physical constraints on the shape and orientation of the garden impose a high level of uniformity. The gardeners themselves recognize this prescribed similarity:

> Sure, that's what they say: the lawns and the fruit trees and everywhere a few flowers, but each is arranged in its own way. The owner plants and so forth. But by and large I would say that the gardens here are the same. Not one of them is something special.[5]

This situation forces families to emphasize the individuality of their gardens through secondary features:

> But there are no gardens that are exactly the same. I have the only one with a bricked terrace. All the others have embankments. So my garden is really the only one that looks different. I believe that I am the only one who has a flower bed.[6]

Another approach is to see each garden as developing its own propensities and qualities. In this case, the owner may have to work to ensure that it does not become too different from the surrounding features:

> The garden, however, should develop its own design, and we have also tried in the main, especially with the tree plantings, etc., to hold to a certain look that fits with the surroundings. It shouldn't stick out like a sore thumb.[7]

Still another approach inverts the desire of individuality by emphasizing the importance of the communication between neighbors. In this case, the exchange involves plant cuttings.

> Yes, it is similar. Because one imitates the other. When one does something that beautiful, then the other says, "Look, that's beautiful. I'll do that

too." After that, of course, the garden is similar to the other one. For example, we have grown large dahlias. The neighbor said, "Can I have a few bulbs from those dahlias?" So I gave him some bits right away. Now it will happen that next year, we will both have the same flowers with the same colors in the same places. So, from that one can say that they are in any one form the same.[8]

This exchange enhances the similarities among gardens. The consistency in plants and forms stands as an index of the community's integration and vitality.

The element of surprise was a central part of the gardens of domesticity, as it was in the gardens of liberty which preceded them. We do not often think of swimming pools or swing sets as surprises, but in the 1820s they were quite a marvel. In contemporary gardens an equivalent level of surprise is often in a sentimental vein. A common example is a corner alpine garden in which the gardener cultivates the flowering plants of high mountain meadows. One interview partner grew six bonsai trees. Another grew pineapple and kiwi in a greenhouse. Such rarities are echoes of Biedermeier sensibility. Plant breeding as a hobby became widespread among upper middle-class gardeners in the Biedermeier. Local plant breeders were held in high esteem. This passion is not as widespread today but still remains alive among many gardeners:

> I'm a fanatical gardener. I love to breed plums, always looking for new varieties. I've been involved for a long time in new rose varieties, especially tree-roses. As we say, I'm a fanatic for plants. I spend a lot of money on them, and I'm happy when something succeeds. On vacation, especially in Italy and Greece, I bring plants home. I have cacti from Greece, Italy, and Yugoslavia. I bring them home and try to develop them further. If something comes of it, it makes me happy.[9]

Another way in which contemporary gardens create an element of surprise is to imitate the spirit of well-known places. The most common theme is to recreate the atmosphere of the Viennese vintner's garden, or *Heurigen*, in the house garden. One enthusiast in a vineyard district equipped his garden with a *Saletti*, or pavilion, for drinking wine. He built a wine cellar under the Saletti, and a dumbwaiter allows him to retrieve bottles directly in the Saletti without having to go through the house. The garden is fenced with twisted wire, exhibiting the owner's craft and imagination to those who wander by. It is a self-conscious space.

> It is very beautiful in the summer to sit in the open, invite guests, and set out simple things like in a Heurigen. Sure, drink some wine, eat. And I've tried to rearrange the terraces to serve as tables.[10]

The space is as evocative of the Heurigen atmosphere as one could hope for. It imitates the oldest and most visually conservative of them. Today, one finds such Heurigen in the northern vineyard communities of Stammersdorf and Strebersdorf. Unlike the more famous western Heurigen districts around Grinzing and Nussdorf, the northern communities have remained unchanged since the early 1800s. In the western districts, the boundary of the wine garden closes the field of view. One sits in a spacious, open-air room. But in the northern district, the garden opens up to include the vineyards themselves, as if one were sitting among the arbors.[11] In the designed garden, the elaborate effort to recreate the traditional Heurigen atmosphere reveals a gardener who is as fanatic about wine as the previous interview partner was about plant breeding. The ideal is manifest in the form, much the same way that nostalgic longing for a republican society was manifest in the Roman ruins of the rococo gardens of liberty.

Most garden owners have only the time or the resources to suggest the atmosphere they find most appealing. Another gardener of my acquaintance also strove to recreate the Heurigen atmosphere in his garden. He had to work with a much smaller space with far fewer resources:

> One can't do much with 150 square meters. I've set out a few strawberry plants, and for fun, a grape arbor. But that is merely symbolic. Because my father is a farmer, a vintner, I set out a few vines. And a wooden table stands there. Wooden benches and a table stand there. That's it, right?[12]

The wooden table and benches became the basic equipment of his Heurigen. The garden itself is a small rectangle on the end of townhouse row. A shrub wall seven feet high encloses it, and the garden floor is a grass lawn. This gardner placed the arbor and wooden furniture two thirds of the way to the back of the garden. The evocation of the Heurigen is highly personal and sentimental, without the conspicuous attention to imitative detail of the first garden. The hedges close the garden from public view; only the gardener's family is intended to enjoy its form. It presents a complete transformation of the rococo elements into a garden of domesticity. The difference between these two contemporary gardens demonstrates the historical drift of garden forms from the 1820s through the 1850s, from imitation of the publicly known garden themes to the miniaturization of the forms in increasingly private landscapes.

DISCOURSE ON GARDENS OF DOMESTICITY

For the absolutist aristocrats, the boundary between nature and culture in the garden obliged them to subdue nature and chasten its force. For the aristocratic gardeners of the Enlightenment, nature was an artist creating picturesque compositions. They sought to transform culture by making the coexistence of nature and culture their garden model. For the emerging Bürgertum of the early nineteenth century, the central problem was to bring greater harmony between the order of culture and the chaos of nature into the garden. Nature produced monstrous vegetative growth and vigorous variety through free mating. Culture generated the form of the garden and the careful selective breeding of separate varieties within a species. The main task, as the *Neues Allgemeine Gartenmagazine* put it, was as follows: "Art without nature is impossible. Nature without art is unfocused. At least the latter is something the pleasure-seeking person can bring to a fuller perfection" (Anonymous 1826, 2:25; cited in Althöfer 1956:73).[13] These gardeners sought a form wherein the separate plants could realize their natural qualities and create a cosmological picture of nature which reflected their class values:

> There is nothing so comfortably undemanding and at the same time so incontrovertibly magical an object in nature or art as that perfect, thriving, lush, fully developed blossom, streaming forth light and bliss. The eye and senses turn themselves to this simple, yet ennobling sensation and attach themselves to it as inspiration and as denial of the self. (Bürgerstein 1907; cited in Althöfer 1956:73)[14]

This celebration of the beauty of nature invoked through human device and design offers an approach very different from that described for the French and English styles. In form, they are quite distinctive. The first person to emphasize this distinctiveness was Franz Althöfer in his 1956 dissertation. He summarized the unique features as follows: irregularly shaped beds, in which highly varied and colorful vegetation grew freely; low, interlacing iron bows or a row of very low bushes enclosing the beds. The gardens were breeding beds for inspired amateur horticulturists and often included large glass house complexes. They were also the first gardens to include playground equipment. These were warm weather gardens. They required sunshine to bring out their charm: the tiniest details of juxtapositions of color in the flower beds and the artifacts of domestic intimacy, class representation, and sentimental naturalism.[15]

The Viennese were in the process of inventing modern urban lifestyles for themselves, including the reorganization of time to include defined, specialized periods of leisure activity (Baltzarek 1982:135, 145). Along with walking through the Wienerwald and parkscapes of the noble estates, in their free time many Viennese families visited private gardens in the warm months. This contact helped spread the elements of the Biedermeier aesthetic widely through the city's inhabitants, many of whom built their own gardens to imitate the larger ones. Topographic drawings of gardens of houses that were for sale and drawings in garden pattern books of the period reveal that the vegetation patterns and play elements from the larger gardens were copied with precision in many of the contemporary house gardens (Althöfer 1956:41–42).[16]

The most famous showcase of the Biedermeier style was the Rosenbaum'sche Garten. Joseph Rosenbaum bought an 86.4-square meter piece from the subdivision of the Strahemberg Palace garden for 1,200 gulden. The total area was 7.5 hectares (three acres). The ground was enclosed on all four sides partly with a masonry wall and partly with a high wooden fence. Irregularly shaped beds were defined by three cross-cutting, curved paths. The bed layout is visible in the Behsel lithographic plans of the district of Wieden in 1823 and 1834. Contemporary views of the garden are available through four-color engravings by Josef Gurk.[17] The lithography and engravings reveal a studied irony in the design of Rosenbaum's garden.

The first print (Figure 9) focuses on the house side of the garden. We see a few benches and a potted tree; a large grass bed fenced with low iron circles containing smaller flower beds and shrubbery; and two posts, one of which supports a glass ball. In the background is a laburnum plant and a narrow stair leading to a Gothic tower. The tower opens toward the house and is crowned with a mansard window and an unfenced balcony with a large flag. The open hallway at the ground level is covered with a tarp. The second print (Figure 10) shows a side of the house with the door flanked by two trees, a large

FIGURE 9. *Gesselschafts-Platz, the entrance to the Rosenbaum'sche Garten, by Josef Gurk. This plate and the next three are among the few contemporaneous images of an influential Biedermeier garden. Shown here are the proximity of the garden to the house, the pavilion, the tower, and some of the front beds.* (Weidmann 1824)

pavilion and building behind it, a flower theater, and a high mast. Behind the green fenced beds the Gothic tower rises, surrounded by blooming leafy bushes and trees. The third print (Figure 11) is of a garden party near the Gothic tower. On the right and left, low, thick vegetation grows, with a semicircular bed and frame fencing it off. In the bed are many kinds of flowers, blooming bushes, and two poplars. A curving path separates the two beds and leads from the stairs of the Gothic tower to the entrance of the grotto. Along the path is a bench set in a niche formed entirely of tall shrubs. The last print (Figure 12) shows a party in front of the statue Flora, a clothed figure standing in the middle of a round bed on a raised mound surrounded by small trees. Next to this bed is a swing. A path weaves around the bed.

In each of the beds, the flowers grow out of the grass lawn, which

FIGURE 10. *Kleines Parterre, by Josef Gurk. Shown is the view of the Rosenbaum'sche Garten from the right side. Also visible are the hoop fences, the wooden bridge, the tower, and some of the fabriques. The variety of trees is also evident.*

is no longer the self-standing element it was in the English garden. The free-flowing growth of the flowers could not happen in a baroque garden. Many of the rules for visiting gardens carried over from the baroque estates. Visitors had to stay on the paths and could not step onto the beds or lawns. The collection of architecture and sculpture in the garden was eclectic. The Gothic tower, the square Turkish tent, and the Italian saletti were all nods toward the rococo tastes of the aristocracy. The statues of Greek Muses and of Flora, the swings, the tent, the glass balls, the memorials, all derive from different stylistic periods: the classic, the mannerist, the romantic, and so on. It was as if the Bürgertum had taken over the romantic's taste for historical allegory but allegorized the domestic experience instead of the aristocratic.

Dr. J. P. Rupprecht, an imperial book censor, established a garden similar to Rosenbaum's in 1822 in Gumpendorf on the site of a for-

FIGURE 11. *Ansicht des Thurms*, by Josef Gurk. Shown are the left side of the tower and path leading to the goddess Flora. The stone walls of the ruin are visible as is the variety of flowers in the beds.

mer baroque garden.[18] Rupprecht emphasized flower breeding and the cultivation of specific plants. This garden's ground plan, visible on the Behsel lithographic plan of 1826, also featured irregular, curving beds. A visitor would enter the garden through an alley between two houses and would be greeted first by a pool of water with water birds and lily pads. The pool and surrounding potted trees and blooming bushes are visible in a drawing by Kisch (1883). A balcony from the left of the house featured a long sun awning that opened onto the garden. The grass lawn spread outward from the pool area with hundreds of potted flowers.

Rupprecht was a flower breeder of renown, and his garden was a central point for garden enthusiasts throughout the empire. Botanical variety was the chief attraction here as were the particularly lush, blooming flowers. Rupprecht was also a famous developer of grapes, carrying forward the combined character of the Viennese garden.

FIGURE 12. *Flora Parthie, by Josef Gurk. Shown are the left side of the garden with the bed devoted to the veneration of the goddess Flora. The swing is visible on the right side of the bed.*

According to a contemporary account, there could be fifty thousand flowers of the same species grouped together in multiform patterns in the same bed (*Theaterzeitung* 1833:990).[19]

The Biedermeier did present something essentially new, and owners of smaller house gardens slowly redesigned them to follow the fashionable new ground plan. In the 1830s and 1840s, the core areas of new garden development were the new suburbs of Döbling, Heiligenstadt, Hohe Warte, and especially Hietzing. The succession in garden styles is clearly visible in the lithographic plans from the period. The 1819 lithographic Katastralplan of Hietzing reveals highly varied garden designs, some resembling the irregularly shaped beds of Rosenbaum and Rupprecht, whereas others used the older perpendicular crossing paths pattern with four or more rectangular beds, often with round beds in the intersections.[20] These older garden types began in the Middle Ages but are typical of no specific epoch. Private gardens merely repeated these established bed designs in smaller form, without much innovation. With the Biedermeier, the variety of garden forms suddenly multiplied. Inspiration for this profusion stemmed from the taste for imitating other bürgerlich gardens as a representation of class identity. The imitators would then add idiosyncratic elements to give their gardens a unique identity.

The main variations among these gardens were the shapes of the beds and the length of the small vegetation strips along the edges of the garden. No garden was identical to any other, and not only did the form and size of the beds differ, but also the relationship of the beds to each other. Within these variations, three subtypes emerged. Type 1 was a completely irregular ground plan (the Rosenbaum model); type 2 added irregular details to a regular schema, such as rectangular beds with scalloped borders that curved in and out without violating the geometry of the path; and in type 3 the symmetric forms dominated close to the house, becoming curved and irregular in the back half of the garden. Type 1 was seldom found outside the four largest gardens of the period, the Rosenbaum, Rupprecht, and von Hügel gardens in Hietzing, and Pronay's garden in Hetzendorf, all open to the public. Type 3 was found only rarely, lying entirely within the village of Hietzing. Type 3 may have been a variant of type 2. The tension among these competing approaches confused some Viennese. The *Allgemeine Deutsche Gartenzeitung* spoke derisively of contradicting forms created by "paths of crooked geometry" (1826:174). The combined pattern (type 2) became the departure point for garden design around and after the middle of the century.

The garden must be considered a part of the interior of the Biedermeier home, which so completely reflected the bürgerlich cosmos (Klauner 1941).[21] The garden provided all of the elements for life inside the private circle. Whereas the English garden tossed all anthropomorphic elements out of the garden, the Biedermeier restored to it the privacy of the domestic sphere and expressed the essence of the period more completely than the house interior. The love of play and the wish for surprise and special effects found new and special expression in the garden. New leisure interests, such as collecting things, the love of flowers and botany, here had their own time to develop. Flowers in their multiform combinations appeared throughout the house as its most common decorative theme (Althöfer 1956:47).

The domestic importance of the garden was also apparent in the special designs that served the needs of children. Gardens became the setting for toys and games and playground equipment of various kinds: swings, seesaws, hoops, badminton, *Blinde Kuh* (blindman's bluff), butterfly hunting, round dancing, soldier games, and dolls and doll wagons. Children began garden work very early; it was considered good childhood training, especially for boys. The first kindergarten (Fröbel'sche Garten) was founded in Blankenburg in 1839 on these principles. It was a garden for children to plant and care for by themselves. The garden work was moral and aesthetic training as well as physical exercise. Through the long hours of work, the children learned that meaningful leisure came with a price. At the same time they learned that the recreation available in the garden restored them for effective commercial work. The gardens were the backstage area for rehearsing the business of social life.

The Biedermeier were symbolically gardens of domestic love: the happy couple sitting with their children under the leaves, surrounded by roses. Even allegories lost their effectiveness when one entered the Biedermeier. The style sentimentalized everything; a common drawing of the time was of a stork bringing the newly married pair five children at once through the branches of the trees of their garden. But the pathos and heroism of images forfeit their strength through overuse and in time become kitsch. These images of the garden offered the symbolic solution of the private world to counter the anxiety and tragedy of the Biedermeier world—one that was thwarting the hope for economic improvement through industrialization and republicanism. At no previous time did the garden have such a critical meaning for the propertied middle class.

SOCIAL PRODUCTION OF GARDENS OF DOMESTICITY

Between 1770 and 1840, the population of Vienna grew from 160,000 to 440,000, with an average annual increase of more than 40,000, largely as a result of immigrant labor (Bobek and Lichtenberger 1978:25). This expansion changed the way in which space in the city and the immediate suburbs was used. Known as the manufacturing period, this era witnessed the rapid growth of small industries that employed fewer than twenty people. The labor involved was highly skilled and often organized into guilds. Each workshop had its complement of master, journeymen, apprentices, and helpers. A sizable portion of this labor force was native to Vienna. But as the economy grew, productive capacity outstripped the supply of skilled labor, and so journeymen from Italy, the Low Countries, Germany, Bohemia, Silesia, and Hungary came to work in the shops.

The growth of factory-based production with its large volume of semiskilled and unskilled labor began after 1820 and experienced its fastest expansion in the 1830s and 1840s. The factories were themselves exports from the regional centers of the empire and arrived in Vienna complete with capital, machinery, and disciplined provincial labor. They became an external social force, primarily responsible for reshaping the landscape on the edge of the suburbs in which there was a steady supply of water for the mills. This process involved a degradation of the environment from agricultural to industrial production and introduced low-quality worker housing and pollution.

However, the workshop economy was an internal social force, primarily responsible for shaping the landscape of the immediate suburbs during the Vormärz. This involved the beautification of the environment with tree plantings, Biedermeier house gardens, and new public parks. The workshop economy sustained this landscape in three ways. First, it determined the primary architectural form of the period, the *Gewerbehaus*. Next, it sparked the growth of a new class of landscape patrons, the *Grossbürgertum*. Finally, it produced new wealth in the city which could be invested in public parks. The primary impact of society on landscape during this period was the steady rise in the wealth generated by the early phase of the Industrial Revolution. The effect on the cityscape was to polarize further the central city and fast developing outer suburbs.

Although the industrial economy of the outer suburbs also produced new wealth, it did so through a very different architecture—one that stressed large shed-type structures that made little use of the open-air space. The industrialists were also members of the Grossbürgertum, but their immediate concern was the capitalization of their firms. When they finally were able to pull resources away from production to begin their own private landscapes, they focused on new landscape forms on the hilly suburbs adjoining their industrial areas.

The Gewerbehaus made its appearance in Vienna in the early seventeenth century. For the next two hundred years it was the primary form of bürgerlich housing in the city (Hösl and Pirhofer 1988:17). The building was of two or three stories, with a street façade filling the entire lot. A large door opened onto either a central courtyard, a *Hof*, or a large backyard, a *Hinterhof*, permitting carriage traffic to move goods into and out of the house. The street front also included space for a store. Windows on the second and third stories illuminated the living quarters of the master and craftworkers. Back rooms on the ground floor were used for storage and heavy craft activity, and those on the upper floors housed apprentices and additional workshops. These structures integrated the craft workshop into a complete living and working unit. The important feature for the production of landscape was the existence of the integrated courtyard or backyard. It was used for the loading, unloading, and temporary storage of produced goods, for productive activities in good weather, for ventilation of the workshop, and for the kitchen garden.

Rich entrepreneurs and manufacturers, bankers, wholesalers, commercial agents, and the top levels of the bureaucracy wanted to find a way of expressing their new affluence. They had seen the importance of public displays of wealth among the aristocracy and sought ways to imitate that display. The restrictions imposed by the reactionary administration on the middle classes hampered them to some extent. By the 1820s, most of the families that had built the large baroque palaces were out of money and began to subdivide and sell their holdings in the inner suburbs. On these parcels, the Grossbürgertum built home and rental properties in the style and scale of the traditional Gewerbehäuser. These parcels were hard to come by. More typically, a rich Bürger would buy a Gewerbehaus and rehabilitate it to the new classic revival and Biedermeier tastes. The buildings were often quite old, with the better residential properties lying in the Landstrasse, Wieden, Leopoldstadt, and Alsergrund and summer houses in Hietzing, Döbling, and Pötzleinsdorf (Schediwy and Baltzarek 1982:140). This gentrification was restricted primarily to the propertied middle class. The working classes often did not have rights to land and could not build gardens.[22]

The Hof or Hinterhof was rebuilt into gardens. This is where the four large-model gardens discussed previously made their greatest stylistic impact. The gardens of Rosenbaum, Rupprecht, von Hügel, and Pronay were all located in districts that were undergoing the greatest gentrification (Map 4). All but von Hügel's were Hinterhof gardens. They demonstrated the ideal pattern for garden building. Thus, it was the architectonic homogeneity imposed by the func-

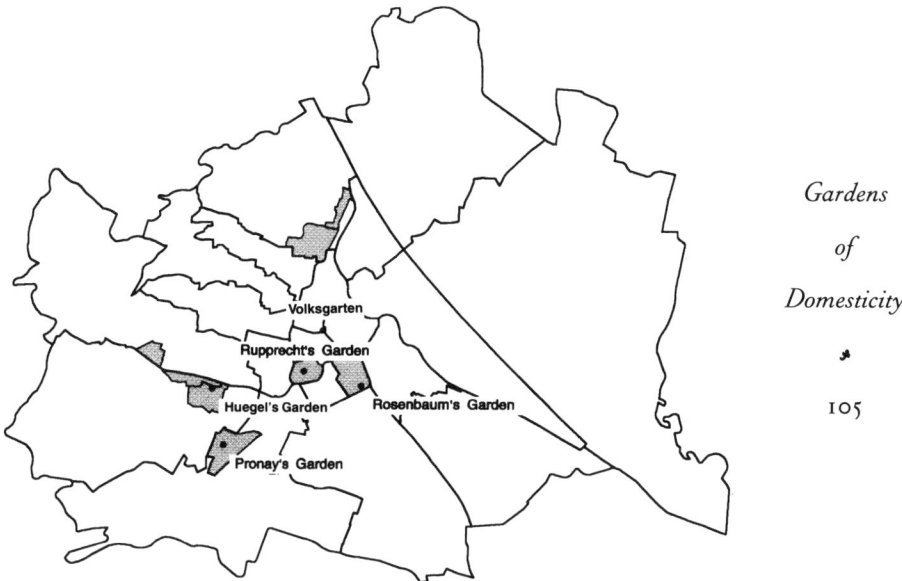

MAP 4. *Biedermeier gardens of the early nineteenth century. Shaded areas indicate precincts in which the largest concentration of Biedermeier gardens developed. The four gardens discussed in the text are indicated, together with the location of the Volksgarten.*

tionally designed Gewerbehaus which led to the stylistic sameness of the Biedermeier.

The members of the aristocratic class who had managed to retain their family fortunes continued to build parkscapes in the estates, at least through the 1820s. This permitted bürgerlich commentators to attack the politics of reaction fostered by the aristocrats without incurring the attention of the censors:

> English parks are depraved in the views of most people. Every possible way for executing these perfect indecencies and nuisances should be expressly denounced by the highest authorities. (Böckh 1823:148)

With the exception of commercial gardeners who happened to have titles, like von Hügel, most aristocrats stayed away from the Biedermeier forms. The aesthetic was too playful and nostalgic for their tastes. The politics of the reaction set aristocratic families against most bürgerlich interests, creating gaps in shared culture which extended far beyond landscape and garden tastes.

The Biedermeier was a time of flower mania (Auböck 1975:53). Many spoke their feelings through flowers, and not only through flower beds in gardens. Paintings of flowers commanded high prices and made the reputations of painters such as Johann Knapp (1778–1833) and Franz Xaver Gruber (1801–62), who specialized in flower painting. Flowers were the favorite motif on porcelain, glass, jewelry, furniture, and wallpaper, permitting a closer integration of garden exterior and house interior. Besides the symbolic elaboration of familiar species, the Viennese hungered for new ones. Between 1755 and 1821, six major expeditions to the Western Hemisphere brought back exotic species, many of them publicly exhibited in the botanical gardens of Schönbrunn. A new building, the Palm House, was built to contain the collection of exotic trees and cacti from these expeditions, which were financed by public funds and must be counted among the socially productive efforts aimed at creating the urban landscape.

The K. u. K. Gartenbaugesellschaft, the Royal and Imperial Garden Society, founded in 1837, is a strong indication that the house garden had firmly established itself in the consciousness of the Bürger (Mollik, Reining, and Wurzer 1980:294). The Biedermeier garden became interesting not only for its own formal elements, but as a forerunner of the villa gardens of the mid nineteenth century. The first president of the society was von Hügel, also a commercial gardener who bred and sold plants for use in the Hofgartens of the Bürgertum. The yearly garden exhibitions of the Gartenbaugesellschaft were as much an advertisement for the commercial gardeners as they were paroxysms of garden enthusiasm. With the right property located in the appropriate district, with plants supplied by the commercial gardeners, and with the models of garden form provided by Rosenbaum and others, the Bürgertum was able to define itself in space and landscape design that was different from both the reactionary and enlightened aristocrats, as well as from the foreign and domestic workers who were quickly filling up the suburbs.

Habsburg Emperor Franz I was himself an avid gardener, and it was partly his patronage of gardening which allowed it to remain free of the bureaucratic intervention permeating everything else in the city's life. During his reign, thousands of trees were planted along the major city streets and the Glacis, creating shady, cool, baroque alleys. The effect of the tree planting and the hundreds of domestic gardens in the inner suburbs was to magnify immensely the gardenlike appearance of the city.

THE HETEROTOPIA OF DOMESTICITY

A common feature of preindustrial European households was the cultivation of a kitchen garden. If space permitted, children played and families socialized there. The domestic becomes extraordinary when there is a perceived threat to the family or its members from outside forces. Placing the garden with the house, as well as the design of the space itself, produced a feeling of seclusion. The garden and house fused. Garden colors and floral patterns permeated the house. Double doors on the ground floor and balconies above opened wide to blend the spaces. Furniture littered the garden, which was organized as a room would be—not so much for efficiency as for comfort. Merging the house and garden this thoroughly produced the garden of domesticity.

The needs of the household to participate in a culture of domesticity will vary with the nature of the threat. In the case of Vienna, the threat was political and ideological. The very people who could afford to build such spaces also participated in social projects that threatened the existing power structure. People who made their money from commerce, and especially industry, were seen by the aristocracy as naturally favoring republican political values. This imposed a group consciousness on a portion of the city which might not otherwise have recognized common bonds, and in this way, the aristocracy first defined and then militarized the Grossbürgertum. The aristocrats curtailed political activities by threatening the leaders of the new class, sending agent provocateurs to undermine trust in public discussions by censorship and by secret police surveillance of public activities of members of this class. The one place where such oversight was ineffective was the home and garden. The new class poured resources into making these protected precincts as comfortable and as pleasing as possible. The garden in particular was to serve as a surrogate for the arenas of public play which had become so dangerous.

Having established their gardens as separate preserves, the Biedermeier Viennese then filled them with elements borrowed from the experience of the enlightened aristocrats. Gone were fabriques such as Chinese bridges, Roman ruins, and Gothic castles. In their place, the garden patrons erected striped canvas pavilions, statuary, mirror balls on pedestals, swings, miniature fish ponds, and hundreds of species of flowers. These elements conveyed many layers of meaning, beginning with the playful, the childlike, and the disinterested. Choosing to follow the rococo taste over the classic revival favored by the aristocrats was a subtle statement of affiliation with republican ideals. The flowers were a novel element. They set the Biedermeier apart and nominated it as a third stylistic force in the unfolding of future Viennese gardens, alongside the baroque and the English.

In Europe, flowers are the part of the plant which is customarily consumed only through the senses. They are rarely eaten. They contrast with the edible fruit of plants. Their color, perfume, sweetness, and shape attract not only people, but animals as well. There is a fascination about them which they share to some extent with feathers and swimming fish. Flowers are delicate. In the winter and spring, one can anticipate the beauty soon to arrive. In the warm months, they bloom and die within a short time. In autumn, one thinks about the loss of youth and beauty. Contemplating flowers links the symbolic with the material, the living with the dead, and the supernatural with the human. Flowers are sexual organs. There was nothing of the sexual repression in the Biedermeier which we find in the later decades of the nineteenth century. On the contrary, the period reflected a lusty preoccupation with the pleasures of the flesh.[23] The variety of the flower bed reflected the variety of the marital bed. Flowers spoke a language of vice and virtue. The selection of specific species in the same bed could tell a tale of friendship betrayed, of love unrequited, of ingratitude, of sacrifice, and of devoted attachment.[24] The flower beds, like the rococo elements, were texts. But unlike the political messages of the rococo, the Biedermeier flower texts spoke of personal longings, satisfactions, and disappointments. The capacity of a domestic garden to express both the rational and emotive sentiments of its owner is the lasting contribution of these gardens of domesticity to the received meaning of the Viennese landscape.

The public world operated according to the structure of the calendar and, increasingly, the clock as well. The garden of domesticity was timeless. It cycled through its seasons with wondrous regularity. Originally, the Viennese spent the darker, colder months enjoying the garden within, surrounded by the cool shades of green and the delicate images of flowers. In the sunshine months, the family moved out of doors and enjoyed the bountiful colors of the mixed floral beds, the toys, and the surprises of the garden. It was a place where seasons revolved and people and plants grew, but where childhood was always available through sentimental attachments.

Because threat from the outside world defined the place, its boundaries were concrete and impermeable. One could only enter the garden through the house. Its walls were high and offered no hint of the activities within. Historical records show that the garden fence was a wooden wall of considerable height. From the inside, trees, shrubs, and tall bushes hid the wall from view. At the edges of the garden, the density of plants increased until they became so thick that nothing more could be seen. With enough fantasy, one could pretend that there were no walls at all.

The gardens of domesticity shut out the predatory political world. They created a fantasy world in which life was lived solely within the joys of the family circle. In so doing, they mystified family life, imbuing it with a harmony and peacefulness that were at odds with the lived experience. The Viennese families were highly patriarchal; their ideology was influenced strongly by Counter Reformation Catholic Church doctrines, Italian social mores of honor and shame, and later, Napoleonic legal strictures on property relations and family law. As such, they had no room for the economic and intellectual strivings of younger sons, daughters, and wives. The family was merely the most acceptable value to justify the need for privacy in a society whose rulers were suspicious of all private communication among men. The gardens were indeed camouflage for such communication. Like-minded people could come together in the private gardens as opposed to the public places and not be observed by the secret police. This was especially true of clubs and organizations that were officially banned. In his memoirs I. F. Castelli wrote that just such a dismembered club met in the farther reaches of Rosenbaum's garden. The group included the remains of the Ludlam Club, a society of artists which had been banned in 1826, to which the playwright Grillparzer had belonged (cited in Kaut 1975:58).

Even if the gardens functioned as private political space only rarely, maintaining the ideology of domesticity was necessary. This had to be the reason for the garden's existence. The ordinary guests to the garden had to be within the circle of acquaintances of the family and not merely business associates or political cronies. No member of the class could be certain that using the garden for other purposes was totally out of the question. The symbolic elaboration of the gardens as preserves of domesticity was, therefore, a necessity for the progressive and ambitious sections of the middle class. Since the affairs of Vienna were the most visible social actions in the entire empire, the government concentrated significant police activity there. They saw all nonpublic communication among members of the propertied class as subversive. This engendered a more comprehensive elaboration of the theme of domesticity, producing a stylistic system that was wholly identifiable with Vienna. After the 1848 Revolution, a new government reconstituted the reactionary state to accept a greater role for bürgerlich politics. The Austrian Liberal Party became increasingly in command of municipal affairs. With greater enfranchisement, the Bürgertum slowly gave up the cozy domesticity of the Biedermeier for a more cosmopolitan garden style, one that reflected the pride they took in their accomplishments for the empire, for German speakers in Europe, and for their families. These gardens of pleasure connected the Austrian Bürgertum with their peers in Northern Europe.

Gardens of Pleasure

In the language of the history of landscape design, the gardens of liberty, gardens of domesticity, and gardens of pleasure are all romantic effusions. All participated in the romantic vision that prevailed in European garden design from the beginning of the eighteenth to the beginning of the twentieth century. Ordinarily, distinctions within this epoch refer to individual interpreters of the vision rather than to coherent stylistic movements. In this study, the focus is as much on the consumers of the products of landscape design as it is on the producers. These consumers vary in the quantity and quality of space they can provide to mount a garden. As new opportunities arise, even if only for a few decades, there is an upswing in garden building activity. Cities establish public gardens at a different pace than domestic gardens. The production of public space develops from a different social process than the production of domestic space.

Gardens of pleasure illustrate this process quite neatly. The name derives from the German word *Lustgarten*, literally a garden of pleasure. The word has been in use since the late medieval period to describe a garden that was not intended to produce food (Hennebo

1962, 1965). These were always the possessions of the elite. In Vienna, the Renaissance palace of Maximilian, the Neugebäude in Kaiser Ebersdorf, was the largest palace garden north of the Alps until it was destroyed by the Turks in their second siege. The term continued to be used to describe villa gardens, such as those designed by Furttenbach for the aristocratic and mercantile elite of Augsburg and other Upper Rhine towns in the mid seventeenth century. In this regard, this landscape taste was the immediate precursor of the gardens of order. The immediate roots of the nineteenth-century form lie simultaneously in Repton's reinterpretation of the romantic English garden as a pastoral and Sckell's clarification of parkscapes in the Munich English garden. Both of these designers worked in the first two decades of the nineteenth century, at a time when Viennese landscape tastes still ran to the French and the English. When Pückler-Muskau and Lenné were building the gardens that would exemplify the new form in Central Europe, the Viennese were exploring the Biedermeier style domestically and the classic revival style publicly. Only in the 1850s, as a new political configuration began to reshape the cityscape and new opportunities began to swell the numbers of people in the garden-building class, did the Viennese embrace this new variation in romanticism. In so doing, they established the garden of pleasure form as the definitive interpretation of the English style in Vienna. The discourse on urban landscape received renewed vigor and maintained its influence through much of the twentieth century.

A garden of pleasure can be identified by its size, layout, and plantings. It is built on a relatively large plot of land in which the house is the most important design element. The house itself is in the garden, unlike the Biedermeier, in which the house fronted the garden and closed it off from the street. One of the major debates among designers in this era was over the most effective way to integrate the verticality of house with the horizontal line of the garden. The garden was open to view from at least two sides of the house and from the street as well, even though it was designed to serve as a domestic space. A carriage path brought the household and its guests first to the house and then past the house to the orchards, flower beds, and lawns. Circling through these plantings, the path then rejoined itself near the house, completing a circuit. This created the central oval bed that is the characteristic feature of the garden of pleasure.

In the eighteenth-century English parkscapes and the Biedermeier gardens, the craft of the garden designer lay in systematically violating the regularity of geometry. Not only were straight lines banished entirely, but the highly prized atmosphere of surprise was heightened by violating the expected angle of a curved path as one walked along. Visitors could never predict how a path would twist around an unseen curve. In the gardens of pleasure, the line of the path and shape of the beds followed regular curves. There was geometric certitude to the layout, but never a straight line. The design instrument of choice was the French curve, not the straight edge. Instead of surprise, the visitor was comforted by the predictability of movement through the garden. If space permitted, the path could make secondary circuits, crossing the main circuit at well-defined points, producing the characteristic *Brezelwege*, or pretzel paths. This return to regularity in layout is the primary distinguishing feature of the vernacular gardens of pleasure in Vienna.

The general plan involved a contrast between the central oval and the outer beds. The center was primarily a lawn of manicured grass surrounded by a tree border, broken in places to allow an unrestricted view of the lawn and the tree border on the other side. Within that border, fruit trees alternated with nut trees and broadleaf trees. The portion of the border closest to the house was often a small orchard of mixed fruits, offering a view of flowering trees in the spring and branches heavy with fruit in the autumn. Broadleaf trees were clustered in the back of the oval and along the return path. The outer beds near the house featured complex floral plants backed by shrubs. Toward the back corners, the designers favored evergreen trees and higher bushes, often arranged with niches, complete with benches, for viewing the lawn or a statue. They might also place a Salettl, or pavilion, along the back of the border on the axis at the main path, permitting the destination to be glimpsed from the first entry into the garden. The entire effect was one of a miniature parkscape.

The full design could be mounted on plots as small as eight hundred square meters. On these smaller plots, the central oval expanded at the expense of the border until the circular path itself was absorbed. The result was not a tree-ringed lawn, but a more complex pastiche. Smaller beds and other design elements, such as a gazebo, chosen from pattern books, could be added. The gazebo was placed at the back of the lawn, away from the house, and the path between the two was straight. In smaller spaces, the garden of pleasure style gave way to the Biedermeier.

Because so few people could participate directly in building this kind of garden, the garden of pleasure contributed far less to the language of landscape than the gardens of order, liberty, and domesticity which preceded it. Today, looking for echoes of this discourse in people's descriptions of their domestic gardens is disappointing. The gardens of pleasure were less independent of the house than even the gardens of domesticity in the Biedermeier. They were part of a complex of bürgerlich ideas about the meaning of owning a house and the land on which it sat. Hösl and Pirhofer called this complex *Hausdenken*, house thinking (1988:39). Vienna had always been a city of renters. Only the aristocracy and a thin layer of the merchant class had the resources to purchase and maintain land for a house. As industrial expansion worked its way through the regional economy, the range of Bürgers who could afford to buy land and build houses increased. With more homeowners, Hausdenken began to pervade bürgerlich culture. This trend involved viewing the house as interest-bearing capital in the form of goods. The investment was understood as safe and one that would insulate the owner from economic cycles over the long term. Maintaining the quality of the building and its grounds protected the investment—which is where the garden form became important. The garden had to develop and beautify the land, but it also had to frame the house and display its charms in the best possible light. One important element in this charm was the feeling of seclusion—but not Biedermeier domesticity among Bürgers hiding from a hostile state. That danger was now past. The new threat came from foreign workers crowding the industrial suburbs a mere twenty-minute walk from the villa districts, which was one of the reasons that villas were built in only a few districts. No one wanted to share space with the newcomers. The code for talking about a property in a segregated district included such phrases as *Heimlichkeit*, secludedness; *Behaglichkeit* or *Gemütlichkeit*, coziness; *Bequemlichkeit*, comfort; *Vergessenheit*, forgetting; *Abgeschiedenheit*, seclusion; *Eleganz*, elegance; and *Ruhe*, quiet.

The Hausdenken complex characterized the high Bürger class in this period. From his ability to make such an investment, the Bürger could expect a high rate of return at the sale of the property. Because of such a fine investment, he could also expect a high degree of status, including political clout, political enfranchisement, and entrée to the better society. In the idiom of the city, these were *die besseren Leut*, the better people. The concrete expression of success was bound up with the possession of property.

Today, only a small portion of the people with whom I spoke looked at their gardens in this light. Even among the gardeners who possessed detached houses, only four responded positively to the notion that a garden could symbolize their success in life. These positive responses automatically included the house with the garden as the basis for the significance:

> No, the garden is certainly not [a symbol of success]. Perhaps the house and garden. One can accomplish it only when one has money. To build a house costs a lot of money. Unfortunately, we didn't inherit any, so we had to . . . [earn all of it].[1]

The vitality of Hausdenken lies not merely in building or buying a house, but in creating an investment. There is another, related idea concerning the feelings of security when one possesses a small piece of land; it has less to do with investment and more to do with life security and will come up in the discussion of gardens of security. Echoes of Hausdenken are rarely heard today. In this response, one can hear the idea clearly expressed:

> Well, in a way, yes. If I didn't have it, didn't have the house. . . . It is the case that I can live from it still. That I have to live from it already makes me somewhat of a victim. Sure, if I was to sell it, I could live essentially better. I already feel the urgency of doing that. I'm no one's fool, but as long as you live, you should hold onto that bit of earth.[2]

The entire passage is Hausdenken, but the last thought makes the connection between the investment and the self in a very dramatic fashion. To live without the investment, even if it means a materially better life, is to live without the class identity that possession confers.

Many of the phrases that one would expect to hear from people who were fully participating in this Hausdenken complex, such as references to house or garden as cozy, comfortable, or secluded, are not there. The exception is the image of quietude. I asked people directly if they found their gardens to be loud. Only those unfortunate enough to live in settlements near heavy traffic agreed. There was less elaboration on the experience of quietude than had occurred for other questions that tapped a sensitive issue. Everyone took it as self-evident that gardens were quiet. Few viewed the quiet as extraordinary; those that did interpreted the question as referring to noise, rather than as a code for segregation from the undesirable mixing of classes in residential space. Even among those interview partners who had attained the social level equivalent to the high Bürgertum of the mid nineteenth century there was no reflection that preservation of property values depended on maintaining residential segregation.

For most of Vienna's residents the city's public parks were the place to experience gardens of pleasure. The parks were specifically designed as icons of the values of liberal culture in the city. Sheehan described Central European liberalism as a family of ideas incorporating notions of constitutionalism, individualism, and progress, through which a noncorporate *Öffentlichkeit*, the politicized public, struggled to replace the established corporate power structures, especially the linkage of absolutist aristocratic interests with the church (Sheehan 1979). The landscape style for these parks associates the liberal ascendance with the goals of the Enlightenment through an imitation of the form of the gardens of liberty. Although labeled English parks, these are neo-romantic gardens of pleasure. Their size, structure, form, and function are different from the earlier parkscapes. What both styles have in common is a banishing of the straight line geometry of the gardens of order which are so closely associated historically with the aristocracy and church. At the time of their design, these parks were considered provocative and radical. Later, reformers and reactionaries targeted the garden of pleasure form as the liberal government of the city lost its popularity among the populace. The gardens had become symbols for the now old-fashioned and self-aggrandizing bürgerlich political agenda.[3]

DISCOURSE ON GARDENS OF PLEASURE

The fundamental problem for the mid nineteenth-century garden designers was *Landschaftsverschönung*, the improvement of the landscape. The phrase *improving the landscape* has similar connotations in English and German. In *The Country and the City*, Raymond Williams noted that "an estate passed from being regarded as an inheritance, carrying such and such income, to being calculated as an opportunity for investment, carrying greatly increased returns. In this development, an ideology of improvement—of transformed and regulated land—became significant and directive" (1973:61). There are enormous differences between the English and the Viennese experience. First, the English experience began a half-century earlier and developed in a fully mature liberal political environment. More importantly, it took place in an industrializing countryside. The Viennese experience with the ideology of improvement happened in an unstable political environment in which power was held by the liberals with the acquiescence of a strong aristocracy. It occurred on the expanding edge of a metropolis, whose land prices were inflated by the rapid immigration of thousands of industrial workers.

In the second half of the nineteenth century, the house garden became an income-producing investment among the economically expanding Bürgertum. This new group of patrons had grown in number, in purchasing power, and in the ability to influence public taste. As priority tasks, they returned to the English parks, which had lost all of their former meaning among these industrialists and had become the model of the improved landscape. The garden of pleasure defined the aesthetics of improvement. The design principles alone came to symbolize the social power of the liberals, and the plainly decorative function of these gardens went hand in hand with the general decline in intellectual achievement during this era (Hoffmann 1970:274–76).

The garden of pleasure was English in its basic layout and in its support of the natural growth patterns of plants. It differed from the English in its size and its unboundedness. The garden of pleasure was defined primarily by the limits of a piece of property, and it permitted the eye to view the house and land as a unit. The pathetic, the heroic, and the ruins lay outside this space. Instead of the softly modulated light and shadows of the English park, the neo-romantic favored the bright sunshine and flash that would best display the multicolored array of flowers (Hoffmann 1970:186–87). The style had the character of the unfinished or the sought after, the digression into literary or exotic contents, in the excessive expression of details, in the impression of the totality of the natural in the artistic point of view, and in the movement toward refining the neo-romantic canon of nature-referring forms (Althöfer 1956:186–87).

As more and more Bürgers benefited from the expanding economy, they began to invest in country estates. In doing so, they imitated the one garden style available to them which was not tainted with the economy-stifling reactionary tendencies of absolutism: the English parkscape. So many demands being made on the limited number of English style garden architects in the region meant that some modifications in the original style were inevitable. The variety of formal elements was reduced, simplified, and assembled into pattern packages that the patron could select from *Schablone*, pattern books, and garden magazines. What had been a series of design principles capable of producing infinite varieties of composed landscapes became a canon of forms applied repeatedly in bürgerlich estates. At the same time, the technicalities of executing the designs became easier. It took a great talent to construct a freely curving path that pleased the eye. In the garden of pleasure canon, French curves were substituted, as is evident in Figure 13. These satisfied the eye, but their advantage lay in the ease with which they could be built by less talented gardeners armed only with a knowledge of geometry. These designs were copied by gardening firms and hobby gardeners, who learned of the designs from the books themselves and from garden magazines. One of the earliest magazines for gardeners, *Ideenmagazin*, was published by the Leipzig professor of philosophy J. Grohmann in 1796. A later publication, *Neues Ideen-Magazin zur Verschönung der Gärten*, edited by C. Menzel, was published in 1825, and Hoffmann credited it with effectively disseminating the forms of the canon (1970:269).

The fate of elements in the canon can be illustrated by the treatment of the stand of trees. In the English original parkscapes of William Kent and Capability Brown, the stand of trees was composed of the same species grouped together to emphasize the height of the tallest tree. The stand celebrated that species and set it off against a background of others. It caught the viewer's attention and led the eye to the next element in the composition. In the garden of pleasure, the stand became the arboretum, a section of the estate which used only trees for its design—collections of trees that would never occur together in nature. By planting them together the architect formed an assortment, not out of botanical interest, but as a *Naturphysiognomie*, a face of nature (Meyer 1859).

The style of the garden of pleasure is associated with the design regime of the English gardener Humphrey Repton, who believed that nature had to be subdued and made comfortable for people to

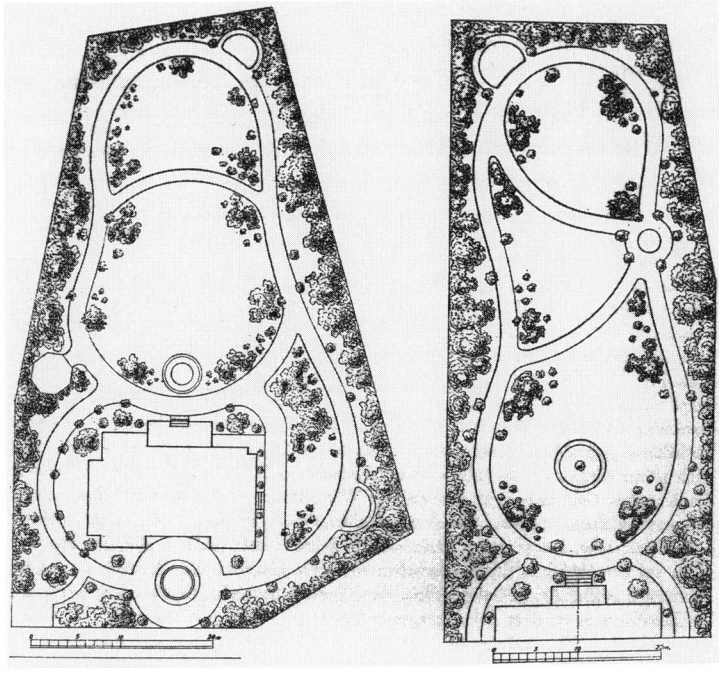

FIGURE 13. *Neo-romantic villas at the end of the nineteenth century, ground plans by Hampel (1902). The plans reflect the domestic landscape designs that dominated throughout the second half of the nineteenth century. The French curve paths and open central bed are typical of the Hausdenken landscapes that patrons preferred as a way of making their estates attractive to the widest possible market, ensuring a stable investment.*

live in. This meant that the garden needed to contain "formal" elements in the vicinity of the house, so that the house would not appear to exist in the middle of a wilderness (1982:141). This pattern was quite similar to those of the Biedermeier gardens in which regular beds and geometric paths defined the part of the garden closest to the house but lost their strictness with greater distance from it. Repton emphasized an unmistakable geometry in his design of flower beds, hedgerows, and bosquets. Repton's ideas about design were expansive. He thought in terms of integrating the elements into a total landscape and coined the term *landscape gardening*.

In German-speaking lands, Repton's ideas were influential in the development of the new canon. Three designers, Sckell (1750–1823), Pückler-Muskau (1785–1871), and Lenné (1789–1866), developed parkscapes that were influenced both by Repton's pleasure grounds and by Biedermeier gardens. Sckell was the designer of the English Reptonesque garden in Munich. The architecture of the central house was the focal point of the design, and the garden form reflected its regularities and then slowly developed into a parkscape. For Sckell, the garden was a place where nature appeared in its best attire, an appearance that it could never attain outside the parkscape (Sckell 1818:8).

Pückler-Muskau was even more strongly influenced by Repton, whose gardens he visited in the early 1800s while he toured England. Pückler-Muskau found the older version of the English parkscapes monotonous. His writings expressed his desire to fence the landscape to support the feeling of *Heimlichkeit*, secretiveness. On principle he opposed curved paths, thinking instead that the path through the landscape should produce very definite sensations of *Behaglichkeit*, coziness; *Zweckmässigkeit*, practicality; and *Bequemlichkeit*, comfort. He thought these feelings were best elicited by direct paths. His interests went beyond parkscapes to include the small private grounds where fresh vegetables and flowers were grown. These only breathe "seclusion and secrecy, quiet, and the forgetting of worldly cares" (1830: no page given; cited in Althöfer 1956:66). Instead of varying the landscape garden, he built comfort, charm, security, and *Eleganz* into the gardens at his family's estate at Hermannsbad-Muskau.

Lenné was a student of Sckell's. He redesigned sections of Berlin after the inspiration of Repton. In his Peacocks Island garden of pleasure at Sanssouci Palace (Figure 14), the grass beds were cut into irregular shapes, and flowers were grouped in homogeneous patches of color. The paths were redesigned for practical and aesthetic purposes. Lenné often took contracts that enabled him to redesign older French style estates into more up-to-date parkscapes. He always tried to retain the symmetry of French pattern while finding ways to unify its underlying regularity with natural forms (Lenné 1826). The public garden of pleasure also included flower beds, something the eighteenth-century English gardeners would never have tolerated. The flower craze of the early 1800s had affected the patrons of large gardens as well as small ones. In popular preference the tulip came first, but soon people were demanding large and unique collections of hyacinth, crocus, anemone, daffodils, iris, lilies, gladioli, peonies,

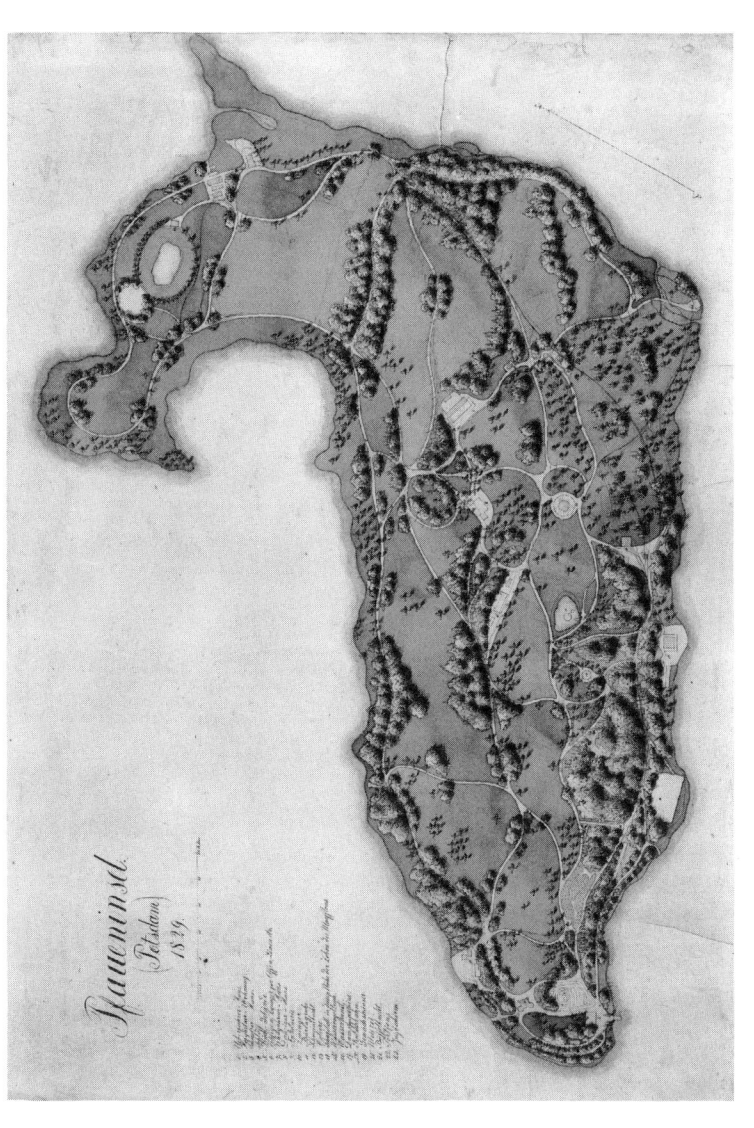

FIGURE 14. *Peacocks Island, at the Sanssouci Palace in Potsdam, plan by Lenné (1829). This was a redesign of an older, French style garden. Part of the old garden remains in the far left corner of the island. Three large flower beds lie just to the right of the old garden. The paths define irregular beds, and the trees are grouped together by species.*

dahlias, daisies, and hortensia. Loudon's book contains two illustrations of how these beds can be made to fit grass fields (1850:932). Both Pückler-Muskau and Lenné designed flower beds for their gardens. Flowering bushes such as magnolia, rhododendron, azalea, heather, along with roses, became more popular. As the canon developed during the century, confining the flowers and bushes to flower beds was replaced by having them border the property or by placing them in a central oval; they were also used to connect the house to the horizontal line of the ground.

Of the three influential designers, Lenné was the only one connected directly with Vienna. In autumn 1812, he came to Vienna for the festivities surrounding the Wiener Congress. Because of a longtime friendship between his father and the imperial garden director, Joseph Boos, Lenné stayed with the Boos family. He intended to become a professor of botany or a botanical garden director and planned to work toward those goals in Vienna. In Vienna, Lenné met the old professor of botany and founder of the university botanical gardens Jacquin and in 1814 worked for the garden department at the royal Lustgarten at Laxenburg Castle. Two surprises awaited Lenné in Laxenburg. First, the estate manager asked him to submit plans for the redesign of the garden. Second, he was honored with the title *kaiserlich Garten-Ingenieur*. His Laxenburger plan strongly resembled his first large plan for the work at Sanssouci. He left Vienna in 1815 (Günther 1985:14).

Lenné's student Meyer is credited with codifying the garden of pleasure canon in his 1859 *Lehrbuch der schönen Gartenkunst*. Another popular pattern book, *Die Landschaftsgärtnerei*, was published by Pückler-Muskau's chief gardener, Ernst Petzold, in 1861. These books became the standard references for the garden of pleasure style for the entire second half of the century. Two locally influential pattern books preceded the publication of these German gardeners: *Schlüssel zur Bildenden Gartenkunst* by Neubert in 1853 and *Das Decameron oder 10 Darstellungen vorzüglichen Formen und Charakterverbindungen Aus dem Gebiethe der Landschaftsgartenkunst* by Hügel's student Rudolph Siebeck in 1856. A third pattern book, *Garten-Architektur* by Hügel's co-worker Lothar Abel, was published in 1876 and was even more influential than the other four within Vienna.

Neubert's 1853 pattern book included thirty-five color engravings. There were several differences between these and the contemporary

Biedermeier gardens: Neubert's beds were irregular but no longer free and natural; they were instead mathematically constructed in free curves. The beds were not fenced. Like all parkscapes, the grass and tree beds invited walking and sitting. Finally, the colorful flowers and botanical variety of the Biedermeier gardens became negligible elements in Neubert's designs, in which the lawn and the shrubbery dominated.

The change in the bed form resulted from a process of stylization, already prefigured during the height of the Biedermeier. For example, in the house garden of F. A. Engels in Grinzing from the 1840s, there was a small side garden and a main garden. The little garden contained two beds in fish bladder form, had no enclosure, no flowers, and two chestnut trees. The main garden was in two parts, one with curving beds and one with straight beds with an axis in the middle. None of these beds was enclosed, and they were composed of trees instead of flowers. The curves were harder and less natural. A strip of high shrubs surrounded the main garden, a feature carried over into Neubert's drawings as well.

Another difference between the garden of pleasure and the Biedermeier is the closing out of economic possibilities in favor of purely decorative uses (Neubert 1853: plan 14). Some of the drawings show that there were rococo elements, such as labyrinths (ibid.: plan 31). There were greenhouses, but they were smaller and more isolated. The few play toys that remained were collected in specific places designated as playgrounds (ibid.: plan 21). The most archaic type of house garden design, the symmetrical Paradiesgarten of the Middle Ages, was still available in Neubert's pattern book, with two crosscutting axes and two round beds at the cross (ibid.: plan 1).

Siebeck's book came a few years later (1856) and developed further the second Biedermeier type: regular lines near the house, irregular curves further away. For Siebeck, the point of departure was the house, and the garden merely surrounded it. He stylized the cut-lawn carpet patterns and offered designs to suit a number of purposes including commercial gardens, botanical gardens, and parks for entertainment and recreation. In this way, he divided the functions of the garden into autonomous plots (1856: plan 4).

Changed social realities undermined the ideal naturalism of the English garden. The period when an eternally good nature mirrored an open society ended in the 1820s. Soon after 1830, the revolution in material lifestyle, increased population pressure, and a rising set of expectations among the Bürgers produced more crowded spaces and more legal barriers to the creation of parkscapes. In the second half of the nineteenth century, the house garden became an investment in property among the socially mobile and grew thereafter in frequency, size, and expense. Alfred Weber characterized this new group as having a penetrating, naive, growing optimism about life. The scientific positivism and naturalism, which had conquered so much of the outer being, also shaped the inner being. This mind set was no longer inclined to interact too deeply in the dark world of its own assumptions (1960:417).

The Viennese Enlightenment aristocrats ushered in the English parkscape style. The next generation of emerging Bürgers admired this vision of nature and society and participated in it. By the third generation, industrialization had transformed this vision. For this generation, the garden of liberty was an anachronism, a form too unwieldy to represent properly the old-fashioned and weakened nobility. Acceptance of the continued domination of society by their reactionary cousins under Metternich appeared as a betrayal of their grandfathers' republican ideals. Pückler-Muskau said it succinctly when he described the need to move away from the older English style: "Let the poor, useless aristocrat have his poetry. It's the last thing he has. We must respect the old Spartans" (1834:178). The form of respect was the appreciation of natural growth. The new form, however, was a return to geometric lines.

The developing garden of pleasure canon was not without its critics. In an assessment of the artistic importance of these gardens by Jakob von Falke, there are descriptions of ornamental forms rivaling the gardens of liberty: coats of arms and names cut into the lawn, and juxtapositions of statuary of differing historical styles. Falke argued for a return to design compositions that emphasized the solitary tree and naturally shaped beds dominated by lawns—in short, a return to the more rigorous and demanding principles of the eighteenth-century designers (1884:84). Another critic, Schultze-Naumburg, argued for a new stylistic development, one oriented toward the forms from the pattern books of the period around 1850. His examples immediately before and after the middle of the century are neither beautiful nor sublime. In some of his statements one can hear the echo of the Biedermeier taste: "A garden is not a forest and it is not a meadow. It is the humanized form of nature. . . . The plant itself strives to develop freely. The form of the totality of plants in the garden is one imposed by humans." In place of the gardens of pleasure, he offered natural growths, using for ground cover plants that were both beautiful and useful, such as the strawberry (1909).[4]

By the latter half of the nineteenth century the gardens of pleasure had lost all of their former meaning among these right-leaning industrialists. As improved landscape, however, the parks could reflect their newfound social power. The forms themselves became increasingly devoid of meaning, and eclectic forms were patched together with historic garden elements into a smooth pattern. With the narrowing of the scope of garden design to that of only representing social class—whether through natural forms or through a collage of all available styles—the weakening of garden art mirrored the decline in artistic work, including the corresponding effects in painting and sculpture. The stage was set for the search for new paths (Hoffmann 1970: 274–76).

SOCIAL PRODUCTION OF GARDENS OF PLEASURE

The period 1840–90 witnessed a relatively rapid redistribution of activities in space, as the number of factories and foreign industrial workers increased. Unfortunately, housing to accommodate this increase did not keep pace. Table 2 illustrates the increasing gap between population size and housing units. Historians have proposed a number of theses for why the gap developed and why it persisted as one of the most pervasive of social problems in the city through the 1930s.

Baltzarek suggested that the problem began as an artifact of feudal land ownership. The area that could potentially be developed for housing was the *Burgfriedensbezirk*, the castle precinct, or settlement area that could legally claim protection within the fortifications in times of danger. This was the so-called *Linien Wall* (Map 5). New residential areas were based on the capacity of the fortified area to support the population during an attack, a requirement taking on concrete urgency when we remember that Vienna lay under siege by the Turks on two separate occasions in the sixteenth and seventeenth centuries. This protected area grew slowly between the two Turkish wars. After the second siege, more villages were incorporated, and the area expanded more quickly. By 1750, Vienna had the largest

TABLE 2

Nineteenth-Century Population and Housing Growth within Present-day Municipal Boundaries

	Housing		Population		
Year	No. of Units	Total	Index (1,700 = 100)	Increase between Years (%)
1700	5,030	123,500	100	
1750	6,630	191,330	154	1.1
1795	10,930	249,380	201	0.6
1830	13,710	378,510	306	1.4
1869	21,580	875,460	708	3.3
1880	28,390	1,147,260	928	2.2
1890	34,210	1,404,800	1,137	2.4

Source: Baltzarek 1980:13.

metropolitan area in Central Europe. An outer defense wall built in 1704 defined the area.[5] Land rights within the defense wall were owned by the municipality of Vienna and by twenty-one feudal and church corporations, who used the rights to block the development of new housing, forcing new residential spaces beyond the defense perimeter. Table 3 shows the effects of this obstruction on the residential geography.

In the 210 years described in these tables, the central city stagnated. All of the dramatic growth was in the suburbs, where housing units increased 900 percent and the population 1,650 percent. Pressure on the available housing, measured by the number of inhabitants per unit, doubled. This pattern of suburban growth was already established in the earliest manufacturing period, and by the time of the 1848 Revolution, the pattern had become irreversible.

In the aftermath of the 1848 Revolution, the old feudal landowners lost most of their legal right to obstruct land development. The major beneficiaries of this shift in land control were the municipality and the large military districts surrounding Vienna. The municipality began to exercise administrative control over the local communities neighboring it, an oversight that had grown slowly from the early 1700s onward. The earliest areas of foreign worker settlement,

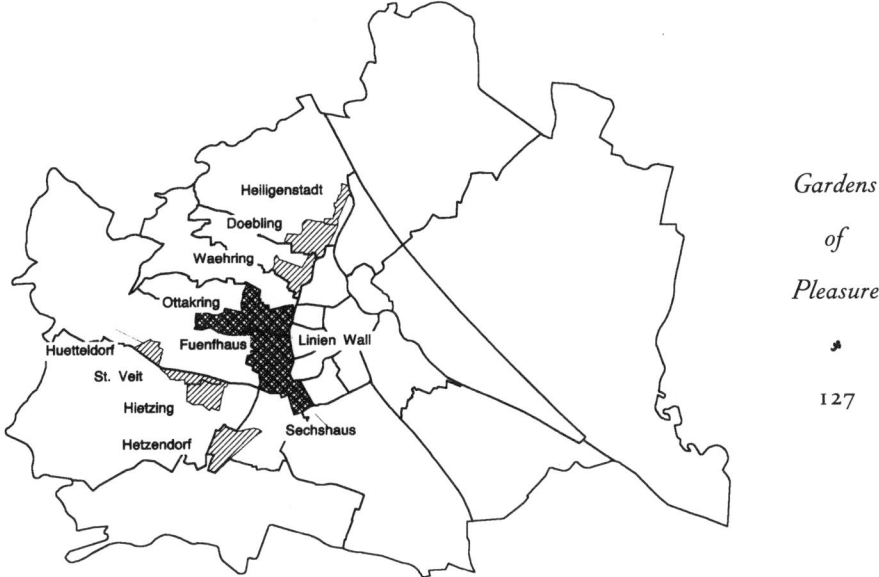

MAP 5. *Neo-romantic gardens of the mid nineteenth century. The* single cross-hatched areas *indicate precincts designated in the text as middle-class villa developments. The* double cross-hatched areas *indicate named workers' districts. The Linien Wall separating these outer districts from the Burgfriedensbezirk is also indicated.*

Währing, Hernals, and Neu-Lerchenfeld, and later the manufacturing district of Gumpendorf, had presented to the municipality the specific problems of transportation, health, security, and fire protection in the unincorporated villages.

Until 1820, aristocratic and religious landowners had managed to ensure the increased value of their property by obstructing the building of workshops and factories within the municipality. That year the restriction was lifted, and communities could choose freely to grant building permits to factory owners. The increasing population of workers in the suburbs upset the conservative bürgerlich residents of the central city and nearest suburbs. They were especially concerned about the rising costs of providing services to these untaxed communities. Populist politicians of the period fanned this resentment. In the hope of pushing the workers' settlements farther away from the municipal services, measures such as the 1832 Ordinance

TABLE 3

Housing and Population in Linien-Wien within the Boundaries of the City between 1849 and 1890[a]

Housing Year	Central City	Castle Precinct	Index (1,700=100)	Areas Outside Defense Wall	Index (1,700=100)	Suburbs Total	Index (1,700=100)
1700	1,150	1,000	100	780	100	1,780	100
1750	1,150	1,370	137	1,490	198	2,860	160
1795	1,310	2,190	219	3,090	396	5,280	296
1830	1,210	3,180	318	3,520	451	6,700	376
1857	1,220	3,550	355	4,340	556	7,890	443
1869	1,170					9,010	506
1880	1,380					10,950	615
1890	1,410					13,050	733
1900	1,350					14,750	828
1910	1,350					16,060	902

Population Year	Central City	Suburbs	Suburb Index (1,700=100)	Suburban Persons/House
1700	50,000	63,000	100	35.3
1750	54,340	121,000	192	42.0
1795	51,340	159,070	252	30.1
1830	54,230	230,000	365	39.3
1857	57,500	418,730	664	53.0
1869	63,810	543,610	853	60.3
1880	69,640	641,490	1,018	58.5
1890	67,030	746,590	1,185	67.2
1900	58,500	924,560	1,467	62.7
1910	53,100	1,042,160	1,654	64.8

Source: Baltzarek 1980:14.

[a] In 1869, the outer defense wall boundary was abrogated, and new boundaries were established which incorporated many of the residential districts within the municipality.

forbade the building of new housing within two miles of any village center under municipal control (Koch 1842:339).

The modernization of the streetcar and light rail systems made eventual incorporation inevitable. One transit line tied together in a semicircle the outer boundaries of the developing areas from Heiligenstadt to Hütteldorf. The availability of swift connections to the light rail system led to a jump in new factories and other enterprises on land that was actively involved in agricultural production. Factory owners converted existing buildings into smaller housing units for new workers. In 1890, incorporation did come, even though the city had extended services in a piecemeal fashion in the three decades prior: police jurisdictions in 1850, welfare services and postal delivery beginning in 1865, and market ordinance jurisdiction in 1870 (Baltzarek 1980:20).

After 1848, the bulk of the residential building in the suburbs involved rehabilitating existing structures in the old village centers. No profit could be made building worker housing, partly because of the economic outlook of the era. Anyone with any capital to invest looked to the future with great optimism. Land prices, the housing market, and mortgage interest rates were rising. Taxes on rental income were dropping as the currency slowly inflated. Modern building codes allowed the use of cheaper materials and less involvement by guild-based inspectors. New housing was logically the safest interest-generating investment available (Hösl and Pirhofer 1988: 37–40). The frenzy of apartment building initiated by the Ringstrasse project demonstrates how swiftly housing capital could be mobilized; in the case of the Ringstrasse *Mietpaläste*, apartment houses, it was always housing for the higher income buyers.

Districts in the suburbs that received this investment included the western vineyard villages of Ober- and Unterdöbling, Grinzing, Ober- and Untersievering, Pötzleinsdorf, Neustift am Walde, Dornbach, and Neuwaldegg, and the southern villages of Hietzing, Ober- and Unter St. Veit, Hacking, Lainz, Hütteldorf, and to a lesser extent Penzing. The western villages were wedged between the teeming working class communities of Heiligenstadt and Ottakring. The southern communities lay north of the working class districts of Fünfhaus and Sechshaus and the agricultural community of Meidling. Collectively these became known as the villa districts, which had, for the preceding two hundred years, attracted the attention of the well-to-do as summer holiday areas. The stream and river valleys that cut through the woods remained cooler and less humid than the Danube valley itself. The royal summer palace of Schönbrunn was in the village of Hietzing. The Wienerwald villages of Neuwaldegg and Pötzleinsdorf were the former sites of celebrated gardens of liberty.

Building gardens of pleasure was undertaken by a very narrow population segment: those who could afford to develop large parcels of land for domestic use. These households were concentrated in the outlying districts. Döbling was the preeminent district in the period for gardens of pleasure. By 1869, the residents of this district had the lowest percentage of gainfully employed persons (20 percent) and the highest ratio of household employees: sixty-three per hundred households (Schimmer 1874; cited in Bobek and Lichtenberger 1978:83). These new villas opened opportunities for creating gardens of pleasure. The estates were investments. The family lived in the house and garden. The father commuted to his office downtown. Servants kept everything tidy and well ordered. If the market changed and it was possible to sell at a great profit, everyone moved temporarily to an apartment while the new villa was being built. The upper levels of the Bürgertum built villa after villa in this fashion. They did so for three reasons: to avoid the high cost of rents in the city, to take advantage of the eroded cost of skilled labor, and to ensure long-term growth for their capital. Except for the low labor costs, the rationale for home ownership has not changed very much. In mid nineteenth-century Vienna, this thinking conveyed a tremendous amount of status, a certain degree of political clout, and economic as well as symbolic security. In 1873, the Viennese stock market suffered its greatest crash, destroying the paper fortunes of those foolish enough to be sucked into the speculations of the previous decade. The crash crippled the greater Viennese economy, which did not recover fully until a century later. Those with their capital invested in villas survived with their fortunes intact. The real estate market dropped but rebounded relatively quickly with no loss of pre-1873 value (Hösl and Pirhofer 1988:39).

To hedge against any differences that might arise between the ground price and the housing market, the villa estate required sufficient land and a house large enough to be subdivided into apartments if necessary. The structures were usually three stories high with a staircase at all entrances to facilitate easy conversion. The investor had to develop the land to maintain an attractive setting for the house. Each element played a role in maintaining the market value of the investment: the garden protected the value of the land, and the house protected the value of the rents.

The Viennese produced most of their gardens of pleasure on large, privately owned spaces in the outer suburbs. Private gardens were not the only examples of this landscape consciousness; the municipality advanced gardens of pleasure as the form of public garden fit to exemplify the ideals of the modern, liberal state. Primary examples of these parks were the those built within the Ringstrasse itself: the Stadtpark and the Rathauspark.

The Ringstrasse was the most ambitious urban redevelopment project since Haussmann's reconstruction of Paris. It signaled a new, more powerful role for the planner-architect in determining the cityscape. The walls of the city would be razed, and the Glacis would be redeveloped for public, commercial, and housing uses. The extent of the area involved is shown in Figure 15. The planning commission held an international competition, and eighty-five of the leading architects of Europe submitted projects to the jury. The project description stipulated that it was the desire of the city to create a major traffic corridor that linked all of the districts while defining areas for commercial property development and the sites of a specified list of public buildings. There were three prizes. The first prize went to the architect Friedrich Stache, whose plan was based on a wheel-and-spoke model. Specifically, Stache proposed an inner ring boulevard surrounding the walled district near the inner edge of the Glacis, a second ring at the outer edge of the Glacis, a third ring (not built) between the second and the fourth, the conversion of the Linien Wall to a fourth boulevard (today's Gürtel), and a fifth boulevard encircling the fringes of the outer districts (not built). Radial streets connected these five belts to each other. The ratio of built to open space in Stache's plan was 1:2, which would have produced a total of 67 percent open land compared with the existing 56.3 percent. The result would have placed Vienna in the first rank of open space in European cities. The second prize went to Ludwig Förster. He, too,

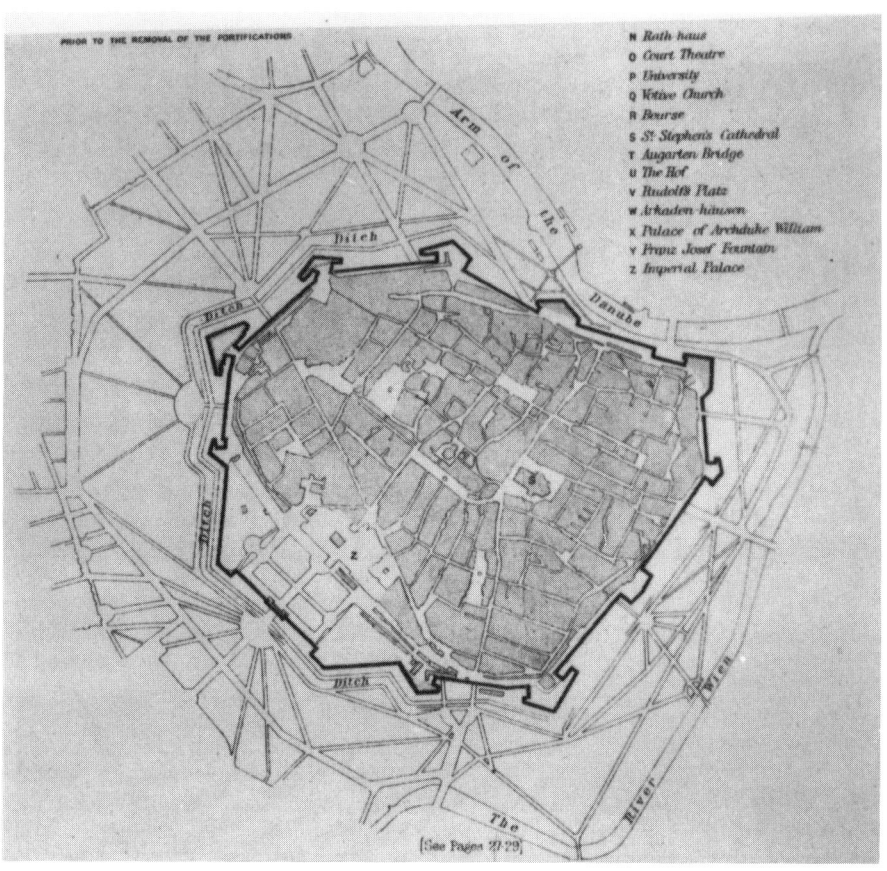

FIGURE 15. *Map of Vienna showing the fortifications and the Glacis as they were in 1857.*
Royal Institute of British Architects 1888:28

suggested a single broad boulevard linking the inner districts (today's Ring Boulevard) and proposed that the ring be divided into three sections in which parks would dominate. Two of these were expansions of already existing parks, the Volksgarten on the left side of the palace and the Hofgarten on the right. The third section was the Wasserglacis, the section of the Glacis whose water spring was purported to have curative powers. This became the site of the Stadtpark. The third prize went to the architect team of van der Nüll and Sicard von Sicardsburg. They placed the boulevard at the bottom of the existing moat and lined it with trees. They also suggested a park in the area of the Wasserglacis.

All of the other projects used the ring motif to link the districts, with one exception. Lenné, the champion of romantic gardens of pleasure in Germany, submitted a project that systematically denied the importance of a traffic corridor as the linking element. It substituted a park the size of the existing Glacis in which the public buildings were placed and commercial development was specifically banned. The project shared a minor prize, but the commission incorporated none of these ideas into the final plan. The final development plan incorporated the general outlines of Stache's wheel-and-spoke design, using Förster's single-ring boulevard. This boulevard was lined with the trees from the design of van der Nüll and Sicard von Sicardsburg. The final plan did bow to some of Lenné's ideas of the importance of green space, incorporating strips of plantings whenever possible and establishing eight major parks, six of which exist today.

Efforts began with the razing of the fortifications around the city, filling in the moat, and digging up the Glacis. The city council administered the redevelopment, debating the form of every park, even to the extent of deciding which species of trees to plant. This project was itself a fully conscious effort to link ideology and environment. In this case the logic of the metaphor was reversed: the parks would confer value on the city as a whole. The redevelopment would proclaim publicly the universality of human liberty, the progressive effects of the money economy, and the irrevocable commitment of the municipal culture to furthering the liberal state.

Before the revelation was possible, the concealment had to begin. This project involved a tremendous loss of unbounded space in the form of the Glacis. In the final plan, 48.4 percent of the Glacis became streets; 32.8 percent became buildings; and 17.4 percent became parks, green strips, and tree rows. By this reckoning, the Ringstrasse project caused an 80 percent reduction in the green space in the center of the city. The completed redevelopment plan can be seen in Figure 16. In his study of this era, Fischer concluded that green space politics had a great deal to do with the debates on the city's right to dispose of the entire Ringstrasse zone in whatever way it saw fit (1971:71). The loss of 80 percent of the area of the

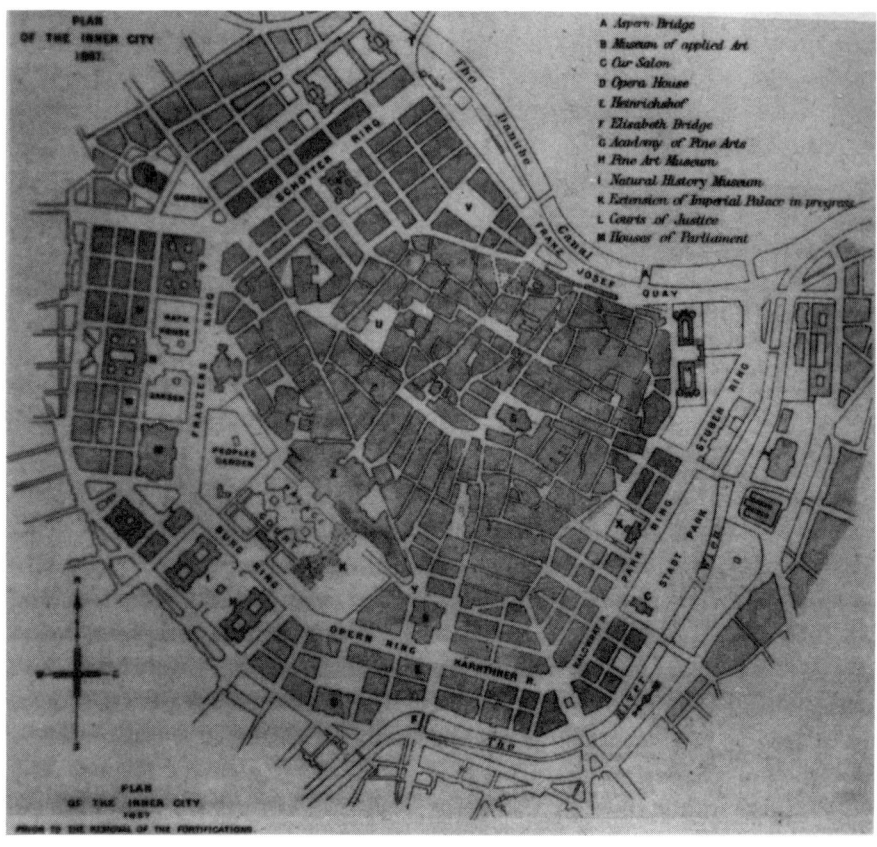

FIGURE 16. *Central city of Vienna after redevelopment (1887). Shown are the Ringstrasse, the location of the public buildings and parks, and the new residential streets.*
Royal Institute of British Architects 1888:28

Glacis during the construction of the Ringstrasse was repugnant to many of the city's powerful imperial officers, as well as to the local public. Newspaper editorials, like the following, reflected this distaste.

> The bastion has fallen. The moat is filled in. The city is free from its stone corset. At the same time that the fortifications were razed, the diverse alleys of the bastions, the grassy places and trees of the esplanade, the alleys and grassy places of the moat, the alleys and broad meadows of the Glacis

fell, as well. We can hardly take the pain felt by so many Viennese as they watched the vast green space in the middle of the city destroyed, as the cool, shady alleys were cut down, as the tumbling places of children, their asylum on humid, summer evenings, were taken away forever. (Anonymous 1869:1)[6]

From the arguments offered at council meetings, it appears that giving up marketable land for green space was not a high priority. The emperor himself reaffirmed the need for portions of the Glacis to remain intact as parks against the frenzy of the redevelopers. He deeded the Wasserglacis to the city on the condition that it remain a public park forever. This became the site of the Stadtpark.

The Stadtpark had priority over many of the planned buildings because of the public uproar over the destruction of the Glacis. Large numbers of people who did not own significant property, and therefore could not vote, used the Glacis. They had little to gain from the Ringstrasse project but stood to lose the most important open space available to them. There were no riots, but the memory of the violence of the 1848 Revolution encouraged the ruling Liberal Party to respond by completing the Stadtpark first. The park was an immediate success. A contemporary observer described its appeal: "Most, perhaps all, go there to find a place where shade, fresh, dust-free, soft breezes, a beautiful view, quiet, the smell of flowers, or all of these can be found together" (Harry 1869:2). By 1905, the city had built eighteen public parks within the Ringstrasse zone.

The recreational qualities of parks were acknowledged but not considered in the landscape designs.[7] The city council built these parks, like the public buildings on the Ringstrasse, to represent the battle between the ideologies of absolutism and liberalism (Schorske 1981:26). Selleny, a landscape painter from Hungary, originally conceived the Stadtpark.[8] City gardener Rudolph Siebeck executed it (Figure 17). The liberals ruling through the city council associated this style with the values of liberty they believed they had inherited from the Enlightenment republicans. Like Shaftesbury, the midcentury Viennese Bürgers perceived the connection between a society that embraced the "mixed government" of liberal pursuits and a landscape that supported a variety of structures (see Chapter 3, note 1). The trees and meadows designed to mimic a picturesque landscape untouched by human design or industry mirrored the political

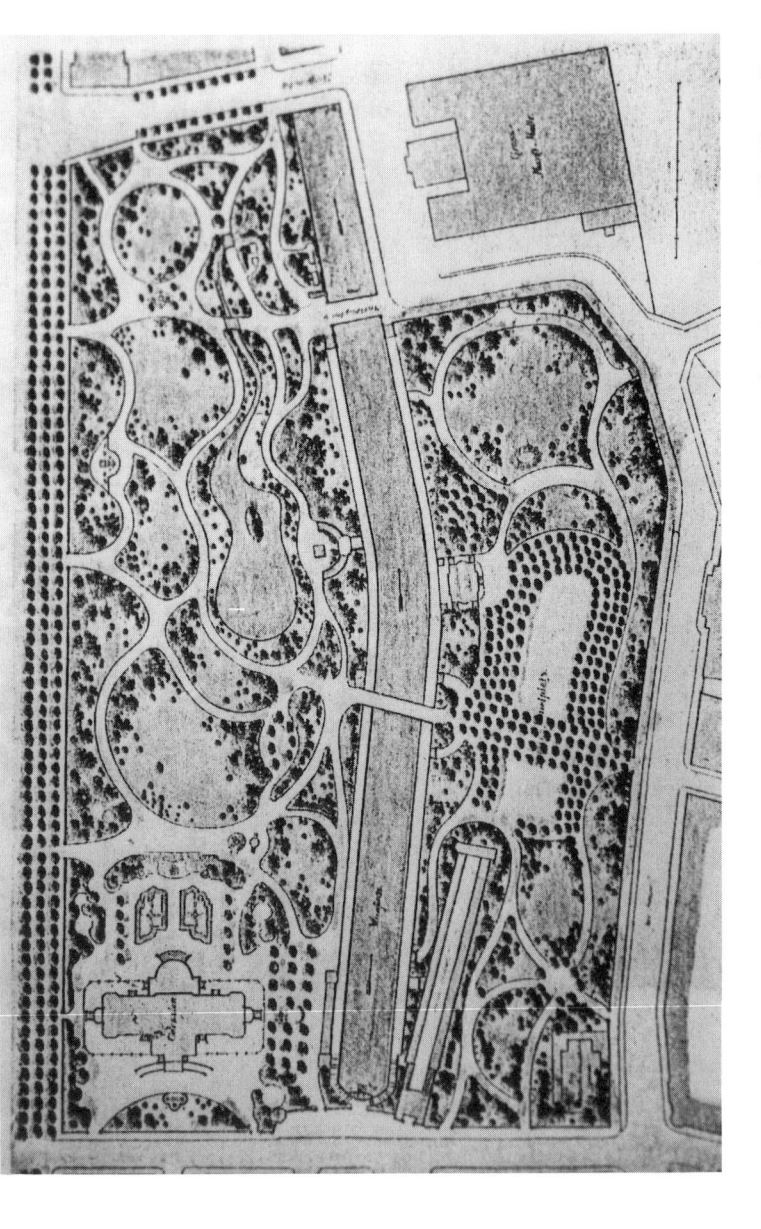

FIGURE 17. *Plan of the Stadtpark in 1905. The older portion designed by Selleny and Siebeck is at the top. The Vienna River flows through the middle. The new Kinderpark is at the bottom. The similarity between this and Lenné's designs (Figure 14) is readily apparent. The design of the central playground in the Kinderpark is a more modern feature. The scale is 1:3,300 meters.*
Mossbäck 1905:349

values of the wealthy Bürgers: equality with the aristocracy; liberty in the disposal of private property, in the practice of religion, and in the freedom of the press; and fraternity in the face of political competition from other classes and with all liberal movements throughout Central Europe (Sheehan 1979). The English style as interpreted by the neo-romantic canon was an icon that linked the free growth of plants with the unleashing of every person's potential—to make money, unfettered and unregulated by the bureaucracy of the absolutist state.

Contemporary commentators noticed this ideological insistence on the neo-romantic. Second only to objections to the high cost overruns of building the park was criticism of its style by newspaper commentators. Many saw the English style as insulting to the emperor and offered the French style as a more loyal design for a faithful imperial capital. Defenders of the English style argued that the aristocratic French design was even more expensive and more limiting:

> Sir Haussmann stands in particular favor with his lord, the ruler of the French, precisely because he holds to the view that future generations will not worry about the cost, but instead will be satisfied with the shiny products of an irresponsible money economy. Thanks to the bürgerlich mentality, this thinking has not yet spread as far as the docks on the Vienna River, and should not do so. We would become victims of its demands, limiting the projects that could be presented to us in the future. (*Morgen Post* 8.XII.1861a; cited in Mollik, Reining, and Wurzer 1980:300)[9]

The Stadtpark was not only a reminder of the beauty of the Glacis, it was also the first opportunity for the liberals to portray symbolically in landscape their commitment to economic and political freedom. It was the first space on the Ringstrasse to concern itself explicitly with representation of any kind. As such, many officials were more interested in keeping it low key by building in as many unobtrusive features of order and ornament as possible.

In theory, these parks granted people permission to use the places in ways that were not allowed in absolutist parks: they could sit on the grass, there were no closing times, and free concerts were offered. The liberals in the city council were divided in how far they felt they could unleash ordinary citizens on public property. Some city councilors were unsettled by the openness of the park, fearing that the use of such permissive parks would lead to a breakdown in public order and morality. Some city councilors saw the parks as an opportunity for increased criminality, especially prostitution (Uhl 1861:4). Other members of the city council were concerned that people would destroy the park by walking on the grass, urinating on the trees, littering, or stealing the flowers. They argued not only for tighter police controls, but for a return to the accustomed taste for ornamental landscape designs. They were able to alter the original landscape of the spa building at the north end of the park, reintroducing French design elements that restored order and control at least to this section. The English style gained a political edge through these discussions, and efforts were made to limit the number of parks built in this style. Maria Theresaplatz, the park for the twin museums of Natural History and Art History, was designed in the aristocratic French style. Since it stood opposite the imperial palace, the argument of erecting a style that would not offend the sensibility of the emperor was more appropriate. Park supporters pointed out that investing enough money in maintenance to keep the parks beautiful was the best way to ensure public pride and care. The sight of a self-regulating, self-disciplined public was the best advertisement for the virtues of liberalism (Mollik, Reining, and Wurzer 1980:287).

The Ringstrasse parks cannot be understood in isolation. They were an element in the evolving cityscape in which green space provided the backdrop for architecture. This cityscape as a whole was intended to have a powerful pedagogical effect on the inhabitants. The design tried consciously to forge a connection between the beauty of the built environment and the political maturity, and the physical and psychological health of the people.

Visiting parks provided health benefits, not only because of the dust-free air, but also because the landscape helped people exercise their bodies naturally. Only a few city councilors felt that the first purpose of the park was to provide recreation for the people. As the city became more congested, this attitude began to change.

Typically, the parks are separated from the street by a tall hedge wall, as in the Stadtpark, or by arrangements of low *Taxus* or juniper bushes that deny access to the inner grounds except through the gates placed at cuts through the hedge wall where the park path meets the sidewalk. Entering the park, the visitor feels a change of mood. The vista is wider than that available on the street. The air is heavy with the scent of grass and evergreen. Pigeons coo audibly.

Traffic sounds recede into the background but never disappear completely. All senses indicate the park to be a different kind of space.

These parks work as landscapes, but they are isolated. The decorum of the place is evident even in the most unstructured of them, the Stadtpark. People sit on benches even though they are permitted to sit on the grass. When children or young adults use the lawns for tumbling or playing catch, the stares of the bench people quickly bring them off the lawn. One late spring, I observed a young couple some fifty meters behind the benches attempt inconspicuously to make love in the sunshine. Instead of turning away and respecting the couple's right to appropriate the space for private activities, the bench people turned toward them, reclaiming the public nature of the space. The couple gave up after a short while and left the park. In the formally contained space created by the Ringstrasse designers, anything that is not specifically permitted is denied. In the old Glacis, the activities of the young couple would have been commonplace and of no consequence to the other users. Thus, although the Ringstrasse parks asserted the ideals of liberalism in an aristocratic world, they never recovered the actual freedoms that had been available in the Glacis.

The Rathauspark opened twelve years later in 1873. Not so much landscape as part of the cityscape surrounded by monumental architecture, the park fronted the Rathaus, a large office building with a late Gothic façade. The park included two square tree gardens separated by a wide alley leading to the front of the Rathaus. The alley was lined with statuary of men who had in some way contributed to the protection of Vienna. Across the Ring from the alley was the Burgtheater. To its right was the Volksgarten and beyond that Heldenplatz and the imperial palace. On the left side of the Rathauspark was the parliament building. On the right side was the university. To be here exposed the visitor to the power fields of art, politics, science, and history. One experienced the city as a total work of art.

In planning the Rathauspark, the city council showed that it had learned something about financing and about the politics of park design. The arguments over the Rathauspark centered on the issue of whether a park should be an architectural element attached to a building or should it have its own separate formal purposes. The council again selected Siebeck to design and execute the park. He believed that a park should frame a building by connecting it to the horizontal in a pleasing manor. This was especially important with the imposing buildings of the Ringstrasse. Without a well-designed linkage between architecture and ground, the buildings would appear naked and isolated in the broad vista provided by the Ring. Photographs of the buildings under construction confirm his observation. The alternative view, championed in the city council hearing by Lothar Abel, was that the parks should have their own stylistic integrity, not relying on a building to develop an integrated arrangement of space. Abel believed that the Rathauspark could do this and still perform the function of visually linking the buildings in this quarter of the Ring. He urged the council to use an Italian mannerist style: free growth and trees of medium height in concentric, geometric beds separated by French curves. The council chose Siebeck's plan to use the English, neo-romantic style again. In a tribute to Pückler-Muskau, Siebeck placed two decorative rondos with fountains near the entrances to both gardens from the central alley. The decision was considered a victory for the side that viewed the architectural environment as primary and the planted environment as secondary. The neo-romantic was perceived as less visually competitive with the monumental buildings (Mollik, Reining, and Wurzer 1980:286).

Debates over the Ringstrasse park styles were not a sideshow to the business of redeveloping the downtown space of Vienna. The Ringstrasse as a whole is a masterful piece of camouflage. The parks are part of that serious effort to give public value to what was a government-supported land grab of enormous proportions. One sees the monumental office buildings, theaters, and museums. One does not see the hundreds of Mietpaläste, apartment houses, built behind these buildings. They were the real business of the redevelopment effort. Born of the housing crisis, apartments exacerbated it by focusing public investment into housing forms that could not serve the needs of the city's new residents. The rents were too high and the location too far from the place of work. Today we have become accustomed to commuting to work, but in the middle of the nineteenth century in Central Europe, people expected to work close enough to home to return there for the midday meal and still get back to work within the hour (Rotenberg 1992b:114). The Ringstrasse apartments would house the Bürgertum, isolating it even farther from the proletarian suburbs. The Mietpaläste were a melting pot that fused the cultures and the agendas of the aristocracy with the emerging upper ranks of the middle classes. Left out of the scramble for control of residential property were the lower ranks of the Bürgertum and the workers.

The Rathauspark was a fitting space for the needs of the bürgerlich apartment dwellers around the Rathaus quarter. Here they could sit on the benches or walk on the paths. Here they could escape the midsummer heat and humidity. But this was all that was permitted. The park's curving walks lined with benches permitted easy visual surveillance of anyone who entered the grove. The tall trees provided a shady canopy but did not obstruct the view. Unlike the free-wheeling spirit of the Stadtpark, in which one experienced the illusion of having left the city, in the Rathauspark the Gothic towers of the Rathaus itself loomed high above, startling the visitor with intrusive glimpses of them. The building was very close to the walk—just behind a stand of tall trees, which exaggerated the height of the towers. Only visitors who were already comfortable with the monumentality of the Ringstrasse and who participated in its celebration of the money economy could find the atmosphere relaxing.

The site from the Ringstrasse period which offers the densest array of representational elements does not sit on the Ring itself, but some eight kilometers to the southeast in the Kaiser Ebersfeld precinct of Simmering. The Central Cemetery, or Zentralfriedhof, was designed under the same regime as the Ringstrasse but was freed from the constraints of space and function which the central location imposed in the Ringstrasse project itself. In 1863, the city council decided to build a new cemetery. The main cemetery for the city, St. Marx, was full. So, too, were the *Linienfriedhöfe* established in 1782 (see Chapter 6). In 1866, a site selection committee was appointed and was headed by Dr. Anton Glickh. The committee chose Kaiser Ebersdorf over two other sites (Rannersdorf and Ober- u. Unterlaa) because the terrain and the quality of the soil were more appropriate for internments, and the distance from the central city was shorter. In addition, transportation lines, parcel size, and burial capacity were well within the guidelines established by the city council. A competition was held to design the cemetery. The first prize of 2,000 florins went to Mylius and Bluntschli of Frankfurt am Main, the second prize of 1,500 florins was awarded to Alexander Wiedermann of Vienna, and the third prize of 1,000 florins went to Gustav Kovompay of Vienna (Stadt Wien 1872). Unlike the Ringstrasse competition, the planning committee implemented the plan as Mylius and Bluntschli drew it, without adding the attractive pieces from the other prize-winning designs. Work started on the cemetery in 1873, and the cemetery opened in 1874. It contained sections specially consecrated for Catholic, Protestant, Jewish, and Greek Orthodox rites and was expanded in 1882, 1888, 1896, and 1905. The final plan is shown in Figure 18. The size of the cemetery was determined by a formula based on the population of the city. As the population of the city rose in each census, the city bought more of the surrounding parcels to ensure that the cemetery could accommodate all of its inhabitants. The larger the cemetery got, the farther people had to travel for burials and the graveside visits during the week of All Saints Day, November 1.

The basic design of the Central European cemetery is based on the medieval cloister cemetery, with two lines of eight trees facing each other in an enclosed space. At the base of each tree, eight monks would be buried. By the time the 128th monk was buried, the corpse in the first position would be sufficiently decayed to permit a new burial in that space. This pattern has remained the norm for twelve hundred years. Central European cemeteries are designed around ranks of trees. The still extant, early nineteenth-century St. Marx cemetery is a good example of how these gardens of the dead looked until the opening of the Central Cemetery. St. Marx has a central path with ten crossing paths, defining twenty banks of trees, with a maximum of thirty trees per bank. There may have been more trees before the cemetery was closed and part of it destroyed to build a highway. The Central Cemetery retains the patterns of banks of trees but places them in a grid that offers far more variety. The overall plan looks like a baroque garden gone mad. A strong central axis links the front gate with the features of the cemetery which symbolize closely held virtues: the Arcadian crypt, the Resting Place of Famous Men, the central chapel. At this chapel, a perpendicular axis extends outward to two rondos. A third rondo behind the chapel completes the symmetry. The three rondos and the main gate form a square that is linked diagonally by cross-cutting paths. These axes and diagonals define areas within the cemetery which resemble the districts of a

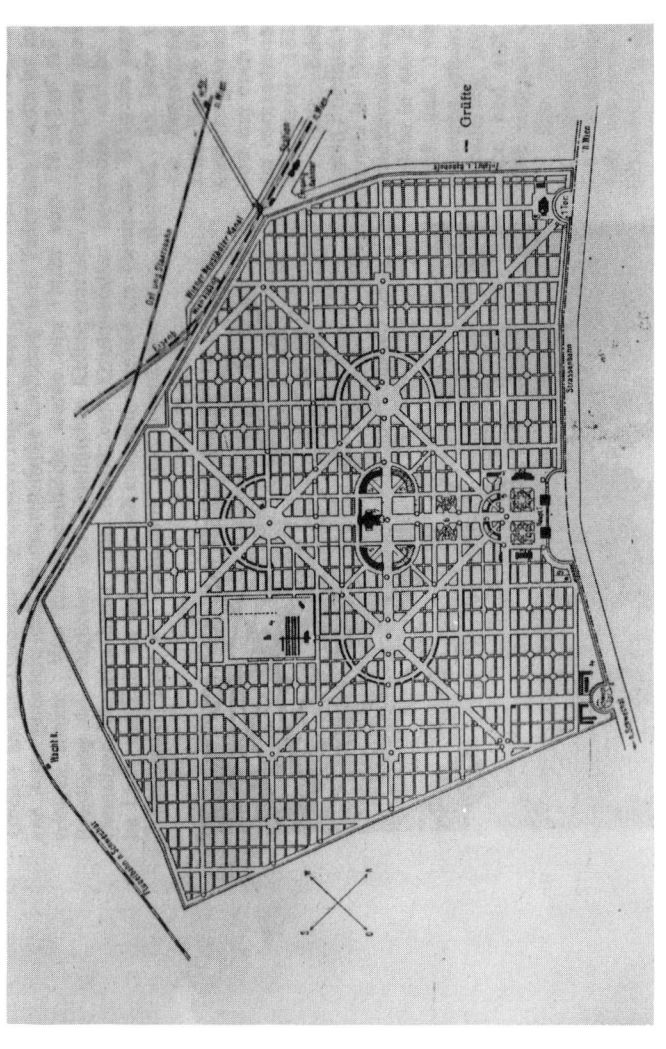

FIGURE 18. *Ground plan of the Zentralfriedhof (1905). In the center of the design is the church. It is surrounded by an arcade of crypts. The main axis leading toward the main gate at the bottom of the drawing is lined with the resting places of famous people. Around the main gate are the funeral chapels and another arcade of crypts. The Jewish funeral rooms and grave area are in the lower right corner. Transportation links at the top of the drawing are railroads. Streetcar and automobile access is along the road at the bottom.*

Filippi 1905:361

city. The intersections themselves are celebrated by statuary, fountains, and specialized architecture. The front precincts are the most prestigious. Second in status are the banks that front the major axes and diagonals. Low in status are the back sections, far removed from the excitement of the specialized architecture. Plantings reinforce the status of the different sections. Stately trees surrounding beautifully carved stone memorials give way to well-trimmed bushes that define the metaphorical tree row at the head of each grave. These then are replaced in the poorer sections by the single tree or bush at the entrance to a row of naked grave markers.

THE HETEROTOPIA OF PLEASURE

The gardens of pleasure build on the naturalism of the Enlightenment in a perverse way. Instead of offering a contemplation of a power that remains beyond the human capacity, the designers of the neo-romantic landscape turn nature into a contemplation of emptiness. The garden of pleasure is a place where nature has no power—where it has been structured so that it can be controlled. The garden does not represent nature so much as it does the gardener's view of how nature works. The gardener decides what is natural. As a view of culture, this image of nature is both oppressor and liberator. If nature is politically disinterested and undirected, it undermines the rule of law, especially property law. The windblown seed knows no property lines. If nature is contained by the garden, it reassures people that powerful forces have been domesticated. This becomes a liberation from fear. Nature has been brought into the garden, partly through the assimilation of its power and partly through the "neutralization of everything that is alien, strange, savage, rude, and unpredictable" (Pugh 1988:62).

As the gardens of pleasure were added to the new villas through bürgerlich Hausdenken, they were executed as elements in a canon. Pattern books and fashionable garden firms were favored over idiosyncratic designs and amateurish executions. Value could only be conserved by conforming to a uniform system of implementation. The garden seemed to have a purpose. The path through it appeared to lead to something. The assignment of space outwardly projected the appearance that different functions were supposed to be taking place. Nothing in these gardens actually happened; there was only the impression of functionality, the simulacrum of purpose. Its reason for existence was the repetition of the forms from garden to garden, which reassured the potential buyer that there was nothing in the property which would detract or diminish its future resale value.

These gardens were about taking pleasure in landscape. Their ability to express a dense and many-layered symbolic narrative was bound up in the ambiguity and ambivalence of pleasure taking. Speaking of the English country gardens of the early eighteenth century, Pugh wrote that

> they are where we are supposed to want to be rather than working, making money; they are a principal Western image of retirement from public life, of rest from work on the seventh day, from the world after a hard life.... Such "pleasure gardens" are also an image of recreation, literally re-creating what has been lost or destroyed by self-interest.... Yet there is something curiously synthetic about this experience, as if it were something that has been marked out as pleasurable in advance of the experience itself, as if we would be somehow lacking if we were not to find the experience pleasurable. (1988:102–3)

This applies to the Viennese pleasure gardens of the mid nineteenth century as well. The gardens were undoubtedly used, although not in the same way as the gardens of domesticity. With the threat of police surveillance removed, public men no longer found necessary the political retreat to the garden. Men spent less time in the garden. Children could use the garden, but provision for specialty playground areas was avoided. It did not fit the canon. Women of this class did not have to rely on a kitchen garden for soup greens; they could instead hire cooks and gardeners to make the soup and care for the garden. Professional help was preferable since it ensured conformity to the most comfortable design. All of the members of the mid-century family used the garden less often and in less intensive ways than was true in the previous two generations. The garden did not require actual pleasure to be taken to be a garden of pleasure. Just to possess it was pleasure enough.

The pleasures provided by such a garden can only be taken for short periods of time. One is a stranger in the garden, not an architect of its life. It provides merely a rest from the activities that really underlie the garden's existence: wealth and power. The garden of pleasure is out of time with the rest of the city. It resonates with the landscape history of the premodern era. It is the *hortus conclusus* of ancient Rome: the garden set apart for the pleasure of the patrician. It is the monastic cloister garden, the personal refuge from the cares of the world. It is the virgin's rose garden of the medieval troubadours, in which youthful love can blossom. It is the garden of love, the allegorical *amor matis*, where one can love and be loved, but also where the labors of love can procreate. All of these images were available in the painting and poetry of the period. For the midcentury Bürger, the garden was a link to a timeless European identity. It transcended provincialism in the same way that the market transcended national boundaries.

Like all gardens, gardens of pleasure were defined by their boundaries. Unlike other gardens, these boundaries also defined property lines of immediate interest to the owners and carried symbolic weight. They confined the family's activities, but they also contained and protected the family's ideology, its property, and its pleasure. The walls of the garden were high shrubs, often reinforced by a fence. They stopped the gaze from both the inside and the outside. From the outside, the walls kept out trespassers both physically and socially, by proposing pleasure as something that only a few could enjoy.

The gardens of pleasure shut out the industrializing city from the view of the families that were extracting the greatest amount of profit from the transformation. Even as the countryside around Vienna was being polluted by factory smoke and workers were being housed in cold, dangerous barracks, the Bürger could gaze upon the semblance of nature from the upstairs window of his shiny new villa. He could occupy the villa knowing that the garden around it preserved and protected its value by signaling to potential buyers that it was a coherent property, unconnected to the volatile development properties of the nearby industrial suburbs. Nature was being destroyed as the Bürgers sat in gardens that painstakingly repressed nature by forcing it to pose as the likeness of itself. This was the true meaning of *Landschaftsverschönung*, the improvement of the landscape, which underlay the design ideology of the neo-romantic canon. In this way the garden of pleasure was linked to the fields of pain in the industrializing suburbs. There, too, landscape was being "improved" for the benefit of the Bürgertum. The result of that improvement, too, was a valorization of productive land and people into productive capital and labor, but it was matched with a devalorization of social values. Eventually, the social problems generated by industrialization caught up with the Bürgertum. By the end of the century, the Viennese were forced to create landscapes that included their burgeoning population, rather than excluding it.

Gardens of Reform

Throughout the latter half of the nineteenth century, Central European cities faced the full force of the social disruption wrought by industrialization. The land speculation and housing shortage discussed in the previous chapter were only two facets of the state of emergency facing planners and architects. The remaining aspects of the disruption, such as the inflationary cycle, unemployment, crime, trade deficits, and an increasing gap between rich and poor, are with us still. The effect on Vienna was the general degradation of the urban environment to the point of jeopardizing the public health. In 1866 and again in 1873, devastating epidemics of cholera swept through the city. Between 1855 and 1857, 27 percent of all deaths in Vienna were from tuberculosis, the highest morbidity in Europe from the disease. Breathing foul air exacerbated the contagion, and bad air was not hard to find in overcrowded residential districts with unpaved streets, wood-burning kitchen stoves, and soft coal as the major source of winter heat. Bad air ignored class distinctions, as prevailing winds distributed the soot and dust throughout the districts. One critic crowned the city the dust capital of the continent (Harry 1869:1). The only hope of stemming this plague was to open up the densest settlements with green space; by so doing, fresh air could mix with the foul, and the public health would improve. The city built these green spaces. The public health did improve. Death from tuberculosis dropped to 23.9 percent of all deaths in 1891, a 0.3 percent annual decline, which has remained remarkably steady over the last century and in 1973 stood at 16.3 percent. Because of its ability to filter dust and distribute fresh air, green space acquired a new quality: purposefulness. Green space was seen to serve a function for the city itself, and not merely for the citizenry. These spaces are the gardens of reform.

At the turn of the century, what had been a unified discourse on landscape in the city began to fragment and diversify. Agreement on the beautiful and the sublime in landscape dissolved into acrimonious conflict among groups who, thirty years hence, would fight a civil war in the metropolis. It was this period that gave birth to the profession of landscape architecture. Landscape had become too volatile an issue to be left to politicians, engineers, and architects. Parks were suddenly seen not merely as a dispensable addition to buildings, but as a necessity for the public health. They became as important as sewage and waste disposal, clean water, and safe energy. For the first time the municipal governments were solving all of these problems in newly incorporated areas. These infrastructural elements had never before required such large-scale planning. Instead of providing water for the eighty thousand inhabitants of 1800, the city found itself designing and financing water resources for two million by 1900. Until the 1870s, the city had *reacted* to technical problems affecting its population, funding solutions only after the human toll had begun to rise. After 1870, the city became more *proactive*. The technical means for solving the problems had existed for fifty years. What was new was a set of standards for a safe and healthy urban environment. The key to all of these standards was governmental intervention and inspection of private development of lands and buildings. Landowners, builders, architects, and landlords had to be restrained from unrestricted uses of their property.

The prime example of this shift in governmental attitude was the movement to salvage the Wienerwald. The forested hills were teeming with game, which the aristocracy claimed as their exclusive right to hunt. The imperial house declared its ultimate authority over the Wienerwald as its game preserve and its source of lumber and firewood. Of these resources, the firewood was the most strategic. Lumber was the only cheap fuel available for home heating and cooking, and the Wienerwald was the nearest large forest. By monopolizing the wood that could be taken from the Wienerwald, the throne regulated the price of fuel for the entire metropolis. If the price rose, the throne could offer more of its reserves for sale. If the price fell, the throne could restrict tree cutting, lowering the supply.

During the reign of Maria Theresa, the throne began to withdraw its control, and a slow process of privatizing lumbering in the Wienerwald started. Direct administration of the forest moved to the office of the state bank, which let contracts to private firms for cutting lumber. Initially, the contracts carried with them the obligation to restore and protect the cropped areas. However, under the pressure of the rapid population increase, the reforestation mandates were ignored. In 1866, during the Franco-Prussian War, complete control of large areas of the Wienerwald was transferred to the private corporations to try to stabilize the war-inflated price of wood.

Within four years, the entire area was in danger of irreparable deforestation. In April 1870, the city council passed an ordinance calling on the finance minister to stop the "incalculable and incurable danger to city, province and empire," and to take all measures possible to protect the climatic, sanitary, aesthetic, social, economic, and commercial outlook for the threatened metropolis. In July 1870, a scientific committee was dispatched by the city council to evaluate the state of the Wienerwald. The committee found that the forest performed essential functions in protecting the quality of life of the metropolis, including reducing the amount of precipitation, leveling temperature extremes in both winter and summer, and weakening the fury of storms, thereby permitting higher yields for the fruit and wine industries. Deforestation had already resulted in the erosion of humus in many places and a noticeable change in the climate of the forest, making some areas barren. Highly degraded forests were evident in Karst and Tyrol, and the committee pointed to them as models of what lay ahead for the Wienerwald if nothing was done to protect it.

The Wienerwald lay between Vienna and the surrounding province of Lower Austria and was itself under the jurisdiction of that province. The Vienna city council accepted the report and asked the

Lower Austrian council for action. In 1870, twenty-one forest villages petitioned the provincial parliament for relief from the unregulated destruction of their environment. The Lower Austrian council responded to the pressure from these communities by passing a law giving authority over the economic use of the forest to professional foresters and taking away from the ministry of finance the right to lease large tracts of lands to private interests. It also called for a general plan for the economic development of the forest which would protect the environment. Finally, the resolution created a department charged with the day-to-day administration of the forest. The Vienna city council then immediately invalidated existing lumbering contracts and established a committee of experts to devise a development plan.

Intervention to stem the abuses by private enterprise was distasteful to liberals. Their political philosophy prized nonintervention. The emergency saving of the Wienerwald exposed the contradictions in this philosophy and set in motion a political opposition that would seize control of the municipal government in 1890. By then, the wholesale incorporation of poor residential districts beyond the outer defense perimeter and the enfranchisement of the lowest rank of taxpayers, the so-called five-crown taxpayer, guaranteed the liberals' fall from power. These developments brought into the political process tens of thousands of new voters who were alienated and angry. They had seen their quality of life suffer over the previous thirty years as successive liberal governments protected the interests of wealthy commercial barons and land developers. The winners in this new political climate were the Christian Socialist Party members under the leadership of Karl Lueger. This party was the first to capture the new voters and unite them around the interests of safety, health, and security. The party took control of the city council in the election of 1890. Lueger was elected mayor.[1]

The Christian Socialist government was reform oriented. The new regime instituted a central office, the *Regulierungsbureau*, to develop further the *Generalregulierungsplan*, the general expansion plan of the city. The bureau was specifically charged with maintaining free space and developing publicly accessible green areas (Mayreder 1895:3). The bureau was influenced strongly by Josef Stübben's ideas about urban green space. His textbook on architecture was one of the first modern German treatises on city planning. Many of the ideas in the textbook were themselves the product of a circle of architects in Germany, the Verband Deutscher Architekten- und Ingenieur-Vereine of Berlin, who were concerned specifically with using zoning codes, building codes, and engineering standards to make cities more sanitary and healthy. There was a similar architects' society in Vienna, headed by Ferstel. Stübben used green space to open congested areas of traffic and population, vent them, reduce dust, and through photosynthesis increase the oxygen supply.[2] Included in these principles were suggestions for widening streets, creating regular open spaces in the traffic network, mandating the building of garden space inside the courtyards of apartment buildings, planting trees and grass wherever possible, building parks and playgrounds from five to one hundred hectares, mandating *Vorgärten*, front gardens, in the building codes of zones with high population densities, and ultimately achieving a green cover on a minimum of 10 percent of the city area, or three square kilometers.

This Generalregulierungsplan would lay out the long-range development for the city, concerning roads, housing, industrial areas, urban renewal and preservation, a standard building code, and zoning. An international competition for the plan, similar to that held for the Ringstrasse project, was announced in 1892. The leading architects of the day, including Otto Wagner, Eugen Fassbender, Karl Mayreder, and Johannes Lehnert, submitted plans. Stübben himself submitted two different plans. Although aspects from all of the submissions were ultimately incorporated in the Generalregulierungsplan, one suggestion by Eugen Fassbender had a lasting impact on the cityscape and resulted in the dedication of the Viennese side of the Wienerwald into a permanent protected greenbelt extending around the city. The forested hills of the Wienerwald, the fields of Simmering to the east, the Danube swamps, and the fields to the north were incorporated into the city as a permanent nature preserve, the Wald und Wiesengürtel.

Fassbender's design was based on the view that the scarcity of parks and garden zones had to be remedied for the long-range health of the city: "It will turn out to be smart for the future of Vienna if one suggests that some portion of the city area remain undeveloped, reserving certain areas. These are especially desirable as reservoirs of air" (1893:18). Further on in his plan he wrote of the need to create a belt of green commons and protect them from every kind of construction. This belt surrounds the entire city and is already one of Vienna's most important bases of public health. Together with the Danube channel that completes the encirclement, this area certainly provides a belt of health for the city. (1893:84)

These ideas appealed to the functionally oriented planners in the Regulierungsbureau. Through a series of city council actions, the Wald und Wiesengürtel was dedicated in 1905. In the text of the city council report that established the preserve, the need for protecting the public health was reiterated.

The report included four separate reasons for creating the preserve, only one of which was public health. The other three were the need for accessible recreation areas in the populous outer districts, the need for recreation areas that were large enough to accommodate the growing population, and an aesthetic function that was rarely found in other municipal architectural writings of the day:

> [the greenbelt] supports and preserves the beautiful for the cultural development of the city population. The beauty of a city is not only found in its buildings and artistic monuments, but also very often in the appeal of its landscape. Everything that contributes to the beauty of a beautiful city will strengthen the people's love, and those deeds which make the community bloom and the state grow large and powerful are always created out of this love of Heimat. (Motivenbericht 1905)

Aesthetics usually took second place to considerations of public health and diverse recreational planning. The author of these words was municipal parks director Heinrich Goldemund, the moving force within the government for the establishment of the forest preserve. The quote is significant not only as transition to the next few decades of landscape discourse in the city, but also because it signaled a reversal of role. No longer was the city seen as providing the necessary services to keep its citizens healthy and successful. Now, those citizens would have to serve the city through deeds inspired by a love of community. To make them want to do so, the city had to remain in their imaginations as a place of beauty. Only such nostalgia would generate sufficient loyalty and generosity in its populace to make the city great.

The assumptions about the necessity for civic pride which underlay Goldemund's ideas were present throughout the development of the discourse on reform landscapes, but the arguments related to sanitation were far more prevalent. They described the primary focus of municipal planning efforts from the 1890s through the beginning of World War I. This effort to take control of urban development and vest it in the hands of planning professionals meant that the city council had to give legal definition to the idea of an *öffentliche Platz*, a public place, specified ultimately as an area in which the city reserved the right to build, plant, or leave open. Previously, land within the city limits belonged either to private title holders or to the imperial family. The city had no legal standing to claim ownership or impose its zoning restrictions; its right to do so was only upheld by the constitutional court in 1914. Even then, it was not held to be a full right of eminent domain. The city could not yet appropriate private property for municipal purposes. Streets and squares were recognized as municipal property for the first time. The city could come into possession of additional land only when the owner sold it freely to the city or when, as a condition of the parceling of large holdings, the city received land for additional roads or when confiscation proceedings against a landowner for nonpayment of taxes were decided in the courts. The restrictions these decisions placed on the city meant that parks could only be built when the land was given or sold to the city.

DISCOURSE ON GARDENS OF REFORM

In the last two decades of the nineteenth century, Central Europe experienced the second phase of industrialization. Through manufacturing, commerce, and government service managerial positions were professionalized. Managerial employees were expected to have certain educational and experiential credentials before embarking on their careers. Because managerialism was understood in the same way in every sector, the educational prerequisites often coincided regardless of whether the students were future steel executives, bank vice presidents, or city bureaucrats. The new managers became the designers' chief clients in commercial, municipal, and private projects. To satisfy these clients, managers learned to speak the new language—the idiom of functionalism derived from Bentham and Ricardo, from Mill and Coleridge, from Saint-Simon and Comté, and from Hegel and Haeckel. It was a culture that saw the world as an interrelation of parts, in which each part took its meaning from what it contributed to the whole. Function was meaning. The premier science of functionalism was engineering—problem oriented, context sensitive, and generating real-world solutions. The science offered such a positive contribution to the modern search for new solutions to social problems that specialists in the merging role of manager in manufacturing, administration, and planning sought ways of incorporating engineering models and methods of inquiry into their professional practice.

Even though architects, particularly garden architects, continued to be trained in academies and gardening schools, they could not avoid participating in this emerging engineering-managerial culture. They studied engineering formally, taking classes from professors whose practical experience was gained in manufacturing. Engineering in the second half of the nineteenth century had developed functionalist thinking more fully than any other science. In the two generations before World War I, this expanding managerial component redirected the tastes of the Bürgertum by imposing the functional worldview on their workplaces, their commercial operations, their cities, and their homes.

Functionalist garden design placed the highest priority on the use of the garden by people. There was a difference between the usefulness of the garden as decoration, as a source of vegetables, for exercise, and so on and the immediate use of the garden for tumbling on the lawn, for sitting quietly, for having a grill party, and for cutting flowers to bring in the house. Functionalists moved away from a conception of gardens as an enclosure for cultivating plants or as some idealized version of nature and instead asserted the primacy of people's relationship to space in the hierarchy of functions. The functionalist garden was divided into rooms, each of which was assigned an activity. The plants, architectural elements, the formal connections between them, and ground plans for these rooms followed specific requirements necessary to fulfill these functional needs. As Louis Sullivan, one of the earliest of the architects serving these new tastes, put it: "Form follows the function!" More importantly, these designers spoke in a language of design which the professionalized class of high-skilled bureaucrats, medical doctors, engineers, and lawyers could understand. Functionalism was the dominant paradigm in the universities that certified the qualifications of these occupations. Through this shared language, functionalists increasingly dominated municipal landscape projects and the homes of this emergent professional class.

The earliest statement of functionalist garden architecture principles belonged to Lothar Abel, co-worker of the Biedermeier gardener Hügel and one of the most active garden architects of the 1860–90 period. In his 1878 book, *Die Gartenkunst in ihren Formen planimetrisch entwickelt*..., he wrote:

> The individual parts of a garden must causally connect to each other. They must appear so ordered that one can reach each part at a leisurely pace and without obstruction. Then all the parts of the garden could be used to serve necessity [*Notwendigheit*] and purposefulness [*Zweckmässigheit*], as well as ornament and decoration. Without good economical use of space, a garden will offer fewer comforts for its owner, in spite of the correctness of the form of the individual parts. A garden must be calculated for the desire and comfort of the owner to realize its purpose. The opinions and needs of people are varied. This produces a great difference in the form of gardens, even when they seek the same ends. (1878:13)

This was written at a time when the ornament and decoration of the neo-romantic style were still very popular among the Viennese. *Notwendigheit* and *Zweckmässigheit* became the key words for functionalist manifestoes in garden art throughout the next thirty years. Abel's insistence that it was space and not plants that were the issue was an important departure from the neo-romantic canon. As developed by Meyer and Petzold, the neo-romantic filled the space left empty between the house and the lot boundaries. What became important for them was not how to use the space, but how to adapt its size and shape to fill it with plants in the best way. Abel's statement suggests that he had already begun to subdivide this space in his mind. In these rooms, the comfort, opinions, and needs of the people were parts of the garden system. Their integration was accomplished through a variety of forms.

The architect credited for having the greatest impact on the practice of functional garden design is Alfred Lichtwark.[3] Klausch credited him with formulating the succinct statement on the functionalist garden principles: *Zweckmässigheit*, purposeful by design, *Brauchbarkeit*, useful for achieving an end, and *Benutzbarkeit*, usable as an ongoing means.[4] For him, the garden was an extension of the living room, a connection between the natural reality, which grew from necessity, and the various demands and inclinations of the inhabitants, who had to be satisfied with the garden. For this reason he reintroduced flowers in the garden: the flowers of the old house gardens, roses, and new varieties that brought color and variability to the garden.

Lichtwark believed that gardens were products of human design and should bear the stamp of human essence and will. Thus, the faux landscape of the neo-romantic had no place in functional gardens. Lichtwark was especially critical of Siebeck's Stadtpark in Vienna, thinking that the effort to produce an imitation of nature by building bosquets and stands of trees and laying out an organically shaped lake were absurd for a park surrounded on all sides by six-story houses.[5] The architectural enclosure imposed by the wall of houses defeated the suggestion of unlimited landscape in the park. Instead the park should have used the *Kursalon* as its architectonic center and developed geometrically from it. He noted that Vienna already had an excellent formal park in its center, the Belvedere, and that its planners should have looked to that as the model for park development.[6]

Lichtwark wrote that the essence and the desire of people were for order to define the area from the house to the edge of the garden. His model for this order was the farmers' garden enclosed with hedges. He also cited the Hamburger patrician gardens and English rural house gardens, both Reptonesque pleasure grounds, as examples of a new canon of forms for the functional garden (Klausch 1971:100). The garden of Max Liebermann in Wannsee was an example of his functional designs. Lying behind the house, the garden was divided into three segments arranged along a straight axis. The first segment was a flower garden with a fountain in its center. The second was a vegetable garden with a fish pond, dwarf fruit trees, and berry bushes along its edges. The third was an orchard of large fruit trees. At the end of the alley was a *piazzetta* terrace, a raised rounded platform surrounded by a low wall facing a lake (Schellenburg 1947:217). In unexecuted drawings of the tripartite garden, the alley culminated in a summer house (Lichtwark 1909:77–78). The central walk from house to culmination point was continuous; the fountain and pond were placed to the side. High hedge walls surrounded the entire garden, and extensions of the hedges and arbors also divided the segments of the gardens from each other.

As Lichtwark's personal influence over the discourse on garden forms declined, Leberecht Migge took up the functionalist cause. In his *Der Gartenkultur des Zwanziger Jahrhunderts*, Migge refined and popularized Lichtwark's ideas:

> A good garden simply repeats the movements of the household, extends them and situates them in the garden. Is the comparison really so far-fetched when I describe a lawn surrounded by trees as a "green gym," a light-filled flower garden as a "garden boudoir," and a wide terrace as "healthy reception and party room?" We have always had kitchen gardens and we can endow the line of arbors in a garden as "corridors of destiny." (1913:62–63)

The reconceptualizing of garden space into highly suggestive areas was typical of the passionate arguments Migge used to cajole colleagues and patrons alike into building functional gardens. He defined the design principles as follows:

> To build a good garden is a simple matter: one must organize it. This can only be accomplished when its parts, its elements of more or less lasting value, are known. These involve the daily needs of the owner's everyday life in the open: playing at sports, walking and sitting are the direct uses; the beautiful joy of flower, tree and bush, the breeding and dabbling in plants, the rhythmic unfolding of shape and color of the garden are values of a higher sort. . . . Whether higher or lower, we always want to fill specific purposes with the furnishing of gardens, purposes that will prolong the performance and the form. How can we do this? (1913:64–65)

He answered his own question with an analogy to tools. A spoon is specifically designed for eating. It is *Zweckgerecht*, justified by its purpose. In this way, he hypothesized, people long ago discovered the essential form of a garden which justified its purpose. That was the geometric form, which one saw in gardens throughout the world. He suggested that the gardens of the modern household include at least three specific divisions of space: *Gesellschaftsrasen*, a lawn serving the play needs of children and the social needs of adults; *Terrasse*, a terrace planted with evergreens and spring flowers and providing a shaded place to sit and look at the garden as whole; and *Rosengarten*, a space using roses as the element that binds together the arbors, the hedges, and the shade trees (ibid.:68–69).

Aesthetically, functionalism produced a sense of incompleteness when viewed without human actors. This is the basis for the feeling of emptiness one experiences when viewing modern gardens. With people in them, modern gardens reveal a comfort and domesticity reminiscent of the Biedermeier. With strong geometric, and later organic, lines, the ground plan of the modern garden imitates the house.

As an ideology, functionalism forced the architect to design for living. This was positive in that people could enjoy their spaces more fully. It was negative in that it determined the uses of spaces and, at least in the early period, did not allow for flexibility. The message that designers and owners of the functional garden sent to their neighbors was one of control, efficiency, and a domestic order that rivaled the control of managers in the workplace.

The most successful of these managers became the patrons of a small group of highly architectonic gardeners associated with Vienna's Sezession movement. These young, middle-class intelligentsia were encouraged in their taste for these gardens by their upper middle-class and aristocratic employers. Their gardens were typified by a series of small articulated areas, each offering a clearly defined function. Special attention was paid to separating the decorative from the domestic. Decorative spaces were given over to the organic imagery that characterized the Jugendstil movement as a whole. This involved a process of stylistic transformation in which the natural was humanized and the human was denaturalized. Special attention was devoted to creating a third dimension to what otherwise would have been a vertical wall—a feat accomplished by layering in order plantings of different heights from lowest to highest. The depth of the wall was often reinforced by low masonry retainers, stair units, and pergolas that cut through the vertical (Wahmann 1990:454–56).

There was a public taste for these gardens as well. Joseph Ohmann's parks, such as the Wienportal in the Stadtpark and the Kaiserin Elizabeth Memorial in the Volksgarten, are the most important examples of this landscape school which still exist today. In addition, Franz Lebisch published a series of postcard-sized drawings through the Wiener Werkstadt (1908). Figure 19 reproduces one of Lebisch's postcards, depicting an architectonic approach to gardens which borders on the theatrical. A new energy appeared in these drawings, perhaps reflecting the rediscovery of the garden architect's control of space, form, and color. Contemporary writers seemed aware of this. J. A. Lux, writing in 1904, spoke of a feeling that "the development of a new garden architecture must develop from the tra-

FIGURE 19. *Design for a Jugendstil garden by Franz Lebisch (1908).*

ditions of the Kleinbürger and farmer" (Rainer 1982:226).[7] These traditions included the preference for straight instead of curved lines and clear functionality instead of multifunctional or nonfunctional space. Architectural elements such as stages, columns, statuary, arbors, and gazebos were integrated with plants to create outdoor rooms.

Ohmann's gardens are good examples of this style. Their function was primarily decorative. Each included a wall or canvas of high bushes which framed an object and set it off through contrasts. In Wienportal, the wall is the façade of the bridge over the river. Concrete and marble features, including allegorical statuary, decorate the façade, giving it the look of a gate in a fortification. Ivy grows across the façade but is trimmed carefully so as not to obscure it. The ivy also connects the façade to the vegetation along the banks of the river; its color sets off the whiteness of the portal and directs the eye toward its central focus: the river flowing beneath the arch of the bridge. The construction is clearly a portal, but the fortifications that it permits the river to breach are botanical walls rather than masonry.

In the Kaiserin Elizabeth Memorial, three square bosquets are placed in a line in front of a fourth bosquet in which the center has been crafted into a fountain pool. Each bosquet is planted with a different combination of flowering and leafy plants around its edge. Behind this pool rises a statue of the empress on a marble stage, and behind the stage stands a curved wall of bushes twelve feet high. Bush walls on the sides of the stage block the eye from seeing the different landscape of the Volksgarten behind the memorial. As one enters the memorial at the first bosquet, the eye is drawn from square to square before settling on the stage with the statue. Because of the green wall, the statue appears larger and whiter than it actually is. The function of the design is to focus all attention on the statue while creating an environment that is regal, meditative, and quiet.

Those familiar with Viennese architectural history will recognize the name Camillo Sitte, who championed what are generally characterized as archaic artisan values in a world increasingly dominated by rationalized approaches to architecture and urban planning (Schorske 1981:62–66). Appointed director of the municipal trade school in 1883, he used his position to publish critiques of the Ringstrasse style and the emerging modernist style of his contemporary Otto Wagner. In 1900, one year after the publication of his magisterial book *Der Städtebau*, Sitte and his collaborator T. Goecke published an essay entitled "Greenery within the City," which was significant in exposing the strains that had developed in the discourse on urban landscape through the second half of the nineteenth century. Sitte explicitly divided the design of urban green space into *Dekorativ*, the decorative, and *Sanitär*, the sanitary, for the first time. *Decorative* referred to plantings whose purpose was to enhance the visual appearance and hence the value of a property. *Sanitary* green space was a pure, late nineteenth-century idea. It was a movement centered within the community of architects and planners to make cities cleaner, healthier, and more livable by building self-cleaning and self-renewing functions into the environment. The sanitary encompassed the idea of the garden of reform much as the decorative embodied the idea of the garden of pleasure.

Sitte located the origin of sanitary green space with the discovery in 1860 that human beings take in oxygen and give out carbon dioxide, whereas plants take in carbon dioxide and give off oxygen. After having some fun with those who thought they might suffocate in closed rooms unless those rooms included potted plants, he noted that scientists had demonstrated that the actual percentages of oxygen and carbon dioxide in the atmosphere varied very little from forest to city. How, then, could we justify plant growth in the city-as-machine? For Sitte the sanitary use of green space by the professional planners and reformers was founded on a misconception.

He substituted a psychological motive for the physical in his argument for more green space: people needed to feel close to nature precisely because cities deprived them of contact. His portrayal was of a romantic longing or nostalgia for an unfettered nature, a desire inflamed by experiences in which

> the last spark of the poetic in town building was intentionally and forcibly extinguished. . . . Instead of carving out bits of one's own little place with appropriate surroundings—either through the curving and deviation of a street opening or through the arrangement of a peaceful corner of a plaza for a mighty tree—all was wiped out relentlessly and en masse. . . . It is precisely these elements that represent the irreplaceable loss because one cannot produce artificially the spontaneous originality of that which has slowly grown on its own. In the face of this there is just one rule to follow, namely to preserve such invaluable heirlooms at any cost and to fit them harmoniously into the new townscape. This procedure is embedded deeply in the popular consciousness, so that every town builder who adheres to it can certainly count on the support of his fellow citizens. (1900:309–10)

This passage exposes five new elements in the discourse on landscape. In the first sentence we learn that the expansion of the city had continued, at the expense of the existing landscape. Sitte may have had in mind the Ringstrasse planners' destruction of the Glacis. He may have seen the old suburban village centers losing their coherence as old gardens with their ancient trees, or the occasional commons, were built over. Like Faust, whose blind desire to enlarge his town destroyed the kindly old couple in their hut by the river, Sitte saw the planners of this period expanding their city at the expense of everything that was worthwhile in the existing landscape.

Next, he consciously employed the image of the curving street. This was not a reference to the Ringstrasse, which for him was a symbol of the betrayal of the promise of modernity. He valued as positive features the visually closed-off squares and dead-end streets in dense residential areas, and he prized curving streets because they, too, produced a greater sense of visual enclosure for people. There was no greater irritant to late nineteenth-century planners than the curving street, which was, for them, a symbol of the archaic, irrational life in the city which modern people needed to redesign. Such streets hindered traffic, caused problems of public safety, and were more expensive to maintain.

For Sitte, curved streets exemplified spontaneous originality, and this loss of the original, the unique, and the peculiar was the third theme in his critique of technical rationality. Precisely an environment filled with such spontaneous originality is what gave a city its character and provided residents with a standard aesthetic for evaluating the quality of their cityscape. Without these elements, architecture lost its human scale and became merely a box to contain unrelated activities. If this were to occur, Sitte argued, all psychological comforts in the city would be lost, and the heightened alienation of the citizen would lead to a breakdown in social order. Sitte wrote at the same time as Georg Simmel and shared the Berlin social theorist's penchant for seeing society as the sum of individual actions. Even though Sitte's worst nightmares happened, all of the plagues of modernity cannot be ascribed entirely to the production of straight streets and to the destruction of spontaneous elements in the cityscape. The redesign of the city to accommodate the demands of traffic need not have been so hostile to the traditional designs. An underlying flaw in the reform planners' consciousness was the distrust of the archaic forms that Sitte championed. The reflex to doubt the value of anything old made enclosed squares and curving streets discomforting to the reformers, but the loss of these features deprived people living in the densest parts of the city of spaces that were scaled to their lived experience. The streets became places of danger rather than places of community. Children were forced to the parks to avoid playing in traffic, and in the process, something positive disappeared.

Sitte was taken less seriously at the turn of the century than he might have been today because of his trust in the emotional value of preserving the urban environment. He criticized the reformers' uncritical allegiance to the rational pursuit of efficiency as blinding them to the value of the existing environment. This point, too, fell on deaf ears. The chief proponent of rational architecture was Otto Wagner, who acquired political appointments, design contracts, and students while Sitte was relegated to teaching restoration technique in a trade school. The appeal of Wagner's architecture lay in his understanding of both the overall structure of buildings and the detailed attention to the necessities of a life that was poised to embrace the possibilities of the future.[8] Existing green space did not fit into the overall structure. It was too undisciplined to belong. It was prefunctional in that it did not reveal its purposes to the visitor. It had to go, perhaps to be replaced in a different time and scale more appropriate to the overall design.

Finally, Sitte reminded planners that the consumers of their work were not other planners and architects, but their fellow citizens. He saw clearly that the development of the landscape had fallen to professionals. By insisting that the city was primarily a technical problem, all those who did not have the credentials to solve technical problems were no longer competent to offer views on the outcome. This attitude eliminated the opinions of the people, depriving them of control in shaping the everyday places of their lives.

The problem of the expanding city carried with it the problem of building new green space while preserving the old. Here Sitte revealed that the debate on the relationship between the horizontal plane of the garden and the vertical plane of the building still raged unresolved:

> For planting trees, a design in harmony with the architectonic surroundings is of basic importance, and this demands that the trees should not hide from view architecture or sculpture of artistic value, such as portals, niches, niche figures, façade mosaics, etc. Besides, a gradual transition from the plant forms to the architecture is required, such as when a musician combines musical chords quite dissimilar in character through harmonic transitions. This can be achieved by a close harmony in silhouette—of buildings as well as of trees and shrubbery—and by the installation of minor architectural forms such as we find in gardens or in the country, where they are combined with natural forms and harmonize with the growing plants.

Sitte sided with Siebeck in the larger argument about which element should take precedence when he offered a balanced arrangement of buildings and trees. His position was that buildings and gardens were part of a *Gesamtkunstwerk*, a total work of art, like the operas of his personal culture hero, Richard Wagner. It followed then that the solution to the debate was to view the buildings and gardens as an ensemble, rather than as specific sites.

Sitte was a Jeremiah whose voice carried moral weight with the next generation of architects and planners, the ones who would found the gardens of security. In 1900, he was a small annoyance to the juggernaut of rational planning which was sweeping German-speaking cities. The chief spokesman for this movement was Josef Stübben, whose first edition of his architecture textbook *Der Städtebau* had appeared in 1890. It contained the first set of city building codes intended to increase health and safety.

These ideas did not originate with the engineers in the 1880s and 1890s; they were part of the discourse on the environment extending back to the Biedermeier. Hügel reflected the changing attitude of the city leaders toward the function of parks as early as 1825 in his address for the founding of the Gartenbaugesellschaft:

> The Chair looks upon the increasing number of parks as a favorable development, one that will contribute to better planning by the municipal government. For example, they now realize that protected areas that encourage people to take their *exercise in the open* belong to the important public health facilities of the city. Clearly, these parks also provide the opportunity and the means to increase the enjoyments of the beauty of nature, the sum of life's pleasures. In this way, parks can ennoble the people and improve their morals. (1825; cited in Koch 1914; emphasis added)

Hügel began with the view of park development as no longer the domain of the crown, but of the municipality. He then turned to a concern that the Enlightenment theorists did not consider: sanitation. In this speech, we hear the phrase *Bewegung im Freien*, exercise in the open, attached to landscape design for the first time. It refers to a theory of wellness widely expressed throughout Central Europe in the nineteenth century which equated good health with the salubrious effects of fresh air. The use of this phrase in 1825 is among the earliest on the public record.[9] The speech also cited the use of parks as a public health institution. The most common public health contribution of parks was believed to be as an air filter and reservoir of fresh, clean air, the *Luftreservoir*.

In the generation before Sitte and Stübben, commentators used language that the engineers would later claim as the basis for technical control. In a *feuilliton* on the public gardens of the city published in the newspaper *Die Presse* in 1869, the pseudonymous observer Harry wrote:

Gardens are called the green lungs of the city and that they certainly are. They are the first and last health resource, the most important regulator of the breathing process of a city. One cannot control the winds, but one can widen the streets and provide room for the air. One can build new houses to help the overcrowded to move out of the old houses. One can plant trees and gardens. One can finally, and for Vienna this is certainly the ideal, combine all the favorable resources to adopt the English cottage system.[10]

This idea of the green areas as necessary for breathing was widespread enough for the city council to use to secure grassy places around schools and markets from the Stadterweiterungsfond in the 1890s, ahead of the publication of Stübben's textbook and building codes.

SOCIAL PRODUCTION OF GARDENS OF REFORM

Population growth and industrial expansion fueled the production of new urban space. The focus of activity was the space between the old, seventeenth-century outer perimeter wall, which became the second ring, or *Gürtel*, boulevard, and the new, late eighteenth-century outer perimeter wall, which served as the customs boundary of the city. People who entered the metropolitan areas at customs stations along this wall had to pay *Verzehrsteuer*, a consumption tax, the effect of which was to limit access to the city by poor groups and migrating laborers, who were encouraged to settle outside the perimeter wall. Soon large colonies of poorly housed, unemployed, and unruly people developed on the edge of the metropolitan region. At the other end of this band, new mass housing forms based on the rental palaces of the Ringstrasse, but with smaller units, were increasing the population density in areas that had begun to develop in the previous decades. Behind them, thousands of small, *Hinterhof* (backyard) industries were started, each attracting labor from nearby residential housing. These constituted a de facto industrial zone. In the middle and at the far ends of the area, especially in the valleys of the steeper hills, the newly enriched families were joining societies and building detached houses on small plots of land in so-called cottage communities, which increased in size as the land values declined in the farthest reaches of the region. In the established inner districts and along the major streets leading to the new developments, land prices skyrocketed, creating an uninterrupted building line that still

TABLE 4

Turn-of-the-Century Population and Housing

Year	Housing Units	Total Population	Index (1,700 = 100)	Increase between Years (%)
1890	34,210	1,404,800	1,137	
1900	38,900	1,742,720	1,411	2.4
1910	43,440	2,057,140	1,665	1.8

Source: Baltzarek 1980:13.

characterizes the commercial streets of the city. Thus, at the beginning of the 1890s, a social geography had developed in this second band of regional development which concentrated the poor working-class families around the Gürtel, distributed the middle classes behind them in tightly bounded communities, and banished the industrial underclass to districts beyond the tax wall.

Then, demographic hell broke loose. The baby boom of the pre-1890 economic immigrants combined with a new immigration from Bohemia and Slovakia. The population growth by almost one million people in twenty years is summarized in Table 4. However, in 1900, fewer than one third of the residents had been born in Vienna. The immediate result of the increasing pressure was the incorporation of the area between the Gürtel and the tax wall into ten new districts—a process that began in 1890. The still unrelenting pressure forced the incorporation of two additional districts fourteen years later on the left bank of the Danube, which increased the number of people and the area of land under direct municipal authority. This expanded scale of municipal operations, combined with the coming to power of the reform-oriented Christian Socialists, led to one of the largest municipal efforts at improving the education, public health, and welfare institutions of the city, catapulting Vienna into the forefront of municipal activism in Europe.

Ironically, the production of space during this period was fed more by speculation in the real estate market than by the growth of capital. These forces continued through the three decades culminating in World War I. The damage created by building speculation reached its peak in the first decade of the new century. Private development was responsible for almost all of the housing built in the period. In spite of this powerful contribution to the regional economy, there was one sector in which the city found itself reacting to demand, rather than play a proactive role. That sector was housing.

The need for intervention in this area is apparent when we consider the anarchical swings between the demand for and the supply of housing in the new suburbs. Table 5 illustrates these developments in eight of the newest suburbs of the late nineteenth century. Private investors were not able to establish a balanced market.

The intervention of planners in the development market began during the optimistic days of the Ringstrasse. The city expansion committee was composed of architects, bankers, and politicians, whom the city council entrusted with subdividing the parcels, putting them out for bid, and establishing the standard codes for the residential buildings.

In 1860, Eitelberger and Ferstel published a book that was quite influential in directing private investment toward single-family homes. They knew from the critical essays in Viennese newspapers that the Mietpalast, the predominant form of housing investment and the form that would dominate the Ringstrasse period, did not meet the needs of apartment renters. Most employees, workers, and pensioners could not afford to lease apartments in the Mietpaläste. To combine their public offices and their homes, the burgeoning number of physicians and lawyers needed a different organization of space than that afforded by the Mietpalast. Eitelberger and Ferstel's book offered a unique model of housing which tried to attract investment away from the Mietpaläste. The key to their design was that every middle-class family could have a space that was theirs alone (1860: 9–10). "We seek a domicile in which the bürgerlich purposes of life can be realized. In addition to health, these include housing that is comfortable, livable, and cheap. . . . A comfortable domicile means a family house that is self-contained" (ibid.:13). They called the architecture for this domicile the *bürgerlich Wohnhaus*.

Ferstel had toured Belgium, the Netherlands, and England in 1851. The efficiency, comfort, and low cost of the middle-class rowhouses he saw there impressed him. From this, he put forward a new way of building residential communities known as the cottage system, which involved a consortium of house buyers who pooled their capital to buy and develop a large tract of land. After laying down the streets and amenities, they subdivided the lots and hired a construc-

TABLE 5

Percentage of Yearly Increase in Houses (H) and Population (P) in the Western Suburbs between 1820 and 1886

Year	Fünfhaus		Sechshaus		Rudolfsheim		Gaudensdorf		Unter-Meidling		Ober-Meidling		Hernals		Währing	
	H	P	H	P	H	P	H	P	H	P	H	P	H	P	H	P
1820–29	1.5	6.7	1.9	3.9	5.3	4.0	11.0	15.4	0.4	0.5	0.4	0.5	0.9	2.2	0.3	1.2
1830–39	13.6	8.7	0.2	3.9	1.3	3.7	2.7	7.8	0.8	6.0	0.8	1.7	3.4	3.2	1.5	0.7
1840–49	3.8	6.8	1.3	8.1	11.9	6.5	1.8	5.2	1.5	7.6	0.2	2.5	6.2	10.8	2.4	3.1
1850–56	0.2	4.0	0.7	5.1	4.4	4.0	0.5	4.6	9.7	9.6	1.8	5.9	4.3	5.0	0.7	6.5
1857–68	0.2	8.2	0.9	3.8	4.5	3.7	0.9	2.8	6.7	17.3	0.7	0.7	6.7	10.6	11.2	17.8
1869–71	6.0	11.5	2.8		0.3	6.1	0.6	3.9	3.4	14.6	1.5	11.2	8.2	19.0	10.5	25.7
1872–74	0.3	3.1	0.3	2.3	3.6	0.7	3.9	2.0	3.5	3.4	2.3	3.3	4.1	3.3	10.2	8.4
1875–79	1.8	0.1	−1.8	1.12	1.8	2.5	1.4		2.7	2.0		2.2	1.5	1.3	1.6	2.5
1880–85	4.0	2.7	1.8	0.5	3.7	1.7	0.9	0.5	1.2	3.5	6.6	1.6	1.3	1.9	3.6	5.0

Source: Mischler 1887; cited in Baltzarek 1980:21.

tion firm to build detached, single-family homes. Ferstel developed a four-story rowhouse design for the cottage communities based on his study of the Atlantic communities. In this design, the ground floor was a commercial shop. The family lived on the second floor, and the workshop and storage room occupied the third and fourth floors. The functions are the same as found in the seventeenth-century Gewerbehaus described in Chapter 4. The differences lay in the greatly reduced area of the rowhouse. Each family's floor was thirteen hundred square feet (thirty-six square meters), with four floors per entrance. The Gewerbehaus area, including Hof, averaged fifty-two hundred square feet (144 square meters), with three floors per entrance. Ferstel's solution for multifamily housing used the same model but provided living space on the third and fourth floors. For sufficient living space, privacy, and boundedness to family life, he insisted that there be no more than one apartment per floor (1860:32–33, 41).

The intent of the proposal was to reform society. Noting the high levels of crime, illness, and poverty in the city, Eitelberger and Ferstel blamed the increasing population size that had outstripped the capacity of the city to provide proper housing. They compared the number of people per house in 1856 between London (10:1) and Vienna (55:1). They then noted that the situation in Vienna was worsening. In 1821, Vienna had a ratio of thirty-four people for every house. This was the root of the social problems Vienna was experiencing. Solve the housing problem, and all other problems would disappear. Banik-Schweitzer noted that this argument neatly ignored the situation in Naples, which had the same person-to-house ratio as London in 1856 and a much higher crime rate than Vienna (1967:241).

The Wohnhaus idea set in motion a series of responses by architects and critics. Architect Ferdinand Fellner responded in the same year. He agreed with the principle of one family/one house, but he did not concur that architecture alone could have the social effects claimed by Eitelberger and Ferstel. Eitelberger and Ferstel believed that the spatial coherence of the family permitted people to connect house form, custom, morality, and civic responsibility, and in this belief they appealed to the liberal need for architectural forms that reflected liberal values. Fellner condemned as inadequate the model that combined workplace and apartment. For the successful businessman the space would be too small, and for the small businessman it would be too large (1860:14–15). He criticized Ferstel's use of expensive nonlocal materials, such as sandstone for the façades (ibid.:31). But his most effective point was scale. Drawing the public's attention to the enormity of the housing problem, he asked if society could build these single-family rowhouses fast enough to meet the need. In their place Ferstel offered a greatly reduced scale to the rowhouse model (ibid.:25). These ideas would eventually find expression in the garden city settlements of the 1920s.

The defenders of the Mietpalast never offered excuses for their small, cramped, expensive apartments, emphasizing instead their temporary nature. The apartments were intended as transitional housing for upwardly mobile families, who would eventually build villas in the suburbs. Art historian Karl von Lützow saw them as temporary in another sense. Unlike other metropolitans, the Viennese lived in the city only in winter. In warm weather everyone headed for the countryside to their little family villas surrounded by flowers and grass. Other cities had to create such garden suburbs, whereas the Viennese had them all along (von Lützow and Tischler 1874:9). Although interesting for its recognition that Vienna's road to urban development was different than that taken by other European cities, von Lützow's perception was somewhat limited: only the very rich could afford two houses.

Engineer and architectural critic Elim d'Avigdor also emphasized Viennese exceptionalism. Unlike the Londoner or the Parisian, the Vienna city dweller had a built-in desire to flee the stone walls of the city. No other metropolitan, d'Avigdor asserted, felt as uncomfortable within the four walls of an apartment as the Viennese did. People tolerated their inadequate apartments because they could escape from them on lovely days for the beautiful countryside (1874:30). This particular generalization about the "Viennese" is a bit more apt. As essayist Siegfried Weyr put it, "the euphoria of trees accompanied the Viennese from the cradle to the grave" (1969:20; cited in Posch 1981:17). These apologists for Mietpalast architecture had no idea of the shortcomings of the form for the overwhelming majority of Viennese.

One critic who did understand was Prague economist Emil Sax, who championed the program first offered by Eitelberger and Ferstel without actually citing them. Instead, he developed his idea of the social benefits of one family/one house from the earlier German housing reformers Viktor Huber and Julius Faucher. Like the Viennese, Sax wanted to link the single-family house with family values, morality, private acquisition of property, and civic responsibility. Using Faucher to assert the importance of the English model as the best solution for Central European industrial cities, he anticipated the garden city movement:

> Break through the periphery of the city to develop systematic projects in new districts of significant scale in open fields, providing families with their own house and garden under strong legal protection. Then tie these residential communities to those who were left behind with cheap and effective transportation facilities. (1869:7–8)

The core feature of his model was not merely a house for every family, but a house and a garden for every family. His motives were entirely within the reform movement:

> One means that offers to raise the general health lies within the realm of reform and for that reason should be stressed: the garden. It is not only because of the rich sunlight and fresh air that people have gardens, but also to be able to have the opportunity and the means to move their bodies about freely in the fresh air, which the owner and his family take into consideration. For factory workers this is particularly important. (ibid.:39)

He called his model the cottage system and contrasted it with the barrackslike, impersonal, unhealthy density of the Mietpalast. Sax was widely read throughout Europe and influenced an entire generation of architects.

One of those was d'Avigdor, who saw the housing problem in specifically Viennese terms and in a series of writings proposed infrastructural changes that would open up more districts to the single-family rowhouses envisioned by Eitelberger, Ferstel, and Sax. His primary contribution was his plan for public transportation. This system of light rail trains would tie people living beyond the Gürtel to the economic activities of the central city. Since the land prices in these outlying areas were quite cheap, he believed that it was possible to build affordable houses for workers there (1873:76–79).

Friedrich Engels criticized this entire line of development. Arguing that these were all middle-class solutions to a working-class problem, Engels called for cutting the ties between the workers and the land—ties he saw as evident in the ownership of a house and garden. He argued that only a social transformation of the relationship between people and property could solve the housing problem. All solutions that tried to transform proletarians into Bürgers through property ownership were doomed to failure. Capital would never permit sufficient housing for every proletarian family. To try would devalue the house as commodity. Engels looked back to the socialist architecture of the utopian planners Owen and Fourier as the kind of housing which might be possible once the issue of property ownership was resolved. People lived communally in these buildings, but families were housed in architecturally defined units within larger structures. The opposition of city and countryside was eliminated by integrating productive gardens with the communal house: some members of the community cultivated food, while others worked in industry (1955:16–17, 36–37). Since the middle classes were not likely to opt willingly for revolutionary change that would result in a net advantage to the working class and since its success depended on the prior conclusion of a widespread revolution, Engels's critique had little effect on the immediate situation. Where Engels was influential was in shaping the housing policies of the workers' parties. When one of these came to power in the early 1920s, many of Engels's plans were implemented immediately, and projects sharing some of the features of the utopian socialists were tried.

This debate between the architects and the social critics set the tone for subsequent discussions of the housing problems that dogged Vienna until the 1960s. The implications for the urban landscape of a full commitment to single-family detached homes were quite different than a mixed strategy or one that favored collective or cooperative housing. Each form encouraged the development of certain kinds of gardens and discouraged other kinds. The surrounding ground performed different functions for detached homes than for rowhouses. As noted in the preceding chapter, gardens sustained the resale value of private houses. However, gardens that were part of cooperative or collective property were likely to conform to different values.

One of the first attempts to realize one or another of these positions was the Cottageviertal in Währing.[11] Beginning as a group of Bürgers interested in implementing Ferstel's ideas, the association was founded in 1873 with Ferstel as its honorary president. Members included government officials, teachers, military officers, and pensioners and widows from these categories, as well as other employed persons who had fallen victim to the severe housing shortage. They contributed start-up capital along with gifts of cash and loans to the association. After looking at a number of different parcels, they bought one on the far side of the Währinger cemetery, an area that had little productive value. The far end of the parcel bordered a sand quarry, the Türkenschanze, so-named because the sultan had erected his tent on that hill during the last siege of the city. Their development was a purely residential district, with no provision for shops or other amenities. The site was selected for its excellent public transportation possibilities: four different streetcar lines were an easy walk from the development. House lots varied from 600 to 2,750 square meters, with an average built portion of 25 percent, leaving substantial land around the cottages for gardens (Banik-Schweitzer 1967:245–48).

According to the national census of 1880, eleven hundred people had completed their houses and were living in the district. The person-to-house ratio was 16:1. Crowded as this may appear by late twentieth-century standards, it was a dramatic improvement back then. Houses were often occupied by extended families, which not only benefited the housing needs of several couples and their children, but also helped to defray their costs. For a small house (a lot of 600 square meters), the association expected the member to put up capital of 7,000 florins. For a middle-sized house (a lot of 680 square meters), they expected 12,000 florins. For the largest house available (on a lot of 2,700 square meters), they expected owner-contributed capital in excess of 26,000 florins (ibid.:250). Around 1870, the closest year for which statistics are available, the average yearly income for a factory worker in Vienna was between 500 and 700 florins (Scheichl 1885). An amount equivalent to ten years' wages was too high a requirement for wage-earning families who were immigrants to the city. For that reason, housing of this type never became the general solution to Vienna's housing problem.

Gardens played a very interesting role in the Cottageviertal (Map 6). All residents were expected to sign a covenant that they would maintain gardens on the land surrounding their homes and that they would not reduce the garden from its size at the time of purchase. The purpose of the covenant was to prevent people from subdividing their parcels into additional houses, thus increasing the build density

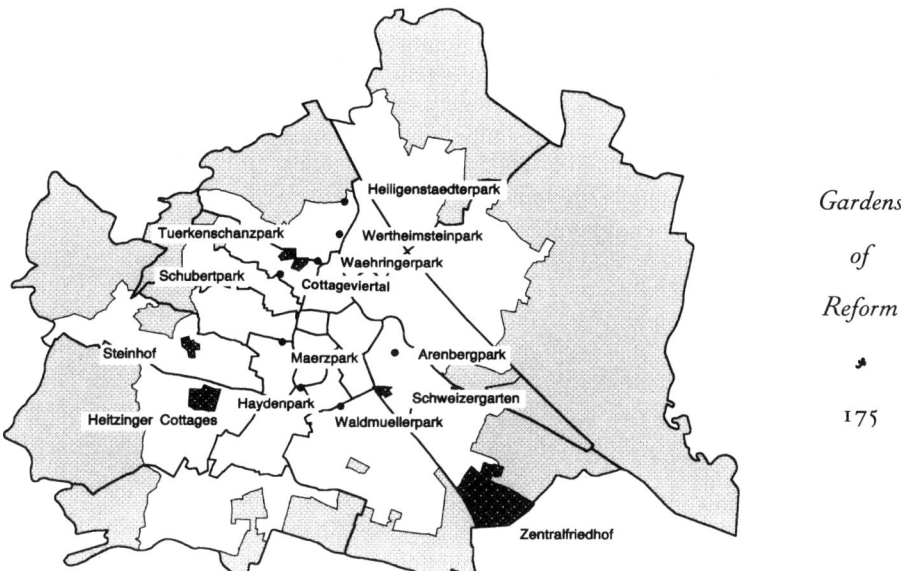

MAP 6. *Reform landscapes of the late nineteenth century and the Wald und Wiesengürtel. The* light shaded areas *indicate the different sections of the Wald und Wiesengürtel. The sites discussed in the text are indicated as the* darker shaded areas.

of the settlement and "preventing one's neighbor from taking enjoyment from the fresh air and view of fresh green space" (from the Foreword to the *Third Building Campaign of the Cottageverein*; cited in Banik-Schweitzer 1967:251). The requirement to keep a garden raised the residents' desire to have more green around them, and this led to the efforts to rehabilitate the Währinger cemetery into a children's park and to assess residents for capital to build on the Türkenschanze the first private initiative park in the city.

Ferstel initially proposed building the Türkenschanzpark in the last year of his life (1883). He observed the need for a public park in the rapidly growing bürgerlich suburbs of Döbling and Währing and selected the Türkenschanze because of its view of the city of Vienna. Near the stellar observatory that the city had erected in 1879, the Türkenschanze was famous for its view, although the Viennese themselves rarely visited it because access to the steep hill was through dense undergrowth. The entire area had been neglected for decades, and only the local children knew the safe paths through it.

A committee was formed to raise public and private funds for the venture. The Cottageverein itself raised more than 84,000 florins from its members and bought 40,000 square meters of the Türkenschanze to contribute to the park. The Cottageverein, the city of Vienna, the village of Döbling, the village of Währing, and the state of Lower Austria all committed themselves to specific yearly contributions for construction costs and upkeep. Gustav Sennholz, the city gardener at the time, designed the park. Using the hilly terrain to his advantage, he created winding paths and filled two depressions with water. As illustrated in Figure 20, the style combined elements of the neo-romantic on the front portion by the pond, with the denser tree growth of an older English parkscape in the back. Sennholz placed numerous rococo elements in the English portion, including a grotto, three waterfalls from two brooks, decorative bridges, fern gullies, and an alpine garden (Kaut 1975:64). Trees and shrubs from the Sanssouci Palace garden in Berlin, Lenné's most accomplished neo-romantic garden, as well as from the most famous nurseries in Germany and Bohemia, were brought to the park through private donations. The collection of botanicals was so extensive that the park had the feel of a modern garden. It included a restaurant, two music pavilions, and a lookout tower. The park opened in 1888 as part of the celebrations of the fortieth anniversary of the reign of Franz Josef. The emperor himself spoke at the dedication and in his speech expressed the wish that the young garden and that residents of these new suburbs would soon overcome the physical boundary that separated them from the mother city. The province chose the adjoining parcel as the site of the Lower Austria School of Soil Sciences. In the following year, Lower Austria ceded the two suburbs of Währing and Döbling to Vienna (Banik-Schweitzer 1968).

Following the lead of the Cottageverein, small cottage building associations in Hietzing and Döbling initiated parks of their own. Of these, Hügelpark in Hietzing still survives. Park superintendent Goldemund reflected the city's view that these areas fulfilled the need for park space in the growing suburbs (cited in Banik-Schweitzer 1968:348). Up to this point, park space had developed through imperial fiat, through redevelopment planning, and through private initiative. In the 1880s the city had not yet learned to plan and execute parks in districts that could not afford to initiate them. The workers' districts, which were every bit as needy of park space as the affluent

FIGURE 20. *Plan of the Türkanschanzpark in 1905. The park was designed on a former sand quarry in the neo-romantic style by Gustav Sennholz. It features a sequence of beds deployed through a complex terrain of low hills, gullies, and a pond.*
Mossbäck 1905:351

TABLE 6

Conversion of Cemeteries into Parks between 1874 and 1928

District	Cemetery	Park (Year)	Size (m²)
Favoriten	Matzleindorfer Friedhof	Waldmüllerpark (1923)	35,000
Währing	Währinger Friedhof	Währingerpark (1923)	52,000
Währing	Währinger Pfarrfriedhof	Schubertpark (1924)	14,000
Floridsdorf	Donaufelder Friedhof	Donaufelder (1924)	7,000
Floridsdorf	Florisdorfer Friedhof	Paul Hock-Park (1924)	7,880
Margareten	Hundsturmer Friedhof	Haydnpark (1926)	26,500
Fünfhaus	Schmelzer Friedhof	Märzark (1928)	16,000
Total			158,380

Source: Fischer 1971: 40–41; Kratochwijle 1931: 21–34.

suburbs, received none under the liberal city governments. This changed with the election of 1892. The scarcity of parks was a major part of international competition for the Generalregulierungsplan in 1893. Stübben included 220.3 hectares of new parks in his submission. Otto Wagner included 1168.5 hectares in his. Fassbender's greenbelt was his solution to the park scarcity. In the Generalregulierungsplan that developed from the competition, the city planned to create park space by buying and redeveloping tracts of private property near dense residential districts and by converting closed cemeteries to parks. In 1782, the city had established a number of cemeteries just outside the outer defense line. Over the ensuing ninety years, these so-called Linienfriedhöfe had filled up. Table 6 lists the parks built on these cemeteries. The opening of the Central Cemetery in 1874 made the future use of these cemeteries unnecessary. The Generalregulierungsplan provided the timetable for transporting remains to the Central Cemetery, and by 1908, the process of sanitizing the spaces was finished. However, other municipal projects preempted the redevelopment of sanitized land into park space, and when work did begin, it was interrupted again by the start of World War I. Economic problems after the war delayed the return to park building. Thus, many of the parks that had been planned in the early 1890s did not open until the late 1920s.

The Christian Socialist landscape policies did succeed in establishing four new parks before the war ended their control of city government. These were the so-called Volksparks, designed to function like the public parks in New York, Chicago, and New Orleans, which had attracted worldwide attention. The parks would be both pleasing to the eye and inviting to the body. Although the parks would preserve some of the symbolic functions of the Ringstrasse, they would also contain playgrounds for children. They made no provision for adult play. The models followed by park superintendent Goldemund were the Hamburger Stadtpark by Lichtwark's disciple Fritz Schumacher and the parks in Paris designed by Eugène Hénard (Fischer 1971:46–47).

Two of these Volksparks were conversions of aristocratic estates to public use: the Arensbergpark in Landstrasse and the Wertheimsteinpark in Döbling. Originally laid out in 1785 as an English parkscape on the grounds of a palace owned by the Esterházy family, the Arensbergpark had been redesigned by the owner into a neo-romantic garden just twenty-five years before it was bought by the city in 1900. Like the Türkenschanzpark, it combined both the English and the neo-romantic styles (Kaut 1975:74). The city revamped it for public use, adding a children's playground and benches. It opened in 1906. The Wertheimsteinpark was the former Arthaber garden in Heiligenstadt, dating back to 1830. Originally a late rococo parkscape, the Wertheimstein featured a mill on the central pond, a small portion of which was still visible in the late 1920s. The city bought a third park, Kuglerpark (Heiligenstädterpark), in 1900. Since the 1780s when people discovered hot steam and a mineral spring coming from the rocks on its slope, the property had been a curative bath. Beethoven visited the site in 1804 in hopes of regaining his hearing. Over the years, the area had acquired a neo-romantic parkscape and a hotel and swimming pool. Eventually other baths with curative powers attracted people. The city built a four thousand-square meter playground on the site of the old swimming pool. It opened in 1905 (ibid.:47, 49; Kratochwijle 1931:14–16).

The fourth park in the city's social reform effort was the Schweizergarten. Unlike the others, this area had been a former warehouse and freight storage district next to the South Railroad Station. It lay on the other side of the Gürtel from the Belvedere Palace. At 114,300 square meters, it was double the size of the Stadtpark (Kaut 1975:73). Goldemund had designed a neo-romantic layout. Unlike most parks, it was cut into thirds by two streets that provided access to the railroad yards and could not be closed or moved. Its central portion featured a rose garden and a fern gully. There were three ponds, a sledding hill, many benches lining the curving walks, and after 1905, a dairy bar. Most importantly, visitors could use the two large grass playgrounds for whatever purpose they wanted. These were the first grass fields in the city specifically designed as playgrounds. The first portion opened in 1904 (Fischer 1971:47; Kratochwijle 1931:12).

Another element in the Generalregulierungsplan was the implementation of Stübben's designs for decorative plantings. He called these plantings *geschlossenen Schmuckplätze*, closed, decorated plazas, through which "the gardener slowly conquers the surrounding solid enclosure [of the building walls] in order to get on with his planting and entertaining" (Stübben 1907:581). The champion of sanitary green space was not revealing a Sitte-esque emotional side in these plantings; he perceived the space as contributing to the overall sanitation of the city's air. He developed green strips down the center of streets and planted triangles at the point where three streets converged. The central strips included trees of medium height and occasional benches. Shrub lines defined the curbsides. For the planners, their purpose was to trap dust. For the critics, they provided "a memory of landscape and nature in a gray street" (Mollik, Reining, and Wurzer 1980:317). They served another purpose as well. These Schmuckplätze defined the öffentlicher Platz, the public place. As discussed earlier, these newly recognized municipal resources symbolized the emerging metropolitan identity. Marking them with plantings set them apart from private and imperial space. They were less ornaments than emblems. The first such spaces were planted in 1890. By 1917 more than thirty-five thousand square meters of Schmuckplätze dotted the Ringstrasse, an area equal to the Kinderpark portion of the Stadtpark (ibid.).

The city had used the same rationale to plant the large boulevards with trees. The Ringstrasse itself was a variation on the theme of the baroque alley. The ranks of trees increased or decreased depending on the stature of the functions designated by the nearby buildings. Thus, the section of the Ring near the imperial palace contained four ranks of trees; the section by the parliament and Rathaus, two ranks; and the section by the canal, none. The Ring looked like no other street. Under Bürgermeister Seiller an effort was made to line with trees most of the boulevards that left the Ring. Seiller believed that if the boulevards looked like beautiful, purposeful promenades, the people would more readily journey between the central city and the near suburbs (ibid.:320–21). The difference between the Schmuckplätze and the tree-lined alleys lay in their design. The Ring tree ranks were as much an application of the principles of historicism to landscape as the Gothic façade on the Rathaus or the Renaissance façade on the university. The façade of a baroque alley planted by moderns self-consciously invoked the spirit of the baroque on a street whose function was the unfettered movement of traffic. Just as the original function of the baroque alley was to point the eye toward the institutions that exemplified the lord's political power, the style of the Schmuckplätze was functionalist. Tree and shrub lines pointed the traveler down the street. Their height trapped dust. They denied as many actions as they permitted: there was no room for walking and no accommodation for children's play. One could look at them, but nothing about them was visually interesting except the splash of green color they offered against the gray stucco of the downtown building walls.

The final innovation in the Viennese cityscape wrought by the functionalist reformers was the landscape of the public sanitarium. The city built the largest of these institutions on the Baumgartner Hill in 1907. This was the Lower Austrian Provincial Healing and Nursing Institution for Psychological and Nervous Patients on Steinhof, or more simply, the insane asylum on Steinhof. On a neighboring parcel of land the city built a sanitarium for tuberculosis patients a few years later. Following the centralized cemetery, the centralized market hall, and the centralized slaughterhouse, it was the last in a series of efforts to bring under managerial control the delivery of municipal services. This was to be the centralized insane asylum. Like the Central Cemetery, the location of the asylum permitted easy expansion in the future if the city continued to grow.

Steinhof had a sister institution built in 1913 in the Lower Austrian town of Mauer-Öhling. Like Steinhof, it was the care facility of last resort for people too sick, too poor, and too confused to care for themselves or to be cared for by their families. The landscape of the two institutions was the epitome of gardens of reform.[12] Although designed by different architects in the provincial planning offices, the two settings reflected common elements, and these common elements provide the best examples of the use of functionalist landscape design principles to create gardens of reform.

At first glance, Steinhof looked like the ground plan for the Central Cemetery in Vienna: boxlike residential buildings for the patients arranged on crossing paths that meet a strong central axis. The axis led from the front gate, up the hill to a chapel. Instead of having an unobstructed view of the chapel, the eye first met an imposing double-wing administration building. Behind and above it was the kitchen, and behind that was the residence of the staff backed by thickly planted trees. Behind and above the trees, the chapel was barely visible.[13] The intention of this arrangement was to emphasize the functions that kept the institute working, rather than the divine help that would bring each patient through a troubled time.

As with the Central Cemetery, Steinhof gave license to the planners to reproduce the essential qualities of what became known as the "White City."[14] The residential buildings on the cross-paths were arranged symmetrically. Twelve residences lay on either side of the central axis: men's residences on the left and women's on the right. Each residence sat on the highest elevation for its section, and below it, the slope fell away into a garden. Trees and shrub walls in these gardens effectively hid the residential buildings above and below. Each garden featured a different form, some with angular bed shapes, reminiscent of the baroque, and others with regular curves of the neo-romantic. The beds were laid out formally, making the landscape predictable and removing any element of surprise which might have upset a patient.

The residences were differentiated by status as defined by the physicians. For psychologically disturbed people this involved the degree of control they could exercise over they bodies. Violent patients were segregated from semiviolent and nonviolent ones. One residence served as a *Pensionat*, a self-commitment facility in which neurotic or overstressed citizens could receive acute care. These patients had the freest movement and the highest status of all, since they were in the institute voluntarily (Haiko, Leupold-Löwenthal, and Reissberger 1981:11). The planners viewed this social differentiation among patients as necessary for effective therapy and good administration.[15] Through it, the patients from the upper classes could remain separate from those of the lower classes, reminiscent of the differentiation of burial spaces in the Central Cemetery. Both places permitted the reproduction of class-based power differences even as they contained the socially accepted functions of internment or commitment to the asylum.

Mauer-Öhling was built on a flat plane rather than a steep hillside. It featured a central axis leading from the front gate to the administration building and continuing through the center of a large diamond-shaped neo-romantic meadow to the chapel and behind the church through another diamond-shaped bed. The figure was distorted by a flattening of the far end, where the staff residence was built. The residence halls were deployed along the sides of the two diamonds, each in its own square section. Within the square the building would front the paths that described the sides of the diamond. Behind each was a large garden. The ground plans of the gardens were not drawn in detail, but published photographs indicate that the landscape was consistently neo-romantic throughout the institute (Anonymous 1914:10–11).

The design principle found in these otherwise different landscapes was the assertion of function over form. In an unsigned article, probably written by Franz Berger, the planner of the Steinhof project, how the design of the landscape took the function of each residence into account is clearly indicated:

> With the exception of the two in-take halls, all the residence halls of the patients are provided with richly proportioned gardens, which are designed reasonably to serve the specific needs of the patients living in each.... The garden for the violent patients is walled, not to protect the patients, but to afford them privacy from the hundreds of visitors that stream to the institute on Sundays and holidays. (Anonymous 1912:5)

The author provided no further examples because ultimately the logic for choosing one garden form to meet the needs of tuberculosis sufferers and another for nonviolent psychiatric patients was arbitrary. The overall ground plan was decidedly a human product, with no illusion of a natural landscape. Tree sections served a purpose. Here one could see the influence of Lichtwark and Migge—that strongly geometric gardens are products of human design and should bear the stamp of human essence and will.

Steinhof was a self-sufficient village of the insane, containing all of the functions necessary for the day-to-day life of any village. As a therapeutic colony, the institute featured the progressive "open-door" approach to patients, permitting the family members to visit during the day and participate in the patients' care. As dusk descended, the families would leave, the gates were locked, and the control paradigm that Foucault described for asylums in *Madness and Civilization* (1965) reasserted itself. This village embodied the most advanced ideas available about the relationship between psychological health and architecture, including the need for a friendly and rural environment (Roller 1831:63); the opportunity to observe the entire layout of the grounds (Burrow 1822:57); and the incorporation in the landscape of such restful points of visual interest as lakes, rivers, waterfalls, mountain, and fields, and also nearby cities and villages (Reil 1803:459). In all of these respects, Steinhof qualified. As an English language description of the planned institute prepared by the Lower Austrian government observed:

> [i]n all directions the eye has an open view to a distance of 30 kilometers from every point of the institution. In the West and Southwest expands the evergreen "Wienerwald." . . . Towards the East extends the panorama of the City which, especially in the evening, when its thousands of lights are blazing, presents a grand sight.[16]

Haiko and his colleagues argued that this village also manifested the dislocation of the psychiatric sufferers in the city. As a sign of the prevailing ideas about treatment, one isolated the insane and took responsibility for their care, often for their entire lives. Although it was done with kindness and lack of malice, the assignment to Steinhof was a form of incarceration. Stripped of their freedom of movement, these victims were at least offered a sanitized social order and the opportunity to experience the pleasures of nature (Haiko, Leupold-Löwenthal, and Reissberger 1981:10). This, then, was the ultimate purpose of landscape in the social production of gardens of reform: to serve as a surrogate for personal freedoms forgone in the name of social progress.

On the whole, the reform movement succeeded in increasing the publicly accessible green space in the city as a whole by a factor of a thousand. The increase in every district of the city varied by several hundred to several thousand percent. By 1913, 1,095.6 hectares, less than 4 percent of the metropolitan area, were publicly accessible (Fischer 1971:43). At the same time, housing investment put more garden land in the hands of individual bürgerlich families. Neither of these developments was sufficient to restrain the effects of industrialization on the landscape. As coal-based factories continued to mar the nearby environment and the population growth continued to outstrip the housing base, the public and private funding for reform gardens appeared less effective.

THE HETEROTOPIA OF REFORM

The content of these gardens is one of *Natürlichkeit*, naturalness. This differed from the Enlightenment naturalism, in which nature was the concrete manifestation of a rational universe. Naturalness interpreted nature as a commodity for people to consume with their eyes and ears and with the movements of their bodies. Nature was a resource to be used, an opportunity for growth, a common inheritance of all who claimed native attachment to a place. This ideal united the otherwise highly varied accomplishments of the planners of reform gardens: the Wald und Wiesengürtel, the Volksparks, the cottage system, the Schmuckplätze, and Steinhof. Each landscape strove to include as much nature as feasible in a form that transformed nature itself into the uncommon and the exceptional.

The essence of the reform aesthetic was that nature should take its proper place in the emerging industrial landscape. To do so it had to become objectified and abstract. Nature itself was too clumsy. It did not fit into the program. When projected onto a human geometry and placed in the appropriate line of sight, it framed human works. The goal of the design was to optimize usefulness at the expense of overt ideology and natural growth. The garden was always part of a larger plan in which it played an integral part. It was configured so that its meaning did not become clear unless the context for its existence was also known. Buildings and their gardens were to be viewed as an ensemble. A house garden, extracted from its house, was meaningless. The highly organized landscape at Steinhof was senseless unless one knew that it was a large insane asylum. Gardens of reform were justified by their purpose. In order not to compete with its function, the form of the garden had to remain simple: straight lines, regular curves, uncomplicated shapes. Users were not to be distracted from their purpose, but rather guided toward it by the most efficient use of the space. What made these gardens extraordinary was the commitment of their designers to this utilitarian ideology.

Gardens of reform fulfilled the specific function associated with the building to which they were attached or the district of the city in which they were found. They were designed to be of sufficient size to contain all of the activities necessary for that function, and only those. In some cases, expansion potential was built into the plan in case the function would grow. Often this function was quite specific, as in the misguided belief that tracts of green produced a higher level of oxygen in the dust-choked atmosphere of the city. In other cases, the function was polymorphous, as with the playground lawns of the Schweizergarten, which could be used for any kind of play. Even here, there were limits. Open cooking fires were not permitted. People had to leave the park at dusk; they could not use it as a campground. Picking flowers and taking plant cuttings were strongly discouraged. Different functions were allocated to different spaces within the garden, all contributing to the overall function of the larger space. A dream was being fulfilled by this design—a dream of a city in which all of the parts fit together harmoniously; a dream of integration and cultural similarity.

The gardens seemed to form as if the city were wrestling with the forces of industrialization to retain a foothold on the rapidly disappearing Gegenden that the Enlightenment had so idealized. Each garden proclaimed the rescue of nature for people. They were symbols of plenty, of deprivation denied. Instead of suffering the loss of contact, the teeming population could thunder to the few large parks in the hot humid summer months to remember other places in other times. Behind the progressive social policies of the reform landscape lay a baroque attitude of rule from above. This was not a nature free and unfettered, but one that had been domesticated. This collection of botanicals toed the line, obeyed the demands of the users, and showed discipline in rebounding after hard use. They symbolized a human facility with materials which was uncanny in its effectiveness. Bare patches might show through a well-used lawn in a public park by the end of the season, but the repairs were made, and the patch was gone the next spring. The message of the garden was a hymn of praise for the good that could be wrought by human control. It was a hymn to the power of the manager.

Temporally, the gardens produced under this regime were no different from other functionally conceived systems: they retained their qualities through frequent iterations and seasonal cycling, but they were ultimately ahistorical. Visits to these gardens rarely contained surprises. Flower beds were rare, and when they existed, they were planted once a season. Lawns, trees, walks, and benches were never redesigned from year to year. The layout was predictable from the last visit. Nothing ever seemed to change. Unlike the urban apartment that was quietly falling apart or the factory that was frequently outfitted with new technology, the garden had no time limits. It restored itself in the off-season and readied itself to sustain the needs of the visitors during the warm months.

The boundaries of these gardens were evident from without. A tree and shrub line separated the public garden of reform from the street. Ostensibly, it filtered dust. More probably, it defined the limits of the public space. Like the Schmuckplätze, the gardens needed to have the mark of the municipality stamped on their boundaries. Private gardens, too, presented walls to outsiders, functioning to protect privacy and to separate the affluent cottage owners from the luckless lower classes. From inside the gardens, the boundaries disappeared. Wall heights and terrace and lawn elevations were manipulated to give the private garden owner the best views of his surrounding countryside. The techniques were established in the early 1700s, but here they were applied to very small cottage gardens. In the public parks, the tree and shrub lines blended into the neo-romantic parkscape, obscuring the limits of the park and giving the impression of unboundedness.

The ordinary places of the city already in a process of decay remained embroiled with the gardens of reform. Too many people, too much pollution, insufficient infrastructure, and a scarcity of capital to make timely improvements ensured that the quality of life in the city would deteriorate steadily throughout this period. The gardens denied and mystified this degradation by creating preserves in which the environment did not collapse but rather renewed itself from season to season. This was not the only way in which the gardens of reform were linked to everyday life. The gardens stood as well-run organizations. They testified to the legitimacy of the role of professional managers in parks, in city planning, and most assuredly, in factories and offices. Functionalism was their worldview. Reform programs reflected their optimism in the power of the paradigm to correct the problems of society. Gardens of reform embodied this worldview as it transformed nature. They were doomed to failure.

Gardens of Reaction

The continuing decline in the quality of urban life produced more radical currents than those expressed in the gardens of reform. Distrust of civil institutions, especially the market and the forces of capital, pervaded all of the reactionary movements of the era. Antimoderns targeted Jews and other minorities as the agents of capital. Lueger transformed the Christian Socialist Party's original reactionary platform into a reform movement that attempted to rationalize rather than remake the metropolitan economy. Other reactionary parties, such as the Deutsche Volkspartei (1882), the roughneck ward organizations of the right wing of the Liberal Party in the 1894 election, and later, the National Socialist Party, stubbornly pursued the radical reconstruction of a preindustrial utopia.

These movements had comparatively few activists. They succeeded only by appealing to resentment over the decline in quality of metropolitan life and by providing specific targets for that resentment. Their rhetoric influenced all public discourses in Vienna at the turn of the century, including the discourse on landscape. As with many ideologies that shaped this discourse, contemporary Viennese were barely aware of the relationship between their landscape aesthetics and reactionary rhetoric.

When the meaning of a particular garden is described in the language of reactionary utopianism it does not mean that the owners of those gardens themselves are reactionary. I have met victims of fascism who have used these phrases. Migge wrote passionately about the need to return cities to nature and employed rigorously reactionary language to envison a society that put food production in the hands of small urban gardeners. He died in 1935, isolated from the policies of the new Nazi regime and hostile to its aims (Michelis 1990:416, 420). It is in the nature of discourses that ideas present themselves to the participants as internally consistent and based in an objective reality. Verbal formulas that embody the discourse on reactionary landscapes today have lost their historical reference. What remains is neutral and unthreatening. The phrases claim special legitimacy even as the neutral context in which they resound masks their original meaning.

To a modernist, the word *reactionary* is clearly pejorative. Yet, it means nothing more than to believe that in some of its aspects, however secondary, the past was better than the present (Kolakowski 1990:5). This attitude is a direct challenge to the presupposition of modernism that the new is always better, and stasis cannot be tolerated. To be a self-conscious reactionary, even when it is appropriate to negate the dominating direction of cultural development, is to inherit the stigmatized historical legacy of previous reactionaries. It is much easier to hide one's dissatisfactions and romantic yearnings for a less complicated, less threatening life in the acceptable rebellions of mainstream public discourse. The discourse on landscape serves this end. By 1988, the owners of a family garden in suburban Perchtoldsdorf redesigned it as a *Wildgarten*, a garden so ecologically balanced that human cultivation was no longer necessary. It was nestled among neighboring gardens of well-manicured lawns and carefully pruned fruit trees. Compared with these, the Wildgarten was a jungle. The owners had uprooted native plants from the sides of the surrounding hills of the Wienerwald and replanted them in the garden in the same density as their original site. A *Biotop*, a stagnant pool, was carefully constructed with water from a town water pipe. Left to its own processes, the pool soon supported algae, a few frogs, and many mosquitoes. A sign near the garden gate proclaimed the owner's intentions to create a garden that would sustain itself without pesticides, fertilizer, or human cultivation—a garden that would mirror nature's own cycles and yield the fruits that nature intended. There were many messages in this garden, the most important of which, as far as the neighbors were concerned, was the arrogance of the garden owner to impose this biological nuisance of weeds, pests, and chaos upon others. Garden walls are relevant to humans only. Seeds, parasites, and mosquitoes pay no attention to them. The garden was the horticultural equivalent of crying fire in a crowded theater. The owner was completely surprised by his neighbors' reaction. He assumed that everyone saw the logic of a return to ecologically balanced gardening. The rhetoric of the organic gardening movement legitimated a revolutionary praxis, the redesign of the idea of the garden in purely ecological terms. He soon learned that this view was perceived by his neighbors as reactionary.

The meaning of reactionary garden aesthetics lies in a specific set of verbal formulas. For example, when Herr Hasenauer explained why some aspects of a person's garden appear so similar to those of the neighbors, he said: "Somehow they become similar to each other *because some things grow especially well in the area and others not.*" Herr Kolowrat elaborated further: "One plans a garden so that one projects one's own imagination into it and not merely to copy or imitate. But, through the similar positions of the gardens, there is *a certain automatic similarity, because the position of the gardens are practically the same.*" Frau Hasenhut concurred:

> That [the similarity] occurs actually through *the type of plants which are best suited to this soil.* This is an alkaline soil, and not very much is successful here. And for that reason one comes back to the same plants that are strong enough to grow here. The neighbors realize that just as we do. We experimented out of ignorance and attempted to transplant things. We had to be satisfied with what grew.

All of these statements empower the environment to select between plantings that are suitable and not suitable. In Hasenauer's formulation, the selection is seen in the different degrees of successful growth. For Kolowrat, the selection derives from the microclimate of the gardens. In Frau Hasenhut's statement, the soil selects the plants that thrive. Earlier schools of gardening would have made more of an effort to manipulate the plants and the environment so the garden would conform to the gardener's choices. These remarks are influenced by a product of reactionary landscape ideas first formulated by a Alwin Seifert in the 1920s and grouped under the rubric *Bodenständigkeit*, nativism, in which the gardener must restrict his choices of plantings to what the environment will support.

The search for a bodenständig garden is not all-pervasive. It coexists with the older criteria, and gardeners have recourse to the variety of systems in selecting their planting. Herr Leiter, for example, said:

> We have very good communication here in the settlement. And as a result, the neighbor gives me her plants, and I give her some of the ones that I breed. And then, if there is once something that is particularly pleasing, then one has only to ask if one can maybe have a cutting. Through this process there naturally develops a certain similarity.

Herr Pahl agreed:

> They are similar because we imitate each other. When one has something beautiful, then the other says, "Look. How pretty. I'll do that too." And after that the gardens naturally look quite similar. For example, we have some large dahlias. The neighbor said, "Jeez, Mr. Pahl, can I have a few bulbs?" Now, recently we split a few in half and gave them to the neighbor. It will come to pass next year that he will have the same color in the same dahlias in the same place as we do.

Both of these gardeners could have ascribed the similarities of their neighbors' gardens to the selections of the environment, but they chose to focus on human taste. They are participating in an older discourse on the selection of plantings, one that depends on the cultivation of either an architectonic or a painter's criterion for the composition of the beds. Without the moment of reactionary ascendance which occurred in the first half of the twentieth century, the alternative of Bodenständigkeit might have remained a concern for specialists and never have penetrated the popular discourse on landscape.

Among the oldest informants, it is still possible to hear the echoes of the reactionary rhetoric as it may have sounded fifty or one hundred years ago. Eighty-year-old Frau Czermak, reflecting back on a lifetime in the oldest small garden colony in Vienna, spoke about gardens in this fashion:

As I told you at the beginning, the garden movement is a treasury of a people's knowledge. I should never have continued one. We are the trustees in our generation. After World War II I rebuilt the garden after my own taste, but I never should have done so. My parents would have said the same thing. As the inspired ones, they wanted a piece of land, a piece that bound them to nature.

For *treasury of a people's knowledge* she used *Volksschatz*, a word that privileges a locally circumscribed group of people as possessing a special knowledge of their local environment, embodied in their landscapes. The notion of trusteeship, *Betreuung*, refers to the continuity in knowledge which gives a *Volk* its meanings, a continuity that modern life destroys. The lack of trust in the appropriateness of one's own taste compared with the established patterns of the community is a reference to the greater importance of the group over the individual in reactionary thought. Finally, the idea that one can bind oneself to nature through working a piece of land is a complex formula that rejects urban life as unnatural, idolizes farmers as living the most natural lives, and encourages imitation of the farmers' life on the land as the best alternative to modern life.

DISCOURSE ON GARDENS OF REACTION

The language of reactionary landscapes originated in the critique of the romantic landscapes of the nineteenth century. Like the functionalist and reformist critiques before it, the reactionary rejected romanticism as too much art and not enough real value for the modern sensibility. The language of the reactionary critique began in the same way that the functionalist critique of Lichtwark and Migge began: the garden must return to a focus on usefulness to defend its place in the modern urban landscape, and the need for strict geometric lines and useful plants must take precedence over decorative, exotic, and fanciful motifs. The reactionary critique then took that one step beyond the modernist functionalists by specifying the political goal of the new gardens: a return to the agricultural Gemeinschaft.

Reactionary ideologies are expressions of antimodernism; that is, having experienced modernism and its consequences, antimoderns view the present, on balance, as less desirable a place to live than the past. Sometimes the rejection is piecemeal, as in the *Lebensreform* movement, which sought to correct the more pernicious elements of modern city life by fostering older patterns of dress, nutrition, and activity among urbanites. More often the rejection is total. Unable to live with the consequences of modernism, the reactionary actively seeks to implement a utopian alternative in which the contemporary city and its life ways are eradicated from the possibilities of human choice. It is one thing to write a novel imagining an alternate society; it is quite another to carry out the revolution that will remake the world in the utopian model. Yet this is precisely what the German nationalists, through their political movement in the National Socialist Party, did. In their haste to make their evolution complete, they simultaneously engaged in multinational warfare while refashioning the landscape of the territory they controlled. The singlemindedness of their vision to uproot, destroy, and re-create the world in their image, as well as their failure to win the war, branded the movement an outlaw of history. In the process, reactionary ideologies acquired a bad name. In spite of the label, the antimodern impulse is as important today as it was at the turn of the century. We label the movement by different terms that hide what is common to the separate ideologies: a rejection of the present and the future as the moments of the highest cultural strivings of the society. Thus, religious fundamentalism, intellectual conservatism, environmentalism, the New Age movement, and some postmodern artistic movements share more through their rejection, respectively, of secularism, progressivism, capitalism, positivism, and functionalism, than either the social origin of their adherents or the legitimating doxa of their movements might suggest. In the discourse on landscape, the work of designers during the Third Reich represents the highest development of thinking about the antimodern landscape. If any of the current reactionary ideologies wanted to make a statement about landscape, they would turn to the landscapes of Schultze-Naumburg, Meyer, Wiepking, and Seifert.

These ideas were extremely influential beyond the areas in which the designs carried ideological weight. Stripped of their ideological trappings, the landscapes appeared rational and attractive to modernists in other political environments who saw them only as the "new" or as the novel model for regional planning. In both of these guises, designers produced the reactionary landscape in the United States in the 1930s; in the cities of Africa, South America, and South Asia in the 1950s; and in corporate developments today, where they mix nicely with the same international style buildings that were the anathema of the reactionary architects who first designed the landscapes. The reactionary discourse is as "true" as any of the previous ones; that is, it has the power to present reality as an understandable whole.

The specific features of the reactionary contribution to the discourse on landscape involve four elements: a view of nature which includes humans (*Biologismus*); a search for the native ecological system in which plants, climate, human culture, and soil evolved codependently (*Bodenständigkeit*); a view of landscape as the primary battlefield on which the forces of pollution, both environmental and cultural, must be defeated (*Naturschutz* and *Heimatschutz*); and the support of small agricultural activities (*Siedlungskonzept*). These landscape principles came together in National Socialism, where they combined with the principle of the strong leader (*Führerprinzip*) and racism.[1]

Some of these principles combined with other ideologies that were developing simultaneously. For example, many members of the Social Democratic movement in Central Europe supported the Siedlungskonzept as a solution to urban overcrowding and the housing crisis. The difference between the reactionary use of the Siedlungskonzept and progressive use of it lay in the location of the settlement and cultural direction of its population. The next chapter will discuss these progressive ideologies. The reactionary approach was to tear down urban agglomerations, reconstruct viable communities on a rationalized regional scale which permitted them to remain as small as possible, and populate the communities with as culturally homogeneous a population as possible. This was an antiminority, antiurban, anticlass approach to constructing settlements. It was a return to a premodern European model in which cities were greatly reduced in cultural power and were the exceptional form of housing for Europeans. Instead, most people would be housed in peasant villages clustered around a defensible market town. In a similar fashion, the Lebensreform movement was pure Biologismus but served the ideological ends of both the left and the right. Born out of the soot, tuberculosis, and cholera of the industrializing centers of the mid nineteenth century, this movement looked to involvement with nature as a health-maintaining and healing force in people's lives.

A good example of how the progressive and the reactionary approaches to Biologismus differed is nudism. Originating at the turn of the century, this practice sought to improve people's health by permitting their bodies to move freely about with no restrictions whatsoever.[2] The underlying premise, that free movement is healthier than movement that is restricted by culture, is a central principle in Biologismus and is usually ascribed to Schreber (see below). For the reactionaries, the principle provided a means for criticizing the physical qualities of the population. Members of the movement had a moral obligation to free their bodies from clothing to fortify the community as a whole. For the left, nudism was an expression of the rejection of bürgerlich morality and the assertion of the modernism and cultural daring of emerging working-class culture. Thus, the same practice signaled a rejection of order by one group and the fortification of order by the other. Both the Siedlungskonzept and Biologismus impacted the landscape whether practiced by the right or the left. In this chapter, the focus will be on the effects of right-wing practice. The next chapter will be devoted to progressive outlooks.

Although World War II provided the laboratory for experimenting with reactionary landscapes on a grand scale, the formal principles on which the landscapes were based were set in the early decades of this century. All landscape theorists at the time were trying to discover alternatives to the formal canon of German neo-romantic gardens enshrined in Gustav Meyer's 1859 *Lehrbuch der schönen Gartenkunst*. Already in the 1890s, Lichtwark (1892) and Avenarius (1899) had dismissed the clichés of the dwarf hillocks and of the pretzel-fenced flowerbeds that were shaped like interlocking rings. The new direction for the twentieth century was first signaled by two theorists, Muthesius (1904, 1907) and Zobel (1905), and by the first three garden exhibitions of the century, Düsseldorf 1904, Darmstadt 1905, and Mannheim 1907. Their designs featured very strong architectonic forms in the use of built and botanical elements, arranged in small, closed garden rooms with rich appointments. The spaces were designed both for comfort and use (Schiegerl and Stiegler 1985:27–28). These forms never took hold in Vienna, although Lebisch's Jugendstil postcards typify the garden designs of this Art Nouveau approach (see Figure 18).

The architectonic gardens were criticized as elitist, crowded, and prohibitively expensive almost as soon as they were exhibited. Several critics felt that because too many ideas in a small space created confusion, the modern garden rooms should reflect a single idea. Others believed that the return to topiary shapes violated the public's accustomed taste for natural growth patterns. Most importantly for the future development of reactionary ideology, the architectonic gardens brought the issue of plant type into sharper relief. The garden exhibitors incorporated the newest breeds of exotic plants with native varieties to produce sharp contrasts in leaf density and color. Using simple field and meadow flowers together with blooming fruit trees, they argued, would increase people's awareness of the ecology and local conditions of their surroundings. Although referred to in 1905 as *Natur zur Idee* (Schiegerl and Stiegler 1985:29), this was the origin of the Bodenständigkeit ideology in reactionary landscapes.

In articles published between 1929 and 1937, Seifert developed the principle of Bodenständigkeit and defined it as the intimate contact between the landscape and its historical descendants (Seifert 1927:45). The role of Bodenständigkeit was to alert the architect to the myriad environmental and human factors involved in the design of the garden. These human factors included the desires of the owner, the form of the house, and the provision of useful access (*Benutzbarkeit*), productivity (*Wirtschaftlichkeit*), and simplicity (*Einfachheit*). Consideration of these factors would yield a single solution to the garden design. At the same time, the architect was to avoid any foreign elements that appealed merely to him. Only then could a "complete harmony between the landscape, the house and its owner be achieved" (Seifert 1933:849). The landscape itself would be addressed through the properties it exhibited, including the elevation, size, cross-section, and morphology of the lot; the local climate; the geological development of the soil, together with the analysis of its chemical and physical makeup; the existing botanical community; and surrounding land use patterns (Seifert 1927:44).

The discipline of Bodenständigkeit required an ever-vigilant care that "any trace of fashionable or modern, and therefore intolerable, forms" be removed from the garden (Seifert 1962:271). This could be seen most explicitly in the area of botanicals: "Bodenständigkeit is every plant in the garden which finds its best success in ground that nurtured it (angestammten Boden).... Bodenständig is any garden in which the selection of bodenständig plants permits that it naturally and artistically fits with its surroundings" (Seifert 1929:34). For this reason, the designer also had to analyze the surrounding environment to find the best fit between the garden plants and their milieu. Similarly, the basis for the garden was always the plants that were growing there before the house was built. Using newly bred varieties and foreign species was permitted, but only to enhance the position of the native varieties. If foreign varieties were used, they were to be composed in such a way that they could not obscure the views that linked the garden with the surrounding landscape. Seifert differentiated between the local and those plants similar enough to belong together according to their biological sympathy or antipathy. To help both specialists and amateurs, he composed one of the first plant charts based on the growth conditions and requirements of various species (Seifert 1929:5).

All of these propositions seem reasonable enough. The composition and selection principles he put forward are so common today as to seem self-evident. There was, however, no absolute necessity to follow these principles in garden design. Indeed, all of the eighteenth- and nineteenth-century schools of garden design violated these principles with astoundingly beautiful effect. Seifert's formulation was an aesthetic one. He found the landscape equivalent of contextualism more pleasing than the botanical eclecticism of the earlier schools. After 1934 Seifert was simultaneously an instructor of garden and landscape design at the Technical Institute in Munich and a consultant on landscape problems to the general inspector for German streets in the building of the Reichsautobahn. It is difficult to separate the development of Bodenständigkeit from other ideas about native qualities in the discourse on racism within Nazism. Seifert's biographers point out that he was not responsible for the metaphorical extension of Bodenständigkeit and linkage to the landscape (*Landschaftsverbundenheit*), the *Blut und Boden* of racial rhetoric. They also argue that his development of this design criterion was neither opportunistic nor fashionable, but part of a universally applicable rule that grew from the new awareness of botanical communities (Schiegerl and Stiegler 1985:41). This raises the interesting paradox that Seifert may have been the only one who did not understand the implications of his ideas. For him they came from direct observation of natural processes. How could he then prevent the application of this natural process to the affairs of society? If foreign elements should be banished from the garden for good ecological and aesthetic reasons, why should foreign elements, such as Jews, Communists, the handicapped, and homosexuals, be tolerated in the garden of the Third Reich?

The term *Heimat* means the place where one feels oneself to be at home. By *being at home*, most speakers of German do not literally mean the parental house, but rather the home community, the people with whom the speaker shares the greatest portion of experience and meaning in common. One does not become aware of one's Heimat until one leaves it or until it disappears. The dislocations and immigrations of the last fifty years of the nineteenth century produced the feeling of having lost one's Heimat. This term then took on important spiritual value among the antimoderns. For most of them, the search for Heimat began in their mid teens, around the turn of the century, and continued through the Third Reich. Even today, the term is a rallying point for antimodern sentiment.[3]

The relationship between Heimat and landscape may not be immediately apparent to the non–Central European. Indeed, the antimoderns themselves had to learn to make the connection. The mechanism for antimodern socialization at the beginning of the century was the *Jugendbewegung*, the youth movement, and especially the central activity of almost all youth organizations, wandering.[4] Through their club magazines, speeches of leaders at mass meetings, song lyrics, and most importantly through the experience of meandering through the countryside, these young people developed a view of landscape as moral geography. The search for Heimat became a quest for the ideal community, most likely to be found in the countryside, since the city was the location of modernism, cultural heterogeneity, and moral vacuity:

> Wandering is the greatest corrective against the deteriorating and soul murdering poison of the metropolis. The metropolis with its encroaching technology and its cunning pursuit of gain robs us of the belief in our own essential goodness and our own good will. The metropolis supports the belief in the pursuit of pleasure as the only true faith of disconnected egos. (Habekern 1926:90)

The ideal landscape for the ideal society was a place as far from the metropolis as one could get. In this fashion, the social critique became a critique of landscape. As will become apparent when the Siedlungskonzept is discussed below, when the reactionaries did gain power, they immediately moved to dilute the size and power of the metropolises.

The appeal of the youth groups for the Viennese did not begin with antimodern resentment. People were attracted to the clubs as a way of getting away from their parental homes. In the groups they could be in the company of people their own age, unchaperoned, and beyond the rigid behavioral constraints of their bürgerlich parents. This may have been the first generation in history to experience a communication gap. Differences in perception between the generation in their forties in 1900 and the generation in the twenties were, in cultural terms, greater than the twenty years might signify. The older generation had grown up in well-to-do parental homes during a depression. They experienced the decline of liberal power at the time when they themselves were preparing to take over their families' businesses. They profited from the growth of the city's population and resources. Because they also had a strong consciousness as a class under threat, they retreated into social, political, and religious conformity. The parallel experience of the middle class in England and the United States during the latter half of the reign of Queen Victoria is well known. Like their counterparts in the English-speaking world, the children of these staid families rebelled against the social conformity and against the worldview that held that class warfare was necessary to preserve the independence of capital which, in turn, preserved the family wealth.[5] By joining the youth groups, the children of these families could reinforce each other's rebellion and begin to seek their own solutions in their lives.

The name of one of the most important of these youth groups was the *Wandervogel*, the wandering birds. The magazines and newsletters of these clubs are an important source of information on the language and images that the youth were absorbing. These publications efficiently distributed the new discourse and ensured a high uniformity of value among the Wandervogel groups throughout Central Europe. Pictorial and literary images of the landscape were pervasive in these publications, scenes frequently of a young male standing on a high point overlooking a valley, with the sun rising or setting behind a distant hill. As illustrated in Figure 21, the reader sees what the viewer in the picture sees. In the literary images, one also viewed the landscape as from a lookout point:

FIGURE 21. Blick von Gipfel, *or view from the summit. This view of the landscape characterizes that prized in gardens of reaction aesthetics. The masthead vignette is from the youth magazine* Der Wandervogel *(1910). The postcard at the* bottom *was also produced by the Wandervogel organization.*

> Does my entire being not quicken when I look out upon the sublime beauty of the German beech forest? The red-brown fields give me a feeling of delightful quiet. Worry and fears depart as I stare into the swaying motion of the field-river. Does my inner being not savor the harmonious beauty of this landscape: its fallen ruins, the mighty drifts, the checkerboard fields, the abrupt change from field to forest through which winds a little brook, the charming villages with their straw roofs and their building style adapted to the land? (Goebel 1909:80)

Perceiving the landscape in this way was prevalent in the baroque and Enlightenment gardens. In the baroque, straight alleys directed a viewer to look toward the buildings or property that celebrated the powerful. In the Enlightenment, lookout points were built into the paths, often including benches from which to enjoy a particular view. Landscape as a composition of divine nature was pleasurable. But the antimodern perspective was no return to baroque theatrics or Enlightenment pantheism. Instead, the *Blick von Gipfel*, the view from the high lookout, permitted the wanderer to see the interrelationships between landscape and human community, between Heimat and Landschaft, in their completeness:

> We burn with impatience and homesickness for mountain beauty and the free view of the land.... There above the sun breaks through and prepares the way through the silent wood, where it must be free and shining indeed! Suddenly we stand before a wooded slope, where a small path lined with raspberry bushes leads us to a height. Our cheeks burn and our eyes flash as they are now open and are able to gaze below into the valley. (Rogge 1919:24)

It was precisely this view that was abrogated by the closely built environment of the metropolis before skyscrapers. The phrase I translated as *homesickness* is *heimlicher Sehnsucht*, literally the *desire for home*. It refers to the same concept of home which is at the root of Heimat. It is a desire that is fulfilled only by viewing the landscape and not by any other means. In both the German periodicals and in the English-speaking world of the time this was often expressed as the search for Arcadia (Schmitt 1969). In this view, society was reduced to nature, whose laws and process then supplanted modern, urban culture as the primary criterion for value. Racial theories of the time delivered a biological basis for this concept of Heimat, that "there are genetically differentiated human races which reflect not only physiological difference, but also possess different cultural preferences and practices" (Sieferle 1984:194). Thus, the nonurban landscape that the young wanderers viewed from on high offered the hope of discovering a place where harmony existed between humans and nature. Of necessity, this harmony could only exist if the people living there had become genetically, and therefore culturally, adapted to the local conditions. Harmony meant cultural homogeneity.[6]

True natives who had managed to avoid the upheavals of the Industrial Revolution and who led social lives that had evolved through close association with the natural condition were the *Stamm*, tribe, or *Volk*, folk. They were most often the farming communities of a not yet rationalized Central European agricultural system. Their beatification as people untouched by modernity meant that their practices and values, their *Volkscharakter*, were specifically selected for by their landscape and thereby served as a model for those who would leave the city and restore themselves through the Arcadian community.

The Volk were under duress. The urban world was slowly undermining the basis of their community through modernization: the mechanization of agriculture, the migration of farm children to the city, and the extension of social legislation from the city to the countryside. These threats called for efforts to protect as an endangered species this source of all value. Viewing the pristine landscape was not enough; youth were urged to organize themselves to protect the landscape and the Heimat from the destruction that would surely follow if the metropolis expanded without resistance. Thus were born the movements of the *Naturschutz*, protection of nature, and *Heimatschutz*, protection of the home community. Rudorff, founder of the Naturschutz movement, wrote as early as 1880 that preserving nature was the only way of saving the customs of the people and that this was the real basis for loving the land (1880:268). Gradmann, author of an influential 1910 book linking Heimatschutz and landscaping, defined the former as the support of only those human structures (built or planted) that were natural, *unauffällig* (modest), *heimisch* (homey), and *bodenständig* (native). Under these criteria he suggested that everything built since 1870 be leveled (1910:3).

The primary theorist of Heimatschutz was Raoul francé. A biologist by training, he was a dedicated monist[7] who provided the rationalist paradigm for Heimatschutz and laid the basis for today's ecology movement. He also linked the natural legitimacy that Biologismus enjoyed among Central Europeans to the programs of Landschaftsschutz and Heimatschutz. Francé was one of the most widely published German natural scientists of the first three decades of the twentieth century. Through seven books and hundreds of articles that appeared primarily in periodicals in the youth and Wandervogel movements, he popularized a view of nature which appealed to the emotional as well as the rational needs of the antimodern bürgerlich youth. His writings avoided abstract discussion and provided instead a knowledge of nature based on concrete observations that the readers themselves were able to share. This gave his ideas a greater legitimacy since the readers believed that they could test the truth value of his assertions through their own experience.[8]

The specific link between Biologismus and Heimat appeared in one of Francé's earliest articles, "Das Gesetz des Waldes" (The Law of the Forest), published in a Wandervogel magazine in 1908. In it, he asserted that the law of ecological interdependence was the appropriate model for evaluating living human communities (1908:50). The goal of the human community should be to create a "harmonious organism" that "always responds to the ever-changing occurrences of the struggle with the environment, and is the result of all the adaptations that derived from the struggle for existence" (1908:40). "Every Volk, every tribe, conforms to the universal environmental laws, from which they cannot extract themselves" (1923:37), and as a consequence they are adequate for specific ideal landscapes (Wolschke-Bulmahn 1990:89). In this view "the understanding of Heimat is grounded in the living law of ecology" (Tenschert 1982:8). "Heimat, humans, animals, plants, and soil build a living unity" (Rust 1924:165). According to this model, the city is clearly pathological.

The meaning of this point of view for the entire antimodern movement cannot be overstated. In a 1923 article, Bronsart wrote about the Law of the Forest as follows:

> He [Francé] can teach us to find the laws of life in nature, in a form that permits us to use them directly to shape our lives. You evolving citizens, who interest yourselves in public matters, learn to see the forest, the ecological community of nature, through Francé's eyes! Read *The Path of Culture*, *The Eternal Forest*, or *The Culture of Tomorrow*. Then you will know the way to heal our society. (1923:5)

The call to arms in this passage exemplifies how the youth movement was manipulated in the 1920s to serve adult interests. Under the legitimating rubric of "objective philosophy," Francé's followers applied his ideas to social problems.[9] And because Francé's solutions were consistently anticity, antiminority, and pro-Heimat, they were used to justify racist policies and to forge the Siedlungskonzept applied in western Poland during World War II.[10]

The implementation of the Siedlungskonzept originated in a secret October 7, 1941, order from Hitler which named Heinrich Himmler the Reichscommissar for the Strengthening of the German Volk. The purposes of this commission, known by its German initials RKF, included transporting Germans living in other lands back to the Reich, "sanitizing" the influences of foreign people on German culture, and designing a German settlement to receive the newly arrived Germans. It was this last provision that spawned an agency to seize land in western Poland, to demolish existing towns and villages, and to reconstruct the region as a purely German landscape, complete with new villages and towns. The landscape architects and regional planners running the agency were all former members of the youth movement: Konrad Meyer, director; Erhard Mäding and Josef Umlauf, assistant directors. Working as consultants to this agency were specialists from German universities, also former youth movement members, notably Walter Christaller from the University of Heidelberg, best known for formulating the central place theory in geography.[11] Heinrich Wiepking, special consultant to the RKF for landscape design, was the only policymaker in the group not himself involved in the youth movement, although he admitted to co-workers that his planning was strongly influenced by the landscape ideals of the movement (Lendholt 1973:476).

Under the Third Reich, the scope of landscape design and planning was very broad. For Wiepking, the entire territory of Germany was one big garden (1941:23). For Mäding, it was the *Lebensraum*, space for the full development of a group's culture, which was the garden of an entire Volk (1942:200). This enlarged vista meant that garden design could now take into account an entire region. Since the goal was the preservation of the natural forces that shaped Heimat and Volk, there could be no property limit, zoning ordinance, or political boundary to hinder the design or impede its construction. There was only the Siedlungskonzept, nothing less than the total reconstruction of a landscape as it may have appeared in the time of Goethe. The actual target date varied with the planner. Mäding was convinced that the Goethesque landscape had begun to disintegrate in the face of industrial capitalism in 1830. Wiepking thought it was 1860. Only by retreating that far into the past could the planners retrieve a landscape free from foreign influence and thus, one that truly reflected the Heimat of the German Volk. Landscape painting, literature, and poetry of the period between 1750 and 1830, the very gardens of liberty discussed in Chapter 3, were the models used by the planners imagining their ideal landscape (Mäding 1942:94).

SOCIAL PRODUCTION OF GARDENS OF REACTION

Something very similar to the Siedlungskonzept was advanced for Vienna as early as 1908 by Hugo Hassinger, the founder of urban geography. For him, the growth of urbanization was naturally limited by traffic flow. He promulgated the idea that a one-hour traveling distance from the center of a city by whatever means defined the traffic boundary of the city and the most rational limit on its growth. Analyzing the differences between the political boundaries and the natural traffic boundary in Vienna, he concluded that the city could easily develop substantial residential areas in the Lower Austrian country adjoining the city in the south, Mödling (1910:5–88). Southward growth was advantageous for several reasons. First, the population density would be dissipated, preserving the historic center of the city by reducing the flow of traffic around the ancient buildings. The cost of transportation would be reduced because more people would be forced to use it. Residential space would be enlarged, permitting more settlements of affordable single-family homes in areas of cheap land, reducing the unhealthy congestion in the tenements, and opening up space between ethnic enclaves (1912:27).

Hassinger was a Christian Socialist more interested in reform than in reactionary landscape policies. After World War I his ideas about expansion set off a debate that would have dramatic effects on Viennese life. The opportunity to change the boundaries of Vienna, and with them the area that municipal planners could control, came immediately after the war. Stripped of its role as capital and first market of the dissolved Habsburg monarchy, Vienna and the other Austrian provinces negotiated new political boundaries. Social Democrat leader Karl Renner suggested southward expansion as the solution to the economic problems of the city (Figure 22). Including the Vienna Basin as far south as Wiener Neustadt in the city would create a province with better balance among the industrial, commercial, administrative, and agricultural sectors. The larger area would permit the decentralization of the city by creating smaller residential settlements modeled after Ebenezer Howard's garden cities in England. The ideology was evident in the argument that incorporating greater amounts of rural landscape improved the quality of life for all Viennese. In a reversal of the positions that the parties would normally take, the Christian Socialists opposed this suggestion for political and not ideological reasons. Because it was the site of many factory towns, the Vienna Basin had more workers than farmers. Renner's party was a majority in the Lower Austrian assembly, and this legislative power frightened many conservative farmers in the expansion region. They were afraid they would be unfairly taxed to support Vienna in the grandeur to which it was no longer entitled. By opposing the expansion, the Christian Socialists hoped to capture the farm vote and put forward a plan to expand the city northward to an area that was sparsely settled and had comparatively fewer towns than the south. Their plan would increase cheap residential land without creating political conflict. The third largest party, the reactionary Grossdeutsche Volkspartei, also fought the Social Democratic plan, favoring one that would have given them greater influence on the final boundary lines. Eventually, the city acquired home rule as a province but did not expand its borders into significant portions of Lower Austria. This decision froze in place many of the problems of industrialization. Lack of room forced the professional planners to measures that increasingly alienated one or another group.

According to Posch, at this point Vienna embarked on a historical course through the twentieth century which led to two separate worlds. One world he called the English-Democratic, which emphasized the self-rule of citizens in a cooperative state. The other was the Roman-parliamentary state, which itself remained only a short step away from the fascist Roman-imperial state. These two worlds were symbolized by different house forms: the common tenement with its democratic sympathies and its appeal to cooperative solutions versus the settlements of single-family detached houses with their fear of

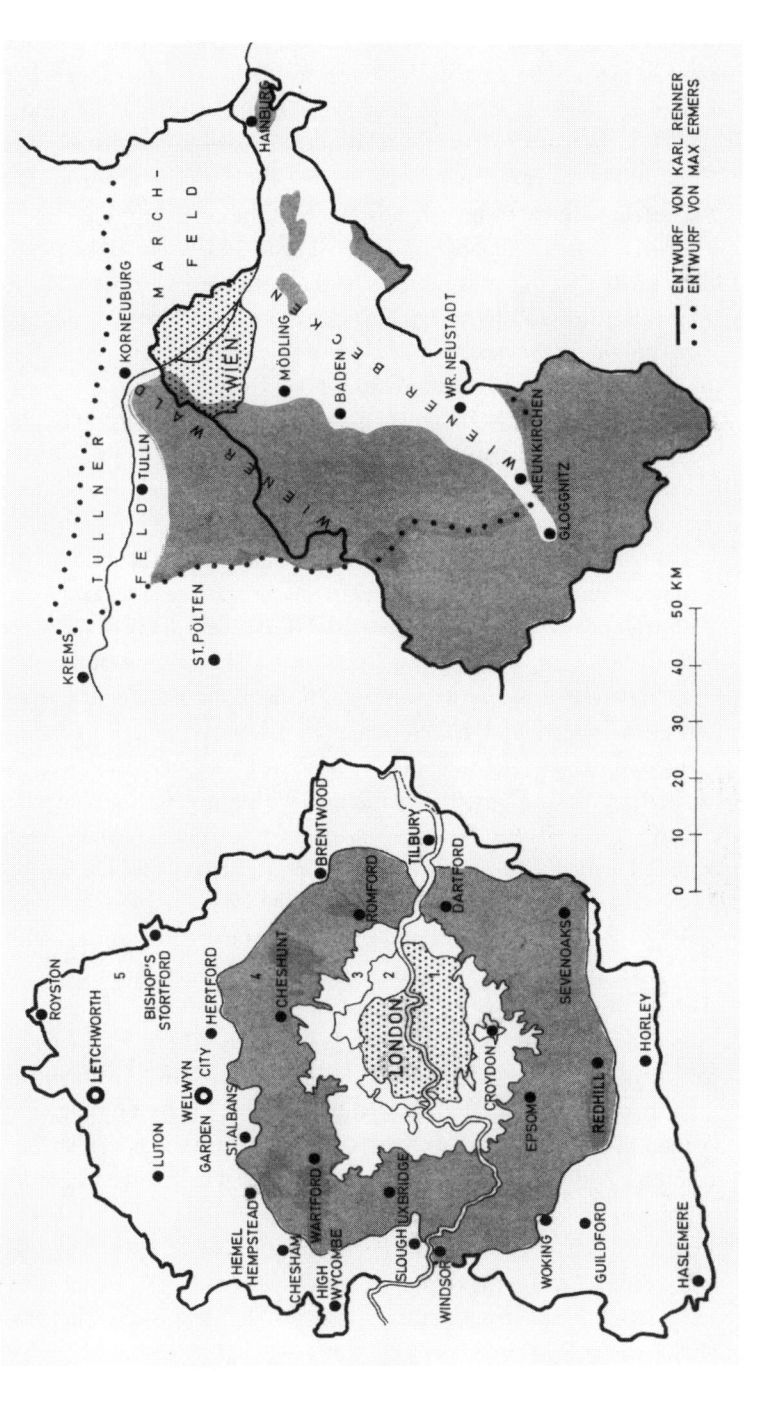

FIGURE 22. *Expansion of the metropolitan area in the 1920s. The expansion was a response to the increasing importance of reactionary designers in government. The drawing at the right by Wilfred Posch contrasts the alternative plans offered by two progressive members of the Social Democratic Party, Karl Renner (solid line) and Max Ermers (broken line) during the 1919–1922 debates. The principle that municipalities had natural boundaries was not confined to Central Europe, as Posch's drawing of the successful implementation of the 1944 expansion of the city of London (left) makes clear.*

Posch 1981:59

democracy and reliance on strong central leadership. Public investment to expand the area available for one form over the other was a core plank in the party platforms throughout the period (Berchtold 1967:228, 367, 458). Botz argued that the seizure and redistribution of desirable housing were reasons for the public's ignoring the wholesale removal of Jewish citizens from the cities (1975).

After closure of debate on the new borders for Vienna, the possibility of solving the metropolitan land use problems through decentralization and southern expansion evaporated (Posch 1981:60). Party politics in the next four decades would swing the emphasis first toward tenements and then toward cottages, with increasing tension. When civil war broke out between 1929 and 1931, the biggest battles were waged in the streets outside the tenements of Vienna. Victory by the reactionary coalition led to Anschluss with Germany and Austria's slow descent into the maelstrom of World War II.

The resentment and xenophobia that gave the reactionary discourse its persuasive power earlier in the century seem weak and inadequate today. With the defeat of the Third Reich, many of the more radical ideas completely lost their authority. The gardens of reaction were both very small and very large in that they included the small garden movement and the regional planning movement. Public style mandated the use of native plant varieties. Parks were functionalist in their layout but larger in scale and with a greater emphasis on straight lines. Before the Nazi seizure of power in Germany, reactionary landscape ideas found few political patrons, and the few reactionary landscape architects who found work in the 1920s built private gardens for the antimodern Bürgertum. After 1932, many architects and planners found employment in very large projects, such as the building of the Autobahn or the planning of the communities in western Poland for the Germans returning to the Reich from other countries. Many of the design ideas from the German Autobahn were incorporated into landscaping the interstate highway system in the United States, where the use of ground cover, shrubs, and trees had to provide a connection between the drivers in traffic and the native landscape beyond the bridge abutment.

After the 1938 Anschluss with Germany, planners were concerned with reconstructing the region around Vienna to reflect an antimodern, hence antimetropolitan, ideology. The expansion that had eluded the politicians in 1919 was imposed on Lower Austria by administrative fiat in 1938. This expansion annexed to Viennese municipal control the eastern and southern slopes of the Wienerwald and large sections of the Lower Austrian counties of Schwechat and Mödling. By forcibly removing many ethnic workers to single-factory towns or agricultural villages, their voting strength in Vienna itself was diluted. The intention was to hobble permanently the political and cultural strength of the Viennese working class. The war economy prevented the wholesale reconstruction of the region, but many infrastructural facilities, including gas and telephone lines and the extension of the Viennese street rail system to the southern towns, was completed. Even today, residents of these portions of counties which returned to Lower Austria after the war have Viennese telephone numbers and pay their gas bills to the Viennese municipal gasworks.

The second, and in the long run, most lasting impulse for garden production within the reactionary discourse was the *Kleingarten*, or small garden, movement. A Kleingarten is a garden of modest size, usually between seventy-five and three hundred square meters, on land that one has rights to use but does not own. Use rights come from rent or lease agreements that are entirely separate from the rent or lease agreement on the domicile. Such small gardens have existed outside the walls of the European cities since the Middle Ages and can be seen in North European paintings of the fifteenth and sixteenth centuries. They are evident in seventeenth-century Viennese maps. In the eighteenth century, Austrian soldiers were given garden plots near their Viennese barracks to grow fresh vegetables to supplement the food provided by their regiment.

In the nineteenth century, three separate movements led to the Kleingarten movement in Austria: the *Armengärten* (poor gardens), the *Arbeitergärten* (workers' gardens), and the *Schrebergärten* movements. Armengärten were parcels of land set aside by the community to provide the poor with an area to grow their own food and to have fresh air to combat the tuberculosis raging inside tenement housing. The movement was church based and began after the Napoleonic Wars. Arbeitergärten were garden parcels on the grounds of factories and public utilities for workers and their families and provided a recreation area for poor or large families and those with sick or handicapped members. The gardens involved workers with recuperative and restorative forms of nonwork activity and helped them teach their children about nature and work discipline. The proximity of other gardeners strengthened community ties, and long-term leases for the gardens protected renters from land speculators. These benefits attracted skilled workers in industrial sectors with relatively low wages, such as the light machine and print industries in the private sector, and the post office and railroads in the public sector. The vast majority of Viennese factory workers were employed in low-skill, low-wage occupations, but there is no record of Arbeitergarten complexes on the sites of these factories. Contemporaries viewed both the Armengarten and Arbeitergarten movements as progressive developments in cities. They do not seem to belong to the discourse on reactionary landscapes.

Ernst Hauschild began the Schrebergarten movement in 1868 in Leipzig. He intended it as a method of providing children with physical, social, and moral training by teaching them how to cooperate in the planting and tending of small garden plots. He named the movement after Daniel Gottlieb Moritz Schreber, the founder of Heilgymnastik, homeopathic physical therapy. Schreber wrote extensively on the relationship between physical activity and good health, especially in children. His ideas were very popular in the later nineteenth century in German-speaking communities, where he played a role similar to that of Dr. Benjamin Spock in mid twentieth-century North American families. The Schrebergarten movement spread quickly through northern Germany, but reached Vienna only in the first decade of the twentieth century. By then, it had lost its schoollike character and had become a garden movement in which the entire family could participate.

The Schrebergarten movement had a health and wellness principle at its base. Schreber believed that health came from unrestricted physical activity, especially activity that occurred in natural environments where the obstacles were of natural dimensions, weight, and scale. His *Naturheilkunde* (homeopathic) philosophy is summarized in the phrase *Bewegung in die Natur*, to move with nature. Central Europeans used this idea to describe the appeal of gardens throughout the nineteenth century. Schreber gave it scientific legitimacy. To move naturally, one must first find a natural setting. This was not easy if one were too poor to buy a villa garden or too discriminated against to enjoy visiting a public park. Hauschild's idea was for charitable groups to lease parcels of land for working-class families to garden collectively. His motives were progressive within the context of the dominant liberal ideas of his day. By improving the health of the laboring classes, the health of the entire community would rise, and the German people would be stronger. Thus, charitable groups could support the Schrebergarten movement on purely nationalistic grounds. This strategy proved very successful in Bismarck's Germany, but it was less appealing in Vienna where people viewed liberal nationalism as a provincial plot by Hungarians, Czechs, and Italians to destroy the empire. When Schrebergärten came to Vienna, it was under a quite different set of perceptions: reactionary agro-romanticism.[12]

The nineteenth century produced a school of utopian thought which was sharply antimetropolitan. Writers such as Tolstoy, Fournier, and Kropotkin urged their readers to abandon the immorality of the city and return to the wellspring of social health in agriculture. All three were passionate gardeners. The utopian appeal of the garden dream seduced many socialist movements of the nineteenth and twentieth centuries. Tolstoy and Kropotkin inspired Oscar Wilde and Gandhi but angered Marx and his students. In the year after the Social Democratic Party of Austria was founded (1889), Viennese journalist Theodor Hertzka published his novel *Freiland* about a utopian settlement in Uganda (1890). Hertzka's novel served as the basis for the Freiland movement, a cluster of discussion groups exploring ways of implementing the utopian vision. Theodore Herzl was a member of one of these groups, and this may have led to his vision of Zionist society as the return of denaturalized urban Jews to the garden. This movement was similar to the Bellamy Societies in the United States, which followed Edward Bellamy's utopian socialist novel, *Looking Backward* (1880), and the Morris Societies in Britain. William Morris, besides starting the Arts and Crafts Movement together with Ruskin, also wrote the utopian novel *News from Nowhere* (1890), in which all cities were transformed into tiny agricultural villages. Similar to these utopian novels but aimed at a younger audience were the Winnetou books of Karl May. Set in North America before the destruction of native communities, the books celebrated the virtues of an idealized tribal society.

In addition to discussing the possibilities of nonurban, nonindustrial utopias, these back-to-nature movements channeled the critique of the bürgerlich cultural hypocrisy. The children of this class had realized that their parents could profess the most puritanical and orthodox Catholicism while exploiting factory workers and ignoring massive social problems. The breakaway Jugendstil artists used natural materials and preindustrial handicrafts in the Wiener Werkstatt. Young people involved in the Wandervogel movement imitated the scholars and journeymen of old and hiked everywhere. Members of alpine clubs and similar tourist clubs competed with cows to breathe the pure air of the mountains—social-revolutionary utopians and Volk-reactionary romantics, side by side.

A Viennese natural healing association founded the first Schrebergarten in 1903 in Deutschwald on the Westbahn near Purkersdorf. They bought the land directly from a farmer with funds collected from the membership. The first huts were built in 1904. How the settlement looked in 1906 is shown in Figure 23. Although technically outside the boundaries of the city on the western slope of the Wienerwald, it was inside the customs barrier[13] and accessible from the city by the Westbahn rail line. This was important because these gardeners had regular jobs and housing in the city. According to Frau Czermak, whose parents belonged to the group that built this first Viennese Schrebergarten, the effort was part of this general agro-romantic movement. It approached the need to return to the land through homeopathy. She was four when the gardens were first established and described the group she knew in her childhood as follows:

> The natural healing association, you know, really had been established in the metropolis. It developed around a circle of people who said they wanted to experience nature. Its approach to natural healing was through nutrition and lifestyle. At that time, in the monarchy, it was a groundbreaking affair. Today it is impossible to imagine what a difference it made to live in a metropolis around 1900 and to go out and be in nature. And then to be able to live in nature and not even be a farmer or a rich estate owner! When I was six years old and the children in school asked me what we were doing, I couldn't explain it. It wasn't a farmer's house. It wasn't a villa. What was it exactly? The concept of a weekend house did not exist before World War I. Then it slowly entered the popular speech. The group in Purkersdorf got something in their heads which was quite modern and quite dangerous. For that circle, the gardens were practically their

FIGURE 23. *The first Schrebergarten in the Viennese region, photograph (1906). The Schrebergarten was founded in 1903 by a Viennese natural healing association in Deutschwald on the Westbahn (railroad line) near Purkersdorf.*

religion. Water, sun, and oatmeal, I always used to say. But they were revolutionaries who didn't fit anywhere, even in their own families, in their own kindred. We were path breakers who wanted to be one with nature.

Reforming one's life! Reforming one's life through clothing, eating, and the way one lived one's life. It always entailed spiritual development. And these folks were far from being religious in the sense of the established church.

Of course, tastes also had to be changed. Men started to wear net T-shirts and open sandals. They wore full beards, but never ties or hats. And the women didn't have to follow the fashion of tightly bound corsets. They wore so-called reform dresses that were of tougher material and hung freely from the shoulder, so that the entire body could develop beautifully. Also nudism had come into use then for the first time. So, there were many other improbable innovations.

The group was entirely vegetarian. They ate whole-grain cereals in both porridge and bread and avoided spices and strong herbs. Living and working in the gardens, the group hoped to realize the homeopathic ideal for sustained health which had originally inspired Schreber himself.[14]

The social production of reactionary gardens was halted by World War I, which forced people back to the land to survive, setting in motion an entirely different process for the social production of garden space. These small gardens were primarily gardens of security in a hostile world. As will become evident in the following chapter, agro-romantic ideas were revived in the 1920s and 1930s for community building within large garden settlements. People built these for reasons that indicate a clear break with the pure idealism of groups like the Purkersdorfer gardeners. These earlier romantics did not have to garden; they chose to out of their reaction to the uncomfortable and unhealthy world of the metropolis. The gardeners of postwar Vienna no longer had this choice. They gardened because it was the only way their families would survive.

THE HETEROTOPIA OF REACTION

A significant portion of the young, bürgerlich Viennese population had turned antimodern by the first decades of the twentieth century. They looked at the world that industrial production had created and were repulsed by it. They sought a return to a simpler life and looked to the past for the model for what this life could be. To symbolize it, they evoked its landscape. They defined nature as the antithesis of the industrial city. Unlike those that preceded it, the gardens of reaction could not be constructed by society. People discovered them somewhere outside the city and inhabited them on their own terms. Young people wandered the countryside in search of such landscapes. This cultural movement set in motion a new landscape aesthetic that would influence all of the gardens of the twentieth century. The theorists of this movement worked primarily in Germany. Antimodernism is as universal as modernism, and for this reason, the aesthetic found supporters in Vienna as well as the rest of the industrial world.

Gardens of reaction fulfilled the dream of the return to the preindustrial world. They integrated human society into the living community. This community followed its own rules, without regard for human history. One goal of such a reintegration into nature was to end history. A second was to halt the destruction of nature through pollution; people would return to agriculture and handcrafts as their means of subsistence. A third was to reduce the tension of social life by eliminating ethnic pluralism, the rationale being that not all living communities are appropriate for all human societies. Humans needed to sort themselves according to kind, undoing the mixing of groups which the migrations of the modern era had engendered. Then, properly sorted, groups would find the communities from which their ancestors sprung, reconnect with their native soil, and begin to build the kinds and sizes of settlements appropriate to their natural inclinations. They would finally become *Naturmenschen*, like the tribal peoples written about in the ethnographies and ethnographically inspired novels. By following nature's laws instead of human law, inequality and resentment would disappear. One only needed the strength to renounce the luxuries of the industrial life. With its self-imposed privations, the Wandervogel movement provided people with the confidence that they could live with this renunciation.

The most powerful symbol of the garden of reaction was the view from the high lookout. It wiped away the clutter and obstructions of the cityscape to afford the seeker a clear picture of the interrelationship of landscape and human community. Such a view required effort. New clothing styles, nudism, and hiking reflected physicality and a focus on the body as the point of departure for a new landscape.

The physicality was that of youth and heralded the beginning of a new age. The turn-of-the-century hiking costume, itself modeled on the sturdy woolens of alpine farmers, continues in contemporary Vienna as the clothing of choice for weekend walks in the Wienerwald. The physicality resonated with the rootedness and harmony with nature which people sought in the garden of reaction. The rootedness belonged to the native firmly implanted in the soil of home. Blood and land were conjoined into a single whole. Together with others, the robust native felt the synergy of the community. Their works became the product of the Volk, the romantic ideal of cultural homogeneity and social harmony. At the head of this Volk, concentrating within himself the spirit and energy of the community that nurtured him, stood the leader. He could not do otherwise than reflect in his words and actions the deepest sympathy and desire of the Volk.

The garden of reaction reversed the arrow of history and then suspended it altogether. By returning to the rural landscape of the 1830s, the reactionary planners intended to undo the effects of mechanized agriculture on the rural landscape and the migration of industrial capital and its workforce to the cityscape. The gardens that came the closest to realizing these ideals before the mechanical transformations of the Third Reich turned them into a modernist frenzy were the Schrebergärten of the pre–World War I era. The recollections of those who participated reveal a garden life that celebrated the rhythms of the seasons. Ironically, school and work required that this thorough suspension of city time take place only on weekends.

The gardens of reaction separated themselves from ordinary space by distance. The pristine preindustrial landscape involved years of trekking through forest land. The small allotment garden was a considerable distance from the tenement or apartment. At that distance, the forest lookout or the early Schrebergarten was so unlike the landscape of the city in its transparency, its scale, and its possibilities, that one truly felt oneself in another world.

The gardens of reaction were uninhibited in their condemnation of urban life and were specifically intended to close off the industrial, the multicultural, and the modern. In so doing, they mystified the relationship between landscape and community—a relationship that only existed between certain rarefied landscapes and certain unattained communities. Every garden style discussed up until now saw landscape as a human artifact apart from nature. This distance permitted the gardens to use natural elements as symbols of the unspoken values in the urban community. The gardens worked because their simulation of nature within the cityscape was necessarily selective and incomplete. But when the human community was perceived as alienated from nature, these gardens were no longer possible. The urban itself suffered from incompleteness. In negating the city, the gardens of reaction negated gardens as well. This radical stance could not endure. Antimodernism ultimately could not overcome the appeal of the modern. Industrialism continued to expand and diversify Vienna. In the aftermath of World War I, necessity would triumph over fantasy for a decade, and gardens would proliferate as never before. The motive in this case was not aesthetics, but hunger.

Gardens of Refuge

As described in the preceding chapter, small gardens marked the beginning of antiurban, reactionary movements at the turn of the century. The present discussion traces how a group of planners fashioned these small gardens into a progressive mass movement by adapting some principles from the garden city model to the conditions of the social production of space in Vienna. These gardens of refuge afforded their owners a measure of stability in the face of threats to family survival. They changed the cityscape by securing as garden space large sections of land in some of the most desirable districts. Although not publicly accessible, these garden settlements brought a greater number of metropolitans in contact with green space than did the gardens of the cottage districts.[1]

By 1912, small garden colonies were still not very common. Paternalistic factory owners and reactionary groups established them to fulfill specific goals, including providing food for families; strengthening the community; reducing land speculation; securing open-use areas in the city; establishing a recreation area for large, sick, or poor families; providing a field of activity for unemployed people; developing the physical strength of the Volk; educating the youth; supplying social welfare for employees; and ensuring health. All of these goals reflected the reform or reactionary ideologies of the movements that had given birth to them. To some extent, they also reflected the goals of municipal planners, even though at this point, the city had made no effort to establish its own gardens and had discouraged the creation of garden settlements in open lands. The gardens carried a significant load of historical baggage which made municipal investment in establishing more gardens politically painful. Because Vienna had been an imperial administrative capital, the association of house and garden conveyed a noble, or, at the very least, a bürgerlich, prerogative. The Bürgertum stigmatized the small gardens as the summer homes of little people before the gates of Vienna. Municipal support of garden settlements looked like cooptation to the lower classes and welfare coddling by the upper classes.

According to Siller and Schneider, in 1915 there were approximately 2,000 Kleingärten and an additional 1,200 *Kriegsgärten*—gardens that grew vegetables on land that had previously had other uses. In 1916, the numbers grew to 3,000 and 2,800. By 1919, 40,000 families, more than 200,000 people, had more than 12 million square meters under cultivation. They concluded, "Without a garden, it is practically impossible to lead a humane, healthy life in our time. We always recall the economic value of the small garden, but anyone with vision must admit that the educational and health value contained in the Schrebergarten is even more meaningful" (1920:79).[2]

Right after the war, people converted every available piece of land to *Nutzgärten*, utility gardens. The breakdown of the economy during the war left the city without provisions. Bombed-out roads, scarce supplies of petroleum, disruption of the planting schedule, and lack of labor on the farms for harvesting and delivery all reduced the supply of foodstuffs of every kind in the city's markets. What was available was sold on the black market to avoid the emergency price controls imposed by the government. The working class could not afford to buy food regularly on the black market and depended on their own gardens for fresh vegetables and the occasional rabbit or chicken. All available land, including parks and preserves, was used. Before the war, the housing crisis had forced some people to build squatter settlements in the forest preserves.[3] The food shortage exacerbated this movement. From an estimated 3,000 squatters before the war, the so-called *Wildsiedlungen* grew to 18,500 in 1918, and

FIGURE 24. *Squatter cabin in 1919. A landscape of refuge surrounds this squatter cabin in the Wienerwald. The woman at the* right *is slaughtering a rabbit. From wild settlements such as this the first municipally supported garden settlements developed.*

55,000 in 1920 (Figure 24). Returning soldiers from the fronts and the sharp rise in the number of unemployed fueled this process of inner colonization. Gardening was a crucial part of the squatter camps. When the city finally appropriated public resources to supply water and sewerage facilities to these colonies, many of them were redesigned and rezoned as garden settlement-type residential districts (Kampffmeyer 1926:719–20). In less than five years, these accumulations of stalls and huts approximated Gypsy camps, built by individualistic, solitary, security-seeking people into unified, cooperative garden settlements.

Development of these settlements continued along two lines. The first began as small garden colonies modeled after the Schrebergarten movement. People incorporated themselves to lease a parcel of open land, typically from the city, for a specific time.[4] The parcel would then be subdivided and subleased to members of the colony, who would build sheds and grow vegetables and fruits for their own use. The plots were substantial in size, often exceeding 125 square meters, and offered plenty of room for individual landscape design and food cultivation. Initially, the sheds were used to store gardening equipment, served as shelter in bad weather, and caged small animals raised for food. Stipulations in the leases forbade winterizing the sheds, so they were not intended as year-round housing. The city provided some services, such as water and rubbish disposal, but others, such as gas and sewerage, were withheld. Over time, as the functions of the gardens changed, some people used their sheds as summer cottages. Others installed stoves and used the cottages for winter entertaining. Eventually, some sheds did become unofficial year-round homes.

Today, these small gardens dot the city in various forms: as large colonies and single isolated gardens; as leased or privately owned land; in residential districts and wastelands; on the edge of or in the Wienerwald and the Danube preserves and in the middle of the city's densest districts. Of the more than 34,000 gardens, two fifths of them are on land zoned for other uses. More than 5,000 of these gardens are on public preserves (Weber, Feigelfeld, Auböck, and Lehner 1986). Altogether, more than 8,000 gardens stand in violation of zoning ordinances (Rathaus Pressebüro 1984).

Because the land was and is still the property of the city of Vienna and because it is located on the edge of the city, the small garden colonies have occasionally been the victims of municipal expropriation regardless of their zoning status. This was especially true in the 1960s and 1970s, when the edges of the city were the scenes for highway and park building. Legally, the families who had built up their sheds had no recourse to recovering their investments, which led to intense lobbying efforts by small garden colonies to permit the conversion of the gardening leases into settlement leases, the latter being more difficult to expropriate. The colonists also demanded de facto recognition of the use of the gardens as housing lots.

The second line of development was the cooperative housing movement. Between 1919 and 1930, the city built or subsidized the building of forty-six cooperative colonies on what was then the periphery of the city. These projects used the labor of the future residents as a form of sweat equity to reduce construction costs and created a public corporation to supply the necessary materials. The colonies combined suitable living space with sufficient land for subsistence gardens and generated an increase in quality low-income housing at the lowest possible cost. These gardens are a fascinating phase in the formation of metropolitan culture. Their meaning lies between that of private property, with its unassailable rights of use and disposal, and common property, in which group rights override individual will. Some existing settlements reflect one prevailing ethic or the other. These are the exception, however. In most contemporary settlements, the membership is a tense mix between house and garden as private versus collective property.

By the consensus of those who have analyzed its impact, the cooperative garden settlement movement was a successful housing policy (Marcuse 1986; Taylor 1959), and yet the city abandoned this strategy after six years in favor of large *Superbaublock* projects. Motivated by political pressure to speed up the availability of housing units, the city could complete the Superbaublock design more quickly and provide construction jobs for a higher number of unemployed. The last garden settlement was completed in 1934.

In the Viennese discourse on the meaning of the landscape, people summed up in one of two phrases the ambivalence they felt toward the small garden: *das kleine Glück*, the little stroke of luck; or *mein eigenes Stückchen Land*, my little piece of land. The first refers to the reward of participating in a garden experience which is only possible through one's willingness to cooperate with others. The second speaks of the desire to secure some means of self-determination through the garden. These prove to be complex themes in Viennese culture.

One hears a number of metaphors for the tension between the private and the communal garden experience. People who have gardens can be categorized as *Gärtner*, gardeners, or *Siedler*, settlers. The implications of being a Gartner are that you have committed yourself to the ideals of the Schrebergarten as the source of health-giving exercise and healthy foods and as the symbol of your personal diligence. The connotations of being a Siedler are that you have committed yourself to improving your family's housing conditions by establishing a home in your garden. The garden becomes the miniature estate of the ordinary metropolitan, a source of capital, and a symbol of one's success in life.

Contemporary Siedler are different from the people who struggled to create the garden settlements in the 1920s, even though writers sometimes use the term for both groups. The difference lies in the changing conditions of housing production over the seventy years. The old Siedler, whom I will call by the term they used to refer to themselves, *Pioniere*, or pioneers, were highly skilled, underpaid, and underhoused families who built houses and gardens cooperatively to ensure the shelter of their families.[5] They prized collective efforts, each helping the other to build roads, lay house foundations, make bricks, and plant gardens. Contemporary Siedler are comparatively individualistic. Their primary concern is to bolster the quality of their family's housing. They are moving from standard housing to a high level of adequacy, one in which the possession of a detached house in a garden confers extra status.

Both of these attitudes involve issues of security. In the discourse on landscape, I see these attitudes as producing no new garden styles. Instead, they describe a vernacular line of development between 1920 and 1960. The Pionier and Siedler gardens followed the formal features of the functionalist gardens developed by Lichtwark and Migge. What changed was the meaning that the gardeners attached to their gardening activities. This chapter concerns the earlier meaning of the gardens, and the following chapter picks up the story after World War II.

By calling these gardens of refuge, I choose to emphasize the role of the garden as a response to threats from outside the household. In the case of the Pionier garden, the threats to the family were hunger and social isolation. For Siedler gardens, the dangers were the erosion of housing capital and the loss of status. For those raised on the Pionier values, the Siedler seemed to be rootless, valueless individualists. From the point of view of the Siedler, the old Pionier families appeared to be idealists and also intruders and busybodies who overstepped their bounds with their settlement covenants and endless committee meetings. At the time of my conversations with these Viennese, many settlements had lost their cooperative spirit entirely. Members in some cooperatives had transformed them into condominiums or private property. In other settlements, recruitment criteria for new members had been tightened to ensure advantages for as many young families as possible, especially those who had previously shown an interest in cooperative activities of some sort. Only by recruiting families with Pionier values do these settlements hope to survive as cooperatives (Rotenberg 1992a).

The battle between Siedler and Gärtner was even more hard fought in the small garden settlements. The threat of uncertain expropriation created a certain urgency on the part of Siedler to gain the upper hand in colony politics. In many colonies, the changing functions of the garden made Siedler arguments easier to accept. After two generations of family use of the garden, members had forged significant personal attachments to their specific garden, even if they had not rehabilitated their sheds into cottages. Those idealistic Gärtner who tried to argue that the garden itself was less important than the work one did to make the garden found themselves carping against the emotional current. The Siedler soon had control of the Zentralverband der Kleingärtner, the citywide organization of small garden colonies. From here they promulgated a new concept on small garden policy in the city which emphasized building more garden land and legalizing existing renegade garden colonies inside the Wald und Wiesengürtel.

As related in Chapter 6, Lichtwark characterized the function of gardens as *Zweckmässigheit*, purposeful by design; *Brauchbarkeit*, useful toward an end; and *Benutzbarkeit*, usable as a means. Gardens of both the Pioniere and the Siedler were purposeful by design. Their difference lay in the subtle distinction between usefulness toward achieving an end and usefulness as an ongoing means, usefulness in both cases emphasizing the ease with which the gardener could convert the land to service. The most important criterion for the Pionier was whether his garden would feed the family; all other considerations were subordinated to this. Pionier attitudes oriented the garden toward solving present problems and gratifying immediate needs. The problem of provisioning lasted for years, and Pioniere found that they could enhance the usefulness of their garden beyond its physical limits only by cooperation with neighbors.

Contrarily, using the garden as an ongoing means emphasized the power of the garden to satisfy wants—a concern of the Siedler, who wanted to see the value of their investment in the garden appreciate, the housing quality of the family enhanced, and the representation of their success in life embellished. The Siedler directed the garden toward future problems and deferred gratification of their needs. Their goals would be realized with the passage of time. Their stubborn insistence on building homes in their gardens forced the city to rezone the area and make services available. The actions of neighbors could detract from the future value of the family property if they permitted their own to deteriorate, but only rarely could any collective action enhance it. Thus, Siedler did not grant a very high priority to nurturing cooperative relations with neighbors.

Social Democratic leaders in the prewar period saw the Siedler as that part of the working class which most wanted to imitate the property-owning Kleinbürger. The ideal Gartner expressed a working-class worldview. Siedler wanted houses more than they wanted gardens in which to grow food and flowers. For them, gardens were important only inasmuch as they increased the value of the house. Garden settlements developed during a time when the needs of people for both housing and food were very high. The Pioniere built their own houses and gardens. If class differences existed between Siedler and Gärtner, they survived in the gardens.

Gärtner, Pioniere, and Siedler all built gardens of refuge, but under different conditions and with different goals. All three are twentieth-century types in Vienna for which there were no nineteenth-century counterparts. There are other kinds of gardeners in the city today, but these three types include the overwhelming number of active garden builders. The location of the gardens and the relationship of the house to the garden identify the differences among them. Most have not traveled very far from the districts where their grandparents or great-grandparents first settled. For them, gardens are *Zweckgerecht*, justified by their purpose. When these Viennese talk about their gardens, they invoke its usefulness:

> Yes, one can put it to good use. That means that I can plant vegetables and use them later in cooking. I can plant herbs and use them later in cooking. I can let the children play alone in it, or I can play in it with them.[6]

> [Mr.:] I wouldn't call it a Nutzgarten anymore, because we make no use of it. [Mrs.:] We had one once. We had tomatoes. We had potatoes. We had lettuce. And that's a Nutzgarten. For a two-person family, its all too much. And we can't handle the fruit harvest any more.[7]

Today very few Viennese use their gardens in this way. In the 1950s, many gardeners converted their Nutzgärten into recreational gardens. These are discussed in the next chapter. I could find only one or two gardens in each garden settlement in which the gardener ded-

FIGURE 25. *Classic* Nutzgarten *in 1988. This daughter of a garden city Pionier family continued to cultivate a classic Nutzgarten in 1988.*

icated all of the available land to growing things. A larger portion, though still a minority, planted small vegetable gardens. Almost every garden has at least one or two fruit trees.

Photographs of the old Pionier gardens still in the possession of those who grew up in them show a very different treatment of space: every available inch was used to grow food for the household (Figure 25). Vegetables grew in raised beds separated by narrow crisscrossing footpaths. Raised arbors along the fences and path lines supported grape vines, beans, and tomatoes. Moving around in these crowded gardens took caution. Animal stalls, now converted into television rooms, housed chickens, rabbits, goats, or pigs.

The Nutzgarten also specified the spirit of interdependence which the garden settlement engendered. In justifying the lack of produce in her garden, one woman described the support system that still continued to operate in the settlement.

I cook nothing from the garden. I give it away to families with children, who already look forward to it. We also exchange, which is very pleasant. When someone has too much fruit, then we exchange. We don't need a plum tree because the neighbors have plenty of them. They are happy to be rid of them. It makes it very pleasant that we have such very good relations with each other.

Older conversation partners spoke of the so-called *Kräutergemeinschaft*, the "soup-green" communities of their youth. Women visited their neighbors in the late afternoon, exchanging herbs for flavoring the family's evening soup:

> Everyone knew which neighbors had which herbs and when you needed one, you simply went over and said, "Please, can I have some." And no one was put off if you borrowed something. There was never the feeling that you have to reciprocate immediately. When you borrowed something, you simply said, "If you ever need something, come to us." It was actually very positive. (From a woman who grew up in a small garden in the 1940s)[8]

Through this soup of borrowed herbs, the children of the gardeners virtually drank in the spirit of cooperation in the settlement.

For those who lived in the garden settlements in the 1920s and 1930s, the connection to neighbors is particularly strong.

> In the first place, we lived in the community. We didn't need a kindergarten. We grew up here in the community, the relationship with neighbors. (From the daughter of a Pionier)[9]

A Pionier who helped build the settlement and who still lived in it at the age of eighty-two, explained how this worked:

> We were always together with people. It was, how should I say it, connected with nature. We had this community house out there. It burned down. In it we had a bar, but it was an alcohol-free bar. There was a chess club and a garden club, and they contributed a lot to forming, cultivating the people, as we cultivate plants.[10]

> We connected with each other through these clubs, and performances and each of these contacts helped to make us what we are. It's like in a forest where you see so many trees. They have to grow straight because the others do not allow any single one of them to grow crookedly.[11]

The particular conditions of life in the small garden colonies put limitations on the extent of the community building networks. Nevertheless, they generated the same community atmosphere in them, as this woman, who grew up in such a garden, explained:

> In the winter when we were all in our apartments, it was very seldom that we would get together and visit with the people who had neighboring gardens. Everyone looked forward to the summer. When we first came to the garden in the spring, we ran around and looked to see who had already arrived. And there were already plenty of people there who had moved to gardens very early. . . . We were not friends, but rather very good neighbors. We helped each other. There was no electricity. We used gas for light and heat. There were times when we ran out of petrol, and it was too late to get some more. Then one naturally went to the neighbors and said, "Can we borrow some petrol for our lamps?" And it went without saying that one always lent some to the other. The supply of food was also uncertain then, and we shared what we had with one another.[12]

The preponderance of exchanges based on generalized reciprocity rather than the metropolitan market makes these garden experiences stand out in participants' memories. These were extraordinary social experiences that the garden settlements contained and permitted.

The gardeners could not duplicate these experiences in their metropolitan neighborhoods because only in the garden did the participants completely control the production of goods they exchanged. Several conversation partners spoke of the cooperative atmosphere of the old Pionier gardens. Others spoke of the birth of a true communal spirit in which to raise children. The contrast with the crowded, dark, stuffy city apartments in which neighbors ignored and resented each other was always available. So, too, was the contrast with the tidy functionalist, unproductive lawns of the cottage district. Both those left behind in the apartments and those living in the cottages found reason to criticize the gardens. The nongardening working class saw them as having abandoned their class for the false pride of property "ownership." The Bürgertum saw them as tasteless, crude, and pretentious imitators of themselves. For both sets of critics, the crucial issue was the property relations entailed by gardening.

Contemporary gardeners' feelings about property are varied. When asked if the feeling of possessing the house and garden is important to them, most of my conversation partners said that it is:

Right. That's correct. This is the property where I can say, "this belongs to me," or rather, "this belongs to us." Where I could say that I am on my own land and soil. (From the owner of a detached, single-family, summer house)[13]

That in any case! I always wondered why that question affected me in such an emotional way. When I bought my first property, it agitated me something awful.... Owning the house had never affected me as strongly as that first piece of land did. A piece of the earth belongs to [me]. Today, I don't feel it quite as much, but that first time was quite an experience, I must say. I could base it on the fact that my ancestors were always owners, but I don't really know if that's the cause. Maybe it is that people have or need such a relationship. (From the owner of a private rowhouse)[14]

I believe that. It looks as if it's the case with many people. Sometime in the 1960s some people looked for a parcel of their own or any land they could drive out to. But these people who built [summer cottages] practically in Burgenland or Lower Austria overdid it, I believe. We can enjoy the garden here day and night. When I come home at night and sit in the garden and drink a cold beer, like when its hot, or when its too hot in the house, then I sit out in the garden and can somehow say to myself, I feel myself, "I feel happy." (From a fifteen-year garden settlement resident)[15]

People with whom I spoke repeated these sentiments in the majority of interviews. Property roots one in both the soil and one's own personal history. It is the source of the happiness that comes from experiencing the combination of the house and garden. This language is typical of the Siedler view of landscape. For others, this feeling was not very important. They expressed their dissent in language like the following:

[Mr.:] No, the proper feeling is that one occupies the land. [Mrs.:] It's a little difficult to differentiate between these two German words. [Mr.:] It means that one is in charge of it, that it is exclusively available.... One can have property and still not have anything from it, when it is somewhere and someone else lives in it.[16]

This response transcends the notion of property as mere ownership and looks to the relationship between the land and the person as the true source of meaning. For this respondent, it was the custody of the land which the person held, not the rights to dispose of its use. This is still not as strong a notion of relation as the Pionier feeling that the land binds the community together, as in the following response:

[Mrs.:] No, it is not ours. It belongs to the cooperative. [Mr.:] I don't have that feeling. It isn't pride of ownership, but rather joy of use. . . . We are the users. . . . [Mrs.:] Understood in the broadest sense. . . . We are honest enough to admit that it doesn't belong to us. We are here only as renters and hold it in trust as well as we can. (From life-long residents of a garden settlement and children of Pioniere)[17]

Among the more recently recruited families to the cooperative garden settlement, there was more ambivalence about the loss of equity one suffers by living on land which one has no personal rights to dispose of, as reflected in this response:

No, I have a closer relationship to it than that [of property owner]. I have a close relationship to my wife too, but she is not my property. On the other hand, there is the formal legal history. The garden has its own life. I hope it also has a good relationship to me, or it would be like a house pet, a really well-trained property. Given our professions, and we thought this over beforehand, this form of "not private" ownership is actually a disadvantage. If we ever move, we have to leave everything that we have invested behind.[18]

The two phrases introduced above, *das kleine Glück* and *mein eigenes Stückchen Land*, now appear as starker categories in Viennese thought. The *little stroke of luck* refers to the joy of use, whereas *my own piece of land* expresses the feeling of ownership. As the last comment reveals, the proponents of the garden settlement movement have never completely resolved the tension between these attitudes. To what extent is the gardener humble custodian of the land as opposed to proud possessor of rights to use it? There are moral considerations implied by words such as *humble* and *proud*. Both attitudes see nature as essentially at the disposal of humans to use for their purposes. The custodial attitude socializes nature by incorporating it into the community. Nature becomes the means for the community to thrive. This is the more desirable moral stance among the Pioniere. The possessive attitude socializes nature by transforming it into a resource separate from the community. Nature becomes the means for the individual to realize certain goals. This is the more desirable view among Siedler.

Siedler demand a stronger feeling about property ownership than do Pioniere or Gärtner. All three require some legal relationship to the land to transform it into garden or home. These legal relationships did not exist before World War I. The story of their evolution coincides with the period of Social Democratic majority rule in the city and the implementation of measures favoring the satisfaction of working people's needs over the needs of the Bürgertum. Since property owners had controlled the discourse on landscape for at least three quarters of a century at this point, the gardens of refuge also indicate an appropriation of that discourse from below.

DISCOURSE ON GARDENS OF REFUGE

The form of the small garden is an assertion of self-determination in space. This antiestablishment attitude exposed the small gardener to charges of garish tastelessness. Instead, I view the gardens of refuge as a vernacular landscape in which the gardening community consciously wove together form, function, and content. The small gardeners arranged the space according to their own needs and tastes. Their problems only began to set in when they had to submit to the constraints of external agencies. One research team summarized the vernacular as follows:

> The small garden fascinates us in retrospect. The individual variety in color and form and the personal relationship to the construction stand in crass opposition to our urban apartments. It acknowledges that we could design it ourselves, did so very well, and now take joy in it. . . . The handiwork and building are naturally necessary. The Schrebergartner builds his self-directed construction not for the love of art. He builds and constructs to meet existing conditions. He executes his ideas out of the materials at hand. (Auböck, Köhler, and Mutensky 1972:57)[19]

The small garden was a canvas on which ordinary, often uneducated people could draw their ideas about the relationship between nature and culture and between people and their society. These were the last playgrounds for adults in which even discovering the rules of the game was an adventure itself (Sack 1972:17). It was a game of high stakes. Food for the family often hung in the balance.

It was precisely this insecurity about the conditions necessary to reproduce family life which separated the gardens of refuge from the gardens of reaction which preceded them. The small garden of reaction was a product of agro-romanticism; that is, the projection onto some rural world of utopian ideas that help to resolve contemporary urban problems.[20] When people associate the rural world with the only morally balanced world that existed in the past, the romanticism is reactionary, as was the case with the first Schrebergärten. When the romantic's utopian world is one that has never before existed, the romanticism is progressive, as in the gardens of refuge. These gardens were experiments in socially assisted self-help. The municipality would create the mechanisms to make the land and required building resources available at the lowest possible cost, often including some form of direct subsidy. The gardeners would then contribute significant amounts of time and effort to building the gardens or the garden settlements with their own hands. This provided the opportunity for working people—some of whom were educated and sophisticated about the communicative power of symbolic forms, and some of whom were not—to build gardens that reflected their worlds. The urban working class had come to consciousness in the two generations before World War I. The period of vigorous garden building started after that war and lasted through the early 1930s. In this short time, the gardens built by these Viennese broke all of the rules. Their existence was a breach in the landscape norm, throwing the symbolic forms of the other gardens in the city into unnatural relief. For showing these other gardens to be extraordinary and unnatural at the same time, the nongardening public anathematized the evolving forms in the gardens of refuge, judging them to be coarse and unworthy of serious reflection.

The basic layout of the garden of refuge is that of a farmer's garden. This layout has not changed for millennia. Within the bounds of the garden, usually marked by fences or hedges, the plants grow in beds that develop along straight lines. There is often a central path wide enough for a barrow. Narrower paths lead along the beds to the fence, permitting the gardener to cultivate the beds from two sides without entering them. Variations arise in the placement of the wider path. One common arrangement is to place parallel wide paths at the ends of the rows as well as in the middle, dividing the garden into two halves. Another is to put a water well or fruit tree in the very center of the garden, with the central feature often dividing the garden in four quarters arranged around it. Still another variation aligns the row beds diagonally within the halves or quarters. Each layout appears to use the maximum area required for cultivating specific plants, while reserving sufficient space for the gardener to move (Kunisch 1985:49–50). Migge saw these designs as essential to the urban gardeners as well:

The requirements of the modern garden are practicality, simplicity, and economy. There is no form that can accommodate all of these requirements better than the geometrical. . . . This architectonic design of gardens is for that reason especially necessary among [modern city dwellers] because it is so simple, because people can master its elements easily, and because it is by nature so thrifty. The architectonic alone makes possible some kind of solution in the widest sense to the fundamental problem of our age. I wish for architectonic gardens out of economic, out of social, and out of ethical grounds. (1913:65–66)

Whether the geometry of gardens inculcated the virtues of practicality, simplicity, and thrift among people who feared starvation, the rectilinear arrangement of narrow beds did make efficient use of the limited space. The gardens were lush and verdant at the height of the season. Vines grew everywhere. Only the straight lines of fences, the boards of the shacks, and the brown traces of footpaths reminded the observer that this was not ordinary farmland.

Another element in the evolving small garden aesthetic was the ambivalence of bürgerlich notions of the beautiful in landscape design. Literary discussions of this feature are hard to find, although the pursuit of beauty in gardens is a dominant theme in the contemporary discourse. Gröning found one detailed discussion in the works of the city gardener of Frankfurt just after World War I (1984:756). Writing on the contribution of the small gardens to the future of German gardening, the official wrote:

> Our people in all their social classes stand opposed to the [aesthetic] value and beauty of the garden. . . . It is therefore important that the feeling for the value of beauty in the garden should be supported above all else. We [professional gardeners] must show how beauty can be incorporated in every existing garden with the simplest of materials at the lowest cost. We must convince the people that garden beauty is something different from garden decoration or garden luxury. We must show that beauty can be achieved in even the simplest garden through its spatial development, through careful selection of its furnishings, through elimination of the ugly product of "string-line cultivation," and through cleanliness in its upkeep and unending care. This can be done without requiring more expenditure of money than the ordinary working of the garden would need. (Heicke 1918:68)

The plea came at a time when people were starving and had to devote every ounce of energy to living from day to day. Photographs of gardens in the Wasserwiese colony in the Prater in 1919 show almost no attention to Heicke's formulas for beauty. Instead, they reveal every intention of carrying string-line cultivation to its ultimate and fruitful end (Siller and Schneider 1920:113ff.). All of the features continued to gall the designers—the lack of a system in the choice of establishing the colonies, the undisciplined care for the garden, the building of shacks out of tin sheeting, the use of old bottles or wires to fence the plant beds and birch sticks for garden fences and gates (Lemmer 1927:3).

Professionals contributed as much advice as they could through garden magazines and "how-to" books. Drawings of model gardens were themselves works of art. In their book on Schrebergarten planning Siller and Schneider included drawings by Lebisch of models that would have looked completely out of place in a small garden colony.[21] The four-hundred-square meter model of a "simple" garden had a central axis baroque alley of rose trellises, symmetrical vegetable beds, a hut with a verandah, and geometrically shaped conifers around two sides. Another model of the same size, primarily for fruit cultivation, featured a garden of roses and annuals next to a verandah. In this model the rose trellis alley was on the side. A third model, also of four hundred square meters, included a manneristic terrace stepping down to the hut and vegetable garden level (1920:84–91).

All of these gardens followed the turn-of-the-century, functionalist prescription for dividing the garden space into the rose garden, the terrace, and the social lawn (Migge 1913:68–69). In his gardens of refuge, Lebisch substituted vegetable beds for the social lawn but retained the other two features. None of these models was relevant to the reason for the garden activity: the tastes of the individual gardeners or the size of the gardens. Siller and Schneider admitted early in the same chapter that one rarely found a garden that reached two hundred square meters (1920:81). Almost twenty years later, Pertl included under the title "The Correct Design of the Small Garden" the same normative design principles (1939:234–35). In Vienna, and I suspect in Germany as well, there was very little improvement in the working-class quality of life throughout this period. Pertl's designs were as inappropriate at the end of the period, at the start of World War II, as Heicke's were at the end of World War I.[22] These ideas about garden design would find their way into the small gardens only in the 1950s and 1960s, after the threat of economic instability, war, and starvation had lowered the level of insecurity for the working class.

SOCIAL PRODUCTION OF GARDENS OF REFUGE

The garden city ideal was an outgrowth of the paradigm of single-family homes which had begun with Ferstel and Eitelberger in the mid nineteenth century. The functionalist domination of the design schools coincided with the publication of Ebenezer Howard's book in 1898 and the arrival of the garden city movement in Germany. Proponents of this movement sought to build small gardens and houses together within the city.[23] The movement called for the best of both worlds, realized through the ideal of *Wohnen in Freien*, living in the open. By the time of Migge's book, proponents had already established the garden city as the ideal housing policy in Germany and Austria (1913:6). A garden was a secondary, value-preserving feature, as it had been in the cottage system. This changed with the famines during and after the war. When one had to grow food to survive, the garden became as important, if not more important, than the house.

The socialist alternative to the single-family detached home arose from the experience of the homeless themselves. Housing was not the only scarce resource during this period of industrialization; fuel was also difficult to find. Many people and factory workers would simply go into the hills surrounding the city and cut wood. The hills were nominally the possession of the emperor. The municipality succeeded in stopping the wood cutting for the making of charcoal and paper in the early 1870s, but protection of these forests from lumber poachers came only in 1905. By then, building materials and fuel needs had denuded most of the lower hills, and wild squatter settlements had sprung up on them. The settlement houses were simply one-room shacks of whatever material was handy. There were no city services, such as water or sewerage. However, almost every squatter shack had a kitchen garden to help the family provision itself. The first squatter settlement within the current city boundaries was on Rosenhügel and is believed to have begun in 1911 (Fischer 1971:62).

The Kleingarten movement was a movement in Lebensreform. It

saw nature as the primary means to living the good life: fresh foods, fresh air, and *Bewegung in der Natur*. The idea of living in the garden permanently was alien to this movement. Living permanently in the garden meant bringing the city with you. One did not live in Arcadia; one merely visited there. The Siedler movement took a different tack.

The two approaches of Gärtner and Siedler continue to influence the politics of Viennese landscape planning even today, when the issues are those of Siedler invading garden colonies that previously had not allowed heated houses and building units that are habitable all year. Siedler use gardens differently than Gärtner do. They tend to build more decorative and recreational gardens with little regard for utility and with little interest in the work ethic of small gardeners. Thus, in the colony, they appear to be different people. This sets the stage for some interesting conflicts, at both the local and the municipal level.

The garden settlement movement would never have happened if the housing policies of liberals and the Christian Socialists had succeeded. By the end of World War I, the housing problem was so bad that many employed people with good incomes simply could not find housing of any kind. The Siedler movement was one of three solutions to the housing problem instituted by the Social Democrats after the war. Unlike the other two options, municipal garden settlements (*Gemeindesiedlungen*) or the municipally owned apartment buildings (*Wohnanlage*), the cooperative garden settlements exemplified one of the highest achievements of sustained self-government and community participation.

Gemeindesiedlungen were quite similar in form to the cooperative garden settlements. Because their construction was financed completely by the city, the city retained control of the recruitment of families to be housed in the developments. Because of entrenched Christian Socialist personnel in the city housing office, these families tended to be Christian Socialist activists. In the color symbolism of the language of politics in Austria, these "black" garden settlements had no cooperative functions and relied entirely on city administrators for maintenance and services. The following settlements were Gemeindesiedlungen, with the number of units and the beginning date of their construction in parentheses: Schmelz (765, 1919), Weissenböckstrasse (128, 1923), Hermeswiese (95, 1923), Freihof (99, 1923), Laaer Strasse (307, 1927), Lockerwiese (643, 1928), Am Tivoli (404, 1928), and Spiegelgrund (311, 1931). These represent approximately half of the units of the total garden settlements built between 1919 and 1934 (Posch 1981).

The Wohnanlage was a municipally financed and built apartment house and represented the city's primary strategy for ending the housing crisis. Between 1919 and 1926, the city built 25,000 apartment units. Seventy-five percent of these were minimal housing, providing one large room, one small room, and a kitchen for a total occupation area of thirty-eight square meters. The remaining 25 percent of the apartments were built for larger families. They kept the same number of rooms but increased the occupation area to forty-eight square meters. In 1926, the Superbaublocks began to be built. By 1928, an additional 30,000 apartments became available with three different layouts: a studio of twenty-one square meters, a forty-square meter two-room apartment with balcony, and a three-room apartment of forty-nine or fifty-seven square meters. All of these included use of a space in the cellar equal to the size of the apartment. All of the apartments had separate entry foyers (Weihsmann 1985: 43–44). The occupation area of the rowhouses in the garden settlements ranged from forty to sixty square meters and included the use of gardens of from fifty to four hundred square meters, with an average garden size of nearly two hundred square meters (Novy and Förster 1985:155).

Christian Socialists were not the only group to seize on the possibilities of creating living colonies of people who shared the same political values. Anarchists and Fascists also developed their own settlements, often through a process of squatting and inner colonization. Opposition to these settlements existed on both political extremes. In 1920, the anarchistic settlement society "Neue Gesellschaft" leased forty hectares of land in Mariabrunn and began to build, in the image of Tolstoy and the German anarchists Gustav Lanauer and Heinrich Vogelers, the artist colony Worpswede as a leaderless socialist settlement. Anarchist settlements continued to spring up in the Wienerwald and the Lobau throughout the period. Reactionary parties became more intent on founding their own garden settlements as the political situation in Austria deteriorated in the late 1920s. On

May 26, 1927, a thousand men wearing green shirts and red ties occupied the Kaiserspitz in the upper Lobau and began to fell trees and burn underbrush. The Gemeinde, which earlier had roused wild settlers from the Au with police, finally relented and legalized the occupation, giving the Reichsbund's *Kolonien in der Heimat* 104 hectares of land in the Lobau. The settlers argued among themselves for a while, before sixty-one working-class families received between twelve and fourteen thousand square meters for vegetable gardens and small animal breeding. This signaled the city's retreat from the policy of no support for unplanned garden development. During the 1930s, reactionary control of the city council swung the policy in the opposite direction, and many families received small parcels to help support their families.[24]

There was a history to the garden city movement in Vienna even before the publication of Howard's book. In 1886, Max Steiner founded the Verein für Arbeiterhäuser, whose purpose was to transform the proletarian into a property owner so that he would feel a part of the commonwealth and would combat the effects of anarchist propaganda. These kinds of organizations were grounds enough for the Social Democratic Party to distrust the English garden city movement and its various manifestations before World War I (Marschalek 1985:10). Agreement among the various socialist parties on the garden city formula as the appropriate solution to the housing shortage, especially for working-class families, took a long time to forge and lasted for only a few years. The right-of-center socialist parties, such as the Deutsche Volkspartei and the Christian Socialists, represented the more alienated segments of the German-speaking Kleinbürgertum. In their party platforms they responded positively to the private use rights implied by the lifetime lease of the parcel and the decentralized, communal control of the individual settlements (Berchtold 1967:363–71). These parties saw the garden settlements as an opportunity for segregating foreign elements, especially Slavic immigrant workers and Jews. Social Democrats were initially skeptical of the private use rights issue. Rudolph Müller wrote the party's position on the issue in *Der Kampf*, in 1912:

> The private house brings difficult problems for the entire workers' movement that one cannot overlook. It undermines the consolidation of solidarity and the possibilities for effective [political] organization, and

partially reduces the awareness of class interest. The more workers become property owners and home owners, the more difficult it will be to conduct successful actions for better wages and better social policies. (1912:171)[25]

After the war, the population forgot this issue as they coped with starvation.[26] This fact helped change the party's policy toward the garden city movement in the years after World War I.

When Ebenezer Howard's vision of garden cities unleashed the wave of interest in these settlements, societies formed throughout Europe to carry out Howard's ideas. Heinrich Krebs, a Berlin businessman involved in the original London Garden City Society, brought Howard's ideas to Germany. The first German *Gartenstadt-verein* formed in Berlin in 1902 (Kampffmeyer 1911:5). Howard's ideas came to Vienna in 1907. Here his supporters organized the *Zentralstelle für Wohnungsreform in Österreich* (Posch 1981:30), an organization primarily responsible for sanitizing the garden city idea for the Social Democrats.

The Zentralstelle included well-placed architects and lawyers. It had five goals, each of which suggested the kind of economic and political problems Vienna faced in the prewar period. These goals included decentralizing the planning of city-financed building projects, supporting local over foreign investment in industry, land reform to permit more people to become property owners, building garden cities, and creating a legal basis for reaching these goals. Members of this organization included its founders, politician Rudolf Maresch and architect Julius Koch; city gardener Heinrich Goldemund; architects Karl Mayreder and Siegfried Sitte;[27] Maximilian Ermers, a student of the sociologist Max Weber and the art historians Wöfflin and Strygowski; Hans Kampffmeyer, the founding member of the German Garden City Society who had brought the movement to Vienna; Franz Klein, the originator of the Austrian Civil Law reform and a powerful legislator in the imperial parliament; Eugen Philippovich, a founder and leading economic theorist of the Social Democratic Party and member of the Austrian Fabian Society; and Gustav Scheu, another founder of the Social Democratic Party. Perhaps the most important member of this group was Richard Weiskirchner, a constitutional judge, member of the Christian Socialist Party, and Bürgermeister of the city of Vienna from 1912 to 1919. Never really a member of the group but certainly its most important architectural advisor was Adolph Loos, one of the most controversial visionary architects of the twentieth century. This politically well-connected group bridged the two wings of socialist politics. It included experienced, respected lawyers and politicians who were able to marshal the legal and economic power of the state to support and protect the movement. After the election of Weiskirchner in 1912, the Zentralstelle members influenced municipal planning and housing policy directly. However, the legal problems of establishing semiprivate, semicommunal housing projects within the city were so great that no projects were built during Weiskirchner's term in office (Posch 1981:32–36). By the end of the war, the creation of cooperative housing was possible but still very difficult.

After World War I, universal suffrage enfranchised the working class for the first time in Viennese history. The voters immediately installed a Social Democratic city council and mayor, who moved quickly to set up a dramatic housing initiative that included a commercial tax and an aggressive building program. Squatter settlements were converted into garden cities under the guidance of Gustav Scheu, a founding member of the Zentralstelle. In an article in the party magazine, he announced his policy. In the more densely built inner districts, the city would build five- and six-story apartment complexes (*Wohnanlage*), with a built density of no more than 45 percent. In the periphery of the city, where there was plenty of cheap land, the city would build cooperative garden cities featuring single-family rowhouses with gardens (1919:10).

The garden settlements administered themselves. The cooperative organization mediated the relationship between the individual leaseholder and the municipality. Those insurance companies that wanted to do business with the city would have to contribute free advice to these cooperatives to help them build safely. A building bureau hastened the planning, inspection, and approval of plans. Another Zentralstelle member, Max Ermers, became the first commissioner of this *Siedlungsamt*. Adolph Loos was the chief architect for the bureau. The bureau created a public corporation, the *Gemeinschaftlichen Siedlungs- und Baustoffanstalt*, or GESIBA, to contract for the delivery of tools and building materials at wholesale prices. The corporation then resold the materials to the cooperatives at cost. Members of the cooperative contributed the labor (ibid.:11–13).

Hans Kampffmeyer came to Vienna to head the settlement movement in 1919. On April 4, 1921, there was a huge march of the different garden settlements and colonies in the Ringstrasse. Eleven days later, the parliament created the *Bundes Wohn- und Siedlungsfond* of 1921 (BWSF), a trust fund established through a special commercial transaction tax. The trust fund would finance the building of high-quality housing throughout Austria. The plans of the Siedlungsamt benefited from the money available through this fund. Even though the Social Democrats dominated the Siedlungswesen, they opted for the older formula of building rental units, rather than ownership parcels. By 1928, the BWSF had built units in 8,654 apartments, but only 592 units in garden settlements. Between 1928 and 1932, the city built no fewer than thirty thousand apartments, but only 11 percent were one-family homes.

The first settlement erected under Scheu's program was Schmelz (1919–24), originally a wild squatter settlement built on the former military exercise grounds outside the outer defense wall of the city. Shacks were torn down, and under plans drawn up by Hugo Mayer, an architect working under Loos in the Siedlungsamt, the settlers constructed two-story rowhouses, each house containing between six and eight apartments. On each of four blocks, rowhouses were built around the edges of the block with the gardens in the middle: a garden plot for each apartment and a common in the center of the development. Communal buildings were placed on the east and west sides of the development, including a meeting hall and facilities for eight stores. Here we see the clearest definition of Austrian social realism: a design of such simple construction that the labor supplied by the inhabitants themselves was sufficient to build it. When funds from the housing fund became available in 1924, Mayer built two five-story apartment houses north of the settlement, housing more indicative of the kind Scheu had intended for the denser sections of the city. The garden had become communal, although it still was placed in the center of the block surrounded by the buildings. This complex also included the city's first free swimming pool for children (Weihsmann 1985:319).

On November 20, 1920, railroad workers, postal workers, and

FIGURE 26. *Streetscape of Rosenhügel in the 1930s. All of the houses were built by the residents.*

small tradesmen founded the Gemeinnütziger Siedlungs-Genossenschaft Altmannsdorf und Hetzendorf. One leader defended the socialist principles of Rosenhügel in an article in a party newspaper as follows: "A settlement is not a collection of single houses with a few ornamental gardens. Rather, it is a closed group of utility gardens with residential buildings near the cultural institutions of community house, consumer cooperative, playgrounds, nurseries, etc." (*Arbeiter-Zeitung* 1921:6). The statement indicates the extent of the shift in perspective among the Social Democrats. The community was a closed group instead of a cottage system where individuals used their houses as capital. The gardens were utilitarian and did not merely ornament the houses. The architecture included residential buildings and cultural institutions as an ensemble, instead of the isolation of the houses in a cottage district (Figure 26).

In his capacity as chief architect, Loos was busy devising new and inexpensive construction ideas, including prefabricated, single-wall construction, as seen in the Siedlung am Heuberg. Mayer also worked on a projected 129 rowhouse units, each with a garden on a hillside overlooking the city. However, even though the new construction techniques did save money and work time, the city only built eight units. Having the plan approved as part of the municipal building code took so long that Loos quit the Siedlungsamt in frustration and moved to the United States. About the same time, Scheu left as commissioner of settlements to resume his law practice, and Kampffmeyer was appointed in his place (Posch 1981:64; Weihsmann 1985:313). Kampffmeyer devoted his prodigious energies to consummating the legal basis for the communal organizations.

Within the administration, substantial opposition to the entire garden settlement project arose. This opposition was less political than bureaucratic. The new policies had created bureaus with wide-reaching powers that in many cases had previously been assigned to other offices. As soon as the new commissioners had to interact with these older offices, they met with stalling, mysterious losses of important documents, and nitpicking paperwork—bureaucratic sabotage that drained the resources and the patience of the activists. Outside the government, the massive increase in the number of units available for rent at very low prices undermined the rental market and alienated many small businessmen who had purchased apartment houses to increase they own standard of living and now viewed the socialist government and the Siedlungsamt as a threat to their way of life. This class would later provide the primary support for Austro-Fascism.

Kampffmeyer worked in this atmosphere for four years, leaving the Siedlungsamt in 1928, to be followed in the position by Max Fiebiger. Fiebiger was a party functionary and not a settlement expert and was the first commissioner in nine years who had not been a member of the old Zentralstelle. Under his weak leadership, the bureaucratic sabotage became more effective, and the power of the Siedlungsamt to shape municipal housing policy declined. The city council eventually phased it out of existence in 1931 with Fiebiger still in charge.

Within the architectural community, opposition to garden settlements began as early as 1911 with the publication of an essay by Otto Wagner in which he argued that modern humans demanded more efficient, more centralized housing than that available in the garden settlements. He proposed a system of *Superbaublocks* of apartments, separated from each other to provide light and air and lawn space

(1911:7). The designs were much like those in Le Corbusier's Radiant City drawings two decades later (1935). After the decline of the Siedlungsamt, architects and planners increasingly preferred to build multiunit apartment complexes, five to six stories high, replacing the densely built Wohnanlage of the 1919–26 building period.[28] These were the same housing types that Scheu envisioned for denser sections of the city. Mayer built the first in 1924 on the northern corner of the Schmelz parcel. Other architects had already built more than forty thousand units of Superbaublock construction in the inner districts since Superbaublocks could be built in compliance with the existing building code instead of the inevitable code variances of the garden cities. Superbaublock builders could contract for tools, materials, and labor as any ordinary builder would have. Garden cities required subsidized building material. Perhaps most important, Superbaublocks did not involve the creation of new legal entities, such as the communal organization of the garden settlements. Fewer approvals were necessary and therefore fewer administrative logjams to overcome. As a result, units became available more quickly. By 1926, it took five years to complete a large garden settlement such as Lockerwiese. Pressed by the rightist opposition to show faster results for its social programs, the Social Democrats endorsed Superbaublocks as the appropriate solution to the city's housing problems. Garden city planning ceased after Kampffmeyer left office.

The effect on the urban landscape of the shift to more Superbaublock construction stemmed the built density limits of the municipal zoning code. *Built density* refers to the percentage of the total area of a parcel which is covered by the finished construction; the lower the built density, the more open the cityscape. Every residential zone category has different limits, depending on the number of stories each zone permits. The built density of the Superbaublocks at under 50 percent was much lower than the 65 to 85 percent of existing complexes but did not approach the 18 to 20 percent built density of the garden settlements. The Superbaublocks presented a solid façade to the street; the open space was inside the complex. The first Superbaublocks looked just like commercial apartment complexes. As the administrative alternatives narrowed, architects sought new ways of combining the speed of Superbaublock approval with the aesthetic and social appeal of the garden settlements. They accomplished this by building on larger parcels, which permitted them to reduce the built density to percentages that approached those of the garden settlements.

The first of these low-density Superbaublocks was Karl Marx-Hof (1927–30), with a built density of 20 percent. Built on five parcels of land between a soccer stadium and a railroad station, the complex provided 1,382 apartment units, housing five to six thousand people. It included five large parks, four of which served as the interior courts for the surrounding buildings. The fifth park was a garden in the center of the complex which served as its "front door." This park was designed according to the German neo-romantic canon. It most closely resembled Siebeck's Rathauspark but with younger trees. Instead of the Gothic façade of the Rathaus as its backdrop, the three-story, rose-colored stucco face of the central building framed the back of the park. This was a solid, massive construction with five low arches, a line of apartment balconies, and five suspended statues, symbolizing the virtues of labor. It served as the propaganda vehicle for the entire project. People walking from the soccer stadium to the railroad station to return home had to walk right through the central park with its flags, statuary, and unstinting commitment to the betterment of working-class living standards. The four interior parks were designed under functionalist principles, with a border of shade trees sheltering banks of benches and the central lawn available as playground space. Also provided were kindergartens, central washing stations, twenty-five stores, doctors' and dentists' offices, a post office, public baths, a pub, and a bookstore.[29] The complex permitted the self-governing committees of the garden settlements to develop, and the building quickly acquired the nickname "Ringstrasse of the Proletarians."

One of the last garden settlements to be built was Lockerwiese (1928–32), designed by Karl Schartelmüller, an architect whom Kampffmeyer had brought into the Siedlungsamt to work with Mayer. The design of this project of 643 two-story, duplex houses was quite eclectic. It combined the map of an English garden city, like Letchworth, with the social realism of Schmelz and the representational face of the Karl Marx-Hof. Curving streets, a central alley of trees, and charming squares provided a picturesque, village atmosphere, which must have seemed somewhat anachronistic to the now highly class-conscious, industrial proletariat who moved into the rowhouses a few years before the outbreak of class war in the city.

Gardens of refuge viewed nature as a source of security, a safeguard against the dangers of metropolitan life. World War I and the economic disaster that followed made these dangers real to the most vulnerable group of people in the city, the working poor. In the bounty of nature, these people saw a way of ensuring a steady supply of food. Combined with housing that could be assembled in the garden, nature became a safe haven. Unlike the reactionary back-to-the-land movement of the previous generation, these families saw no moral salvation in nature itself. For them, natural systems became the means toward an expressly social goal: to forge a support community. Membership in this community depended on one's willingness to garden. These were soup-green communities, in which reciprocal exchanges of home-grown ingredients reinforced neighborly ties and kept up the channels of cooperation. The gardener was tied to nature in the same way that a craftsman was tied to his tools. Just as the tools permitted the craftsman to produce things, so nature permitted the families to produce the community and then reproduce daily and seasonally.

The small garden colonies and the garden settlements fulfilled an image of urban life which was very different from any that had preceded it. As self-conscious attempts to build community and urban housing at the same time, they were a serious departure from the bürgerlich model of building the housing first and letting the market determine the core values of people who ended up living together. The garden communities brought people together through their common feelings of jeopardy. These were people who first sought refuge from poor housing, starvation, and alienation and then built their communities cooperatively, taking collective responsibility for the quality of the roads, the common buildings, and each other's houses. Once in place, their common adaptation to the garden life reinforced and reproduced this spirit of cooperation, allowing it to influence all aspects of family life. Such neighborliness may have existed in the regional towns from which people claimed ancestry, but it had ceased to exist for those who had moved to the workers' districts of the city. In large part, cooperation did not exist in the bürgerlich cottage districts or the few, still intact, preindustrial neighborhoods of the central city.

The settlements were not utopias. They could not resolve every urban problem. They contained within them many of the intractable issues that postindustrial cities continue to confront: substance abuse, family violence, constant unemployment, and alienated youth. To their credit, the inhabitants worked on these problems tirelessly, forming chains of organizations which would provide focus and purpose for the residents in greatest danger. The Naturfreunde permitted working-class youth to participate in the liberating activities of the Wandervogel, but with a different political message—one that emphasized the traditional need of journeymen to survive on the road as they traveled from center to center seeking work (Wolschke-Bulmahn 1990:29). The image of nature was not that of a moral treasury waiting for humans to return, but rather that of an extension of the real world of the worker. It was a world that could be a refuge from the necessary but dangerous life of the manufacturing city. Left open, in spite of the constant debate that swirled around it, was the uncomfortable proximity between the bürgerlich value of pride in property ownership and the working-class value of the honest use of the land. Certainly theorists of working-class culture such as Otto Neurath envisioned that development. Neurath wrote: "The detached house [in the garden settlement] is like a brick in a building. . . . The apparent individualism will be overwhelmed by the settlement through the many cooperative features already evident in all of them" (1923: 24, 36). Refuge in the garden may have begun as *das kleine Glück*, but for many families it quickly became *unser eigenes Stückchen Land*.

The use of such gardens by families divided the year into two parts: the garden time and the winter. The garden phases involved complex alterations in people's housekeeping activities, their social relationships, their nutrition, their commuting patterns, and their physical activity. Garden time was marked by positive memories. Winter time was forgotten monotony. Even those who lived in garden settlements remembered their garden lives primarily in the summer phase.[30]

Designers automatically added garden fences; yet in photographs of the wild squatter settlements that preceded them, none was visible. Garden colonies built fences around their leased land to define it and to lessen the temptation for those with gardens on the edge of the parcel to expand into other territory. Fences also defined the boundary between allotments within the colony. Speaking of their fences, gardeners frequently described their role in reducing tension and potential conflict between neighbors. Gardeners could rely on the fence for some measure of security against theft, especially in the postwar periods. To avoid double fences, each gardener was responsible for building and maintaining only the fence on the right side of the garden. In this way, even the fence structures in the colony or settlement were communal. The boundary fence was itself a contradiction of the otherwise communal spirit of the settlements and colonies. Some Viennese who bought privately financed rowhouses beginning in the 1950s desired gardens without fences. The continuous backyards in which children could run free, like the continuous façade of the house wall, self-consciously invoked in conversation, were examples of a cooperative spirit among the neighbors. The backyards provided a different kind of garden, one in which the discourse on renewal replaced the discourse on refuge. In the gardens of refuge, the fences were necessary.

These gardens were linked to the plight of those Viennese who could not afford to lease land or who did not have the trade union connections necessary to become Pioniere in the garden settlement movement. These Viennese remained poorly housed until the Wohnanlage and the Superbaublock buildings provided opportunities for increasing the housing space, light, and ventilation of workers' apartments. They did not solve the provisioning problem, as the threat of starvation by being dependent on the ordinary urban market continued to haunt them.

Gardens of Renewal

The period immediately after the war was one of hardship and famine. Many of the gardens of refuge reappeared around the city as people struggled to keep themselves alive. The war had left the Viennese landscape in tatters. Almost every public park had suffered damage of some kind. Bombing had destroyed or burned old trees. The army had built huge, bomb-proof flak towers in the middle of eighteenth-century parkscapes in the Esterházy park and the Augarten. There were seven hundred bomb craters to fill, four hundred thousand cubic meters of rubbish from bombed buildings to cart away, and more than two million square meters of green space to be restored to their former beauty (*Der Aufbau* 1954:6). Within ten years, most of the damage had been repaired, at great cost to the city.

Capitalizing on the spirit of civic mindfulness which had united the citizenry around the project of restoring the cityscape to it prewar condition, the socialist-led municipal government embarked on an aggressive campaign to create more parks. The motto for the campaign was "More Green Space for Recreation, Sport, and Play." Vienna had entered a new phase in the development of its metropolitan culture, one that emphasized the rewards of labor rather than the process of labor. The word for recreation is *Erholung*, from the verb *erholen*, to restore, to make whole. The gardens of the second half of the twentieth century, whether public or private, would emphasize this act of making whole. A propaganda pamphlet from the city parks department expressed the new spirit as follows:

> Vienna was once famous far and wide for the beautiful gardens of the aristocrat and the Bürger. Unconstrained speculation and blindness destroyed these healthy structures and created a Vienna in which the flash point of ornamentation shrank from its former position of prominence. At the same time, too many monotonous, dusty, rocky, dense residential districts were built for the wide masses, and established an unnaturally formed environment: a sea of stone, without green, without flowers, without light, air or sun and therefore, also, without soul.
>
> This Vienna still exists today—It still stands and it decays.
>
> The New, the Natural, the Living is already sprouting up within this decay: New apartment buildings in the city, kindergartens, free swimming pools for children, public parks and open space. These lie ON A GREEN BED. They are no longer densely packed against one another, as in the Vienna of yesterday. They all include trees, shrubs, fields and gardens, parks and green space, water and the freedom of the landscape.
>
> This all connecting green of nature, which persistently breaks up the hard Viennese granite cobbles and asphalt, the green that the entire city can use, that serves the people, the children, the adults, the seniors, therefore the society as a whole, and heals the wounds of the old urban blight— That is "soziale Grün [social green]." (*Der Aufbau* 1954:21; emphasis in the original)

This strong reassertion of the modernist, pro-city project expressed a boundless confidence in the future of the metropolis. Although the idea of the city in the garden was prominent during the height of functionalist thinking at the turn of the century, the antimodern challenge in the ensuing years had cast doubt on the ability of the modernists to hold popular opinion on the issue. This program could be confident of its public support because of the experience of the postwar cleanup. The viability of Vienna as a vital community was established as people from different classes, ethnic origins, income levels, and educational backgrounds worked together to rebuild the city. The statement was also a strong repudiation of the reactionary landscape aesthetics that drove people to leave the city to find nature. In this program, the city would be integrated into nature. It would live on a bed of green and be nurtured by the healing power of nature. Finally, the program signaled the desire of the municipal government to pay attention to people's nonworking lives. It was no longer sufficient to house people in safe places. The residential districts had to become open, airy, and sunlit and provide satisfaction for the eye as well as for the body. They had to offer the opportunity for rejuvenation and recuperation from the stresses, both physical and spiritual, of the work experience. The principles of this program have dominated the discourse on landscape since the mid 1950s. All garden designers, whether functionalist, progressive, or reactionary, modified their design criteria to take notice of the program of *soziale Grün*.

In previous chapters, evidence of the continuing presence of verbal formulas that were generated by older discourses on landscape had to be extracted from conversation partners through statements that verged from the commonplace to the absurd. In the case of the discourse on renewal, most of the conversation partners offered explicit statements on the content of these garden ideas with little or no prompting. I had only to give them the opportunity to state why they garden at all to elicit fully formed and carefully thought-out statements. Clearly, this is a living discourse in which the actual gardeners are chief participants. The elements of the discourse are contained in the following quotes:

> It is a space for recreation. . . . When people live as we do, then it is a space for recreation. That means it must also always have the proper components. The care of the garden must always take second place. So, I would not work there unless it added to my leisure. If I don't have time, or lack the desire, then I don't have to do anything. So, the work must be enjoyable, or else one would just let it be. It cannot become some kind of duty. My close relationship with the garden is strong enough that I always do something. I would never do it just to have a garden that was more beautiful than my neighbor's. At that point, I leave it alone. That is no relationship. Nature is life. . . . There are people who get up to weed their lawns three hours earlier than they have to, so that when they come from work, the garden will look beautiful. I refuse to allow my garden to terrorize me that way. And I won't terrorize it either.[1]

> [Then] every activity outdoors is good. When one thinks how I am in the office every day, where I have become accustomed to sitting the whole

day, I would need a recreation or a sport to counterbalance it. And here I have both. I come home, leave everything in the house, and go into the garden. There I am a completely different person. I mean, not only that my body restores itself, but spiritually I feel restored as well.[2]

That's right, my garden is a recreational garden. Not because I lie on a lounge chair or in the garden itself, but rather because I can move about freely there. I can breathe in the garden. I can hear the birds in the morning. I can observe nature. I can attend to nature.[3]

Erholungsgärten, gardens of renewal, are those in which the owners garden voluntarily. The rewards of this work are personal—physical and spiritual—instead of economic. The physical reward is a restoration of the body's strength through compensatory activities (moving about instead of sitting still), through breathing fresh air, and through having the sunlight shining on the body. The spiritual reward is the contact with the plants and animals who live their lives alongside those of people. Birds singing, plants growing, fruit maturing, and seasons passing provide a contrasting rhythm of life which the gardener can juxtapose to that of wage work. The ability to participate in two totally different temporalities is liberating because it exposes the dominant temporality, the public schedule of urban life, diminishing its power to define people's experience in time. Urban gardeners are different from nongardening city folk in the same way that bilingual people are different from monolingual people: they have an alternative system of reference by which to measure and judge the events of their lives. For gardeners, the alternative system is the quietude, satisfaction, and challenge of the garden.

Until the late 1970s, the number of Viennese who could afford to live in self-standing houses remained very small. This number increased slightly, but the gardens of renewal were almost entirely identical in location, size, and organization to the gardens of refuge: parcels in garden settlements and garden colonies. People converted them from gardens of refuge when they felt that the emergency conditions of the war were safely behind them. Throughout the postwar period, parcels in garden colonies increased. Within the city limits, these were the greatest source of new gardens of renewal.

One of the developments in the Viennese housing market after

World War II was an increase in the number of families building summer cabins on land parcels, often located in agricultural regions some distance from Vienna. Unlike the leasehold restrictions of the municipal settlements and colonies within the city, these summer cabins permitted Viennese gardeners greater freedom in setting their own limits and represented the culmination of the Siedler movement. The landscape style remained that of the aesthetics of renewal. Those fortunate Viennese who possessed villas and cottages found that the small gardeners had caught up to them aesthetically, permitting a merging of the older, garden of pleasure forms with the new forms of the recreational gardens. The real distinguishing feature between these different styles of gardens today lies in who does the gardening. The gardens of those who design and work the garden themselves have more in common with each other, regardless of their class background, than they do with those gardens that are designed and tended by professionals. We located gardens of renewal through the active involvement of the gardeners as well as their formal properties.

The change in the plantings from edible to decorative species signaled the transition from gardens of refuge to gardens of renewal. For many conversation partners, the key difference between the gardens was the reintroduction of the lawn. This occurred between 1950 and 1960 among all of the gardeners with whom I spoke. Of the hundreds of gardens I observed, only that presented in Figure 25 in the preceding chapter remained a true garden of refuge in 1988. Planting a lawn had great symbolic value. It was the lawn that had occupied the middle of the ring beds in the mid nineteenth-century gardens of pleasure. Across this lawn, one could see the far end of the round path and view the full extent of the property. In the functionalist public parks of the turn of the century, it was the lawn that defined the space for free play. Finally, it was the lawn that provided the green bed for the villa. Migge, for example, included the "social lawn," along with the terrace and the rose garden, as the three essential rooms of the villa garden. The conversation about grass acknowledges these functional issues.

The Viennese distinguish between a *Rasen*, a grass lawn, and *Wiese*, a meadow. Of these, people consider the Rasen the most difficult to maintain and the most ornamental. The gardener and guest

FIGURE 27. *Lawn of a Viennese bungalow row. The original (1964) design did not have boundary shrubs between the adjacent yards, responding to the style of having open domestic landscapes. The shrub wall in the photo was planted only after the neighbors got a dog.*

look at the Rasen. Its soft homogeneous green color is a canvas that sets the variety of the flower blooms and the deeper greens of the hedges apart from the pastel stucco of the house itself. The Rasen is the appropriate ground for both the villa and the small house, whether detached or undetached (Figure 27). Establishing and maintaining a grass lawn requires much weeding and mowing. The more effort one puts in, the stronger the visual effect. One conversation partner who owned a small garden and self-standing house commented on the efforts of the next-door neighbor, whose lawn was almost flawless, as follows:

> He's crazy. His family cannot even walk on the lawn. They sit on the terrace and look at it. If they want to go to the flower bed in the back, they must stay on the walk he made out of small flat stones. He waters every morning by hand. He doesn't use a lawn mower, but lies down on his belly and cuts the grass with kitchen shears. There is never a dandelion, a mush-

room, or any other weed. In the autumn, he picks up any leaves that fall on this monstrosity three or four times a day. I couldn't live like that.[4]

In his defense, he might have responded in the fashion of another conversation partner, whose house garden was the authentic example of middle-class ornament which the first man was trying to imitate. The owner of the authentic ornamental garden said: "The garden is a sort of wallpaper for the terrace. It's a wall decoration for a room that has no walls." As a representation of class, the recreational garden works through sight rather than site.

The possibility that recreation can include the creation of such a highly ornamental garden was recognized by the people with whom I spoke. Many went to great lengths to distinguish between their meadows and the ornamental (*Zier*) lawns. The idea of the meadow is to create a garden space on which one could tread without damaging it. A meadow can tolerate a higher variety of grasses and still please the eye. Meadows are rugged. You can step all over them and they spring back like new.

The key value for both meadow and lawn gardeners is *Genuss*, enjoyability. The idea of Erholung includes the notion of enjoyability, as well as compensatory, voluntary activity. Gardens cease to be enjoyable when more work is required to keep them looking attractive than the owners can afford to spend, and when it ceases to be enjoyable, the garden also ceases to be recreational. One conversation partner developed a strong negative attitude toward her house garden. After a lifetime spent tending to it, she had become overwhelmed by it. The only reason she spent any time in her garden these days was to do necessary work. She admitted that she could no longer even look upon it without feeling as if she wanted to go away. She no longer enjoyed the garden and eventually leased it to a family that had rented the first floor of the house for their residence.

Another formal element that took on ideological weight was the placement of the building on the garden parcel. In the garden of refuge, the building was always on the edge of the parcel, usually in the southwest corner to minimize the number of hours per day which the garden would be in shadow and to provide shade for the gardener in the later afternoon. One of the first changes to occur with the transition to the garden of renewal was the repositioning of the building in the middle of the garden. In the case of garden settlements, the walk was redesigned as a freely curving path rather than a straight line from a central axis. Both of these redesigns made the same statement about the usefulness of the garden, as the following criticism in a newspaper made clear:

> The average well-off citizen of today has accepted the ideology of useless pleasure gardens, which was first offered by the aristocracy. Only the aristocracy, who regarded all meaningful work as an insult to one's honor, could come on the idea of spending money to build gardens and parks that produced nothing. First the established Bürgertum of the previous century supported this by imitating the feudal French palatial building style in a pruned-down scale and built villas like little Versailles in the middle of a useless little park, the so-called garden villa. In most of the contemporary Schrebergärten and single-family homes, the buildings stand in the middle of the property, rendering it useless, and not on the edge of the property, as was once far and wide the case. These are nothing more than kleinbürgerlich imitations of the großbürgerlich villas, which are themselves imitations of the feudal palace parks. (Marschalek 1985:10)[5]

This raises all of the cautions of Müller's argument against garden settlements from the turn of the century. Garden settlements were no longer built by the city, but the line of criticism still applied to the small garden colonies.

It is possible to view all recreational gardens as inescapably ornamental. The small size and the preciousness of a harvest produced with disinterested effort warrant caution in ascribing utility to the small vegetable beds and pair of fruit trees, as this dialogue reveals:

> [Mrs. 1:] What is use? If I want beans (and I don't want them anymore)? It's all child's play. Underuse would be a better word for it. You can't call it a utility garden in that sense. It has again become an ornamental garden, even if they eat their own beans and their own chives. It's all a game. [Mr.:] They cost ten times more than the best available. [Mrs. 2:] Beans do not a utility garden make. [Mrs. 1:] No, No, I have only a small garden. A small garden can only be an ornamental garden.[6]

The central idea here is justification for possessing a garden although the discourse of utility is no longer valid. The absurdity that the family survives through the garden's produce reduces the legitimacy of the claim that gardens are an appropriate object for the working class.

Erholung also connotes a homeopathic flavor in Viennese usage which does not translate directly into the English *recreation*. Gardens of renewal are salubrious places in which health can be restored. A traditional saying among Schrebergärtner goes, "If he hadn't gardened, who knows if he'd still be alive."[7] Schmidt described a banner that one gardener of his acquaintance had tied above the rose trellis gate to his garden. It read, "Every garden frees another hospital bed" (1975:223).[8] Testimony to the health benefits of gardening is often heard in conversations with gardeners. My respondents spoke of arthritic conditions, stress, and respiratory problems disappearing over the course of their lives in their gardens (Rotenberg 1993). Schmidt's respondents mentioned diabetes, heart disease, headaches, and ulcers. Relief from post-traumatic stress syndrome in veterans following World War II is also frequently discussed in this context. Gardeners are likely to be aware of herbal cures, and they will plant herbs specifically for their medicinal qualities. Gardeners even use the earth itself, in the form of a plaster, to relieve headaches and backaches, testifying that the earth immediately relieves the pain (Schmidt 1975:223–225).

School medicine in Vienna recognizes the efficacy of gardening as more than simple exercise. In an address to the 1972 International Congress of Allotment Gardeners held in Vienna, a professor of medicine, himself a gardener, addressed the congress on the subject:

> Today, a great deal of time, effort, and money are devoted to develop and popularize highly scientific methods that are the last word in relaxation technology for preventive health. Active and self-hypnosis, autogenous training, active relaxation therapy, medical yoga, and many other effective forms of psychotherapy belong here. Their importance in combating unhealthy dynamics is acknowledged today. In their many forms, they do nothing other than our beloved gardens can do. Any method that requires us to busy ourselves using continuous force and separates us from the cares of everyday life, even if with a lighter pressure, will be successful. As we [work in the garden], the daily cares fall away from us. The work has its own quiet rhythm of natural events that forces itself upon us. It is a rhythm that forbids excited haste. We learn to wait. We plug in to the quiet work and all-encompassing advance of the natural events. When it is done right—that is, without becoming exaggerated—the personal involvement in designing and experiencing a garden is the best psychotherapeutic technique that we can imagine. (Fellinger 1972; cited in Schmidt 1975: 226–27)[9]

This is the same observation, in twentieth-century language, as Schreber's *Bewegung in Natur*. The difference between Schreber and Fellinger lies in their views of the relation between people and nature. For Schreber, humans were natural objects alienated from their rightful world, which was an independent and self-governing system that would lead people to health if they could only immerse themselves in its processes. For Fellinger, humans created gardens that then took on their own rhythm, which acted like a set of checks on human excess, channeling movement into a pattern that maximized concentration and relaxation. The benefit came not from nature itself, but from working directly in a garden.

The association of gardening with health grew in importance after World War II, which is why I characterize the gardens as extraordinary places for renewal. Efforts to make the gardens clean and healthy places in which to exercise the body produced pockets of places which seem to erupt with salubrity and well-being. The atmosphere of a garden colony in June is one of steady, relaxed movement, the heady perfume of plant growth, and the humidity of cultivation. Where parks are shady and cool, garden colonies are bright and warm. They are very quiet. The leaves absorb sound so that only the noise of a not-so-distant highway disturbs the stillness. Sitting on their benches in the shade of their cabins, the gardeners eat a piece of fruit plucked from a nearby tree and survey their handiwork. The garden is no mere hobby that can be picked up and set down again, an amusement that can be fit into the fissures of urban life; it is a world that demands commitment and care, just as a newborn child would. The garden of renewal is a significant other in the gardener's life. It is a relationship into which the gardener enters freely, and from then on, it is a life-long association that changes the city dweller into a gardener to the same extent that it changes the land into a garden.

DISCOURSE ON GARDENS OF RENEWAL

After the garden owner has become convinced that the world is safe enough to abandon the garden of refuge, the problem of form returns. What is the best way to construct a garden to serve the recreational needs of the family? Answering this question requires imagining ways in which landscape can mediate between human leisure activities and nature. The discourse on renewal begins in the late

1940s. Short, "how-to" books by garden architects and garden magazines summarized completed projects for gardeners, and trade journals discussed the technical particulars for professional landscaping firms.[10] First articulated in the books by landscape architects which were intended primarily for other designers, the ideas began to appear subsequently in the trade journals of professional gardening firms and finally in popular garden magazines. With the growth of institutes for landscape design (originally in the agricultural schools and later in the architecture schools), textbooks written by landscape architects attempted to synthesize these stylistic trends. Although pedagogically sound in their codification of design principles and applications, these textbooks rarely broke new ground. The small volume summarizing completed projects still remains the primary means for communicating design ideas among colleagues.

The shift in the discourse emphasized garden form for the first time since the turn of the century. The designers of the time were aware of this. As landscape architect Allinger observed:

> The most widely found private gardens today include the utility garden of the garden colony, the small garden of the family rowhouse, and the roomy garden of the detached single-family house. . . . The more the garden changes from an economic holding to an idyll of psychological and aesthetic values, the more it is transformed from a vegetable and fruit garden to a domestic and flower garden—depending on the talent and actions of the owner—the more the questions of form and content move to the forefront. (1953:7)

Discussion of the appropriate form for the recreational garden began after the war. Rauch, a successful commercial gardener, was asked by a garden magazine to write a practical guide for redesigning small gardens after the food scarcity of the postwar years had passed. His book, *Der Ziergarten im Kleingarten*, the ornamental garden in the small garden, was the first explicit statement of the formal transformation of garden functions from utility to recreation. In the introduction, he explored the underlying change in attitudes:

> [The garden] should provide the owner with a place where he can recover from troubles and worries of everyday life in his free hours. It is quite understandable that people who spend eight hours a day in closed rooms, and often with difficult work, should want to see themselves in the free-

dom of nature. They search for a piece of land where they can happily attach themselves and begin to govern. They want to have their own garden to bring them closer to free nature, a garden whose care brings them joy. Seen in this light, the ornamental garden for the working person is no luxury, but a necessity for the relaxation of the nerves. (1950:2)

Rauch anticipated the importance of leisure culture in the 1950s and 1960s. He predicted correctly that people would buy automobiles, making it possible for more people to find gardens to cultivate. His gardens were small, incorporating vegetable beds as well as flower beds. His designs included specialized adaptations for every taste: kitchen gardens for passionate cooks, hobby gardens of exotic plants, and purely ornamental gardens of sumptuous color. The botanical variety he offered within the small area of the gardens gave his designs a Biedermeier quality. He was ultimately a functionalist and specified different rooms for different uses. This potpourri hardly constituted a coherent style; its value lay in the practical advice it provided the small gardener on how to select plants to fulfill the new purposes.

Rauch's book was about a half-decade ahead of its time. Many of the settlement gardeners with whom I spoke remembered converting their gardens from vegetable beds to lawns only in the mid to late 1950s. In the meantime, Rauch's recreational motifs were establishing themselves in the larger private gardens. There were more of these in Germany. The Viennese found that the strongest ideas shaping their landscape again originated in Germany. Seifert remained the most important germanophone landscape architect. Turning his attention from the landscaping of the Autobahn to the house gardens of Germany's new Bürgers, Seifert developed design ideas that were widely influential and quite similar to those he publicized in the 1920s. The differences lay in the greater size of the gardens and the greater financial resources of the patron.

Seifert's private gardens were characterized by a clear definition of rooms or subfunctions connected and integrated by a large open lawn. A shelf of natural growth shrubs linked the house to the garden. The house separated the intimate space of the garden from the driveway and the vegetable beds. Seifert's functional areas included a terrace, a lawn, a vegetable garden, and a highly ornamental entry area. In addition, he deployed specialized elements according to the needs of the owner: a swimming pool, children's garden, or a rose garden. The terrace area filled the same proportions as the house, and the plantings surrounding it were formal and strongly architectonic. According to the desires of the owners, the landscape could either open up onto the lawn area or be enclosed for privacy. The lawn area was undifferentiated and contained no walk. It helped frame the wider view of the landscape and contributed to the calm and quiet of the garden. Seifert included a utility area in all of his private designs. These were primarily mixed fruit orchards with gaps in the tree line to stimulate the growth of a meadow (*Wiese*, not *Rasen*). The vegetable beds played an important role in overall design; they were laid out in straight north to south lines and enclosed by flagstone walks. He added a work shed with running water and a compost pile to encourage the owner to keep the utility garden in good order. The driveway and entry area designs complemented the house and followed a planting and design schema separate from that of the rest of the garden. He preferred to have the smallest possible space between house and street and filled it with trees and shrubs. The specialized areas were always separated from the nearby terrace by shrub and bush walls and were laid out with strict architectonic symmetry. The plants included primarily native varieties, especially along the edges of the property. However, in small, well-defined areas, Seifert would employ non-native species to create the desired effects in color and leaf.

Seifert popularized many new design elements in this postwar period. He used wood frame arbors to create transparent rooms and low-rise brick and plaster walls to define functional areas and hide some plants from open view. Simple wood slat fences combined with climbing plants provided absolute privacy and created a uniform streetscape. He grouped trees together on the edges of the garden, especially in the southwest corner, and used topiary hedge walls throughout the garden rather than only along the outer walls. He cut the beds in regular geometric forms whenever they were associated with buildings or recreational use, such as around the swimming pool and the terrace. Other designers immediately picked up and used these elements (Schiegerl and Stiegler 1985:81–119).

The garden style that Seifert popularized shared many of the functional qualities of the gardens of Lichtwark and Migge, most importantly the differentiation of the garden into activity areas. However, Seifert departed from the earlier generation in several important ways. First, the earlier generation left the owner of the garden several options for using the rooms the architect created. Seifert's gardens removed this freedom from the owner and were more strongly ordered with organized designs. Although the functionalists used regular geometric forms exclusively, they employed a variety of them. Seifert reduced geometry to the rectangle, a form that dominated every aspect of the design. The functionalists identified a space for a utility garden. Seifert planted a limited variety of fruit trees and vegetable beds and then made it possible for the owner to continue tending them with minimal effort. These elements gave all of his gardens a rural farmstead atmosphere. His gardens always developed in a direction away from the house and never the other way around. In functionalist designs, the gardens developed in both directions.

One of the most significant departures from the functionalists was the reworking of the garden as part of the larger landscape. For Migge and Lichtwark, the garden ended at the property line. Like the eighteenth-century designers, Seifert incorporated the views of the surroundings into his designs, opening the garden to the countryside. To do this, he had to hide from the longer view of the landscape any non-native plants, which he had employed for color or leaf variety within a specific context. It was for this purpose that he used the low brick and plaster walls and internal hedge walls (ibid.:123–35).

Many of these design ideas and stylistic tropes echoed the reactionary landscape language of the prewar discourse. The ideas were acceptable to the postwar generation because they were submerged in a thoroughgoing functionalism. For patrons, the old ideas reflected their own landscape socialization as Wandervogel. No alternative view of nature presented itself after the war. Instead, Biologismus increased its legitimacy among educated Central Europeans through their acquaintance with the equilibrium systems model promulgated by von Bertalanffy in 1948.[11] For others, these design ideas appeared modern and orderly compared with the drab green of the wartime vegetable gardens. They resembled photographs of suburban landscapes being produced in North America during the period when North America was considered the most important source of design ideas.[12] For still others, these gardens presented an improvement over the narrowly conceived functionalism of the turn of the century. The most attractive idea was the incorporation of the surrounding countryside in a so-called open garden. Accomplishing this in a small urban garden surrounded by other houses and very little actual countryside was no easy trick.

The foremost proponent of open landscape gardening was Harbers, a landscape architect from Munich. In his 1952 book he wrote that the open landscape solved a number of problems faced by the designer in the postwar years: the owner's desire to experience the freedom of nature, the diminishing size of the house garden, and the need to increase the usable space of the living environment. He discovered this principle of design while walking in the mountain woods in Bavaria. Before him in a hollow of an Alpine meadow he saw a single spruce tree not unlike what one would see in a house garden. The tree was surrounded on both sides by wild forest:

> The landscape of the hollow impressed itself through the playing of the sun through the leaves, the change from dark to light, and through the ozone rich, cool, moist alpine air. The most important lesson here was that all of this could be accomplished in a small garden! The example suggested even more to me. The entire scene was surrounded by separate areas. Here around me was the personal space where the observer stood. There in front was the foreign space which the eye observed. The garden would play the role of the personal space while the foreign space would include the view of the surrounding landscape. (1952:20–21)

Harbers concluded that a careful choice of plants in a small space could be combined with an extraordinary view to produce a greater effect. The open garden should include native plants, as in nature itself, and not combinations of the native and foreign. Harbers never claimed to have discovered this principle by himself and included drawings from the 1905 garden exhibition at Düsseldorf in which Bauer had used it. For Harbers the importance of his experience in the mountains was that the open design could work in the small gardens that were the norm in cities. He noted that the position of the viewer to the scene could be manipulated through artificial elevations, such as the Aha, an eighteenth-century English landscape device in which the viewer did not notice a deep depression that separated his viewpoint from the scene, giving the scene a feeling of being farther away. Walls, fences, and the use of trees and shrubs to frame some views and block others were all artfully employed to give the small garden owner the best possible visual connection to the open landscape (Figure 28).

At the same time, some landscape architects were going in exactly

FIGURE 28. *Garden designed for Roland Weber, as seen from the bedroom, by Harbers. Described in his plans as a large enclosed garden, it gives the impression of being anything but.*

the opposite direction. Allinger, another important German architect in the 1930s and 1940s, continued to influence German garden architecture through the 1960s. Allinger championed a closed design because he felt that it most closely approximated the reasons why people had gardens: the possession of property.

> These garden types together with their variations have something in common, namely that they are enclosed all around with a fence or a hedge, and this signifies the enclosed personal property. The garden court shows the special importance of its position in front of the house by being enclosed by the highest section of garden wall or hedges. (1953:7)

There is a remarkable similarity between his solution to this problem and the pattern gardens of the late nineteenth century (Figure 29). Whether the design was for the common lawn area of a rowhouse complex, the small gardens of a garden city settlement, or the backyard of a free-standing house, the principles were the same: an open lawn surrounded by a wall of trees and bushes. The composition was

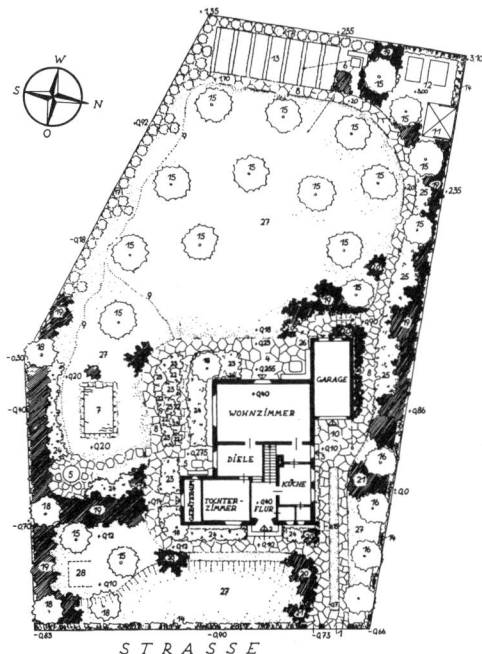

FIGURE 29. *Allinger's design for a house garden in the Ruhr district (1953). The design revives many of Migge's functional elements, including the social lawn, the terrace, and the rose garden. The lot size is 1,490 square meters.* 1, driveway; 2, main house entrance; 3, second house entrance; 4, garden terrace; 5, sitting area; 6, scenic viewpoint; 7, swimming pool; 8, flagstone walk; 9, foot path; 10, work area; 11, open shed; 12, compost; 13, vegetable garden; 14, hornbeam hedge; 15, fruit trees; 16, existing fruit trees; 17, berry bushes; 18, ornamental trees; 19, deciduous shrubs; 20, evergreen shrubs; 21, evergreen trees; 22, roses; 23, summer flowers; 24, flowering bushes; 25, wild bushes; 26, wooden benches; 27, lawn (Rasen); 28, sewerage tank; 29, hydrant.

clearly intended to frame and enclose the family or communal space. This Biedermeier attitude toward the world beyond the property line as frightening and destabilizing had more to do with the defeat of the forces of reaction and the great power confrontations of the Cold War than it did to any modern Metternich.

Allinger accepted the permanence of urban life. Little of the antiurban ideology that characterized his earlier work remained. He acknowledged that "the life and culture of the Volk are so intertwined with the essence of the city that in the future it will be helpful to solve the unhealthy features of urbanization with wholesome growth" (ibid.:16). Finally, he connected the form of these enclosed gardens to what he saw as the meaning of the garden for families:

> It is first a domestic garden in which the person is the center of all things. Second, it is a place of teaching and learning in which the plants become the central objects. And third, it is a garden of wishes in which the connection between people, plants, and architecture . . . finds its realization in its German Heimat. (ibid.:18)

The integration of the person with Heimat through landscape became a wish rather than a concrete goal that the architect could accomplish through design. The garden mediated the connection and replaced the Volk as the dominant symbolic operator in the postreactionary world. *Volk* was transformed into person, and *Boden*, soil, was transformed into garden. The teaching of the plants was the lesson of *Bodenständigkeit*, of nativism, domesticated and miniaturized for the private contemplation of the renewed and reconstructed Bürger.

From the rhetoric of the architects who promulgated these open and closed styles, it would appear that the recreational gardens of owners who still harbored antiurban sentiments would feature a closed design, whereas those of owners who were indifferent to the antiurban sensibility would favor an open one. The differences were not that simple. Local ordinances often required property line fences, even going so far as to stipulate which owners were responsible for which side of adjoining fences. Some gardens were so completely encircled by surrounding buildings in densely built districts that closed designs were the best solution for the garden, regardless of the cultural priorities of the owners. Finally, gardens built on the southern and western edges of the city could take better advantage of the landscape of the Wienerwald rising on its terrace above the property

MAP 7. *Small garden development through the twentieth century. All of the* shaded areas *indicate the locations of the existing small garden associations. Those areas that are enclosed in boundaries are chartered. Those that are unbounded are unchartered.*

than could gardens within the city or on the flat meadows and grain fields of the northern edge. Thus, the position of the garden in the local topography was often the real basis for choosing an open over a closed design. Why gardens came to occupy the particular place in the topography was more a matter of municipal politics than social ideology.

SOCIAL PRODUCTION OF GARDENS OF RENEWAL

In 1982, there were 34,213 parcels of small recreational gardens within 637 colonies, not including settlement gardens, gardens on federal property, and wild gardens, for a ratio of one garden for every twenty households. Sixty-six percent of these parcels belonged to colonies of less than thirty parcels (Magistratsabteilung 1983:293). The colonies dotted the cityscape in the outer districts, providing oases of green (Map 7).

People claimed 8 percent of these parcels as their main residence in 1984. Integrating these homes into the normal zoning and build-

TABLE 7
Changes in Ordinances concerning the Use of Small Gardens, 1928–1985

	1928 Kleingarten Ordinance	1936 Kleingarten Law	1959 Kleingarten Law	1978 Kleingarten Law	1985 Kleingarten Law
Parcel Size	Minimum width: 10 m	Minimum area: 500 m², exceptions permitted	250–350 m², exceptions up to 650 m²	250–400 m², exceptions up to 650 m²	250–400 m², exceptions up to 650 m²
Permissible Construction	In summer cabin areas: summer cabins and uninhabitable sheds.[a] In arbor-only areas: only uninhabitable sheds[b]	Summer cabins and uninhabitable sheds	Summer cabins and arbors	Small garden houses and outlying buildings	Small garden houses and arbors
Habitable Season	Summer cabins: April 15 to October 15	Summer cabins: April 15 to October 15	Summer cabins: April 15 to October 15	No specification	No specification
Built Density	In summer cabin areas: max. of 40 m². In arbor-only areas: max. of 15 m²	Max. of 10% of garden area, up to 50 m²	Summer cabins: max. of 25 m². Arbors: max. of 16 m²	Max. of 15% of garden area up to 35 m². Short-term use buildings: max. of 16 m²	Follows zoning code. Otherwise, max. of 15% of garden area up to 35 m². Short-term use buildings: max. of 16 m²
Clearance (Front/Side/Rear)	No specification	5 m/2 m/3–6 m	3–5 m/2 m/3 m	3 m to entry path; 2 m to side fence, 0 m to rear paths. Follows zoning code for nonconforming plans	2 m to entry path; 1 m to side fence. Follows zoning code for nonconforming plans

Width of Path	No specification	No specification	No specification	Main path: 4 m. Rear path: 2.5 m	Main path: 3 m
Permissible Roof Form	Saddle, tent, or flat	Saddle, tent, or flat	Saddle, tent, or flat	Saddle, tent, desk, or flat. Multiform or curving form not permitted	No formal limitations. Roof balconies not permitted
Permissible Building Height (Roof Edge/ Roof Ridge)	Summer cabins: 3 m/ 6.5 m. Uninhabitable sheds: 2.6 m/4.5 m	Summer cabins: 3 m/6.5 m. Uninhabitable sheds: 2.6 m/ 4.5 m	Summer cabins with saddle roofs: 3.5 m/5 m. Summer cabins with tent or desk roofs: 3 m/3.5 m. Arbors: 2.6 m/4.5 m	3.5 m/5 m, exceptions at the discretion of the colony	Small garden houses: 3.5 m/ 5 m (measured in the middle); exceptions at the discretion of the colony. Max. of 6.5 m for steep, Mansard, or curving roofs. Arbors[a]: 2.2 m/4.2 m, exceptions at the discretion of the colony
Toilet	Free-standing individual installations required for summer cabins. Group installation permitted in some circumstances	Required for summer cabins	Required for summer cabins and arbors	Required	Required
Chimney	Permitted	Permitted	Not permitted	Not permitted	Not permitted

Source: Weber et al. 1986:23.

[a]Summer huts refer to constructions with both walls and a roof but no foundation. The lease did not permit them to be winterized. Arbor-only areas were garden colonies whose leases specified that no constructions were permitted to have walls. This left the gardeners with the possibility of constructing lean-tos and arbors. The German word *Laube* refers to both leaves and arbors and is used by gardeners as a symbol for the garden.

[b]

ing codes of the city was the major impetus for revising the small garden law in that year. This was the latest in a series of postwar garden zoning law changes liberalizing the way in which the parcels could be used; those changes over a fifty-seven-year period are summarized in Table 7. These laws were never retroactive; they referred only to gardens that came into existence after the law went into effect and reflected the current concerns of the city council for the contemporary problems in the small garden colonies. In 1928, the municipal planners thought that parcel sizes were too narrow: the narrower the parcel size, the greater the number of gardens. Specifications for habitable season and cabin size displayed an anti-Siedler bias. Chimney and toilet requirements were public health measures, the former forestalling fires in the colder nights of the early spring and late autumn, and the latter guarding against cholera.

The council reversed itself in the new provisions in 1936, which reflected the strong Siedler constituency of the Christian Socialists who controlled the city council. The garden size was set at five hundred square meters, the largest minimum garden size requirement in the century. The new law increased the maximum built density, permitting larger cabins. Boundary clearances, specified for the first time, forced the buildings closer to the center of the garden.

After the war, the Social Democrats regained control of the city council. Gärtner sensibilities were restored temporarily, and the city retreated to smaller garden plots and smaller cabins. Chimneys were outlawed in an effort to reduce the temptation of people to use the cabins in the winter. By 1978, Siedler domination of small garden politics forced the removal of the habitable season provision, a slight increase in the garden and hut size, a provision to ensure that the main path was large enough for an automobile road, and greater flexibility in the height of huts. These last two provisions permitted people to park their cars in their gardens for the first time and to build second stories onto their huts, if the colony agreed. This was very important because the most common form of rezoning converted garden colonies from *Erholungsgebiet-Kleingarten*, a small garden recreation zone, to *Wohngebiet-Bauklasse II*, a residential district with a maximum height of ten meters (Langschwert 1987:129). These provisions would permit the colony to claim greater investment of city services if rezoning ever took place. The second story would provide additional living space, which is why the shape of the roof was specified carefully. The so-called *Pultdach*, or desk-shaped roof, provided enough ceiling height for the attic level to serve as a room.

In 1985, the provisions did not change very much in detail, but there was a recognition that gardens existed in a variety of different zones. This was especially true of built density requirements, which permitted committed Siedler to construct closer together than permitted in small garden recreation areas in anticipation of rezoning. What is remarkable about this progression was the almost complete invisibility of the Siedler movement in the political rhetoric of the city. Both of the dominant political parties supported a strong Gärtner position in their official programs.

> Garden colonies as green space and recreational areas have an active leisure function in the social and environmental-conscious urban planning. For that reason, existing small garden colonies should be retained as often as possible [from the Socialist Party of Austria (SPÖ) party platform in 1979]. Also the Austrian People's Party [ÖVP] supported the safekeeping of the gardens and "the immediate protection of all areas used as gardens." (Party platform of 1983; quoted in Weber, Feigelfeld, Auböck, and Lehner 1986:17)

Danger to the garden colonies came from two sources. Expanding municipal housing projects, roads, and industrial parks required their destruction; and the Siedler movement sought to convert them first to recreational gardens and then to residential areas. Both political parties emphasized the creation of new gardens; both agreed with the social value of a garden especially for poorer, larger, and poorly housed Viennese. With the passage of the 1985 law, only the ÖVP went so far as to support the establishment of a commission independent of the political process to oversee the application of stringent criteria for the allotment of new gardens to ensure that the neediest families got at least two thirds of them. For these families, reduced leasing costs and mortgage credits enabled them to meet the financial requirements. The city was then supposed to offer the final third as private property for development, ending the deception of residential development under the guise of Schrebergarten rhetoric (ibid.).

A feature of Viennese metropolitan knowledge which is not exclusive to that city is the belief that municipal benefits, such as garden parcels, are not distributed fairly according to uniform criteria: receiving such a popular and sought-after item as a garden settlement house or a garden colony parcel is reserved for the friends of bureaucrats and politicians or loyal party members. Those who want a garden believe that to have a garden is to have powerful friends. Although it is impossible to tell exactly how many Viennese want to have a garden, the waiting lists for the garden settlements and colonies are long enough to guarantee that the demand far exceeds the supply. This belief, whether true or not, influences who will persist in trying to get such an apartment and who will give up after a few years. The belief in special treatment itself has a history that is connected to gardens. In other cities, the belief in political patronage more typically concerns municipal jobs. The historical connection to patronage in gardens helps explain why it continues to persist.

In the early 1920s, the people who participated in the cooperative garden settlement movement were organized through the Siedlungsamt; they were trade union members and stalwart Social Democrats. At that time, the unionized workers would have included second-generation ethnics in high-skill trades or municipal services such as the railroad, post office, or city gas utility. On the other hand, those who benefited from the garden settlements that were managed by the Christian Socialist–controlled Wohnungsamt were primarily activists from that party. Their class background was either kleinbürgerlich or non-unionized craft work families with long-standing Viennese identities, such as shop owners, small workshop craftsmen, and teamsters. The Christian Socialists established the *Wohnungsamt*, or housing authority, during the Lueger mayoralty and staffed it almost entirely with functionaries from that party. Because they were protected civil servants, the staff members continued to perform their office after the radical reorientation in municipal politics following the Social Democratic landslide in 1919.[13] The Siedlungsamt, on the other hand, was created after the Social Democrats came to power and was staffed entirely by their appointees. When the German Nationalist coalition gained control, it also distributed gardens as rewards for loyalty, often evicting Social Democrats and Jews to increase the supply. Because the number of garden units involved was small and because family security was at stake, the parties used the dispersal of these units as highly valued rewards for loyalty. They also resisted any effort to routinize the selection process so as to protect their supply of patronage rewards. In this way, municipal politics operated no differently in principle in Vienna than it did in most other European and North American cities in the first half of the twentieth century. The differences lay in the type of reward which was most appropriate in Vienna.

These party rivalries were exacerbated by the excesses of World War II. Postwar reconstruction saw the outlawing of the National Socialists, the demise of the Christian Socialist Party for its support of Fascism, and the creation of the Austrian People's Party, a liberal democratic version of the Christian Socialists. However, the economic scarcity after the war ensured the importance of gardens as political rewards. Only after the citizens began to feel secure with their economy and their society in the late 1950s did the political importance of controlling who gets the gardens diminish. In the 1959, 1978, and 1984 revisions to the small garden law, the city made available many more parcels by offering open municipal land to leases by new colonies. This increase in supply was not accompanied by any particular political shift that might have justified the rewarding of party loyalty. Instead, it was a recognition that gardens were no longer so crucial to the security of families that party loyalists automatically viewed them as trophies. The reality of the garden life was one of long-term commitment, whether as Gärtner or as Siedler. Not all political activists viewed this commitment as either necessary or desirable.

Still, the demand for gardens outstripped the supply. When the city made available more than a thousand new parcels in 1985, they allotted all of them within three months. Within the garden settlements, the turnover in units as the second generation of Pioniere retired witnessed a landslide of interest from potential lessees, but this demand did not result in an escalation of lease costs. The initial cost for leasing a garden parcel of four hundred square meters in one of the new colonies was around 90,000 schillings ($7,500) in 1980, with a yearly rent of around 10,000 schillings ($833). Administrative limits promulgated by the city and the associations of small gardeners held these costs down. The median yearly income for a Viennese household in 1979 was approximately 200,000 schillings (Figure 30).[14] The garden price accounted for 90 percent of the discretionary income in the first year and 8 percent in subsequent years. The initial costs of a lease for a garden settlement house and garden were around 250,000 schillings ($20,833). Cooperative fees for renewing

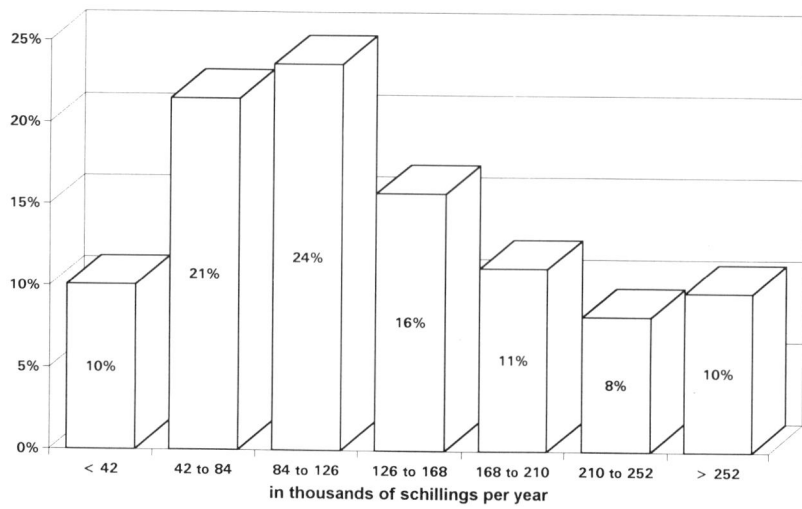

FIGURE 30. *Distribution of household incomes (1974). The bars show the percentage of Viennese households in each earning category.*
Magistratsabteilung 66:325.

the buildings could add another 100,000 schillings. If the previous resident demanded payment for improvements made on the interior of the house or the garden, between 100,000 and 500,000 could be added, depending on the extent and quality of the improvements. In total, it could cost 500,000 to 700,000 schillings ($41,666 to $58,333) for a three-bedroom rowhouse with an average-sized garden.

Compare these expenses with those incurred in buying a house. Inside the city limits, a square meter of land zoned for residential use cost on average 10,000 schillings. A lot size equivalent to the four hundred square meters in the garden colony example was 300,000 ($25,000) schillings. A prefabricated, two-bedroom house averaged 1,000,000 schillings ($83,333) to construct. Building a house, therefore, was more than twice the cost of leasing in a garden settlement (Figure 31), but the house would afford more living space, more control over the arrangement of that space, and fewer cooperative obligations to neighbors. Buying an existing house was prohibitively expensive for all but the highest earning entrepreneurs, managers, and professionals.

Today, there are many forms of housing in Vienna. What makes

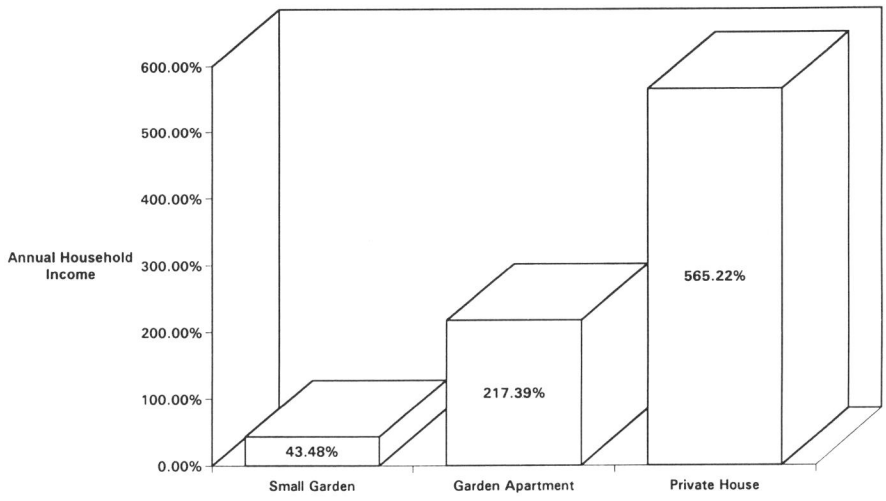

FIGURE 31. *Initial costs for alternate forms of gardens, as a percentage of total household income (1980).*

the garden life so attractive as a residential choice, even if only seasonally, is summed up in this quote from a respondent explaining his family's decision to buy a house.

> I had always had big problems or bad relations with neighbors in all the apartments I lived in. That seems logical, but it was always like that. In the municipal housing flats, you always hear the record player! Or "Stop [the racket] on the stairway!" In a house, no one experiences that as part of the area of life [*Lebensbereich*]. Here the street belongs to the area of life. I always say, "It isn't a street. There is no through traffic. It is actually the garage or the entry path to the house." The street is an intimate space, like the stairway of an apartment house.[15]

The freedom of having one's own area of life does not mean isolation from one's neighbors. The respondent discovered that the garden life dissolved the boundary between the private and public in an unexpected way:

> The social space extends beyond the house. The private sphere extends to the street. Behind the house, it is funny how the private sphere extends into the public. It happened to me that for the first, second, or third week, I always wore a shirt over my belly when I went out in bathing suits. I

stopped doing it when I got to know the bellies of my neighbors. Everyone knows everyone else's belly. One experiences a great deal of the private lives of one's neighbors. When the neighbors argue, you battle with them. And they know when you have argued with your wife. Well, that is already very interesting. First, because your private life is so public, and second because you are so aware of this outside pressure, or rather influence, that it has a very positive effect on the private life.[16]

This is the cost of the garden life. This respondent viewed the destruction of his privacy as a positive influence, even if it took him a while to get used to it. To be cooperative means to give in to the influence of others in your private life. There is a contraction in the portion of the area of life which is truly private and an increase in the portion that is experienced jointly with neighbors. Not all Viennese would feel comfortable in this environment. The problem for the leaders of the colonies and the settlements is to figure out who among all of the applicants for vacant parcels is most likely to adjust most successfully to the cooperative life.

Permission to lease a garden or garden house in a settlement appears to many Viennese today as a gift from heaven. People put themselves on waiting lists and then wait. It is impossible to determine how one's application is evaluated by the local committee, even after one is granted the lease:

We looked for a long time because we didn't want to live in a central district. We wanted to have a garden, if possible with a detached house. We searched hard for half a year and looked at many houses. It was a great stroke of luck that we got this one here. How we got it, I don't know. I've asked about, but no one has explained how the decision was made to give it to us. I can only guess. I was very persistent. I was always disturbing the committee. I had been on the waiting list for a while, but that doesn't mean anything. That is no guarantee that you get anything.[17]

From the point of view of the garden colony or the garden settlement, the problem is one of preserving the cooperative community that is at the heart of the garden life. This community has been under threat of privatization from Siedler families who are at the point in their house building activities to begin to lobby the city for rezoning. In both the colonies and the settlements, this involves the transformation of leaseholds into private property and the destruction of the legal basis for the cooperative community.

According to the chairs of five garden settlements, this threat is sufficiently dire that new families are recruited because of their commitment to the cooperative lifestyle. This commitment has to be demonstrated through previous activities and is not merely taken for granted from oaths or interviews. Young families are preferred to give children a chance to grow up in the cooperatives, ensuring that the next generation will understand and continue to support the values. Patronage has less and less to do with the selection process. Each settlement has a local committee that receives applications and makes selections whenever there is a vacancy. A list of three or four families in order of preference is sent to the cooperative management office, where the cooperative board reviews the applications and ratifies the list. The local committee's selections are usually ratified unless the board knows of an application from another settlement which is even more consistent with the sought-after families ranked on top of the local list. The local is informed if this is the case and given an opportunity to review the other application. The reprioritized list is then forwarded to the city Wohnungsamt, which currently must approve all applications for both city-managed and cooperatively managed housing on city-owned property. At this point, the opportunity for political meddling is greatest. It was the experience of all five chairs that political meddling in new family selections tapered off in the early 1970s and had not been a factor in recruitment during their terms in office.[18]

There was no public side to the social production of gardens of refuge. The gardens of reform discourse permitted the city again to design and build public landscapes for the use of all metropolitans. The pursuit of soziale Grün was seen as a reassertion by the city that the natural environment was an ordinary constituent of the cityscape and not its enemy. The zone between the city and the countryside should be a harmonious transition. The health of the sick, stonebound city could be improved only by opening it up and inserting nature in its very center. Toward this end, the municipality embarked on a green space development project involving the following ten points:

- Every standing viable green space will be kept, and a new tree will be planted for every tree that must be taken down.

- Isolated green space should be integrated into green networks to provide more recreational, play, and sport ground for tomorrow.

- Kindergartens, schools, and recreational centers cannot be erected without an appropriate area of green space.
- All new buildings will include accessible green space.
- The banks of open watercourses in the city will be landscaped.
- The Wald und Wiesengürtel will be enlarged and integrated into the green network of the city.
- Every traffic artery that can technically accommodate it will become a planted boulevard or parkway.
- Sport, play, and recreational areas will become an essential component of the structural planning of the city's development. The absolute and relative value of such areas will be considered equal to that of building lots.
- The wild settlements that developed in response to the food emergency and housing shortages will be incorporated into the city utility network and rehabilitated. Future city planning will take the desire of the people to live in green areas as the key element. The destruction of the landscape through speculation and divergent usage will be fought through better regional planning.
- To implement these basic considerations, the kind of legislative and financial policies must be developed which will support this activist development policy. (Anonymous 1954:11)

The idealism of this plan is so self-evident as to suggest a certain cynicism in those who drafted it. The plan was implemented in those areas that the municipality itself could control: green space in municipal buildings and other projects; the integration of at least some of the wild settlements; and landscaping the rivers, canals, and traffic arteries. In those areas in which the greenery program collided with private development, the developers managed to avoid any new restrictions. The financial and legislative policies did require developers to respond to the plan, which became the first in a series of green space programs occupying the efforts of planners but never overcoming the resistance of real estate interests in the city.

Politicians and developers have an easily discernible self-interest in sustaining the issue of more publicly accessible green space: it helps disguise the actual forces of urban development which disrupt the cityscape. This self-interest is apparent to Viennese critics when they take the time to consider the long-term impact of the city's most celebrated beautification projects. Here, for example, is an assessment by two of the city's landscape critics:

> In a time when the disutility of our cities has become a catchword, green space has become the symbol of an alternative life. This overloads, perhaps, even this symbol with all the desires that remain unfulfilled by modern existence. The struggle to save individual trees has from time to time been driven by a fervor that contradicts the real meaning of the thing. Political parties and newspapers arm themselves with the nebulous motto "More Green for Our City." All too often what happens is quite unrelated, or merely half-hearted. Propagandistic tree planting programs or planting ivy on walls often concerns creating excuses, and in doing so it preserves a naive green consciousness. What is being overlooked, or very wisely concealed, is the quasi-natural process of urban development. That is, the expansion of the concentration of buildings that is the greatest enemy of nature in the city. (Schediwy and Baltzarek 1982:1)

The kinds of planting least offensive to development interests are the modern equivalents of the old Schmuckanlage of the late nineteenth century. These included so-called *Grünkeile*, *Grünzüge*, and *Grünverbindungen*. Grünkeile are wedge-shaped continuations of green space which extend from the Wald und Wiesengürtel into the densely built-up districts of the city. Grünzüge are strips of more than one hundred meters breadth which contain green space devoted to different uses, including small garden colonies, playing fields, public swimming pools, parks, and cemeteries. Grünverbindungen are small, ten- to twenty-meter-wide green spaces, mostly foot or bicycle paths that are bordered by plantings. These may connect to larger green spaces, such as playgrounds, or even narrower ones, such as planted streets.

Planted streets are another category of postwar green space. City planners converted ordinary streets into *Wohnstrasse*—residential streets on which trees narrow the width of the street, decrease the number of parking spaces, and reduce the speed limit of automobiles to a crawl, all to make the street as inhospitable to through traffic as possible. Another category is the *Spielstrasse*, or play street. Here an ordinary street is closed off completely to traffic and converted into a campus between houses (Gälzer 1987a:3).

All of these are relatively cheap solutions to increasing the acreage of protected lands. In Grünkeile the city can simply zone the small valleys of streams leaving the Wienerwald as extensions of the preserve into the city and build around them. The meandering stream defines the shape of the leg and the boundaries of the development zone next to it. Grünzüge are also defined through a process of consciously linking already existing spaces as development takes place around them. The Grünverbindungen are most often the paths between settlements which have existed since World War I. Calling them by a special name and counting their area in the estimate of city space given over to green preservers are the first indications of interest the city has shown in them. To keep them up requires little more than a springtime sweep of debris and undergrowth.[19]

More important than the cost is the noninterference with development. The city is careful not to preserve for green space land that it may someday wish to develop. In the 1980s, small portions of the Wald und Wiesengürtel were rezoned as commercial and residential space. These were adjacent to areas that were already developed, and the people living in the immediate areas approved the removal of the special zoning. The move was not politically popular in the city generally, and the city council approved the rezoning with as little publicity as possible.

In 1986, the city council approved a *Grünlanddeklaration*, or declaration on green space, which in many ways echoed the principles of soziales Grün. The declaration included the following points:

> The long-range plan of urban development in Vienna sets the financial, organizational, and legal resources for green space and open space as a priority. The protection of the greenbelt and the creation of Grünkeile are matters of special concern.

> The existing green space in the densely built areas where green space is scarce are to be protected from environmental threats. The green resources in these areas will be improved through systematic planning of Grünzüge and Grünverbindungen. The purchase and clearing of sites to expand the availability of green space have a special priority.

> In the resolution of conflicts of interest, the preservation of green space has a higher priority than any other use. Existing green space is not to be treated as marginal land or areas of future development, but should be

understood as essential elements in the total regional planning for the future development of the city. Planning decisions with possible negative effects on existing green space, on the goals of the city development plan for green space, or on the zoning law as it applies to green space require special justification. (Magistratsabteilung 22 1986)

Making such a declaration is one thing. Living up to its requirements is another. Within a year of the declaration, memos circulated within the municipal planning departments outlining situations in which the declaration could be ignored.

One memo summarized the various concerns of the professional planners.[20] It was meant to circulate within the city planning offices and assumed a familiarity with the political and economic workings of the city government which is not generally known to the electorate. It might have been embarrassing to the politicians if it had been leaked. The memo revealed a reality that was very different from the motto "More Green Space for Recreation, Sport, and Play," and the writer revealed a sophisticated awareness of the forces that shape the city's production of green space and of the dominant discourse on gardens of renewal. It was an extensive document that I will now summarize.

It began by noting the failure of political will in establishing city-wide control over the planning of green space. Subsequent council discussions of the declaration after it was published affirmed that conflicts between the declaration and the council-approved development plans of the individual city districts were to be resolved in favor of the districts. This created twenty-three separate green space plans besides the one developed by the city planning office. The office with the greatest resources and expertise was assured the least clout to realize its work.

Emphasis on the extensions of the Wienerwald portion of the Wald und Wiesengürtel in the declaration ignored the ecological limitations of the field and meadow sections to the south and the east of the city, effectively closing those sections to further expansion. Other parts of the city's general development plan emphasized the siting of new industries and enterprises in the south, in a development known as Süden Wiens. The memo maintained that localization processes engendered by concentrating industry in a single region unnecessarily would put such pressure on land use that neighboring sections of the Wald und Wiesengürtel and its Grünkeile would be jeopardized. Plans to counterbalance the Süden Wiens enterprise zone with a zone in the northeast were not finished.

Political pressures from developers threatened the eastern meadows of the Wald und Wiesengürtel. In the past, the demarcation of areas as landscape protection preserves often covered up isolated places where development would entail costly extensions of city services. When enough political pressure to build was applied, the landscape protection restrictions were lifted without any fuss.

The memo also acknowledged the effects of Siedler interests in the garden colonies:

> Given the apparent building development in the new garden colonies, it is no longer possible to talk about use of green space. The intensity of the building activity is in many cases greater than in zoned residential districts. One must recognize that neither the revision of the small garden law with its potential differentiation of built areas nor the Kleingartenkonzept with its generalized goals and handbooklike suggestions for gardeners solves the problem of the overbuilding in green recreation zones. In hindsight, the ongoing discussions of a revised building code for areas labeled "Garden Settlements/Living in Green" only serve to further these developments.

These heavily overbuilt garden colonies threatened the function of the Grünkeile, which included garden colonies as a component. This was not the only threat mentioned in the memo. Since the building land neighboring the Wald und Wiesengürtel was among the most highly sought after and, therefore, the most expensive land in the city, considerable pressure could be exerted to reduce the Grünkeile in these districts to insignificant portions, helped by the ambiguous legal justifications for the Grünkeile. The memo cited the pressure for rezoning on the Alsrücken in Döbling as an example of the fate of other Grünkeile.

When the new small garden law sought to normalize the wild gardens that had existed for years within the Wald und Wiesengürtel, the idea was also put forward that park lands were the appropriate places to put new small garden colonies. Given the strength of the Siedler, any attempt to create more garden land without first creating land use restrictions and simultaneously making a massive investment in new residential zones would lead to unplanned settlement in the parklands.

Concerning the statement about the conflict of interests in preserving green space in densely built zones, the memo noted that the principle froze the existing green areas in place without ensuring that more space could be added later. Better planning practice would require a needs assessment followed by a series of short-term and long-term development strategies for fulfilling them. Complicating the issue was the division of the maintenance for green space between the municipal and the district budgets. Most districts would prefer to have new green space included in the Wald und Wiesengürtel because such areas are maintained through the city budget. Zoning the land as a parkland/recreational area requires the district to pay for the maintenance. Nothing in the declaration ensured that district budgets would be insulated against the rise in costs of future increases in the amount of green space. The densely built districts are the oldest, incur the greatest cost in infrastructural improvements, and have the lowest budget appropriations per inhabitant. This almost guarantees that district plans will systematically neutralize any efforts by the city level planners to increase the amount of recreational green space in the densely built districts.

Finally, the memo criticized the declaration because the goals outlined in it were never intended to be realized in the short run. They were to be interpreted as long-term goals and principles. The facts of metropolitan life are such that without specific provisions for instituting the desirable outcomes, none of the ecological and human benefits will ever be realized. The most telling of the missing specifics was the absence of any discussion of the declaration's effects on the city budget. Green space costs money to establish and maintain. It requires personnel and machinery, and the costs are incurred at the municipal and the district level.

Of the two ways in which gardens of renewal can be realized by the Viennese, private conversion of gardens of refuge or public provision of new garden parcels and parklands, political and economic practicalities foster the former and inhibit the latter. The effect is to legitimate further the drive for control of property. The values symbolized in the gardens of renewal fit the landscape requirements of people committed to improving their family's housing conditions by establishing a home in the garden: the rewards of labor, the making of the whole person, and the possibility of living in the city and in green surroundings at the same time.

This bears out the point that one professional planner insisted I take more seriously than any other in interpreting the Viennese landscape: that the Viennese have the gardens they do because of the houses they want to live in. The history of the evolution of the domestic garden in Vienna is the history of the dilemma of supplying sufficient amounts of adequate housing for an increasingly affluent and comfortable metropolitan population. If class consciousness was the prevailing dynamic in the organization of house and garden resources from the Enlightenment to World War II, the dynamic in the period after the war must be characterized as a metropolitan consciousness. Everyone faces the same constraints as they seek to improve their housing at any level: too many people able to buy are chasing too few properties. The countermovement supporting a return to cooperative living is narrowly focused and out of step with the individualism of the contemporary city. What was once a residential cityscape dotted with fruit trees, vegetable beds, broadleaf forests, and meadows is rapidly becoming a lawn dotted with swimming pools, carports, and evergreen bushes.

THE HETEROTOPIA OF RENEWAL

Gardens of renewal project two views of nature. The first sees nature as a set of constraints which affects human actions through the principle of progressive resistance. The harder one struggles to force nature into a certain mold, the greater the friction. Human involvement with nature is mechanical. It improves the physical strength and well-being of the body and the soul and restores one to wholeness and health by providing precisely those movements and rhythms that are missing in the other aspects of metropolitan life. The second view stresses the systemic quality of the relationship between people and nature. Unlike the gardens of reaction, the system is not autochthonous. It is a set of interrelationships that are knowable and manageable. There is no mystery to the workings of the system; the relations can be understood as open, connecting the domestic landscape to the wider botanical community, or as closed, permitting the intimate development of the garden house and family in isolation from others. In both views of nature, human participation is the defining element. Nature becomes important in human affairs only because of the use that people have for it.

Gardens of renewal fulfill a novel view of the possibilities of urban life. Instead of establishing a boundary between the urban and rural, the cultural and the natural, these gardens integrate nature within the constraints of metropolitan life. Architects employ formal devices first devised for parkscape gardens in early eighteenth-century England to create the illusion of expansiveness in the view from the garden. Even those gardens that are enclosed offer people the possibilities of engaging nature's strength through progressive resistance to human movement, shade and sun, and infinite visual variety in color and leaf. These gardens provide the means to realize the century-old vision of the reformist designers of establishing the city in the garden.

Gardens of renewal are symbols of health and vigor. Their beauty lies between the formal elements and the effort required to bring those formal elements to the apex of growth. The beauty of the gardens is an ornament to effort, rather than to status, power, or rank. To look at a beautiful garden is to see the commitment and diligence of the gardener. The gardener is in the garden, and the wise visitor always follows an exclamation of the garden's radiance with a compliment to the gardener's zeal. The well-kept garden is a direct reference to the well-kept body, to self-respect, and self-actualization. One cannot have a beautiful garden without an inner personal harmony. The beauty refers to the positive therapeutic outcomes when the gardener wrestles the garden into its most attractive state. The movements involved are so arduous that only after making the necessary adjustments within themselves can gardeners hope to be successful. Although few gardeners I spoke with could have defined the principles underlying Zen, they embodied those principles.

The symbolic valence of gardens of renewal is social as well as existential. The gardens speak a language of functionalism, both in the sense of use directed toward a goal (health) and use as a means in itself, as a tool with many applications. This message signals the extent to which the value of sound managerial oversight, so prized by the Bürgertum of the late nineteenth century, has diffused throughout the Viennese population. The values of the world of wage work now dictate how every form of work is judged. A gardener worthy of renown exerts control over the space, and he plants in the same fashion as the manager who controls the forces of production. Within this general value, the gardens of renewal permit a wide range of outcomes. Symbolically, the outcomes are described by the continuum of Rasen to Wiese, of lawn to meadow. The refinement and homogeneity of the green carpet become signs of the gardener's managerial style in this latest incarnation of the baroque parterre. The abstract fastidiousness of the lawn free of all variety and clipped to a uniform height tells a different story about its caretaker than the relaxed diversity of the backyard meadow. Both are prized in their purity, but hybrids expose the gardener to charges of neglect or laziness. Gardens become moral duties, responsibilities that once voluntarily taken on cannot later be evaded. The symbolism of the manager cuts both ways.

During this postwar era, a greater number of people than ever before have come to enjoy the weekend period of leisure. Standard work laws reduced the total number of hours per week from forty-eight to forty-five in 1960, then to forty in 1975, and ultimately to thirty-eight for some workers by 1978 (Rotenberg 1992b:68–72). Many Viennese, including many gardeners, chose to distribute those hours to maximize the largest continuous portion of free time possible. This led to a two-and-a-half-day weekend for many employees. The time in the garden became the alternative, complementary portion of the week to wage labor. Eventually it defined leisure for many Viennese, including those who did not own a garden. This not only increased the demand for garden parcels, it also drove nongardening Viennese to seek garden substitutes in summer cottages, wine gardens, hikes in the woods, and vacations to distant landscapes.

The garden time contrasted with work time by turning the organizational features of work into their opposite. Gardeners scheduled activities according to the life cycle of plants, whereas managers scheduled work activities according to the abstract requirements of a project or production process. At work, time was micromanaged and supervised by others. In the garden, effort was entirely discretionary and self-directed. At work, the boundaries between activity segments were defined by clock time. In the garden they were defined by the physical needs of the body for food, rest, and sleep, and the availability of daylight. The differences in time contributed to the idea of compensatory effort by permitting the gardener to produce a valuable object, the garden's beauty, on a rhythm imposed by the progressive resistance of nature to human effort.

Gardens are separated from the ordinary places around them in ways that reveal the contradictions of gardening in the city—the same contradictions that plagued the gardener designers throughout the century: how to resolve the formal distance between the urban life and the processes of nature. The open style in landscaping emphasizes the transparency of the family circle, a radical innovation for Viennese residential landscapes. Previously, the closed style dominated. Gardens of people who wished to advertise their wealth and status did so through the house façade, keeping the garden behind the house, surrounded by shrub walls and wooden fences. The open style is more common along Europe's northern Atlantic fringe, where various permutations of Calvinist worldview have employed uncurtained windows and open gardens as symbolic of the nothing-to-hide freedom from sin of pious families. For the Viennese, who have no feeling for these ideologies, the open style resonates with that other openness, the unclothed *Naturmensch* free to experience the larger processes of nature. The open style returns the family to antiurban romance, creating the illusion of living in the middle of divine nature. In its extreme form, where the family has the good fortune of the Wienerwald as a backdrop for their garden, the open style makes the city disappear entirely. Most open style gardens fall short of the ideal. Their owners are content with the more modest symbolism of living a neighborly life without fences and thereby being open to the commitments and potential conflicts that accompany the growth of a "natural" community. The closed style remains the more common form of gardens of renewal, even in the garden colonies. It emphasizes the values of domesticity, prefiguring a return to the privatism of Biedermeier. The threats in this case are political, involving the humiliation of the defeat of World War II, the need to protect the illusion of victimization at the hands of the Germans, and the East/West confrontation during the Cold War.[21] This new domesticity focuses on the physical well-being of the individual family members, enlisting everyone's participation in the care of the garden. Plants become the source of a shared family knowledge. Unlike the gardens of discovery, to be discussed in the next chapter, in which the lessons of nature are directed at changing people, the knowledge of plants defines the family's collective experience. Everyone remembers the planting of a specific tree or the day that the wild strawberry plant bloomed mysteriously in mid March. The garden links the family to the land, roots it in the soil, and thereby succeeds in creating the spiritual link between the people and the soil which is at the heart of the notion of Heimat. This variant of Heimat is impoverished insofar as the experiences are shared only within the family and rarely with the wider circle of neighbors. The garden of renewal remains a garden of wishes. The romantic realization of unity between human society and nature is accomplished in miniature, even as it continues to be denied in the larger social sphere.

The need to camouflage the realities of urban growth is even more critical in a metropolitan culture that has pretensions to egalitarian policies. It is the peculiar contradiction of Viennese municipal socialism that the appearance of movement toward greater equality in the distribution of resources, in this case green space, must take precedence over the real engine for metropolitan economic growth, the private real estate market. Without question, many Viennese who desire gardens cannot find or afford parcels that meet their needs. The more the city opens up districts to accommodate the needs of these garden seekers, the more the city is agreeing to build on formerly open land. The political parties use the desire for garden parcels as a basis for voter appeal through the programs described in this chapter. None of these programs can reach the stated goals because every move in the direction of public provision of green space, the only actions available to politicians, is a move away from the private production of green space. As the strength of the Siedler movement demonstrates, the private production more completely accommodates the felt needs of the population. The city is faced with a cultural crisis: it must either give over open lands to the insatiable appetite for private residential development or somehow stem the desire for gardens of renewal. The privatization of municipal lands is happening slowly but steadily, depleting the landscape along the way. With less open land available for public access, the future development of parklands and preserves, Grünzüge and Grünkeile, in the city is threatened. At some point, the area of green space per inhabitant will begin to decline. The next chapter outlines the countercultural movement to dislodge the ideologies that underlie the gardens of renewal and replace them with an ideology more conducive to holding green space as a public resource.

Gardens of Discovery

On any extended stay in Europe, one realizes how strong the differences are in the popularity of environmental concerns between Europeans and North Americans. The mass media run documentaries and features on the destruction of rain forests, acid rain, and air quality. Environmental crises on the Continent, such as the Chernobyl disaster, directly affect people's lives. People remember them as the turning points. Politicians incorporate environmental problems into their critiques of current policy and use ecological issues to attract voter allegiance. Although the Green Party exists, whose ideology seeks to redefine state policy around a safe and sustainable environment, no party's platform explicitly assigns the environment a higher priority than economic growth. To be centrist, a party must negotiate among more radical ways of constraining the economy to benefit the environment. This broad consensus on the sensitivity of the voters to environmental issues is known in German-speaking Europe as the *Öko-welle*, the ecology wave.

The Öko-welle is not a coherent ideology; it is a cluster of ideas, some new, some quite old, which raise people's awareness of their relationship to nature. Underlying all of the ideas is a hermeneutic of suspicion; that is, people do not believe that their currently held ideas about nature reflect the most balanced relationship possible. Ordinarily, this uncertainty would produce a period of disinterested experimentation in word and deed among society's experts, with ordinary people watching from the sidelines until a coherent perspective emerges. This is the case with the technology-intensive revolution occurring around the organization and control of information. Ecology consciousness emerges with a heightened feeling of urgency and alarm. People believe that the lives of their children, if not their own, hang in the balance. As a result, a low-intensity cultural crisis has arisen. People doubt the old ways of dealing with the environment, feel some urgency in discovering new ways of working with it, and are willing to experiment personally to discover the new path.

The variety of solutions is large. What they have in common is the view that once released from the constraints imposed by human agency, nature can restore its own balance. For this to occur, both states and families must become involved. At the state level, ecopolitics must prevail, which is why political parties try not to become ensnared publicly in the "ecology versus development" debate. At the family level, the actions include everything from recycling to eating more nutritious *Vollwert* foods. The wave shares much with the reactionary antimodernism of the first few decades of the present century. The emphasis on the need to restore balance, on nature as the only reliable model for a balanced life, and on the pursuit of systemic equilibrium is strong in both movements. There are also important differences. Turn-of-the-century reactionaries had the stark and dehumanizing second industrial wave as a focus, with conditions including abject poverty, rampant tuberculosis, antidemocratic political tensions, and environment degradation as a backdrop for their activities. Today in Austria the environmental effects of economic development are occurring in a period of general public health, affluence for the overwhelming majority of citizens, and a relatively high level of consensus on democratic solutions to political issues. The present situation produces greater clarity in which to envision the environmental issues and the relationship between economic well-being and their eventual solution. The more people become aware of the complex interrelationships between physical comfort and environmental quality, the more they alter the established measures.

The shapes of the discourse begin to emerge through these behaviors, but the process is ongoing. Unlike the previous uses of landscape, this discussion cannot provide a satisfying closure. What we hear in the current language is a testing of the waters, a furtive searching for agreement on which way to turn. Many of the features described in the earlier formations are not yet evident, which is not to say that there is no language for the gardens of discovery. If anything, there is too much language. What is lacking is a commitment to express the underlying meanings of this language in landscape, both publicly and in house gardens. Public landscapes serve as design models that are sensitive to the new consciousness. They are hybrid forms, essentially recreational gardens with the metaphors of discovery. Domestic gardens that employ the discourse on discovery in its fullest sense often evoke public distaste and even anger. This was the case with the Wildgarten described in Chapter 7. Green space is an important issue in the Öko-welle because it is a tangible sign of a healthy environment. The logical solution for ecologically sound gardens remains as difficult to realize in landscape as equitable and sustainable habitats are to achieve nationally.

I have named these gardens *discovery* because their view of nature is that of a system independent of human will, generating novelty and variety through its own processes. Such awesome power should persuade humans to stand out of nature's way and ultimately reincorporate with it. At present, we remain alienated from nature. Our actions work counter to the environment, obstructing and interfering with the autochthonous processes. Discovering nature's unfolding can reeducate people to nature's ways; only then can they stop destroying nature and themselves.

Nothing is new in the basic premises of this discourse. Francé sketched the outlines of this argument after World War I in *Law of the Forest*. Although his generation left the city to find the ideal environment in which to learn about nature, the current generation transforms their lives to discover nature within the city and within themselves. People who attempt to create gardens of discovery do so as part of an overall change in lifestyle. They begin by reorganizing their household schedules, which commonly involves commuting to work by bicycle. They favor homeopathic health systems including natural foods and a wellness-oriented lifestyle. I have also noticed that they structure their memory of the past with nuclear power plant accidents and similar man-made environmental disasters.

The most commonly expressed term for gardens of discovery is *Biogarten*, an organic garden. *Organic* in this case extends beyond growing vegetables without chemical fertilizers or pesticides, even though these are the first things Viennese gardeners mention when asked to define the term. Organic denotes a need to achieve a balance among plants so that the presence of some species benefits the growth of others. Animals of various kinds help check the growth of injurious pests. At this point, the gardener faces a serious design issue: human geometry itself in the laying out of beds becomes a barrier to the effective balance of the gardens, which are no longer properly Biogärten. They have become Wildgärten, whose form must revert to planned disorder. Only then is the promise of discovery possible, as this interview partner found:

> My garden contains only meadows. It is very handy. I am just drawn to the creative untidiness, the planned disorder. Anyway, it is important for my child to know that sometimes things grow which were never planted by people. No one knows where they came from. For example, I like to read the history of my garden, indeed the history of the entire settlement during the year. It is unbelievable the kinds of things that grow. In winter, you see nothing except a bizarre looking bush. Then suddenly in the spring, you see a rare Japanese plant that must have been growing for an eternity (because it grows so slowly), or a peculiar story. I am not the type who rips everything out and plants anew each year. I let everything come up, and then I select what I want. I prefer more weeds to fewer of them.[1]

These gardeners are drawn to the creative untidiness—a creativity living in the garden, not in them. It is important that their children learn the lesson of the garden, that things grow even when they are not sown by people. In other words, nature has its own secrets. These are revealed, or discovered, only when one is patient enough to let the garden express itself. Nature has a history paralleling that of people; but unlike people, nature never forgets its history. Nature produces choices for us to make, and if we select correctly our lives are enhanced.

To discover what nature has built into the garden the gardeners must possess a specific set of techniques and, more importantly, they must practice a discipline. The same interview partner described this as follows:

> If people live as we do, then the garden is a recreation space. That means it must have the components, and the care of the garden must take second place. I would not work there if it didn't bring me leisure. If I have no time or no desire, then I would do nothing. The work must be enjoyable, or it's better left alone. There must be no obligation in it. My close relationship to it is large enough that I return again and again. In the moment when I catch myself thinking about making it more beautiful than the neighbor's garden, I pull back my hand. That is no relationship. Nature is alive.[2]

The shifting boundary between the discourse on recreation and the discourse on discovery is apparent in these first statements. The relation of the gardener to the garden must be leisurely. It must not seem like an obligation, and it must never resemble work. The goal is not to create a thing of beauty, at least not as defined through comparison with the neighbors; rather, the key is *Verhältnis*, relationship, a term often associated with relations among people. For this gardener, the implication is the reciprocity he feels between his work in the garden and the garden's effect on him. If the garden were constantly being forced to higher and higher levels of performance it would impose an artificial standard on that exchange and break the balance. In the following, he explained what he meant by the idea that nature is alive:

> Well, it lives. There are earthworms, hedgehogs, butterflies, and plants of every form of being. There are cells that move. They can't speak, but they have consciousness. Therefore they are alive. And that has nothing to do with obligation. Everything must be voluntary. One must always have peace. There are so many small plants, which are so different. One must watch carefully before pulling something out. Even in mowing the meadow, you must watch out for the tiny mushrooms. You can't move quickly. I don't like this terror that comes from the illusion of making a garden beautiful. There are people who really get up three hours earlier to putter in the garden before coming to work and then putter around again when they get home. I will not be terrorized by my garden like that! I will not terrorize my garden in return.[3]

The living garden produces variety, which is what it gives back to the gardener. To receive the gift, the gardener must observe with patience and care. The gifts are both zoological and botanical. Terror not only negates the possibility of surprise, it also (in this gardener's mind) reduces enjoyment of the gift. The proper relationship between gardener and garden is filled with patience, anticipation, tender care, and respect. In the discourse on discovery, the will of the landscape is every bit as valuable as the will of the designer.

Half of the conversation partners said they tried to maintain a Biogarten, a practice hardly without controversy. The following remarks are typical of the futility some gardeners feel:

> No, [organic gardening] doesn't work. Now first, yesterday the trees were sprayed there. So, if this was an organic garden, I couldn't allow the spraying with poisons. In the spring when they spray, we have to cover the young lettuce plants, if we have them. Besides, I'm not sure I want a garden that is completely sterile. It isn't anyhow.

Others said such an attempt is futile since the world itself is polluted:

> I guess because I don't think very much of the whole movement. By my calculation organic materials no longer exist anywhere. I can do nothing about it. It doesn't matter if from today on I only use organic fertilizer or something else. If I use pure cow manure, the cow has already grazed in a chemically fertilized field. I think the whole organic gardening movement is just a big business with nothing behind it. By my estimate pure organic potatoes or organic cabbage cannot exist. And there is nothing one can do about it.

Fertilizing the garden and protecting its plants from parasites are paths for introducing artificial, and therefore harmful, elements into the garden system.

> Organic gardening is certainly important, but then there is the problem that the insect pests come anyway, especially if one is not experienced. And most gardens are so infested that whatever one puts out becomes full of lice. If I don't spray with chemicals, it only gets worse. Then I don't want to eat the produce. But I won't eat insect-infested stuff either.

These contradictions force the gardener either to abandon the organic program or to permit the creative chaos of a Wildgarten. The first option forces the gardener to renege on strongly held beliefs about the enhanced quality of life which results from living in a balanced environment. It implies a reduction in the overall well-being of the domestic environment. To permit a garden to de-

FIGURE 32. *Wildgarten*. This *Wildgarten* is appreciated for its lack of tidiness by this woman and her daughter and a friend. The four other families in their apartment building supported the woman's efforts to build the garden on the condition that it require very little effort on their part to maintain it. This approach was well suited to her taste for ecologically responsible gardening.

termine its own direction is so nonconforming that a gardener can expect to endure a high level of criticism for the decision. Since both solutions run counter to the contending landscape values, the solution most gardeners have worked out is to garden as organically as they can, accepting the futility of the effort, but refusing to give up entirely.

One partner refused to compromise (Figure 32). With the collaboration of four other families living in the apartment house, she cultivated a Wildgarten on an area of approximately 150 square meters on the side of the Biedermeier period house. Formerly the outside work area for a glass factory, the yard had been a recreational garden until the 1950s. By the time the current residents decided that they wanted to do something with the garden, it had become wild. The garden is full of trees of various ages, most of them saplings. A mixture of field plants collected during the gardeners' many hikes through the Wienerwald covers the ground. The atmosphere is cool and shady. When one is in the middle of the garden, it is impossible to see the house that looms a few meters away. Noises from traffic on the street filter in, but the street itself is invisible behind the garden fence. In the middle of the garden is a kidney-shaped plaster pool ringed with small stones. The pool is full of algae and a few water plants. This is the *Biotop*, the marsh element in the natural system.[4] Scattered among the trees are a few rickety chairs and a wooden table. One large tree has a few boards nailed to its limbs to form a tree house. There is no lawn to speak of, although the area next to the walk leading from the house door to the street gate has grass growing on one side. Around the street gate are a few rose plants.

The garden was designed without the help of professionals. There were no plans. A city hall initiative known as *Hofbegrünung-Förderungsaktion*, a program to support the planting of courtyards, provided funds to help the neighbors restore the garden. This program will provide up to 20,000 schillings ($1,670) toward the cost of planting the interior courtyard of residential buildings in the older districts of the city (Mathias 1985). In our conversation, this gardener explained how she and her neighbors came to accept this form of a garden:

> Yeah, [it's] something not completely tame. My idea of a garden has nothing to do with mowing the grass. I prefer something a bit more junglelike. This is more of an imitation of nature. . . . One neighbor wanted everything planned, the ground leveled, everything pulled out, grass planted, and all the trees cut down and new ones planted. Then lots of the others came saying, "No, we want nothing other than a wilderness here, in which everything can grow." The way the garden had developed enchanted us. . . . We wanted to leave everything a bit wild so we could sit in it. I'm not interested in technical gardening. I'm not a gardener. I like to work in the garden as long as it pleases me. But not when I must do something specific every day. The others feel the same way. So, the garden is half-wild. It looks quite pretty, but not all the time. Sure, we could do more. . . . If the five families gave five hundred schillings each, it would still not be enough to do anything with. Not so? . . . It doesn't disturb me when the branches hang down. It's all the same to me. We have said that we like to have grass, but not a Rasen. We prefer plants or different grasses or some such. We needn't have a tidy lawn free of all weeds.[5]

Her explanation for why the five families made the formal decision to leave the garden in its wild state involved several elements: the existing state was so enchanting that no one wanted to change it; any other kind of garden would have required more obligation than any family was willing to undertake; the amount of money they could raise was insufficient to make a real difference; and they had an explicit aesthetic preference for wilderness. Among the five families there seemed to be only one dissenter.

In spite of its small size, the garden contains a large variety of plants, including ten different varieties of perennials, six different species of fruit trees, grape vines on the fences, and five different flowering bushes. The grasses and leafy ground cover are highly varied. One of the apple trees and two of the plum trees had been so-called trellis trees—trees forced to grow along trellis lines to create a branch pattern that conforms to human geometry. The trees had long since become wild, but the effects of the earlier growth patterns are still apparent. The fruit trees are both a benefit and a problem, as the partner described:

> We benefit by letting the fallen fruit lie around. For example, many birds come and eat or pick at it. There is plenty of food for small animals there. And no one misses a few plums. We let them hang there and I think that's OK. Only lately we've had a plague of rats, and we had to spray with rat poison. Because of that we couldn't use much of the garden this summer. I was very sorry about that.[6]

The joy of seeing the animals who come and eat the fruit is a gift from the garden to the residents, who have to do very little to receive it. But the rats also eat the fruit and then become a nuisance, a problem so severe that they had to use poison and lost the use of the garden for an entire summer. The rat poison introduced toxins into the garden, just as the chemical insecticides and acid rain interfere with the efforts of the organic gardeners. Even the committed Wildgartner must endure the contradictions of gardening for balance in an unbalanced world.

DISCOURSE ON GARDENS OF DISCOVERY

The most influential Central European designers of gardens of discovery are Louis LeRoy (1978a) and Urs Schwarz (1980). Founders of the Ökogarten movement, they insist that nature is in danger of being lost completely. Effective gardening can rescue it. Their strategy is to have gardeners protect native species of plants in home gardens until the industrially damaged and unbalanced systems can be rejuvenated. LeRoy's writings have provided the mottoes of the movement, including "Just let the weeds grow!" (1978b; cited in Burckhardt 1981:264) and "In the garden, nature must be the master and the gardener the apprentice. The apprentice is merely a guest of the master. As a guest, he submits himself to the rules of the house" (1978a; cited in Spitzer 1981:271). Schwarz provides the principles of the movement as follows:

> the avoidance of poison and artificial fertilizers, the replanting of native plants and the construction of specifically threatened ecological communities. The house garden can be a refuge for threatened species. But it is not enough. An entire network of ecological gardens must be developed through the city. (Breitenmoser and Schwarz 1981:224)

Ecological gardeners argue that gardens are not natural: the variety of plants in the small space of the garden would not occur in nature. This assemblage is at war with nature, and this is the conflict that the ecological designers want to manage. The most difficult conversion from conventional to natural gardens, in their sense, is the disavowal of order. Using poisons and artificial fertilizers is only justifiable if one is trying to maintain order; and by disavowing it, the gardener gives up the need for introducing toxic materials in the garden. In time, native varieties of plants will reconquer the garden left to the creative disorder. The ecological program goes farther, asking gardeners to replant regional flora actively. One must understand the regional community by observing those spaces that are still intact. Primal forests, marshlands, meadows, alms, and deserted farms are repositories of the regionally appropriate plants, and protecting them from development is to keep them as a biological trust. In the future these plants will reproduce the balanced community.

The native species requirements described in this argument are different from those developed in the reactionary movement at the turn of the century. Schwarz discusses the issue as follows:

> By native, we mean regionally patriotic throughout. For an inhabitant of the Swiss piedmont, plants from the Alps or the Jura Mountains are no longer native, and a gardener in Cologne should not bring home plant materials from the North Sea coast or the slate mountains of the Rhine.

> This "narrow thinking" goes even further. Those who live in a glacial moraine should leave plants from nearby limestone hills where they are, even when the distance is only a few kilometers. There is good reason to do so: With the exception of certain universal species, plants do appear in different places by accident. This comes about through the combined special effects of climate, soil characteristics, sloop, and competition between different species. For this reason, one cannot stipulate a list here of appropriate plants for a nature garden. Every garden should look different from every other one as long as it fits with the local system. (Breitenmoser and Schwarz 1981:226)[7]

This passage differs from the older version of Bodenständigkeit in two ways. First, it sees the native variety as adapted to a regional system. The boundaries of this system depend on the physical characteristics of the environment and not the cultural characteristics of the people. A well-defined human community can settle astride two, three, or even four different botanical communities. Gardeners get into trouble when they see the boundaries of the human communities as identical to those of plants. Thus, there are no "German" plants that grow only in Germany. Even people living in the valley of a mountain system cannot assume that the plants growing at a higher altitude are appropriate species for their garden. The earlier understanding of Bodenständigkeit narrowly mapped the human community onto the plant world. Second, there are species that thrive in every environment. They are not under threat, and no special effort needs to be made to protect them. They, too, have a role to play in the nature garden. There are no trash plants or weeds. They balance and strengthen the narrowly adapted species when they grow together. This view of the relation between the native and the cosmopolitan went unobserved in the reactionary form of Bodenständigkeit.

To execute these principles in their entirety means that one must surrender design. Throughout the early 1980s, landscape architects struggled to find a role for themselves in the creation of nature gardens. Peter Wirth provided one of the most explicit statements of the direction taken by most of the Central European designers for private homes:

> The shapes of garden design always establish themselves as a result of contemporary views of life. Our requirements for the garden today are most probably [to fortify] the individual garden life and [to facilitate] con-

tact with living nature. The result should be a garden for daily use. . . . The finding of a convincing overall design for a garden that organically integrates everything and connects to the house with optimal usefulness is exhausting intellectual work. . . . It is always correct in garden planning to develop the small [landscape] from the larger one. The more one works for a simpler and more independent garden, the more difficult it is sometimes to find the way to the solution. (1984:11)[8]

Wirth's gardens appear to be less extreme than those called for by Schwarz. For Wirth, gardens are still essentially recreational, but he also has a desire to reach a balanced natural system. By emphasizing daily use, he reproduces the symbolic forms that often compel the recreational gardener to force greater formality upon the garden. He admits that the solutions to this problem require great effort; there is no specific design principle that satisfies every case. He invalidates the pursuit of the independent garden by declaring that embedding the small garden in a wider landscape, essentially breaking down the garden walls, is always the most effective design solution. One can hear the echoes of Harbers's open landscapes in this formulation.

Hans Schiller-Bütow has adapted environmental contexts for gardens in larger estates. For him, gardens are pure ornament. He makes no provision for use. Such designs must appeal to wealthier patrons who have accepted the importance of being environmentally correct. His gardens are playful and innovative but require the well-defined surroundings to work effectively. In his writing on landscape, he struggles against formalism to find a connection between usefulness and the beauty of nature:

> The purpose of the garden has become ornament. Gone is the inspired woman gardener in her straw hat in a dense garden strewn with flowers and fruit. The battle against weeds, that she always lost, has become a sign of pure purposefulness. . . . On the other side, a number of indices suggest that people seek alternative ways to live in a "healthier" world. Many abandon the city and go into the countryside. The life in the open has again become an adventure worthy of aspiration. The garden with its ancient responsibilities is an important device for achieving a new relationship to life in and according to nature. One of its original responsibilities was to collect cultigens [from the wild]. Use is not absolutely identical with edibility. Use also includes the joy that comes from working with plant materials in living green spaces, the encounter with nature, as well

as the harvesting of the plants. The real desire for nature projects from the self to the naturally useful garden. The next step is from a nature garden to an artificially designed garden [that abstracts the natural forms]. (1979:3)[9]

Schiller-Bütow accepts the garden as the device through which people come to an understanding and respect for the workings of nature. He supports the idea of building the garden from wild, native plants and redirects the emphasis to the end rather than the means, the latter of which predominated in recreational gardening. Unlike the security of the harvest which justified the gardens of refuge, his ends include working with plants and encountering nature. Theorists of the gardens of refuge also recognized this possibility. For them, the lessons to be learned from nature included plant and soil cultivation as well as an unspecified appreciation of nature's beauty. Discovery gardeners specifically rejected Pertl's and Heicke's aesthetics.

Schiller-Bütow is a professional designer who must sell designs to practice. Those able to patronize him participate in the discourse on discovery but reject the creative chaos of a Wildgarten. With this in mind, he has developed a design style that incorporates native plants in local soils and local topography to create artificial gardens that borrow from the landscape outside the garden through imitation and abstraction. He selects and amplifies for the garden the features that he observes in the natural landscape. He explains how he does this:

> The naturalism of the enclosing landscape is transplanted by the planner to the garden. There nature becomes an artificial landscape. The planner sees nature from his position and ascertains the main focus. . . . Every landscape has its special focus. It is this special quality, which the observer fixes on, which appeals to him, to always seek the place out again, which when it is named appears spontaneously to him as a picture. The structure of the surface of the land, the color of the materials, including the color and habitat of the plants belongs to it. (1979:5)[10]

The design develops from the landscape outside the garden through imitation and abstraction. Schiller-Bütow produces gardens that include mountain streams, deserts, glacial moraines, and marshlands, in each case replicating the essence of the original landscape with uncanny detail. The hand of the designer disappears. The limitations of this program lie in the location of the garden. One cannot create a desert, a moraine, or a marsh in a city. Only those who can afford to live in undeveloped regions can enjoy the artistry of Schiller-Bütow's designs.

Both Wirth and Schiller-Bütow struggle with the problem of design whose very success requires its disappearance. The last time the discourse on landscape attempted to hide the hand of the designer occurred in the eighteenth century, in the parkscapes of William Kent and Capability Brown. They, too, solved the problem by imbedding the smaller space in the larger one. As Horace Walpole put it, "[Kent] leaped the fence, and saw that all nature was a garden" (1798:536). For Kent and Brown, nature was an unspoiled region that had escaped human intervention and rationalization (Pugh 1988:136).[11] For Wirth and Schiller-Bütow, there is no pristine nature. There is the danger that retrieving the design of the larger environment within the smaller one will only reproduce imbalance.

This imbalance goes well beyond the condition of the environment. It is a critique of contemporary society symbolized through the degradation of nature. Nowhere is this critique more appropriate than in the domestic garden. According to critic Klaus Spitzer, there is a continuity of design from the baroque to the contemporary recreational gardens, and the outward sign of this continuity is the requirement of design, ranging from the specific imposition of geometric forms to the general compulsion to organize. The garden becomes the product of its creator. It demonstrates the triumph of the will of the individual, just as the baroque garden exhibited the overarching power of the absolutist nobility. Nature itself is lost in the process. The garden is not about nature. It is an optical illusion, a work of art employing natural materials. In this passage, which gives some hint to the passion and vehemence of the ecological gardeners, Spitzer explains how this habit to abstract nature for design purposes has undermined the sensory experience of real nature:

> Before the front door of the house, as well as throughout the urban environment, people have replaced the last remnant of nature with surrogates. Our dulled consciousness doesn't react anymore if valuable open lands are rigorously planned and desolated with cotoneaster, or if a few plants are set out on the street cobbles in ungainly concrete troughs like animals in a zoo. In the balcony boxes, plastic geraniums bloom. On our

streets, the leaves are coming out on the plastic trees. And deodorant sprays with forest scent replace the experience of real forests. While hybrid roses lose their scent, people have perfected the replacement: In the department stores, we sniff plastic flowers with embedded perfume. (1981:269)[12]

In Spitzer's view, we seem to have lost the capacity to differentiate between nature and its surrogates. For this reason, when we do encounter nature it shocks us.

This is nowhere more evident than in the definition and treatment of weeds. Weeds are uninvited guests, intruders upon the illusion of individual control in the garden. As "seeds of the devil," they symbolize nature's resistance to the gardener's will. They are polluting and must be pulled out. The tidy garden bed, the well-tended lawn, and the cared for shrubbery are monocultural cultivations. Their value to the gardener lies in their becoming healthy specimens of their kind. All competitors, all detractors from this uniformity are useless, dangerous, and repugnant. This is why LeRoy, Schwarz, and Spitzer place so much importance on letting the weeds grow. When a gardener can perceive a bed as full of nature's variety rather than full of weeds, it is a victory for the ecological consciousness.

In these initial decades, it is hard to discern who participates and who does not. Among the generation born after 1970, the consciousness of the environment is very high. The Green Party in Austria draws its strength from the youngest voters. Among the forty-five gardeners I interviewed, only the two people quoted in the introductory section reflected the kind of commitment to gardens of discovery which these theorists demand. One social scientist who has attempted to gauge the impact of the ecological movement on public aesthetics is Werner Nohl. In a series of studies conducted primarily in Munich, he surveyed visitors to public parks to understand what it is about the contemporary experience of landscape which people find meaningful (1974, 1977, 1979, 1980, 1982).[13] Of primary concern to him and to other critics in the latter half of the 1980s was the role of aesthetic considerations in the emerging discourse on ecological landscapes. Early in his research, Nohl established that aesthetic interests accounted for 21.8 percent of responses to a survey on why people use public parks compared with 19.3 percent for recreational interests and 17.4 percent for those seeking peace and quiet (1977:14).

The aesthetic component in his survey focused on two verbal formulas in the discourse on landscape: the delight in the paintedlike character of green space (*malerischen Charakter einer Grünlage geniessen*) and the enjoyment of the beauty of nature (*mich an der Schönheit der Natur erfreuen*). Both of these formulas have multiple resonances in the history of discourse. Both originated in the English parkscape tradition. Beauty of nature is enhanced further through association with color and variety in the Biedermeier and the reactionary yearnings for pristine landscapes at the turn of the century. The Reptonesque tradition that prevailed throughout the nineteenth century elaborated the painted character of beauty in landscape. To say that the aesthetic needs of the park visitors slightly outweigh their recreational needs and the need for quiet is the same as saying that people delight in the meaning of the parkscape to at least the same degree as they do the opportunities for movement and for resting. The message of the English parkscape continues to speak to metropolitans across the centuries.

Nohl relies on the psychology of perception research tradition to explore the aesthetic dimension of parkscape in more detail. He concludes that supporting the aesthetic needs of an urban population requires designers to install the highest degree of naturalism (*Natürlichkeit*) in the park while providing an ever-changing alternation in form between variety and novelty (ibid.:31). By *novelty*, he means the perceptual comparison that discovers a break between a current structure and some previous experience. This can either be in the form of a surprise, the discrepancy between the present and the past, or uncertainty or indecision between two or more possibilities which leads to the loss of a possibility (ibid.:10). By *variety*, he means building the landscape with plants that vary in growth patterns, color, and mass. Because one moves around in the park, novelty and variety can present themselves in a temporal sequence, permitting people to develop an interest in exploring the space and discovering pleasurable perceptions. At the same time, people have a need to feel secure in public space; they do not like to become lost. This requires that the exploring movements take place in an environment that permits a certain degree of openness with outlook points from which to survey the layout of the space. The layout itself should be simple (1979:638).

For Gälzer, the combination of exploratory and orientation behavior of park visitors requires contradictory design principles. Exploratory behavior demands variety and novelty, whereas orientation behavior is best served by certainty and openness. In design, it is almost impossible to be open and surprising at the same time (1987b:76). Thus, no single design would completely satisfy Nohl's aesthetic requirements. The scenic qualities of a parkscape are also dependent on the visitor's ability to receive and process the information the park designer has built into it. These will vary with the visitor's age, education, and experience with landscape, as well as with the time of day, the weather, and the visitor's visual acuity and imagination (Loidl 1981:9). All of these factors place the aesthetic qualities of the park squarely in the heads of the visitors rather than in the hands of the designers. For this reason, it should be possible for visitors to develop an aesthetic that is tolerant of the creative chaos called for by the ecological gardeners. The question that remains is how to achieve this aesthetic.

Nohl himself supplies one possible solution: the appropriation of space by visitors. The visitor identifies with well-designed spaces that are easily accessible. The description *our park* separates the merely public space and the markedly private space by providing a mediating middle ground: public space that one can appropriate for private purposes. In doing so, the visitor becomes invested in the design of the park as well as in its intended uses. The relation among design, experienced visually, and use, experienced through movement, is not a continuum. Gälzer argues that one does not attain quality in both design and function at the expense of each other. One arrives at them independently. In the appropriation of park space for personal goals, the initial attraction can be through design or use. Subsequently, the commitment to identify oneself with the space can take place simultaneously through a heightened appreciation of design and use. The key is self-involvement. Users of public gardens should be involved in the planning, building, and maintaining of their parks (Gälzer 1987b: 77–78). One historical example of the power of self-involvement in forging positive values toward the landscape is the Pionier movement in Vienna in the 1920s. A contemporary example is the movement to plant the courtyards and roofs of inner-city apartment buildings (see below)—principles that could apply to any design. Since the principles promulgated by the ecological school stand in such stark contrast to the values of the recreational gardeners, self-involvement appears to be the most effective way of proceeding with the revolutionary program.

SOCIAL PRODUCTION OF GARDENS OF DISCOVERY

The program of the ecological gardeners is a ticklish political problem. No political party wants to appear openly antienvironmental. On the other hand, the forces of capital are on the side of unfettered economic development. For this reason, the social production of gardens of discovery in the 1980s has continued cautiously. Since landscape planners are far ahead of most other metropolitans in accepting the principles of ecological gardening, the conflicts in the public support of these gardens have taken place between government offices. Not since the 1920s when Christian Democrats controlled the Settlements Bureau and Christian Socialists controlled the Housing Bureau has the municipal government been so divided in its approach to landscape policy. In the 1980s, the split was not between political parties, but between orientations of the politicians within the parties. The municipality had to appear to conduct its planning policies in ways that appealed to the environmental consciousness of the voters. It also had to avoid making planning decisions that would cripple the development potential of the edge of the city or devalue speculative investments that power interests had already made. The by-products of this conflict included the contradictions between the Green Declaration of the city council and the internal memo on planning priorities discussed in the previous chapter. This pattern of publicly expressing commitment to improving the city environment through the mechanism of ecological gardening and then working behind the scenes to protect the interest of economic developers is certainly not unique to Vienna or Austria. In spite of these political realities, the city has managed to produce some publicly financed projects that successfully combine the objectives of both the ecologists and the developers.

The general planning strategy for the city remains the same as that outlined in the Green Declaration. The metropolis will never become a natural ecosystem. The needs of large numbers of people, the urban ecosystem, will always overwhelm the slower moving compensations available through nature. It is possible to establish within the metropolis a gradient in which urban ecosystems shade off into natural ecosystems. In real space, the urban population is located in the centers of activity and the natural systems on the peripheries. Grünkeile that extend from the edges toward the center and Grünzüge that extend from the center toward the edges link the systems. Neither of these forms as currently constituted lends itself to ecological gardening principles. The Grünzüge tend to be tree-lined boulevards, *Wohnstrassen*, and similar splashes of tree plantings within the stone and stucco streetscape. The Grünkeile include small garden colonies, garden settlements, large parks, and playgrounds.

Neighbors tolerate ecological gardening within the colonies and settlements only when the gardener is highly attentive to its dangers to other gardens. People who allow their gardens to become completely wild have the gardens taken away from them. The *Gartenamt*, the municipal parks department, has the legal power to expropriate and expunge any garden on municipal land which has become a public nuisance. This situation occurs only rarely and usually when sickness or enfeeblement makes it impossible to maintain a garden. Such actions have been threatened for gardeners who take too radical an approach to the cultivation of nature's variety. The key to responsible ecological gardening within the colonies and settlements is the perception by neighbors that the garden is under the gardener's control. If that is the case, the colonies support diversity in gardening.

Although rare in comparison with the other elements, there are areas within the Grünkeile which do lend themselves to large-scale ecological gardening. Brooks, rivulets, and marsh areas lying on the borders of colonies and playgrounds could be improved by creative neglect. The most important areas of the city for demonstrating its commitment to ecological gardening are those within the Wald und Wiesengürtel. In the 1980s, the city established as *Biotope* five districts within the Wienerwald. These special preserves are not easily visited by hikers. To permit nature's order to replace that of humans, foresters have isolated the preserves for a time. How future generations of park visitors will enjoy these preserves has yet to be determined. One thing is certain: the areas are currently not in danger of getting in the way of economic development.

The second area within the Wald und Wiesengürtel to benefit from the application of ecological gardening ideas is the riverscape. Most of the economic functions of the Danube River lie either above or below the city itself or along the canal that links the river with the center of the city. The river divides the northern, less developed half of the city from the traditional centers of activity. In the postwar period, expansion of public transport facilities and increased availability of subsidized housing, commercial centers, and the United Nations center have increased both the population and the importance of the northern portion. Several bridges span the river to accommodate communication between the two halves of the city. The last phase of regulating the course of the river (1972–84) created a long sandbar in its center, which serves as a support for many of the bridges. In the 1980s, the city financed the development of the easternmost section of this sandbar and the northern riverbank it faces into three hundred hectares of recreational space. It is known as the *Donauinsel*, the Danube Island.

The landscape of this island emphasizes its terrain. Rising steeply from the water's edge, the island features an edge terrace and a central terrace. Asphalt paths that permit walking and bicycling run around the circumference of the island and in gentle curves that crisscross the central terrace. A similar pattern exists on the northern riverbank as well. The center of activity is the subway station, which is itself part of a large bridge structure. The station includes a kiosk and other public amenities and provides a height from which to survey the entire layout of the park. The plantings are all indigenous to the river. There are a few stands of trees, but most of the plantings are hearty native shrubs and ground cover. Grassy areas are mixed meadows. Other areas are left as sand outcroppings and dunes. On the northern bank, there is a restaurant complex and a boat rental facility. The park is especially attractive on warm sunny days. In the summer, the slopes of the terraces fill with sunbathers. Various groups hold festivals in the area, and it is the venue for big rock concerts. What is more important, the landscape is almost self-maintaining. Apart from tree care and the occasional sweep of debris from park users, the ecology of the river shapes the landscape. Some complain that the landscape is so natural that all one can do is walk in it. As in many other ecological gardens, people have a hard time seeing the Donauinsel as extraordinary.

A second initiative by the city concentrated on the centers of urban activity, rather than the edge. The city invested millions of schillings in efforts to convince residents of densely populated districts to plant gardens in their courtyards, backyards, and on their roofs. It was this program that enabled the woman and her neighbors to maintain their Wildgarten. The objective of this effort was to make use of greater amounts of city space for ecologically oriented gardening. Interior courtyards and roofs are an inseparable part of the city, yet planners have often ignored them as contributors to the landscape. By investing in these ordinary spaces, the city hoped to educate a greater number of residents to the responsibilities of landscape design, provide room for greater individual expression, and create the greatest impact on the Green Declaration with the least public financing (Hala, Karasz, and Kleedorfer 1988:2).

Participants merely had to register with the parks department, which then sent an advisor to evaluate the area and make suggestions. The apartment house occupants then met, discussed the suggestions, and decided how much they were willing to contribute in time and money to building and maintaining the garden. The city would provide up to 20,000 schillings ($1,667) for the delivery and setting of earth and plants. Roof gardens, arbors, sandboxes, and play equipment could not be bought or developed with city funds. The parks department could also offer to provide plants on its initiative and in many cases did so free of charge. Because of the involvement of the parks department, any spaces developed under this program came under the legal protection of municipal parklands (Mathias 1985:23).

After the program had been running for three years, the city financed a survey to see what had improved. The study noted that people had used the resources of the city in very inventive ways. The addresses of some examples of these efforts are in parentheses. People planted trees, vines, and shrubs along the alleyways leading to backyard buildings (Kirchengasse 28). Some fenced off an area and permitted it to grow wild, withdrawing the space from human use (Josefstädterstrasse 79). A less radical strategy was simply to permit overgrowth, especially of vines, to cool the southern exposure of a building (Stuckgasse 5). The simplest form of courtyard garden was a so-called pot-landscape, in which plants were set out in pots and troughs from spring through autumn. Watering the pots usually became the task of a single person (Skodagasse 21). Those lucky enough to have a fully enclosed eighteenth-century, two-story courtyard building could re-create the villagelike atmosphere of the preindustrial suburbs. These courtyards relied on one or two large trees and vines to provide collective space for several families of renters. The narrow intimate space created a feeling of intensive private use (Langegasse 29). In other courtyards, green living rooms were created, complete with outdoor furniture surrounded by a garden and potted plants (St. Ulrich's Platz 2). Some landlords divided courtyards into separate gardens, one for each apartment, a relic of a practice that seems to have begun in the eighteenth century. People rented the gardens separately from the apartment, but only apartment renters could do so (Burggasse 33). For some inner-city buildings the only possible solution was saving a single old tree in the backyard. Even here, the parks department helped to cut old branches and provided nutrients to the leeched soil (Langegasse 34). Sometimes only a flower box on a window sill was possible. Public and private office buildings took advantage of the program as well, adding potted trees and gardens to the views from their windows. Even though the city did not subsidize roof gardens, some top-floor renters constructed modest gardens consisting of a few potted plants and some chairs (Hala, Karasz, and Kleedorfer 1988:53–128). Although fewer people took advantage of the program than was hoped, it is ongoing today. The planners modified some aspects of the initial idea to make it more attractive to people with less time for gardening.

The issue of the roof gardens remains contentious. A city of roof gardens would be a spectacular sight. However, these gardens put an extra, unintended load on roofs, especially if they involve extensive building of plants and tree beds. Many property owners fear for the integrity of their buildings if the gardeners get too carried away. Nevertheless, a wave of penthouse building is currently sweeping the city, which may generate building techniques that would permit the city to invest greater resources in covering the roofs of buildings with plants.

It is frankly less satisfying to discuss the current conflicts in the use of public funds to support the new gardens of discovery than it was for movements with a few more decades of activity behind them. The issues seem far less clear-cut. The battle lines are less fixed. Everyone seems to be on both sides of the issue at one time or another. In witnessing the evolution of this moment in the unfolding discourse on landscape, we see new political alignments. Something is replacing the older, class- and party-based allegiances of the previous two hundred years. New interest groups are coming to consciousness. Their program is so revolutionary that sometimes it even frightens them. Should the ecological gardening movement ever come to power in Vienna, it will usher in the greatest wholesale redesign of urban space since the Ringstrasse. No one I know is expecting this to happen anytime soon.

THE HETEROTOPIA OF DISCOVERY

Ecological conceptions of nature create processes rather than products. Gardens of discovery do not involve making concrete plans. They unfold over time. The gardeners have no idea of what the product will look like; they simply react spontaneously and actively to the possibilities that nature presents. The garden building process is endless. It is a form of design which works dialectically with the changeability of nature itself. In these extraordinary places we discover the formal riches of a healthy native plant community. Such terms as *health, balance, stability*, and *sustainability* all point to a view of nature which is fundamentally antimodern, standing in stark contrast to the rapid shifts in orientation and taste which characterize contemporary cultures. In surrendering one's will to dominate and giving over to nature the management of the garden's form, the gardener must also sever the link between the garden and the market, the garden and architecture, and at least initially, the garden and the city.

Gardens of discovery dominate architecture. Roofs are covered with plants. Vines grow on the walls. If left to the will of nature, in time the building itself disappears under a cover of plants. The functions of the building remain, but the outward form that reflects the domination of humans over the material world slowly vanishes. Architecture becomes a mere human conceit, a ruin waiting to happen. The initiative of the Viennese city council to plant courtyards and walks and the efforts by some residents to plant roof gardens challenge the primacy of built form as the major component of the cityscape.

The implications of how gardens of discovery might change the lived experience of the city go even farther than these challenges to the social organization of space. Such gardens can undo the link between the producer of beauty in the garden and the consumer of that beauty. Everyone who uses a garden can contribute to its design, and every active designer is simultaneously a user. Each can realize a creative potential spontaneously and playfully, free from the dictates of a fixed plan. The creation of the work lies in the creativity of everyone who works on it. Such collaboration requires a different understanding of garden "ownership," one that denotes rights of use rather than rights of disposal.

In this way, the gardens of discovery project a radical image of what the city can become. Following the lead of nature calls into question all property relations as currently constituted. In particular, the idea of the property boundary becomes meaningless. Nature ignores such arbitrary lines on maps. Even more profoundly, these gardens confound the distinction between abstract and lived space. In a landscape that develops along ecological lines, all space is lived space. Any effort to create abstract boundaries, such as zones for use, assessed value, or public access versus private preserve, conflicts with boundlessness of the ecological garden.

Considering all of the symbolic mainstays of the discourse on landscape which the gardens of discovery reject, one might conclude that the ecological garden is devoid of human interest. Gone is the modification of nature through artificially imposed standards of formal beauty. Gone is the rule of geometry in determining the form of garden. Gone is the identification of the garden with the nongardening life of the owner, its value as a symbol of that person's character and social achievement. The symbolic valences that remain have the meditative qualities of both the deistic gardens of liberty, without the melancholia, and the mystical gardens of reaction, without the yearning for purity of essence. The meditation in the garden of discovery is one of partnership between human intellect and natural energy. Some have called it synergy and raised it to a spiritual practice, a unity between the human and universal. The efforts of the ecological gardener symbolize a willingness to engage nature first as an equal, but ultimately as the master of the garden, of the gardener's nongardening life, and of the urban community in which the gardener lives. The garden itself is the material form of the symbolic action.

The goal of ecological gardening is not the seen-from-above, bounded, and closed work that characterizes many of the other gardens discussed here. Rather, it is to permit the variety contained in a miniature unit (Biotop) to reflect fully the variety of the surroundings (Figure 33). The creative idea never becomes frozen; it remains malleable. No condition is static. Every design form is a transition

FIGURE 33. *Biotop. A Biotop is a wetlands system in minature. This master gardener constructed an extraordinary example of one in his backyard. The pool is home to plants, fish, and amphibians that are native to the Danube marshlands.*

stage in an ever-changing game that increases endlessly in time and space. Temporally, the gardener experiences the garden as a series of lineal steps leading from a pre-ecological condition to one of self-sustaining balance. Whether this end is ever reached is questionable. If it is reached, the linear progression of events ceases, and the garden enters a season cycle measured in geological rather than human time. History ends. Many things beyond gardeners' control would have to change before they achieve this balance. What is different about the temporality of this garden is that one feels an acceleration toward the goal of sustainability.

Boundaries drawn on a map have no relevance to the goals of ecological gardening, but they do have relevance to the politics of gardening, especially if one's neighbors are recreational gardeners, and to the experience of the garden. Ecological gardeners must appear to confine the verdant promiscuity of plant life to their own gardens.

Viewed from outside, ecological gardens are dirty. They contain weeds, plants that are out of place in recreational gardens. If the level of maintenance appears to fall below an acceptable level, the neighboring gardeners will not tolerate the wildness in their midst. For them, the boundaries between their own garden and the outlaw are vital lines of separation. The experience of the ecological garden involves multiple sensory stimulation. All gardens awaken the eyes, ears, and the nose of visitors. Gardens of discovery also reach the tactile organs. They are difficult to move around in. Everything is much closer together. There is no room to stand back from a plant and observe its individual qualities. Everything is on top of everything else. This jumble is precisely the desired effect. By combining touch with the other sensations in the garden, the visitor connects with the garden and becomes part of it. What one discovers is not a rare flower or a small animal among the plants, but rather the interdependence of the garden elements, including the humans. This feature alone would make the ecological gardens extraordinary places.

Nothing in these gardens removes the fundamental imbalances in human society which are symbolized there. The gardens are simply statements, like the slogans on the placards at a demonstration. There is no program to invest more gardens in the hands of people in return for a promise to cultivate them ecologically. Such a program would fail. It would fall into the same Gärtner versus Siedler trap as did the city's efforts to create more recreational gardens. The people who currently cultivate ecological gardens are those who have already benefited from the urban system. They alone have the freedom to reject it since they have already gained from its strengths. We can see at the level of this individual city the same arguments that fly back and forth between developed and underdeveloped states over international agreements on the environment. Just as a poor country with severe food shortages is unwilling to forgo cheap refrigeration in the hopes of slowing the deterioration of the upper atmosphere, a poor, propertyless Viennese sees the ecology movement as a bürgerlich ruse to change the rules of the game just as the welfare state has achieved a modicum of social parity among all metropolitans. As these families are a decade or so away from realizing their own garden, and through it a house of their own, the ecologists are undermining the priority of gardens as recreation which ensured continued political support for increasing the supply. One implication of the movement is that these gardenless families may have to content themselves with a city-financed window box instead of the all-important parcel of land. In this sense, gardens of discovery shut out the nongardener, mystify the role of gardening in metropolitan life, and conceal the social contradictions in the politics of gardens.

CONCLUSION

Landscape

and

Metropolitan Knowledge

What the Viennese know about their landscape—and what we non-Viennese can only wait to discover in our own metropolises—is that urban space is filled with ideological messages. Each of these gardens justified its model of the relations of dominant and subordinate power groups through a legitimating concept of nature. Contemporary landscape echoes fragments of meaning from even the oldest among them. The period of absolutist ascendance produced gardens extolling the glories of the aristocratic state, evoking an image of the security and harmony that only could emerge out of imposed order. The period of the Enlightenment produced gardens in which nature was allowed to develop in whichever way it saw fit. Today, too, these gardens call forth unrestrained speech, movement, and thought.

These two extremes remained the wellspring for symbolic elaboration throughout the next two hundred years. Order or chaos, as geometry or natural growth, came to symbolize groups struggling to define their identity in the political landscape. The Biedermeier view of nature emerged from the perceived threat to the family from outside forces. Placing the house between the gardens and street still produces a feeling of seclusion. Instead of offering a meditation of

The cultural categories we live can become vehicles of comprehension not mystification only insofar as we remember just how human and fragile, how recent and porous they have been and continue to be.
Lawrence Levine, 1988

power that remained beyond the human capacity, the designers of the neo-romantic landscape turned nature into a contemplation of emptiness and helplessness, reassuring people even today that the powerful forces have been domesticated. The reform era sponsored an ideology that established nature as a commodity for people to consume with their eyes and ears and with the movements of their bodies. Nature as a resource to be used, as an opportunity for growth, and as a common inheritance of all who claimed native attachment to a place remain the dominant views among most Viennese today.

The dialectic between order and chaos became even more complex in the twentieth century. A significant portion of the young, bürgerlich Viennese population sought a return to a simpler life in the first decades of this century. To represent this life, they evoked landscapes that society could not construct but which had to be discovered somewhere outside the city. This is a very real concern for all those Viennese, and there are many of them, who tramp through the Wienerwald every weekend and in every season. The first era of democratic socialism viewed nature as a source of security, a safeguard against the dangers of metropolitan life. Among the garden settlements and small garden colonies today, nature and community are inextricably intertwined. The view of nature in the postwar era stressed the interrelationships between people and nature which are knowable and manageable. The systemic relations can be understood as open, connecting the domestic landscape to the wider botanical community, or as closed, permitting the intimate development of the garden house and family in isolation from others. Nature becomes important in human affairs only because of the use that people have for it. Finally, in the most recent era, the ecology movement has created a challenge to the existing regime which is every bit as radical as that posed by the Enlightenment gardens to the baroque.

The same model of nature which legitimated the relations of power could be used to justify the special circumstances of metropolitan life. Absolutist landscapes preserved the city as a sacred aristocratic precinct. Baroque landscapes dwarfed individuals and reduced their wills and desires to insignificance while proclaiming the glory of the men who would build and maintain such places. Enlightenment aristocrats saw the city as the realm of the apostate. The appeal to higher, natural law immediately unraveled the claims to special legitimacy by the state. Furthermore, it placed all people on an equal legal and social basis. In the face of this landscape, the absolutist state could not stand.

These polarized views of the possibilities for urban life continued to work their way through the nineteenth century. In the Biedermeier, the people who could afford to build gardens were a threat to the existing power structure. The garden served as a surrogate for the public arena, the *agora* that was now off limits to citizens. Gardens of pleasure shut out the industrializing city from the view of the families that were extracting the greatest amount of profit from the transformation. Even as the countryside around Vienna was being polluted by factory smoke and workers were being housed in cold, dangerous barracks, the Bürger could gaze upon the semblance of nature from the upstairs window of his shiny new villa. Nature was being destroyed as the Bürgers sat in gardens that painstakingly repressed nature by forcing it to pose as the likeness of itself. The essence of the late-century reform program was that nature should take its proper place in the emerging industrial landscape. The goal of the design was to optimize usefulness at the expense of both ornament and natural growth. The garden was always part of a larger, urban plan in which it played an integral part. It was configured so that its meaning did not become clear unless the context for its existence was also known.

In the twentieth century, the possibilities for a city in the garden or a garden in the city were radicalized even further. Gardens of reaction fulfilled the dream of the return to the preindustrial world by integrating human society into the living community. The destiny of the metropolis was to become a large village. On the other hand, the small garden colonies and the garden settlements offered an image of urban life very different from any that had preceded it. Once in place, the common adaptation to garden life reinforced and reproduced a spirit of cooperation, allowing it to influence all aspects of urban life. Instead of establishing a boundary between the urban and the rural, the cultural and the natural, gardens of renewal integrated nature within the constraints of the metropolis. Even those gardens that were enclosed offered people the possibilities of engaging nature's strength through progressive resistance to human movement, shade and sun, and infinite visual variety in color and leaf. In gardens of discovery, everyone who used a garden could contribute to its design, and every active designer was simultaneously a user. Each could realize a creative potential spontaneously and playfully, free from the dictates of a fixed plan. The creation of the urban society lay in the creativity of everyone who worked on it.

The opportunity to define space is a privileged form of symbolic production. Designers of various intellectual inheritances were employed to create links between garden forms and ideas, recontextualizing the forms in each generation to fit better the dominant views of those in power in the metropolis. At times, groups competed to dominate this emerging symbolic economy. Then, the images of landscape rang with multiple references and echoes of the most deeply held meanings. Again, the pattern was first established in the eighteenth century. The baroque landscape was a fantasy palace in which men consecrated the divine recognition of their election to greatness by living in a house that ruled nature the way a carpenter ruled wood, or a mason brick and mortar. On this level, these landscapes were metaphors of construction. The materials were alive and growing in disorderly and anarchic directions. Their movement toward light and water had to be constantly monitored, snipped, redirected, and disciplined. In this sense, the landscapes were metaphors for destruction.

The English landscape was a fantasy world of a wild and unrestrained nature. It was a delusion of freedom hiding the gravest inequities of the industrial transformation of capitalism. The façade was an eternal pastoral, a heaven on earth in which all social contradictions were resolved. The symbolic repertoire stressed emotional place attachments.

Having established the garden as a separate preserve, the Biedermeier Viennese then borrowed from the experience of Enlightenment aristocrats elements conveying many layers of meaning, including the playful, the childlike, and the disinterested. Flowers were a novel element. Contemplating them linked the symbolic with the material, the living with the dead, and the supernatural with the human. Flowers spoke a language of vice and virtues. Unlike the political messages of the rococo, the Biedermeier flower texts spoke of personal longings, satisfactions, and disappointments. The capacity of a home garden to express both the rational and emotive sentiments of its owner was the lasting contribution of the gardens of domesticity to the received meaning of the Viennese landscape.

The pleasures of the neo-romantic gardens provided a rest from the activities that really underlay the garden's existence: wealth and power. The garden of pleasure was out of time with the rest of the city. It resonated with the landscape history of the premodern era. It was the *hortus conclusus* of ancient Rome—the garden set apart for the pleasure of the patrician. It was the monastic cloister garden, the personal refuge from the cares of the world. It was the virginal rose garden of the medieval troubadours, in which youthful love could blossom. It was the allegorical *amor matis*, the garden of love in which one could love and be loved but also in which the labors of love could procreate. For the midcentury Bürger, the garden was a link to a timeless European identity, transcending provincialism in the same way that the market transcended national boundaries.

The gardens of reform appeared to symbolize the city wrestling to retain a foothold on the rapidly disappearing Gegenden that the Enlightenment had so idealized. Each garden proclaimed the rescue of nature for people. Parks became symbols of plenty, of deprivation denied. This was not a nature free and unfettered, but one that was domesticated. The botanicals obeyed the demands of the users and demonstrated discipline in rebounding after hard use. The message of these gardens was a hymn of praise for the good that could be wrought by human control and a recognition of the power of the manager.

The most powerful symbol of the gardens of reaction was the view from the high lookout, wiping away the clutter and obstructions of the cityscape to grant the seeker a clear view of the interrelationship of landscape and human community. Having this view required effort. The physicality was that of youth and heralded the beginning of a new age, resonating with the rootedness and harmony with nature which people sought in their gardens. The rootedness was of the native, firmly implanted in the soil of home. Together with others, the robust native felt the synergy of the community, whose works became the product of the Volk, the romantic ideal of cultural homogeneity and social harmony.

The image conveyed by the gardens of refuge was not a moral treasury waiting for humans to return, but the antisymbolic extensions of the real world of the worker, a world fraught with threat and striving. Gardens of renewal were symbols of health and vigor: their beauty was an ornament to effort, rather than to status, power, or rank. To observe a beautiful garden was to see the commitment and diligence of the gardener. The well-kept garden was a direct reflection of a well-kept body, of self-respect, and of self-actualization. One could not have a beautiful garden without first attaining inner personal harmony. The symbols were social as well as existential. The values of the world of wage work dictated how every form of work was to be judged. A gardener worthy of renown exerted control over the space, and he planted in the same fashion that the manager controlled the forces of production. The abstract fastidiousness of the lawn free of all variety and clipped to a uniform height told a different story about its caretaker than the relaxed diversity of the backyard meadow. Gardens became moral duties, responsibilities that once voluntarily taken on could not later be evaded.

Gardens of discovery reject most of the symbolic mainstays within the discourse on landscape. Their symbols have the meditative qualities of both the aristocratic gardens of liberty, without the melancholia, and the mystical gardens of reaction, without the yearning for purity of essence. The meditation in gardens of discovery is one of an equal partnership between human intellect and natural energy. Some have called this *synergy* and raised it to a spiritual practice, a unity between the human and universal. The efforts of the ecological gardener symbolized a willingness to engage nature first as an equal, but ultimately as the master of the garden, of the gardener's nongardening life, and of the urban community in which the gardener lives. The garden itself was the material form of the symbolic action.

The urban landscape involves the construction of special temporalities. As with the construction of space, the construction of time in landscape is made to serve the needs of ideology. When first designed, the baroque landscape distinguished its special feeling for time by moving to its own rhythm and not the rhythm of nature which governed other gardens. English parkscapes preserved their own feeling of timelessness. In these preserves, one could revisit a presocial, pre-Christian landscape whose historical resonances denied the authority of the absolutist state. In these parks, all moments of history existed simultaneously. Gardens of domesticity were also timeless. There, seasons revolved, and people and plants grew, but childhood was eternal. The uniformity imposed by the canon on the gardens of pleasure alluded to the abstract time through which the emerging managerial class structured planning, investment, and operations. Temporally, the gardens of reform were no different from other functionally conceived systems, retaining their qualities through frequent iterations and seasonal cycling, but ultimately ahistorical. Gardens of reaction reversed the arrow of history and then suspended it altogether. The use of gardens of refuge by families divided the year into two parts: the garden time and the winter. Garden time was marked with positive memories; winter time was forgotten monotony. Time in the gardens of renewal became the alternative, complementary portion of the week to wage labor. Garden time contrasted with work time by turning the organizational features of work time into their discretionary and self-directed opposite. Temporally, the gardener experiences the garden of discovery as a series of lineal steps leading from a pre-ecological condition to one of self-sustaining balance. If it is reached, the linear progression of events ceases, and the garden enters a season cycle measured in geological rather than human time. The end of history hoped for in the garden of reaction is finally realized.

Landscapes mirror an ideal urban world, but they also camouflage and mystify the existing one. Social realities beyond the garden wall can be forgotten only temporarily. Those realities drive people into some gardens and out of others. In each era, the authority of a particular landscape form was created by its linkage to some obdurate social condition that disheartened the gardener. In the eighteenth century, gardens of order were linked to those other gardens in which nature reigned and in which the work of the human hand was unseen. Because the gardens of order came before them, the gardens of liberty defiantly reminded the forces of control that order was fleeting, and chaos ruled the universe. All of these places linked the alternation of freedom and constraint. The one landscape that remained conspicuously apart from the gardens of liberty was the vacant undeveloped land that the gardens were trying to imitate.

In the nineteenth century, the wave of the Industrial Revolution crashed on the metropolitan shore, inverting and confusing established social patterns. Gardens of domesticity shut out the predatory political world and created a fantasy kingdom in which life proceeded solely with the joys of the family circle. In so doing, these gardens mystified family life, imbuing it with a harmony and peacefulness that were at odds with the lived experience. Gardens of pleasure were odd in the sense that they valorized property in ways that had never been possible before. They turned property into a commodity and thus turned it away from the space of lived experience which dominated the residential places of the non–property-owning classes. Gardens of reform struggled to deal with the contradictions in urban life in positive ways. Their landscape attempted to make the richness of nature as publicly accessible as possible. The contrast with the poorly housed and desperately ill working-class families in the industrial suburbs could not have been greater. In the end, there were not enough people's parks to go around.

The contradictions engendered by industrialization were not resolved in the nineteenth century. In the twentieth century, many were ready to abandon the metropolis altogether. Gardens of reaction were uninhibited in their condemnation of urban life. The gardeners specifically intended to prevent the industrial, the multicultural, and the modern from participating in their land, and in so doing, they permitted a relationship only between certain rarefied landscapes and certain unattained communities. In negating the city, gardens of reaction negated gardens as well. Gardens of refuge were linked to the plight of those Viennese who could not afford to lease land or who did not have the trade union connections necessary to become pioneers in the garden settlement movement. These Viennese remained poorly housed until the Wohnanlage and the Superbaublock buildings provided opportunities for increasing the housing space, light, and ventilation of their apartments. Gardens of renewal camouflaged the peculiar contradiction of Viennese municipal socialism, namely that the appearance of a movement toward greater equality in the distribution of resources, in this case green space, could not take precedence over the real engine for metropolitan growth, the private real estate market. The gardens stood as well-run organizations, testifying to the legitimacy of the role of professional managers in parks, in city planning, and most assuredly in factories and offices.

At one level or another, the Viennese know this. They may not be aware that what they know has a coherence. Certainly there are some individuals who command more of the knowledge, and many others who possess very little of it. Only a handful has ever tried to put what they know together into a congruous whole. Yet, to be Viennese means to understand something of this relationship between landscape and power. The context that empowers this knowledge is the metropolis; these forms and these power groups have no existence beyond its boundary. The media for its propagation are the landscapes themselves, read as contrasting images of the garden in the city. The confirmation lies in the clichés of the landscape discourse, repeated by generation as learned from each generation. Here, then, is a true metropolitan level of cultural integration.

These gardens are concrete objects in the world. They are artifacts of the discourse, but they do not themselves participate in it. They are communicative but not linguistic. It is in the nature of these clichés that they retain the same forms performing markedly differently in different periods among different groups (see Levine 1988:240). The only way to know what the landscape empowers is to know who built it and when. Otherwise it all looks much the same.

I think of these gardens as design regimes, complexes of behavior shaped by a particular viewpoint deemed authoritative and definitive in its moment in history. The gardens continue to be consciously reproduced from day to day, and in some cases from generation to generation when the gardener could just as easily produce some other kind of garden. At their moment in history, these gardens are the authoritative and definitive product of human agency acting upon the natural environment, the ideological apparatus for these behaviors being carried in the language, as we have seen. All of these regimes are immortal insofar as the clichés are still spoken, even though a gardener working a particular garden does so under the rubric of the one regime he or she accepts, and not all regimes.

What becomes of the garden of order when one is actively constructing a garden of discovery? The clichés of the garden of order are not forgotten. They can be recalled immediately through *Ziergarten*. Do they go into some sort of shadow regime, influencing the garden outcome through their opposition? It is evident to me that such debates may occur in the heads of gardeners at some point in the planning process, although I do not have the data to prove that at a moment in the creative garden building process one element is rejected and another employed through the juxtaposition of contrasting images. Intermediate forms are even more problematic. One can see the relationship between the Hausdenken regime of the gardens of pleasure and the Siedler regime of the gardens of renewal, and the opposition to both engendered by the Pioniere. The former regimes are concerned with the security of the investment in family property; the latter are concerned with the health and actualization of the individual. These concerns need not be mutually exclusive. They certainly are in some gardeners, but most Viennese would not describe themselves with either label.

What, then, is served, beyond academic hygiene, by abstracting these categories from the everyday experience of the Viennese? The answer is that these categories describe in particular how the metropolitan life is unlike the life lived in smaller settlements. Each of these gardens is an exploration of contexts that could only be produced in their variety and complexity by forces of symbolic production located exclusively in the centers of power. My studious avoidance of the language of discourse analysis belongs to the recognition that this study is about cultural differences between metropolitans and others. The focus on the discourse permits me to tease out contexts that are unique to large cities while grounding them in the everyday experience of a historically emergent metropolitan knowledge in Vienna.

The constituent parts of the knowledge, be they clichés, landscape forms, or authoritative design programs, have disparate origins and spread. Some, like the Biedermeier, evolved in local Viennese conditions, which may have been similar to conditions elsewhere but still sufficiently unique to produce singular gardens. Others, like the gardens of pleasure or the gardens of reaction, developed through processes effecting change across a broad region, entering Vienna through the language streams and shared institutional affiliations among speakers and readers of German, producing gardens that shared many features with those in Munich, Berlin, and Hamburg. Still others, like the gardens of order, liberty, and discovery, were transregional, growing in response to changes in the global system and reaching Vienna initially through its links to other speech communities. In this field, Vienna's gardens can inspire and influence, as well as respond. To view all of these constituent elements from this one metropolis, to see these competing regimes as a seamless experience of the landscape, is to experience the metropolitan knowledge that the Viennese possess.

Notes

INTRODUCTION: THE CULTURAL MEANING OF LANDSCAPE

1. For example, the articles by Mauro and Sessa, Cranz, Pogacnik, and Auricoste seem to be moving away from the connoisseurship paradigm.

2. This entire discussion is taken from Dieter Hennebo's monograph on the garden in the Middle Ages. The occasion for this information is his explanation of the kinds of plants used in cloister gardens, especially St. Gall (1962:32–33).

3. This text was originally published as "Des Espaces Autres" in the French journal *Architecture-Mouvement-Continuité* in October 1984. Although not a part of Foucault's official corpus of work, it was released into the public domain before his death. In the lecture, Foucault raised a number of examples to illustrate the characteristics of these other places. On the whole, the ideas were highly suggestive but not systematically developed. In this section, I try to develop the idea of heterotopia within Euro-American urban design and hopefully do justice to Foucault's original insight.

4. I realize that this argument isolates the development of heterotopic gardens within the Indo-European speech area and that this flies in the face of the existence of heterotopic gardens in East Asian cities. I simply do not have the linguistic sources to explore the same argument for Semitic, Dravidian, Malayo-Polynesian, Sino-Tibetan, or Finno-Altaic languages. Nor do I mean to imply that only Indo-Europeans and East Asians developed het-

erotopic gardens. It would not surprise me to learn that such sites were common in pre-Columbian meso-America, or pre-Islamic sub-Saharan Africa. I just do not have such information at this time. One fact that stands out for me as an exception proving the rule is the complete lack of planted spaces in Machu Picchu. In this high Andean city, there was not enough water or frost-free days to grow heterotopic sites from botanical elements. Their sacred enclosures were made only of stone. Thus, it can be said that all cities have gardens, but not all urban gardens are green.

5. The earliest references to gardens were closely connected to other kinds of enclosed spaces, like villages. As Anne van Erp-Houtepen has recently pointed out, the words that we currently use to refer to gardens, yards, towns, courts, villas, parks, paradise, and curtains can all find their earliest etymological roots in the reconstructed form *gher (1986:230–31; see also Hennebo 1962:16–18; Jackson 1980:21–25).

6. This simple definition was familiar to early landscape writers, who did not have recourse to etymology. Repton, for example, defined it as "a piece of ground fenced off from cattle, and appropriated to the use and pleasure of man: it is, or ought to be, cultivated" (1816:141–42). This last remark signals that cultivation is entailed but not obligated by the enclosure.

CHAPTER 1: THE MAKING OF THE VIENNESE LANDSCAPE

1. The city is currently developing the southeastern section as a new commercial and industrial residential complex, Wien Süd. The project is only ten years old and has produced new housing and a growing industrial park. When completed over the next twenty years, the Wien Süd project will provide new housing for 60,000 to 70,000 and jobs for 25,000 to 30,000. It will also change substantially the portion of the land devoted to commercial production (*Der Aufbau* October/November 1971).

2. I experienced this firsthand in 1990 while living with my wife and small daughter in the twenty-second district on the far northeast side of the city. There was a small, dirt-topped playground across the street from the large apartment complex, but most of the equipment was either dangerous or broken. To take the little girl to play in a "nearby" large park by public transportation required twenty minutes travel each way and a transfer between tram and subway.

3. For those who would like more background on the premodern history of the Viennese landscape, excellent summaries are available in Auböck (1975), Auböck and Makovetz (1975), Auer (1974), Fischer (1971), Klaar (1971), Lichtenberger (1977), and Schediwy and Baltzarek (1982).

4. The garrison saw intense action between 167 and 180 A.D., when the Germanae overran the line of Danube forts and pushed all the way to the Adriatic. Emperor Marcus Aurelius died of infection in the fort on March 17, 180, after successfully pushing the Germanae back across the Danube. The Vindobona was destroyed in the invasion and later rebuilt (Harl 1979). The name Vindobona means good wind.

5. The family was named only in the eleventh century by Bishop Otto von Friesing, son of the Babenberger duke Leopold III. The name of the father of Otto I was Luitpoldinger; his mother's father's name was Popponen. Both were quite undistinguished families. He picked the name Babenberger because the residence of the Popponen was supposed to have been a place called Bamberg.

6. Rather than translate loan words whose meaning is clear from the context into more familiar French spellings, I have retained the German spelling throughout this work. Thus, *bürgerlich* is used instead of *bourgeois* or, in the current context, *Markgraf* instead of *archduke*.

7. According to early nineteenth-century maps, all of these villages were of nucleated form. Those in the Wienerwald developed primarily along important streets with gardens stretching back behind the house gates. Those in the Marchfeld formed around common greens.

8. Wild grapes of the silvestris variety are indigenous to the area. They migrated up the Danube valley from the Black Sea before human habitation. The domesticated Mediterranean grape, vinifera, was brought in during the Roman occupation. The grapes cultivated in the late Middle Ages were a hybrid of these two varieties. The hearty white grape became the anchor of the Vienna wine industry (Zohary and Speigel-Roy 1975:321–23). The name of the city itself, Wien, is believed by many Viennese to derive from the word for wine, *Wein*.

9. The sixteenth-century Austrian ambassador to Constantinople, Ogier Chislain Busbecq, is said to have brought the tulip and other bulb flowers as well as the lilac back to his garden near the Dominican bastion of the Altstadt.

10. A Paradiesgarten (also Paradiesgärtlein) is a particular form of medieval garden. The more famous one was built for Charlemagne at Capitulare de villis and imitated in Frankish manors through the Renaissance. These gardens were square and enclosed by low walls that permitted passers-by to view it from the outside. The dominant feature of a paradise garden was a central rondo with four paths radiating outward in the cardinal directions. The garden was an allegory of the heavenly paradise and contained a number of Asian, especially Islamic, elements. The four paths represented the four rivers of heaven, and the central rondo was the axis mundi. The four beds were then planted with either trees or flowing plants. This form was a popular way of expressing religious piety among the medieval elite and was used as a place of contemplation. It seems to have been introduced into Europe with the Crusades (Hennebo 1962:21–25). It contrasted with the Lustgarten design first promulgated in an essay by Albertus Magnus. As reconstructed by Hermann Fischer from the essay *De vegetabilibus, liber septimus de mutatione plantae ex silvestritate in domesticationem* (Venice 1517), it was essentially a walled space, usually rectangular, with a single entrance on the side closest to the house. The walls could be masonry or shrub trees, but the enclosure was intended to be impermeable. The garden was often divided in half by a grass-covered bank. The side farthest from the en-

trance was devoted to the growing of fragrant herbs, laid out in geometric beds. The other section was a lawn with fruit trees and various flowering plants (planted in the lawn rather than in beds). A spring, well, or similar water feature allowed a small rivulet to run through the lawn (1929; cited in Hennebo 1962:41–49). The *pleasure* label for the garden is appropriate. The gardens were used for eating, bathing, drinking, playing music, and having sex. The wandering troubadours (*Minnesänger*) of the late Middle Ages located the scenes for the consummation of courtly love in such gardens. Thus, the Lustgarten was a profane, earthly site, in contrast to the sacred resonances of the Paradiesgarten. The symbolic attachments of these medieval forms are important in understanding contemporary ornamental gardens and will be discussed in Chapter 6.

11. Responsibility for the ground plan is attributed to Maximilian himself in the folklore. In a letter to his ambassador in Rome, he described himself as finding relief from his governmental chores only in building and gardening. In actuality, the architects on the projects changed frequently. The one who stayed the longest and had the greatest influence over the final form was an Italian, Ferrabosco (Neubauer 1975:9).

12. Two additional gardens of this Italian period lay immediately in front of the garden walls. The Keilmannsegg'schen Gärten in the area near the mouth of the Vienna River included arcades, water fountains, and pavilions in the Turkish style. These gardens were not connected to houses or palaces; instead they were a series of lawns in which the detailed ornaments had been constructed. The Prämer'schen Gärten lay across the canal in what is today the second district. These, too, were ornamental lawns, but they were connected to a colony of noble houses. The only other thing that is known about them is that the lawns were surrounded by delicate balustrade architecture (Neubauer 1975:11). These gardens were also destroyed in the second Turkish siege.

13. These large properties included Buchfeld (Josefstadt, eighth district) in 1700, Neulerchenfeld (eighth district) in 1703, Hungelbrunn (now fifth district) in 1705, Althan (ninth district) in 1713, a part of Wieden (fourth district) in 1732, and Strozzigrund (eighth district) in 1753.

14. For a discussion of the increasing importance of privacy in Europe during this period, see Rybszinski (1986).

15. The term *Bürger* means someone who resides in the Burg, the walled city. This is the same word as the Frankish *bourg*, the root of *bourgeoisie*. Throughout this book, I will call the citizens of Vienna, whether they live within the walls or in the districts around it, Bürgers, describe their ideas and activities as bürgerlich, and refer to their various corporate class actions as those of the Bürgertum. The highest echelons of this group were ennobled with titles such as Baron, for commercial accomplishment, or Freiherr, for military accomplishment. These titles were not hereditary. The lowest ranks of the class could include quite poor families whose only claim to membership was title to a small piece of income-producing property. In the period discussed through most of this book, the Bürgertum was split into factions.

16. A discussion of Wagner's work and his importance in the development of the modern Viennese cityscape is available in English in Schorske (1981). Stübben was the dominant textbook writer for architecture. He also was chairman of the society of German-speaking architects who made recommendations on improving urban sanitation and safety through building codes. A discussion of his importance in the development of architecture as a modern profession is available in Collins and Crasemann Collins (1986).

CHAPTER 2: GARDENS OF ORDER

1. "Ein Ziergarten ist meiner Meinung nach ein Garten zum Anschauen und nicht zum Betreten. *Das ist mehr reine Zierde.* Ich könnte mir vorstellen den Vergleich mit einem Botanischen Garten oder mit dem Garten Schloss Schönbrunn, der gärtnerisch gepflegt und gehegt wird, aber nur rein für den Besucher, für das Auge da ist und nicht für den Zweck" [Kolbinger]. "Unter einem Ziergarten versteh ich, wenn architektonisch das angeordnet ist, das darf nur da stehen, *das muss den Schnitt haben*, das darf nicht grösser werden als diese Höhe, da muss ein Rasenstreifen sein und die Halme müssen gerade sein und *die Kanten müssen abgestochen sein, dort muss ein Steinchen liegen.* Das ist ein Ziergarten, ja" [Prinz]. (Italics refer to verbose statements.)

2. "Ein Ziergarten ist streng angelegt und symmetrisch" [Mach].

3. "Ein Ziergarten ist ein Garten, der zur Zierde da ist, der schön zum Anschauen ist, der schön gepflegt ist, wo nichts herumliegt. Wo kein Unkraut ist" [Hasenauer].

4. "Ein Ziergarten . . . den man nicht betreten darf, nur anschaut, und zu gepflegt" [I. Lahr]. [Mrs.:] "Nåjå, då is alles picobello, net, und Dings. I bin a Mensch, i bin net schlampert, i bin oba a ka Pedant, i muass mi drinn waschn, und des is für mi wichtig." [Mr.:] "Und net der Sklave des Gartens zu sein, net, also er soll gepflegt sei" [Neuhofer].

5. In a garden settlement I visited in the twenty-first district was a man nicknamed Prince Eugene by his neighbors because of the fastidiousness with which he cared for his garden. A neighbor told me that she saw him actually cutting the lawn with paper scissors to get all the blades the same height and walking around the lawn to pick up one stray leaf, so as not to leave footprint impressions in the green carpet. Whatever the man had in mind (and I was not able to ask him), his neighbors believed that his exactness recreated a garden of order.

6. See Chapter 1, note 10, for a description of the differences between these forms.

7. The importance of flower gardens for the Euro-Asian elite is complex. See Goody (1993) for a detailed treatment of the issue.

8. "Dann es haben etliche diesen brauch, das sie am Sontag uff die dörffer ziehen" (Schultz 1892: I, 355).

9. Furttenbach was an Allgäuer who was the city architect for the city of Ulm. He also built many of the country estates and townhouses for bürgerlich families and became the primary architect for the newly rich Bürgers.

His work was influential throughout German-speaking lands, and he represents the most important interpreter of Renaissance garden architecture in the seventeenth century. His use of mannerist elements such as grottos, watercourses, pergolars, and the asymmetric distribution of statues, pools, aviaries, ponds with islands, and broad paths (Nehring 1990:160) so enhanced their popularity that they continued to have a prominent place in German gardens through the nineteenth century. To my knowledge, his designs were not built in Vienna itself, but his ideas strongly influenced both aristocratic and bürgerlich gardens throughout the eighteenth and nineteenth centuries.

10. In 1720, the numbers of noble houses with gardens in the Neustadt were as follows: 200 in the second district, 110 in the third, 58 in the fourth, 137 in the seventh, 119 in the eighth, and 114 in the ninth district (Bermann 1881:392ff.).

11. The Belvedere is the second most important palace grounds in the French style after Schönbrunn (see below). The palaces house two major art collections, and the grounds are so close to the central district that they are easily accessible to tourists.

12. An authoritative view of the ground from 1759–60 is available through a veduta by the imperial painter to the court of Saxony, Bernardo Bellotto (Canaletto). Although small trees are no longer planted along the sides of the two main beds, the overall design of the main parterre is unchanged (Neubauer 1980:22).

13. In 1800, the English landscape style in Vienna referred to any garden laid out to emphasize the picturesque qualities of landscape. In general, the human hand was disguised in the design. This style will be fully discussed in the next chapter.

14. A Swiss garden is a miniature English parkscape with alpine trees planted in beds shaped like steep hills. The paths trace sharp, free curves and emphasize the slope of the landscape.

15. The Dutch style is the label given to those design principles that emphasize the single species. It was developed in the Low Countries at the same time as the baroque garden in France and quickly spread through Europe as the preferred style for botanical gardens and collections of curiosities. It is small and multiform with grotesque tree cuts. It can be quite colorful. The beds are enclosed with low bushes or half-height fences. The paths are of plaster. Inside the beds, the plants grow as they wish. This style is easily identified because it establishes a line in the bed, either at the edge or through the middle. A single representative of a species is then planted on the line, followed by a representative of another species, and another, and so on. Today the style is used most often by rose garden hobbyists.

16. Today there are very few of these. The most accessible is Belvedere (designed in 1721–22 by Eugene of Savoy himself with help from Lukas von Hildebrandt and Dominique Girard), but Palais Schwarzenberg and the gardens of the Theresianum Realgymnasium, both in private hands, also retain the older character. The city is currently rehabilitating the Neugebäude in

Kaiser Ebersdorf. This is one of the few restorable Renaissance palaces and gardens north of the Alps.

17. Schönbrunn Palace and the Belvedere are among the few gardens existing today in their eighteenth-century form. However, in the eighteenth century, there were many more in royal and noble hands. These included the Augarten (royal, designed by Trehet in 1705), the Favorita (royal, designed by Trehet in 1706), Palais Schwarzenberg (1706, designer unknown), Palais Strahemberg (a tree garden designed for this family by von Hildebrandt in 1719), Palais Harrach (designed for this family by von Hildebrandt in 1721), Palais Althan in Wieden (designed for this family by Johann Fischer von Erlach in 1706), Palais Schönborn (designed for this family by von Hildebrandt in 1711), Palais Trautson (designed for this family by Fischer von Erlach in 1760), Palais Liechtenstein (designed for this family by Domenico Martinellis in 1704), Schloss Neuwaldegg (designed for the Strattman family by Fischer von Erlach in 1692), and Lustschloss Huldenberg (designed for the English ambassador by Fischer von Erlach in 1715) (Neubauer 1966, 1980; Neubauer and Auböck 1980).

18. It is important to realize that this effect of the baroque landscape may not be applicable to all of Europe. The baroque gardens that flourished in seventeenth-century Netherlands were produced in a different political environment and yielded a different spatial scale. This contrast is evident in a series of articles produced at the 1988 Dumbarton Oaks conference (Hunt 1990).

CHAPTER 3: GARDENS OF LIBERTY

1. These style names are themselves historically situated. The French refers to the interpretation of Italian Renaissance gardens by royal architects, notably Le Nôtre, in the late seventeenth century. The style is also called baroque, but in this guise it must contend with gardens being built in Italy during the same period. When the Viennese speak of the French style, they mean the gardens of Le Nôtre at Versailles. This style was associated with the House of Habsburg and the leading aristocratic families. The English style has its origins in exactly the same Italian Renaissance gardens as the French. This might surprise those who, like my Viennese conversation partners, view the styles as diametrically opposed. In the hands of its earliest practitioners, the English shared a motif with the French: garden space was organized for viewing the intrinsic forms of natural objects. Hunt noted that Shaftesbury, an ardent theorist of these design ideas, saw no advantage to spatial imagery that favored the primitive and wild over the geometric, perfected, or shaped. If anything, the early influence of English garden design shaped his view of republican England as the inheritor of the cultural tradition of republican Rome. He wrote of the English garden as a "mixed government" of forms and a variety of structures. In the one-sided baroque, all lines are straight and all beds are symmetric, while the wild and untamed are

banished. Just by admitting the possibility that the primitive form had nascent values that could be cultivated and perfected by gardening, the English garden became forever associated with republican society and contrasted with the aristocratic flavor of the French (Hunt 1986:182–83).

2. "Wir wollten gerne ein bisschen Grün, und dann Ruhe, Frieden und dass man in einem Atelier arbeiten kann und dann die Verbundenheit zwischen Natur und Leben" [Dänzer].

3. "Es ist einfach schön, dass man was Grünes sieht, das man selbst gepflanzt hat und das man wachsen sieht" [Larisch].

4. "Alles was wächst und was wild wächst, wächst wild. Das ist nicht viel geschnitten. Also was von der Natur kommt. Ich tue nicht dauern. Die Bäume schneiden so sie einen Form kriegen oder kleiner werden, oder was weiss ich. Das soll wachsen was wachsen" [Pokorny].

5. "Zum Beispiel gefällt mir, wie auch die Geschichte dieser Siedlung, lese ich ja im Laufe eines Jahres die Geschichte meines Gartens. Da wachsen ja Sachen, die sind unglaublich. Im Winter sieht man sie nicht, was ist das für ein bizarrer Busch? Und plötzlich im Frühjahr sieht man ein sonderbares japanisches Gewächs, das muss schön ewig lange hier wachsen, weil s so langsam wächst" [Mittendrin].

6. "Wir haben mehr oder weniger den Garten so gestaltet, dass wir all unsere Wünsche, die wir an einen Garten stellen und an unser Heim hier stellen, eigentlich verwirklicht haben. Wir haben einen gewissen Sichtschutz, einen gewissen Freiraum, also es gibt so heimliche Enkeln, wie man so schön sagt, nicht daheim und doch zu Hause, und es gibt auch die freie Fläche, es gibt auch die Möglichkeit, ob die optische Nutzung des Gartens in Form von Hausgarten und in Form von Erholungsgarten" [Kolbinger].

7. "Und so haben wir Sachen hingesetzt. Also in den Sinne, spielt es eigentlich unser Wünsche wieder. Wir uns, muss ich zusagen, nicht von fremden Einfluss, eh, fremden Meinungen beeinflussen lassen. Nur unsere beiden Wünsche. Wir haben gesagt Wir wollen hier einige Pflanzen. Wir wollen hier schlanke Konifern. Wir werden da Skyrocket. Wir haben Skyrocket.... Also, sind eigentlich der wieder Spiegelung unsere Wünsche der wir, so zu sagen, so wir es anschauen und so haben wir es gemacht" [Klinger].

8. Throughout the eighteenth century, the very wealthy continued to build estates incorporating the principles of Kent's gardens. In the second half of the century, Capability Brown rose to prominence with greatly enlarged (and more expensive) garden designs, called parkscapes, which imitated underdeveloped forest and swampy areas.

9. Joseph himself was one of these radicals, but he rarely let it show in official circles. He greatly admired Rousseau and even arranged a clandestine meeting with the aged philosopher; however, he also saw clearly that the aristocracy of his empire would never allow Rousseauian constitutionalism. He had his summer palace at Laxenburg landscaped in the English style.

10. This is a free translation of Küchelbecker's text. The original, as quoted in Fuhrmann and cited by Hajós (1989:20), is syntactically obscure.

The original spellings are also retained. "Es fänget sich dasselbe bey Closter-Beuburg an der Donau, mit dem so genannten hohen und mit Holz bewachsenen Kalenberg an, und gehet gegen Abend, bis an den Wiener-Wald, und verursachet dem Gesichte im Frühling und Sommer, wenn allews grün ist, kein geringes Vergnügen; weit mehr aber werden die Augen von den lustigen, fruchtbaren, und fast in Form eines halben Circuls an dem Fussgedachten Berge, um die Stadt herum such erstreckenden Wein-Gebürge charmiret, auf welchen ein ziemlich guter Wein im Überfluss wächset. Am allermeisten träget endlich der breite in unterschiedliche Armen sich zertheilende, und viele mit holz bewachsene Insulln formirende Donau-Strom, zu der angenehmen Situation dieser Stadt bey, als worinnen derselben nicht leicht eine andere in Deutschland gleich kommen wird; der vielen Felder, Wein- und schönen Lust-Gärten, von welchen dieselbe, auf der mittagigen Seite umgeben, und gleichsam eingeschlossen wird, vor jezo zugeschweigen."

11. Other gardens established by the nobility and the foreign embassies include the royal Lustgarten at Laxenburg (1779); the gardens of Graf Cobenzel in the Wienerwald (1781); the gardens of the family Fries in the southern village of Vöslau (1777), designed by Hohenberg, the garden architect of Schönbrunn; the gardens of Prince Strahemberg in the eastern village of Alt-Erlaa (1783); the garden of Prince Sinzendorf in the village of Ernstbrunn (1780); Predigstuhl, the garden of the Russian ambassador Prince Gallitzin in the Wienerwald (1785); the garden of the Graf Schönborn in Göllerdorf (1790); the garden of Graf Harrach in Bruck an der Leitha (1789); and the garden of Princess Paar in Hütteldorf (1799). The Geymüller banking family established a thirty-three-hectare English garden in Potzleinsdorf in 1799. It, too, was executed by Rosenthal, together with Franz Illner, the palace gardener of Neuwaldegg. It was a very popular park among the wealthy bourgeoisie in the first half of the nineteenth century and was described by contemporaries as a garden of towering arbors, flower beds in full bloom, and quietly winding paths. Other English gardens that were established by bürgerlich families include the gardens of Feldmarschall Freiherr von Loudon in the western village of Hadersdorf (1789), the garden of the royal jeweler Franz von Mack in Kalksburg (1792), and the garden of Freiherr von Braun in Schönau bei Günselsdorf (1800).

12. Hirschfeld, the leading theorist of garden architecture on the Continent in the late eighteenth century, described the special role of remembrances and memorials in the parks as follows: "During the landscape period, memorials achieved their highest moral effect when they brought attention to the surroundings, were themselves objects of beauty, pointed out the different natural openings and viewpoints, and at the same time ennobled their subject. They were dressed as nature itself would care for its children. The more monumental (size and complexity) the higher the social standing of the owner. They arouse in the observer the thoughts of the beautiful, and of useful merit, and support his moral inclinations" (1779: III, 142).

13. A contemporary witness, Pietro Metastasio, wrote the following to

his brother: "The Prater is one of the public enjoyment areas which most of the people visit.... On a beautiful summer evening, one can meet as many as 1,000 wagon and 15,000 people" (Kortz 1905:151). Noble reaction was more cautious. Here is Fürst Khevenhüller's diary entry on the opening of the Prater: "Today, April 5, 1766, his majesty the Kaiser let it be known through newspapers and placard that entry to the Prater was now allowed for everyone. On the first Sunday, a large number of people in both rented carriages and on foot came in. To serve them, small huts were erected selling lemonade, coffee, wine and beer, as well as kegel bowling lanes. The hunt had used the Prater quite differently, never going on foot and only the most beautiful carriages were allowed. Only the Kaiser, who everyone knows is no friend of the hunt, wanted to provide new amusements for the public. Because of this action, disorder is everywhere. The patrols are constant, but especially intense during the closing time. All this was produced by the insensibility of the first opening. It will only get worse in the good weather of spring and summer" (Brandstätter and Treffer 1986:170).

14. Because this was primarily an architectural movement imitated in landscape only in this one park, I have not included it as an image circulating in the discourse on landscapes. Rather, I have treated it as a forerunner of the gardens of pleasure and the style that evolved in the 1830s and 40s. The classic revival concerned itself with the renewal of highly regular and geometric forms in architecture and to a lesser extent in landscape architecture.

15. The coffeehouses in the parks added to the charm. These were often the destination of people promenading along the Bastai, the Kai, or the Glacis after the midday meal. Johann Strauss Sr. played for the first time in the Tauberl-Wirtshaus on the Glacis. These concerts became so popular that coffeehouses located outside of the Glacis built gardens in their backyards, where patrons could sit outside in good weather and hear the music. The Eipeldauer letters, the richest source of information on Viennese life at the time of the Congress of Vienna, named the Sperl-Wirtshaus in the Leopoldstadt as a particularly popular coffeehouse with a private garden. The Corti coffeehouse established itself in a corner of the Volksgarten. Although it was not the first coffeehouse on the Glacis, it soon became the best known, setting the standard for many of the grand palacelike coffeehouses built in the 1870s and 80s.

16. The phrase *movement in the open (Bewegung im Freien)* and the similar phrase *movement in nature (Bewegung in der Natur)* are formulas that adhere to the meaning of the landscape throughout the nineteenth and twentieth centuries. Both refer to an equilibrium theory of wellness widely distributed throughout Central Europe, which equates good health with work or exercise in the open. This use of the phrase in 1825 is among the earliest on the public record. The text also reflects a concern for the use of parks as public health institutions, a theme that dominates urban planning at the end of the century. The most common public health contribution of parks was believed to as an air filter and reservoir of fresh, clean air, the *Luftreservoir*. The first

use of this term for public parks was by Adelbert Stifter (1844:x). The idea continues in contemporary attributions of public space, as in the phrase "the parks are the lungs of the city." The first use of this image belongs to a pseudonymous critic of the Ringstrasse parks in this 1869 essay in a newspaper: "Man hat die Gärten die Lungen der Stadt genannt, und das sind sie in der That. Sie sind das erste und letzte Heilmittel, der wichtigste Regulator für den Athmungsprozess einer Stadt. Man kann den Winden nicht gebieten aber man kann die Strassen erweitern, um der Luft Raum zu verschaffen; man kann neue Häuser bauen, um der Übervölkerung der alten abzuhelfen, man kann Bäume pflanzen und Gärten anlegen; man kann endlich—das ist freilich für Wien die Ideal—um all die günstigen Dispositionen zu vereinigen, das Cottage-System der Engländer adoptieren" (Harry 1869:1). The city council used this argument to secure grassy places around schools and markets from the Stadterweiterungsfond. Chapter 6 will return to this sanitation theme in the meaning of landscape.

CHAPTER 4: GARDENS OF DOMESTICITY

1. Historians of style refer to this period in other parts of Europe as empire style. There are important distinctions between Biedermeier and empire because of the high level of consumption of decorative arts for the home.

2. There were no public parks designed in this style in this period. The one park that was built was the Volksgarten. I discussed the stylistic features of this park in the previous chapter. Two other public spaces developed through private initiative: the Paradiesgärtlein on the Burgbastei and the Wirtshaus on the Wasserglacis. I introduced the Paradiesgärtlein in the previous chapter. The Biedermeier influenced both of these, especially in the use of artificial flowering trees, small table bouquet arrangements, and the exhibition of botanical curiosities. These were public places, however, and that meant exposure to pressures for a common, nonoffending civic taste. These public gardens were the first evidence of Biedermeier design elements leaving the narrower discourse on domestic gardens and entering the broader discourse of the appropriate shape of urban space.

3. "Ja, als Spielplatz, wenn man in der Richtung denkt auf alle Fälle. Das ist natürlich schrittweise zu betrachten: Zuerst ist der Garten der Standplatz für die Wiege des Kindes. Der Kinderwagen, die frische Luft, die Nähe zur Mutter. Man muss nicht in den Park, man muss nicht irgendwo hinaus ins Grüne. In späterer Folge ist der Garten der nahe Spielplatz, der kontrollierte Spielplatz des Kindes, wo man auch über einiges hinwegsehen muss, wenn etwas zerstört wird, das haben Kinder so an sich und in späterer Folge der Lehr– oder Lernplatz. Da Aufwachsen mit der Natur, das Sehen, wie die Pflanze wächst, was daraus wird, wird spielerisch aufgenommen. Und wenn man dann ins Schulalter kommt, eventuell Kontrollieren, selbst was anpflanzen, lernen im Garten, in der frischen Luft und zuletzt dann, das, was Sie angesprochen haben, das Danach, nach den Eltern" [Kolbinger].

4. "Es is'n zweiter Aufenthaltsraum, ein vergrösserter und ma muss sich

nicht schön anziehen, um ins Freie gehen zu können, ich kann auch im Pyjama hinausgehen.... Ja, kann sogar mit'm Badeanzug hinausgehen, nicht, ja, tut man auch" [Adler].

5. "Ja, jetzt sag ma, die Rasenflächen und die Obstbäume und überall sind ein Paar Blumen, also es wo jeder irgendwie nach seiner Art, nach.... Der Besitz bepflanzt und so, aber im grossen und ganzen möchte ich sagen, dass die Gärten hier gleich sind. Nicht einer irgendwas Besonderes hat" [Kleist].

6. "Wenn man jetzt, das kleine Grundstück, was mein Garten ist, ist die Ähnlichkeit irgendwie soweit gegeben, wo s die natürlichen Voraussetzungen zwingend machen. Aber es gibt keinen Garten, der gleich ist. Aber ich bin der einzige, der die Terrasse aufgemauert hat. Alle anderen haben Böschungen. Also, mein Garten ist wirklich der einzige, der anders aussieht. Ich glaube, ich hab als einziger in meinem Garten ein Beet" [Roth].

7. "Der Garten, sondern er soll individuell gestaltet werden und wir haben auch versucht, nur in den groben Zügen also, bezüglich der Bepflanzung mit den Bäumen usw. eine gewisse Norm einzuhalten, die der Umgebung angepasst ist, nicht extrem aus der Rolle zu fallen" [Kolbinger].

8. "Ja, ja, das ist schon. Weil einer tut dem anderen nacheifern. Wenn einer was Schönes gemacht hat, dann sagt er, du, schau, des ist schön, des mach ma auch. Daher natürlich schaut ein Garten dem anderen ähnlich. Bei uns zum Beispiel wir ham so grosse Dahlien gehabt, soviel, ham die Nachbarn gsagt: 'Könnt man von die Dahlien ein Paar Knollen ham?' Na, jetzt ham ma s heuer gleich zerteilt und ham die Nachbarn dann beliefert. Jetzt passiert s, dass nächstes Jahr die gleichen Farben, die gleichen Dahlien auf an Platzerl ham wie wir. Also, daher könnte man schon sagen, dass sie in irgend einer Form gleich sind" [Pahl].

9. "Die meiste, die meiste ... ich bin nämlich ein begeisterter Gärtner. Ich bin ein begeisterter Pflaumenzüchter, besonders immer wieder von Neuheiten. Ich habe lange Zeit selbst Veredelungen durchgeführt von Rosen, besonders auch von Bäumen. Wie gesagt, ich bin ein Fantast in Pflanzen. Gebe sehr viel Geld aus für den Garten und, wie gesagt, ich freue mich immer wieder, wenn mir was gelingt. Wenn ich eine Pflanze vom Urlaub vom Ausland usw., Italien, Griechenland ... ich habe zum Beispiel die Kakteen, sind sehr viele aus Griechenland, aus Italien, Jugoslawien usw. Wenn ich sie mitbringe und versuche, weiter zu züchten, und in etlichen Fällen gelingt s mir" [Himmel].

10. "Und für das Feierlich hier das mehrere Gäste einlade, und das ist im Sommer sehr schön, und frei zu sitzen, und hier sowie bei den Heurigen einfacher Denke aufstellen. Ja, Wein trinken, essen. Und ... habe ich die Fläche immer gerade gemacht, Terrassen zu Tische aufstellen ... Geräteshtte, Stempel Ziegeln, Weinlauben [Salettl], Swimmingpool, Weinkeller" [Neuhofer].

11. Heurigen that retain the original Biedermeier atmosphere have survived in the north. Wine gardens are discussed in more detail in the chapter on Viennese play in my earlier monograph (1992b).

12. "Ich meine 150 Quadratmeter kann man nicht sehr viel machen, an

und für sich, weil ich hab' dort ein Paar Erdbeeren stehen und ein Paar Himbeeren und zum Spass auch einen Weinstock, aber das ist mehr symbolisch, weil mein Vater mal ein Landwirt war, ein Weinhauer, steht halt dort 'n Weinstock. Ein Holztisch steht auch darin, eine Holzbank und ein Tisch steht drinnen, das kann man sagen, ja" [Adler].

13. "Die Kunst ohne Natur ist ein Unding, sowie die Natur ohne Kunst sehr vieles abgeht, was der nach Genüssen strebende Mensch zu grösserer Vollkommenheit rechnet."

14. This is from the keynote address of Hügel at the Gartenbaugesellschaft's Flower Show in 1836. The German text is: "Es gibt fürwahr keinen, mit so wohltuendem anspruchslosem und doch so unwiderstehlich anziehenden Zauber begabten Gegenstand in Natur und Kunst, als das Wesen einer zur Vollkommenheit gediehenen, üppig erschlossenen Blume, welche Licht und Wonne (Sonne?) strahlend, Aug und Sinn des einfachen wie des veredelten Gemütes an sich zieht und die zur Begeisterung und Hingebung fesselt."

15. "Unregelmässige Beetform, freies Wachsen bunter und vielgestaltiger Vegetation in diesen Beeten, Einfassen der Beete durch Eisenbögen oder Vegetationsstreifen, Glashäuser und das gesteigerte botanische Interesse, Spielgeräte, die Abhängigkeit von der Jahreszeit und die besondere Bedeutung des Sonnenlichtes, die Kleinheit und Intimität. Die Gesamtanlage des Biedermeiergarten, das Ineinander all dieser Einzelformen zu einem unlösbaren Ganzen ist, eine selbständige Schöpfung und es ist das erste Mal, dass der Hausgarten eine so eigenständige Leistung hervorbringt" (Althöfer 1956:71).

16. Literary descriptions of the private gardens of the Biedermeier are rare. Pezzl included a brief reference to garden parties in the suburbs as a prevalent feature of Viennese recreations in the spring. Other than mentioning that this often involved fireworks displays, he provided no further details of these parties (1823:218).

17. The lithographs were published in a memorial to the garden written by Weidmann (1824).

18. Gumpendorf was a small village on the north side of the Vienna River. Wieden, the site of Rosenbaum's garden, was on the south side. The land stretching from the banks of the small river was one of the three areas of residential and industrial development in the early nineteenth century. Eventually, Gumpendorf was incorporated into the district of Mariahilf, today the fifth municipal district.

19. An even more famous flower developer was Karl Freiherr von Hügel. When he arrived in Vienna in 1824, he established a garden in Hietzing, a suburb on the south side of the Vienna River some five miles from the center of the city. It is the neighbor of the imperial summer palace of Schönbrunn, whose gardens were developed throughout the eighteenth century. Hietzing underwent dramatic growth in the early nineteenth century as the favorite summer cottage area of the lower aristocracy and higher Bürgertum. This garden was arranged in the same form as that of Rosenbaum and Rupprecht.

It remained in its original form until 1848, when Hügel gave up his house in Hietzing for government service. The garden was so successful that Hügel started a commercial nursery from it. On his estate, Hügel had eight glass houses in which he maintained the color and variety of his garden through the winter. The fourth major Biedermeier garden was Baron Pronay's garden in Hetzendorf (1817), a north bank Vienna River village slightly west of Hietzing and about six miles from the city center. Pronay was vice president of the Gartenbaugesellschaft and was a specialist in breeding pelargonias. His garden was open to the public, and people could barter and exchange plant varieties with him (see Kaut 1975:57).

20. This lithographic plan was drawn by Sicard von Sicardsburg in four sections. The section containing the area around Hietzing is catalogued as Viertal unter dem Wiener-Wald, No. 122.

21. The characteristics of Biedermeier home decorations were clear, simple forms of furniture; very sparing use of ornaments; an affection for natural *Maserung*, colored woods contrasted with black detail work; colorful upholstery, usually stripped, decorated with stark, colored flower patterns; and padding on all the wooden parts of furniture that people contact. Furniture was designed in sets, rather than each piece for a specific place. Rugs and wallpaper were decorated similarly. Green carpets were particularly popular. Miniatures were the preferred form of art. Porcelain was usually flower patterned. There was a great love for things that were small and playful. Sedlmayr said that this was perhaps the most recognizable movement of the era (1948). All homes had glass vitrines with collections of small objects and souvenirs (Althöfer 1956:44–45).

22. The phrase *to have* (to own) here is being used figuratively. Property rights in Vienna are quite complex. Throughout the history of the city, the overwhelming number of residents in every class were renters (Lichtenberger 1977). Rent classifications included primary leaseholders, or *Hauptmieter*; secondary sublessors, or *Untermieter*; and tertiary users, or *Bettgehe*. Each category had different rights to use the courtyard or garden of the building, which could be leased separately to a nonresident or to any of the three categories of renters. A separate lease could restrict access to the lessor only, or it could preserve access rights to various categories of residents. The most common situation was for the persons occupying the ground-floor apartment in a house to control the design and access to the garden. This was most often either the owner of the building or the most prominent primary leaseholder.

23. The tenor of a city's attention to sexuality can sometimes be gauged by the public displays it tolerates. Adolph Glassbrenner, a Biedermeier journalist, observed love in the Volksgarten in the following passage: "The Volksgarten on the right side of the Palace was very loving yesterday evening, and more love spilled over into the neighboring areas.... I saw very many young men and women; very much love with a special view towards the rapid consummation of their passion. In the morning, a fog hung on the

park. The well-fed citizens let their children play on the grass. Here, where just last night the idea of humanity was aroused, he runs already by himself and laughs. How large everything is when one understands how to see it" (cited in Brandstätter and Treffer 1986:237). The Volksgarten was only a short walk from the Spittleberg district on the other side of the Glacis. This was one of the most notorious brothel districts in Europe. I. F. Castelli, a contemporary poet and raconteur, described them as follows: "There are in the inner suburbs small, unimportant public houses of the common classes, called 'Beiseln,' where the innkeeper offers pretty and saucy girls and where every evening two of three musicians play dance music. The most sought after of these establishments are found in the Spittleberg. Everything there is so arranged that the guests can drink, dance, and caress the girls, in whatever position desirable, as much as one wants, until one doesn't care anymore and one's purse is empty" (cited in Brandstätter and Treffer 1986:234). Finally, this was the period in which the waltz became the most popular form of public dance among the middle classes, in spite of its lasciviousness. The form required men and women, who were most often not married to each other, to hold their pelvises tightly together while whirling around the floor to a hypnotic rhythm for hours on end. No other dance form of the period required such close physical contact. The police state could easily have driven both the brothels and the public activities underground if popular culture had been the least bit puritanical about such things. This was certainly the case in East European countries after World War II. That Metternich tolerated the high level of open sexuality in the city suggests that sexual permissiveness and the patriarchal state may very well have coexisted in the Biedermeier. As Glassbrenner's observations in the Volksgarten show, this permissiveness apparently extended to middle-class women as well as men.

24. I am indebted to Jack Goody for drawing my attention to the language of flowers during a seminar he conducted on that topic at the Newberry Library in Chicago in March and April 1991. For a list of the species and their emotive content, in English, from the period immediately following the Biedermeier, see Dumont (1868). Goody determined that these meanings are quite ancient and widely distributed throughout Europe (1993). Dumont's list can be seen as reasonably reflective of the subtlety and variety of the Biedermeier flower culture.

CHAPTER 5: GARDENS OF PLEASURE

1. "Nein, also, der Garten sicher nicht. Vielleicht Haus und Garten. Man kann sich so was nur leisten, wenn man Geld hat. Das ist eine logische Folge. Ein Haus bauen kostet halt Geld. (Natürlich.) Geerbt haben wir leider nicht, also mussten wir" [Hasenhut].

2. "Naja, irgendwie schon. Was es mich nichts hätte, hätte ich das Haus nicht . . . das ist schon das ich ihn erhalten kann noch. Das zu erhalten davon schon irgendeine Opfer. Na wenn ich schon verkaufen würde, könnte es

mir wesentlich besser. Das ist schon das man das eilt. Eigentlich für niemand da Narrish steht, nur dass so lang man lebt das Stückl Erde noch habt" [Pokorny].

3. The wider public tastes of this period continued to mix the new pleasure garden style with the older, more playful Biedermeier. This is evident in the private commercial gardens that were built. Albert Weghuber, owner of a coffeehouse on the Glacis, built a Lustgarten in what a newspaper report of the time characterized as the English pleasure garden style. This meant that trees were planted in a irregular fashion around the section of the Glacis which Weghuber controlled. The design was executed by the Rosenthal gardening firm, which had gotten its start building gardens of liberty for aristocrats in the first decades of the 1800s. Unlike Siebeck's Stadtpark, which opened in the same year, Weghuber's coffeehouse garden probably had paths constructed from free curves. Two thousand people could be seated at more than three hundred tables. But then the Biedermeier elements start to accumulate. The tables were placed under two small tents and one large one to ensure protection from the weather. Free morning and evening concerts were provided by an orchestra. Running water was available in the garden. Gas lights were installed to permit use of the garden in the evening (anonymous article in *Morgen Post*, January 23, 1861:2).

4. Schultze-Naumburg wrote at a time when Jugendstil gardens were in vogue among the new lower managerial class in the city (Wahmann 1990:454). These young college graduates were usually the first members of their families to have a professional education and carried with them much of the attitudes of economic insecurity which characterized the *Kleinbürgertum*, the lower middle class. Schultze-Naumburg was very much in tune with these values. Although he himself was a member of the lower aristocracy, his critical tastes found favor among the new class. In his writing we find early mention of two concepts that figure prominently in the reactionary landscapes of the 1920s and 1930s: *Heimatsliebe*, love of home community, and *Heimatverbundenheit*, connection to the home community. That these concepts were still held by a broad cross-section of the population is evident in the use of the term *Heimat* in the declaration that established the Forest and Meadow Belt in 1905.

5. Rights to protection within the fortifications did not include uniform political rights within the villages. Some retained complete control over their area, usually through the feudal rights of a duke or bishop who "owned" the village. Others retained control except in times of war, when control switched to the municipal military commanders. A third group was entirely within the control of the municipality at all times (Baltzarek 1980:11).

6. "Die Bastei ist gefallen, der Stadtgraben verschüttet, die Innere Stadt von ihrem Steingürtel befreit worden, aber gleichzeitig mit dem Walle verschwanden die verschiedenen Alleen der Bastei, die Grasplätze und Bäume der Ravelins, die Alleen und Grasflächen des Stadtgrabens, die Alleen und ausgebreiteten Wiesen des Glacis. Wir können den Schmerz so

manchen Wiener begreifen, als er das viele Grün inmitten der Stadt vernichten sah, als die schattigen kühlen Alleen rasiert wurden und die Tummelplätze der Kinder, ihr Asyl an schwülen Sommerabenden, für immer schwinden sah."

7. The city council discovered that the Stadtpark had unintended recreational uses when people began skating on the park pond during the winter of 1867. Skating became so popular that the city council appropriated additional money to build a shelter for the skaters to change their boots and warm themselves. The shelter was completed in 1869.

8. Selleny was a landscape painter. The connection between the painter's conception of landscape and the development of the garden style has been noted by many authors (see Hunt 1990). In this case, his renderings of his design of the park so impressed the city council that only his were exhibited in the council chamber, in spite of submissions from Siebeck, Abel, and the Rosenthal group. Approval was not automatic, however. Fearing renewed problems with the citizens because of their choice of a design, a majority of the council voted to exhibit the four designs for four weeks and gauge opinion. It is not clear how long the designs were exhibited, but none of them gained popular approval. As one visitor expressed it during a council meeting, "der Park tauge nichts, er ist nicht schön und unzweckmassig" (Protokoll der Sitzung des Gemeinderathes, v24.10.1862:1480; quoted in Mollik, Reining, and Wurzer 1980:298; "The park is no good. It isn't beautiful or suitable"). In spite of the lack of ringing popular endorsement, Selleny's design was adopted.

9. "Herr Hausmann steht bei seinem Herrn, dem Beherrschen der Franzosen, gerade deshalb in besonderer Gunst, weil er der Anschauung, huldigt, die künftige Generation werde nicht nach den Kosten fragen, sondern sich mit ein glänzenden Ergebnissen einer verantwortungslosen Geldwirtschaft zufrieden stellen. Allein so weit ist es, dank den bürgerlichen Sinne, an den Ufern der Wien noch nicht gekommen und soll es auch nicht kommen. Wir wollen die Opfer kamen und bemessen welche die uns vorlegten Zukunfts Projekte erreichen."

CHAPTER 6: GARDENS OF REFORM

1. This election was filled with controversy (see Boyer 1981:247–380).

2. The main critic of these principles was Camillo Sitte. He could barely contain his contempt for these naive ideas about the sanitary uses of green space. In his essay on urban green space, he cited scientific studies of how little carbon dioxide is absorbed and oxygen produced by small clusters of trees or even forests. He relished rubbing the Stübben circle, whom he called the Engineers, in detailed analyses of forest air which showed it to be as contaminated with organic molecules and poisonous gases as any metropolis (1900:141–43). What Sitte could not have known, and why this exaggerated condemnation of forest air has never taken hold in the popular imagination, is that contemporary scientific investigations of the human reaction to forest

air have found a class of "monomolecules," like ozone and some organic gases, which have the psychotropic effect of sedatives on the nervous system. This effect is what the Viennese label *frische Luft* and seek out by walking in the woods. This is also what the Stübben circle wanted to recreate in the city with their small tree groups in the middle of crowded streets. Sitte may have been wrong in his understanding of why forest air is attractive to people, but he was right in condemning the planners as naive.

3. Lichtwark was from Hamburg. He worked from 1886 to 1914 as the director of the Hamburger Kunsthalle and built several new parks in that city. He also designed some house gardens for friends but never published the drawings. He was often either the advisor or the judge in many competitions and juries, such as Düsseldorf 1904, Darmstadt 1905, Mannheim 1907, and the magazine *Woche* in 1908. In this last capacity, he forged a powerful group of architects around his ideas, including Camillo Sitte, Josef Olbrich, Peter Behrens, Max Laeuger, Fritz Schumacher, Hermann Muthesius, Paul Schultze-Naumburg, Ferdinand Avenarius, Fritz Encke, Walter von Engelhardt, Friedel Gildemeister, Friedrich Bauer, Leberecht Migge, Harry Maass, and Camillo Karl Schneider. Sitte, Olbrich, Behrens, and Schneider worked in Vienna at one time or another (Klausch 1971:99).

4. These distinctions are subtle but important for understanding the varieties of vernacular styles in functionalist gardens. For an example of this, see the discussion of the difference between Pionier and Siedler gardens of refuge in Chapter 8.

5. "Lässt sich die Illusion einer freien Landschaft auf engen Raum zwischen grossartiger Architektur nicht erreichen, so ist das stilistisch Gegebene der streng architektonische Garten der aus der Noth eine Tugend macht" (Lichtwark 1883:110). A more detailed analysis of Lichtwark's ideas on urban planning and garden architecture is available in Fischer (1961).

6. Lichtwark's most invective rants were saved for the architects and planners who imposed a pure engineering vision on the tasks without including human emotional satisfaction with buildings and spaces as part of the systemic requirements of good design. In this respect he was closer to Sitte's ideas about the compatibility of practicality and taste than to the "Sanitation First" utilitarianism of Stübben (Fischer 1961; Collins and Crasemann Collins 1986).

7. He was right, but the gardens that developed in the twentieth century bear little similarity to the geometric fantasies of Lebisch. The real gardens of the Kleinbürger and the farmer turned out to be war gardens designed to feed hungry children.

8. Wagner's own comments on green space in the city are contained in a short essay, *The Metropolis* (1911), in which he set forth his plans to redesign the twenty-second district to accommodate 150,000 in 30,000 apartments on a thirty-by-twenty-block grid with a 50 percent built density. Here the green spaces would function to break the monotony of the street line every two blocks. These breaks themselves would be two blocks. In the center of the grid woud be a three-by-sixteen-block *Luftzentrum*, airdome. One hesitates

to call it a central park because it would not be a place one would choose to visit. Fixed in its place in a grid by straight lines, it would provide a place for the air to settle. All of the important cultural and institutional buildings of the district would face this park, just as they do the Ringstrasse in the central city. The airdome would offer no obstruction to their architectural precedence but would instead provide the properly reverent setting in which their power could be best appreciated.

9. Earlier views of the sanitizing effects of landscape stressed viewing it, rather than moving around in it. See, for example, Reil (1803) or Burrow (1822). This was essentially the eighteenth-century Enlightenment view of landscape as revelation of the power of nature.

10. "Man hat die Gärten die Lungen der Stadt genannt, und das sind sie in der That. Sie sind das erste und letzte Heilmittel, der wichtigste Regulator für den Athmungsprozess einer Stadt. Man kann den Winden nicht gebieten aber man kann die Strassen erweitern, um der Luft Raum zu verschaffen; man kann neue Hauser bauen, um der Übervölkerung der alten abzuhelfen, man kann Bäume pflanzen und Gärten anlegen; man kann endlich—das ist freilich für Wien die Ideal—um all die günstigen Dispositionen zu vereinigen, das Cottage-System der Engländer adoptieren" (Harry 1869:1). Harry was probably Heinrich Ferstel, the Ringstrasse architect and designer of the university building, who, together with another leading Ringstrasse architect Rudolph von Eitelberger, had published *Das bürgerliche Wohnhaus und das Wiener Zinshaus* the previous year (see below). This book introduced the English cottage system to Vienna. Ferstel would be neither the first nor the last architect to try to drum up business through commentaries in the press.

11. The founding of the Vienna association followed the attempts in other countries to establish the same kinds of single-family detached house communities: Mühlhausen in Alsac; Napoleon III's settlement for workers in Paris; Prince Albert's settlement in England; and in Germany, the Schönberger Wharf settlement in Berlin, the Railroad employees settlement in Stuttgart, and the English Quarter in Dresden, as well as similar settlements in Hamburg and Munich (Banik-Schweitzer 1967:242).

12. Ground plans of the landscapes of Steinhof are available in a psychiatric journal celebrating the opening of the institute (Berger 1907:22). The ground plan of Mauer-Öhling is available in the information bulletin the province supplied to physicians to help them refer patients (Anonymous 1914).

13. The chapel is Otto Wagner's only church, St. Leopold's on Steinhof. It is more a functionalist tour de force than house of spirituality. The furnishings and decorations by his colleagues at the Sezession and the Wiener Werkstatt are among the most beautiful accomplishment of the Viennese art nouveau movement. Because the chapel sits within a still functioning institution for emotionally handicapped people, it can only be visited on Saturday afternoons.

14. This may have been a reference to the Chicago World's Fair of 1893, itself a model of the beaux arts rejection of functionalism. The implication in

the label for Steinhof is that this institution would be both functional and beautiful.

15. The hierarchy was more thoroughgoing than the arrangement of relative degrees of violent behavior. Haiko and colleagues noted the hierarchy among the care providers which was military in form: patient-care provider, patient-physician, care provider-physician, family member-care provider, family member-physician, and among the care providers, ward nurses-head nurses. Inferior-superior statuses were maintained by strict adherence to uniform dress, deferential speech and behavior, and a need-to-know formula for dispersing medical information which rarely included either the patient or the family members.

16. The name of the unsigned, undated pamphlet is *The Provincial Sanitarium of "Steinhof" in Vienna (Austria) XIII*, and the place of publication is Vienna. The passage is cited in Haiko, Leupold-Löwenthal, and Reissberger (1981:10) and seems to be a partial translation of a longer passage of the same nature in the final report of the planning committee of the institute, published the previous year (1909:103).

CHAPTER 7: GARDENS OF REACTION

1. Gröning and Wolschke-Bulmahn researched the history of ideas surrounding professionalization of landscape architecture in Germany from the turn of the century through the 1950s (Gröning and Wolschke-Bulmahn 1986, 1987a; see also 1987b for an English summary of the third volume; Wolschke-Bulmahn 1990). Their work was indispensable in my efforts to understand the relationship between reactionary political ideologies and gardens in general and Fascist landscapes in particular. The discussion of their work in this chapter cannot do justice to the enormous effort they went through to trace individual planners and architects from their initial contact with reactionary ideas in the youth movements of the pre–World War I period through the Third Reich. They showed quite clearly that the reactionary attitude toward the landscape and the romantic return to the agricultural Gemeinschaft preceded the expression of loyalty to Führerprinzip and continued to dominate the work of the most important of these architects through the 1950s. Long after the political means for realizing these ideals were lost, the artistic means for doing so remained.

2. For a discussion of the history of this movement's organization in Vienna, see Eder (1983) and Keller (1985). Both works focus on the colonization by nudists in the 1920s, 1930s, and 1950s of beaches and wilderness areas in the Lobau, a swampy wooded area on the right bank of the Danube. Brandstetter (1981) put the movement in its political context. Nudism is now relatively mainstream in Viennese culture and has lost it power to shock bürgerlich sensibility.

3. In her book Applegate outlined the connection between the emergence of nationalism in early nineteenth-century Germany and the use of the term *Heimat* in this expanded metaphorical sense (1990:1–19). It developed along

with the concepts of *Nation, Staat,* and *Volk* as part of the vocabulary of German public, bourgeois life. It contrasts with the *Öffentlichkeit,* the public life, to bring to mind "the restricted and secure society of childhood memory, the very word would seem to emanate from, as well as refer to, the society of the hometown burgher, the unabashedly local German" (ibid.:8; see also Sheehan 1978).

4. There were two separate youth movements, one for the children of bürgerlich families and one for the children of working-class families. These movements had different rhetorics and different goals, even if the core activities were the same. The working-class movement stressed the very real skills of learning to live off the land and developing the confidence in moving from place to place by foot because the realities of unemployment, lack of housing, and lack of general relief among the poor made these essential skills. Working-class children had no choice but to learn self-sufficiency. They, too, sang songs of the joys of wandering. The lyrics emphasized the solidarity of the wandering group rather than the Heimat they would find at the end of their quest (Wolschke-Bulmahn 1990:29). This discussion concerns the bürgerlich group only. The working-class group will be discussed in the next chapter.

5. For a fascinating account of the attitudes and activities of antimoderns in the United States, see Lears (1981) and Schmitt (1969). The similarities to the Viennese and other Central Europeans is startling, suggesting that at least in the industrial core at the turn of the century there was something very much like the postulated universality of experience for the bourgeoisie.

6. As mentioned in the preceding chapter, this motif was used by the city of Vienna on the cover of the Motivenbericht for the Wald und Wiesengürtel project in 1905. Its use reflects the importance of the symbol very early in the growth of the antimodern movement. The Christian Socialist ideologues who supported the development of the forst preserve were well ahead of their peers in seeing the popular appeal of a program that linked landscape to Heimat.

7. Monism is the philosophical system that attempts to derive all that is knowable from a single principle. In the late nineteenth century, many biologists in Europe, led by Ernst Haeckel, the man who coined the term *ecology,* saw the principle of Darwinian evolution as the appropriate starting point for a new monist school. Francé was a cofounder in 1906 with Bölsche and Stallmeyer of the German Monist Federation (Wolschke-Bulmahn 1990:84). For his work, Herbert Spencer, the British sociologist who coined the phrase *survival of the fittest,* is among the best known monists in the anglophone social theory. The school of social Darwinism which he engendered is a monist system. Francé's impact on Central European thought was as pervasive as Spencer's would be in the anglophone world. There are significant differences between the two thinkers. For Spencer, the ecological dimension, and especially the local community, was of far less importance than the struggle itself. This is quite understandable since Spencer's world was one in which members of his society had established highly successful social

organizations in environments quite distant from the home community. His evolutionism had to take this into account, and as a result individual qualities played a greater role in Spencer than in Francé.

8. In his book *Die Entdeckung der Heimat* (1923), for example, he wrote about how he first came to understand the Law of *Lebensgemeinschaften* (ecological communities) as follows: "You know where I came to understand these ideas? In a small, quiet valley, where the mill stood on the bank of the stream, the discreet forest behind it, the illuminated fields and blue mountains on the edge of the heavens: My true loving Heimat was the key to the secret for me. From its undoing of complexity, I derive my entire philosophy and this work is the basis of my life" (1923:64). The implicit method is that the principles are self-evident once one has broken from the metropolis and put oneself on the vantage point in the landscape from which the interrelationships can be seen. Since his readers had presumably experienced this Gnostic moment, no further evidence was necessary.

9. The three most active Francé followers were Bronsart, Tenschert, and Viergutz, who collectively published a journal in the 1920s devoted entirely to the application of Francé's law of nature to social issues. Francé himself published a journal in the 1920s which was specifically devoted to racial issues (Wolschke-Bulmahn 1990:87).

10. In the reissue of *Die Entdeckung der Heimat* in 1982, Tenschert wrote in his foreword that Francé was one of the originators of the ecology movement. Tenschert affirmed the importance of Heimat and the importance of keeping the idea of the Volk as central to the protection of nature and the environment. He interpreted the contemporary green movement as the outbreak of a consciousness of nature, Heimat, and *Volkstum* (peoplehood) and ascribed to each Volk its own specific natural environment (1982:7–8; cited in Wolschke-Bulmahn 1990:90).

11. Christaller's contribution is particularly interesting. To avoid any of the hazards of spatial crowding or urban sprawl in future generations, the planners wanted to build the most harmonious balance between village size and access to markets. Christaller worked over regional maps, laying down complex combinations of "K" rings to prepare alternative densities of villages and towns. The planners in the RKF could then pick the density they wanted depending on the final population sizes. Christaller was committed to a rational approach to settlement form and was less political than idealistic. He belonged to the Social Democratic Party in the 1920s, when that party led the movement on settlement policy. Through this connection, he led the committee on settler and small farmer settlements. When the Nazis took power, he submitted a settlement plan for the Reich which brought him to the attention of the new powers. He had never shown himself to be particularly democratic and accepted the authoritarian structures of the Reich as the best opportunity to implement his settlement ideas (Gröning and Wolschke-Bulmahn 1987:13–14).

12. The most radical approach to the movement in nature ideal was Frei Korper Kultur (FKK). Based on the notion that any restriction to the body's

movement is deleterious and freeing the body from the constraints of clothing is healthful, this movement initiated the nudism, or naturism, wave in Euro-American culture. Followers of the movement were persecuted as deviants in puritanical bürgerlich Vienna, in spite of the acceptance of the underlying principle. Devotees retreated to the most inaccessible areas of the city, such as the Lobau and the isolated shores of the blind arms of the Danube. One group carried the idea of nudism into a social theory, founding a nudist colony in the Lobau in the 1920s. Calling themselves the Indians of the Lobau, they styled their community after the native communities of North America (Keller 1985). These were among the first of a series of anarchist communities which arose in the aftermath of World War I (Brandstetter 1981).

13. The first inside the boundaries of Vienna was established in 1909 in the Rosenthal near Steinhof and the Baumgartner Höhe. After that, there were no recorded organized efforts to establish garden associations until the war forced people to begin to grow their own food (Siller and Schneider 1920:5).

14. According to Frau Czermak, the group knew nothing about gardening. The farmer sold them a piece of land that lay on the eastern slope of a valley running north to south. It was the first part of the valley to accumulate snow in the autumn and for the snow to melt in the spring. It was in shadow most of the morning, and the ground was always wet. In spite of the unfavorable environmental conditions, the gardens were built and have remained in existence under the auspices of the same organization for more than ninety years.

CHAPTER 8: GARDENS OF REFUGE

1. In this chapter, I am speaking about three different forms of garden district. I use *cottage district* to refer to the development of single-family detached homes in landscaped parcels, in the tradition of the gardens of pleasure. I use *garden settlement* to refer to the 1920s movement to establish leaseholds on rowhouse apartments with attached garden land for working-class families. I use *garden colony* to refer to the allotment garden associations in the tradition of the Schrebergärten. These leases apply to the garden land only. The primary residence of the lessee is elsewhere.

2. "Ohne Garten ist in unsere Zeit eine menschenwürdige gesunde Lebensführung so gut wie unmöglich. Wir betonen immer wieder die wirtschaftliche Bedeutung der Kleingarten, aber jeder Weitblickende muss sich sagen, dass die erzieherischen und gesundheitlichen Werte, die eine Schrebergartenanlage in sich schliesst, noch bedeutungsvoller sind."

3. For a discussion of the living situation of factory workers immediately before World War I, see Bolognese-Leuchtenmüller (1983).

4. Any landowning entity could lease land to the small garden associations. Following the tradition of the old Arbeitergärten, employers with large land holdings were often encouraged by trade unions to provide garden

land for use by pensioned workers and their dependents. The security of providing additional foods augmented the meager size of pension benefits in the early years of trade unions. After the city, the federal railroad was the second largest lessor of garden lands, which can still be seen today along the right-of-ways traveled by the commuter trains. For a fuller discussion of the role of such paternalism in the founding of Viennese garden associations, see Förster (1983). The practice did not play a leading role in this movement.

5. The people who organized themselves into a cooperative building materials buyers' group and built the settlement at Rosenhügel took to calling themselves *pioneers* after the English founders of the consumer cooperative movement, "the pioneers of Rochdale" (Neurath 1923:18; cited in Novy 1981:47).

6. "Ja, Man kann sich ihn zu Nutze machen, das heisst, ich kann Gemüse anpflanzen, kann sich das Gemüse zum Kochen verwenden, ich kann Kräuter anpflanzen, kann die Kräuter auch zum Kochen verwenden. Ich kann drinnen, meine Kinder können spielen oder wir können mit den Kindern spielen, das ist . . . dient zur Unterhaltung" [B. Lahr].

7. [Mr.:] "Einen Nutzgarten würd ich's nicht nennen—nicht mehr—weil wir keine Nutzung ziehen. [Mrs.:] "Ja, wir sind, wir haben's gehabt, wir ham Tomaten, wir ham Kartoffeln, wir ham Salat gehabt und da is es, bei einem Zweipersonenhaushalt wird es zuviel. Und das Obst konnten wir nicht mehr verarbeiten, es wollt es keiner mehr" [Miklas].

8. "Man hat genau gewusst welche Nachbarin, welche Kräuter gehabt hat, und man ist einfach zu ihr gegangen und hab gesagt 'Bitte, kann ich das ausborgen?' Da hat man sich gar nicht ingenirt und nieeinander hat es gestört wenn man sich etwas ausborgt hat, und ohne auch damit eine Verpflichtungen zugehen und etwas zurückgeben müssen. Man hat einfach gesagt, 'Wenn du etwas brauchst, komm' her.' Das war eigentlich etwas sehr positives."

9. "Wir haben erstmals in der Gemeinschaft gelebt. Wir haben keinen Kindergarten gebraucht. Wir sind hier in der Gemeinschaft aufgewachsen, das Verhältnis zu Mitmenschen" [Sinn].

10. Among what we today would call alternative lifestyles, the cooperative garden settlements supported vegetarians and teetotalers, wilderness hikers, nudists, aerobic gymnastics, natural healers, and communal living arrangements. There were women's support groups and free daycare services that began with early infancy. There were nature lovers clubs, music societies, a home guard militia, a folklore society, pigeon keepers, bee keepers, and, of course, a garden club. There were extension classes in gardening and communal living. Adolph Loos, chief architect of the movement, taught a course on the settler as discoverer, in which he exhorted the pioneers to "learn how to live." Greta Schütte-Lihotzky, the century's major innovator in kitchen design, taught courses on social living arrangements. Max Ermers, the leading policy planner for the city's office of cooperative settlements, taught a course on the settlement as a cultural problem. Each cooperative

established homes for war orphans and homeless children, both from the municipality, and once in an emergency action, from Berlin. Teenagers volunteered to "parent" these orphans and involve them in childhood activities such as swimming and ball games, which the war had prevented them from enjoying.

11. "Naja, Bildung, weil ma jo eigentlich immer mit Menschen z'samm kommt, die was, wie soll ma sogn, naturverbunden san, und da hat ma die . . . ma is ka . . . wir ham hier (?) da heraussen net, was abgebrannt is, net, das Genossenschaftshaus, ham wir eine Gaststätte . . . und die war eine alkoholfreie Gaststätte, und des hat bei . . . und da war auch der Schachclub, und so die Vereine, der Gartenverein, drinnen und es hat sehr beigetragen, die Menschen zu formen, kultivieren . . . . wie a Pflanzerl aufbauen, net. Wir ham . . . durch des hamma eigentlich mit de Siedler dann Kontakt gekriegt, ja, und hamma Veranstaltungen ghabt und hat aner den anderen gformt, net. So wie in an Wald, wann viel Bäume san, müssen sie grad sein, weil sie net schief können" [Stangl].

12. "Und im Winter wenn alle in ihren Wohnungen waren, ist es sehr, sehr selten dort vorgekommen dass man sich gegenseitig besucht haben. Aber alle haben sich auf den Sommer gefreut. Wenn wir in dem Garten zum ersten Mal im Frühjahr gekommen sind nach dem Winter, haben alle geschaut wer ist denn schon da oder dort und es hat Leuten gegeben die schon sehr früh in den Garden gezogen sind. . . . Es war keine Freundschaft, sondern eine sehr, sehr gute Nachbarschaft. Es hat jeder dem anderen geholfen. Es hat keinen elektrische Strom gegeben. Wir haben alle mit Petroleum beleuchtet und geheizt. Es ist vorgekommen dass manchen das Petroleum ausgegangen ist und wenn man vergessen hat es zu kaufen, dann hat man natürlich die Nachbarn gebeten 'Borgen sie uns Petroleum für unserer Lampen?' und es war selbstverständlich, dass man den die anderen geborgt hat. Die Nahrungsversorgung war nicht so gut damals und hat man sich untereinander ausgeholfen" [Shirmer].

13. "Richtig. Das Stimmt. Das ist der Grundbesitz, wo ich sagen könnte, das gehört mir oder das gehört uns. Wo ich sagen könnte, da bin ich auf eigenem Grund und Boden" [Klinger].

14. "So ist es! Es hat mich selber gewundert, das war, als ich mein erstes Grundstück gekauft habe, das hat mich emotionell wahnsinnig berührt (?) das besagte Grundstück, das war (?) Quadratmeter, Steinfeld, Wiese, also nichts Berühmtes, war auch kein Nutzgarten, war nix da, nur wenige dünne (?) von fünf cm und mit Unkraut und allem, aber das hat mich emotionell stark berührt, da hat mi net amal das Haus so stark berührt, da hat mi net amal das Haus so stark berührt, wei' wohnen muss i ja wo, net, aber das erste Grundstück, das hat mich . . . es g'hört ein Stück der Erde Dir, so das, i weiss net, das hat mich irrsinnig berührt. Heut' empfind' i das nimmer so (?) gewöhnt ja, aber das erste Mal war's für mi scho' a Ereignis, muss i scho' sag'n! Ich könnt' das begründen weil meine Vorfahren immer Besitzer waren, aber ich weiss nicht, ob das wirklich der Grund ist. Vielleicht ist das also (?), dass

der Mensch also so eine Beziehung hat oder braucht, vielleicht g'hört das dazu. Ich hab' mir immer gedacht, vielleicht weil ich also aus einer Sippe komme, die immer Eigentum hatte, aber das muss net stimmen" [Adler].

15. "Stimmt auch, ja. (Eigentumsgefühl?) Des glaub i. Also wie es jetzt, wie es jetzt aussieht, es haben sich sehr viele Leute . . . also wie es, wie die Zeit gwesen ist, also 1900 . . . also 1965 und 64, 65, 66, so um diese Jahreszeit, hat man getrachtet auf ein eigenes Grundstück, oder irgend auf ein eigenes Land, wo ma a bissl von der Stadt irgendwo rausfahren kann. Aber diese Leute, die jetzt praktisch im Burgenland oder in Niederösterreich oder irgendwo gebaut ham, na also die ham sich übernommen, also mir persönlich da, also wir können jo jeden Tag und in der Nacht und jederzeit kann ich des geniessen. Diesen, diesen Garten. Weil wenn ich da am Abend z'Haus komm und setz mich da her und, und trink was weiss i, a kühles Bier, wenn's sehr heiss is, oder mir ist zu heiss in der Wohnung, dann setz i mi da in Garten raus und da kann ich mich in irgendeiner Art, sag ma, wohl fühlen, net" [Kaschauer].

16. [Mr.:] "Nein, das wichtige Gefühl ist, dass man es besitzt." [Mrs.:] "Das ist ein bissl schwierig, diese zwei deutschen Begriffe auseinanderzuhalten." [Mr.:] "Ja. Es ist . . . heisst, dass man darüber verfügt, dass es einem zur Verfügung steht ausschliesslich (Man kann das haben, wenn man will?)." [Mr.:] "Ja. (Und?)" [Mr.:] "Und dass es Eigentum ist, das heisst . . . .(ist mehr eine gesetzlich?)." [Mr.:] "Ja. Egal ob man im Grundbuch steht oder nicht. Und wenn man kann Eigentum haben und hat trotzdem nichts davon, wenn das irgendwo ist und jemand anderer dort wohnt" [Donnenberg].

17. [Mrs.:] "Nein, das ist nicht, weil es ghört der Genossenschaft." [Mr.:] "Das Gefühl hab ich nicht (lachen). Es ist nicht Besitzerstolz, sondern Benützerfreude. Mhm. (Aber es ist möglich, so wie Herr Brenner? heute morgen dass man, das geschildert haben, dass es sich Ihre eigene Stückchen?)." [Mrs.:] "Ja, das schon." [simult. Mr.:] "Wir sind die Benutzer." [Mrs.:] "im weitesten Sinne gesehen, nicht?" [Mr.:] "Aber kein Besitzerstolz." [Mrs.:] "Wir sind so ehrlich und sagen, es gehört nicht uns. Wir sind hier nur, also, Mieter und halten das in Schuss, so gut wir können" [Michalice].

18. "Nein. Ich hab ein nahes Verhältnis dazu. Ich hab auch zu meiner Frau ein nahes Verhältnis, aber sie ist nicht mein Eigentum. Jenseits der formaljuristischen Geschichten. Der Garten hat schon sein Eigenleben. Ich hoff, dass Sie auch ein gutes Verhältnis zu mir hat oder es ist so wie Haustiere, wirklich dressiert, Eigentum. Es ist ja bei uns mit dem Beruf so schwierig. Wir haben auch lang überlegt, ob wir . . . und eigentlich ist ja diese Form des Nichtprivateigentums für uns sehr ungünstig. Wenn wir mal hier weggehen, ist ja alles weg, was wir hier hinein investiert haben" [Mitterhofer].

19. "Der Kleingarten fasziniert uns in Hinsicht. Die individuelle Vielfalt an Farbe und Form und die persönliche Beziehung zum Bauwerk steht im krassen Gegensatz zu unserer Stadtwohnung. Er beweist, dass wir selbst gestalten wollen, es sehr gut können und damit Freude haben, wenn dir Möglichkeit und Rechtfertigung gegeben ist. . . . Das Basteln und Bauen ist natürlich Notwendigkeit. Der Schrebergärtner baut seine eigenwilligen

Konstruktionen nicht der Kunst zuliebe. Der Kleingärtner baut und konstruiert aus den Gegebenheiten heraus. Er passt seine Idee dem gerade vorhandenen Material an" (Auböck, Köhler, and Mutensky 1972:57).

20. For a fuller discussion of the reactionary tendencies of the early settlement movement, see Hoffmann (1983).

21. Franz Lebisch was the Jugendstil landscape architect whose garden design postcards were published by the Wiener Werkstatt. His work was discussed briefly in the preceding chapter.

22. The Third Reich had its own ideas about what small gardens should look like. Gröning found a widely distributed brochure from the Reichsbund Deutscher Kleingärtner e. V. from 1940 which set out to regulate and normalize the different garden types, giving nonconforming gardens two years to redesign themselves to follow the guidelines (Steinhaus 1940:45; cited in Gröning 1984:758).

23. For Howard, the garden city was a solution to unlimited city growth without loss of community and identity with a specific locale. His proposal had eight features, only some of which related to housing and gardening: (1) the garden city land is held in common, reducing speculation by removing land from the market; (2) the population of the garden city has a 30,000-person limit; (3) the uses of land for residence and industrial development are kept strictly separate; (4) parcel size is controlled by the commons but should be no smaller than 6 by 31, or 186 square meters; (5) public buildings, squares, and streets should be planned; (6) workplaces should be located along the railroad right-of-ways; (7) roads and railroads are thoroughly planned; and (8) the relation between the central city and the garden city is such that residents commute easily in both directions, giving the residents of the garden city easy access to fields, hedgerows, forests, ornamental gardens, and parks. He separated public and private property and had many suggestions for public space but left private space to the taste and needs of the individuals. He saw the need for individual space as part of human nature.

24. For a more detailed discussion of the Innenkolonisation movement among the extremist groups, see Stiefel (1983).

25. "Das Eigenhaus birgt sehr schwere Gefahren für die gesamte Arbeiterschaft die nicht übersehen werden dürfen. Es untergräbt die Solidaritätsbestrebungen und Organisationsmöglichkeiten der Arbeiterschaft und hebt das Klasseninteresse der Arbeiter zum Teil auf oder vermindert es. Je mehr Arbeiter bodenständig und an das Haus gekettet werden, desto mehr werden dem Klassenkampf Kämpfer erzogen, desto geringer sind die Aussichten, erfolgreiche Lohnkämpfe zu führen und gute Sozialpolitik zu machen."

26. Müller's position served as evidence for the conservative apologists of the settlement movement until well into the late 1920s. See Hoffmann (1978) and Cassandra (1926).

27. This was the son of Camillo Sitte. Sitte himself never saw many of his ideas about the rehumanization of the city realized through the garden city movement. He died in 1903. His students were involved in the Siedlungsamt, along with those of Otto Wagner. Of the settlements that were built, two in

particular, Sandleiten and Lockerwiese, reflected the turbine squares, curving streets, and culs-de-sac that he believed provided the psychological security that enabled people to thrive in densely populated cities.

28. See note 25 above.

29. The ratio of inhabitants to number of stores was actually quite meager: 250:1. This led to long shopping lines. As a "city within a city" Karl Marx-Hof was a failure. The ratios of renters to laundry bucket were 96:1; showers, 200:1; and bathtubs, 300:1(!). This led to waiting lines for laundry and bathing facilities (Weihsmann 1985:281). In the 1970s, many apartments were modernized to include private bath and washing facilities.

30. When asked to name in which season they considered their gardens to be the most beautiful, only one respondent said that he preferred the winter. When asked to explain, he said that it was the only season in which he had the time actually to sit and look at it instead of having to work in it. All of the others mentioned spring, summer, or autumn.

CHAPTER 9: GARDENS OF RENEWAL

1. "Es ist ein Erholungsraum.... Wenn man so lebt wie wir, dann ist es ein Erholungsraum. Das heisst, es muss auch immer die Komponente, die Pflege des Gartens muss immer die zweitrangige sein. Also, ich werde nicht da arbeiten, wenn es mir Mühe bereitet. Wenn ich keine Zeit habe, keine Lust habe, dann werd ich das nicht machen. Also, die Arbeit muss lustvoll sein, sonst soll man es bleiben lassen. Es darf keine Pflicht daraus werden. Mein Naheverhältnis ist gross genug, dass ich das immer wieder mache, aber nur um es schöner zu haben als der Nachbar, das muss ich nicht. Dann Finger weg! Das ist kein Verhältnis. Natur ist Leben.... Da gibt's ja Menschen, die stehn wirklich drei Stunden früher auf, um herumzuwühlen, und dann kommen s von der Arbeit nach Haus und wühlen schon wieder. Terrorisieren darf mich der Garten nicht. Ich terrorisiere ihn ja auch nicht" [Mitterhofer].

2. "Denn jede Bewegung in der freien Natur ist gut. Und wenn ma denkt, dass i in einem Büro war, wo i den ganzen Tag eine sitzende Tätigkeit ausgeübt hab, war es ja zugleich ein, eine Erholung und ein Sport und daher hab i des also schön ... ma kommt, legt alles ab und geht in den Garten und ist ein anderer Mensch. Also nicht nur, dass man sich körperlich erholt, erholt man sich ja auch seelisch" [Michalice].

3. "Das ist richtig. Mein Garten ist ein Erholungsgarten. Auch wenn ich nicht unbedingt im Liegestuhl liege, nicht unbedingt sitze im Garten, sondern weil ich mich bewegen kann, frei bewegen kann, richtig atmen im Garten, ich kann die Vogerln hören in der Früh, ich kann die Natur beobachten, ich kann die Natur betreuen und das ist" [Himmel].

4. Petra Kramer, stated in English; June 1988.

5. "Der durchschnittliche Wohlstandsbürger von heute hat sich damit einer Auffassung angeschlossen, die erstmals nur von der Aristokratie vertreten wurde, der Ideologie vom nutzlosen Lustgarten. Nur die Aristokratie, die jede sinnvolle Arbeit sowieso als ehrenrührig empfand, konnte auf die Idee

kommen, Gärten und Parks anzulegen, die Geld kosteten, aber keine Ertrag brachten. . . . Erst das etablierte Bürgertum des vorigen Jahrhunderts konnte es sich leisten, den feudalen französischen Palastbaustil in bescheidenerem Masse zu imitieren und erfand die Villa, das Klein-Versailles inmitten eines nutzlosen Kleinparks (Gartenvilla). Die meisten heutigen Schrebergarten und Eigenheime, bei denen ebenfalls das Gebäude nutzungsfeindlich inmitten und nicht wie in unseren Breiten vormals allgemein üblich, am Rand des Gartengrundstücks steht, sind nichts weiter als kleinbürgerliche Imitationen der grossbürgerlichen Villen, die ihreseits die feudalen Schlossparks imitierten" (Marschalek 1985:10).

6. "Was heisst auch Nutz, wann ich Fisolen und ich möge schon keine mehr. Es ist auch Spielerei, Unternutz wenn Sie wollen. Nutzgarten kann man nicht sagen, in dem Sinn. Es ist ja wieder ein Ziergarten, auch wenn sie die eigenen Bohnen essen, und den eigenen Schnittlauch, ist das alles eine Spielerei, natürlich." [Mr.:] "Sind sie zehnmal so teuer wie die Besten gekauften." [Mrs.:] "Fisolen, aber man kann nicht sagen ein Nutzgarten." "Nein, Nein. Ich habe alle Kleingarten. Ein Kleingarten kann nur ein Ziergarten sein" [Czermak].

7. "Hätt' er nicht geschrebert, wer weiss, ob er noch lebert." The phrase is cited in Schmidt (1975:223).

8. "Jeder Kleingarten erspart ein Krankenbett!"

9. "Es wird heute sehr viele Zeit, Mühe und natürlich auch Geld angewendet, hochwissenschaftliche Methoden zu entwickeln und zu popularisieren, die letzten Endes als sogenannte Entspannungstechniken, wirken sollen. Aktive und Selbsthypnose, Autogenes Training, Aktive Entspannungstherapie, Medizinisches Yoga und viele andere einschlägige Formen der Psychotherapie gehören hierher und ihre grosse Bedeutung zur Lösung viele krankhafter Dynamismen ist heute unbestritten. Sie tun aber vielfach im Grundsätzlichen nichts anderes als unser lieber Hausgarten tun kann. Er zwingt uns so wie jene Methoden, mit viel sanften Gewalt, wenn wir uns mit ihm beschäftigen, uns von den bedrängenden Spannungen des Tagesgeschehens zu lösen. Wenn wir im Frühjahr Bäume schneiden, den Boden düngen, im Sommer die wachsende Pracht überwachen, Schäden beseitigen, dort und da mit sorgender Hand nachhelfen, so fällt geradezu dir Tagesspannung von uns ab; die Arbeit hat ihren eigenen ruhigen Rhythmus des Naturgeschehens, den sie uns aufzwingt, einen Rhythmus, der unruhige Hast verbietet, uns warten lehrt, uns einschaltet in das ruhigen Walten und allmähliche Fortschreiten des natürlichen Geschehens. Den Garten auch nur besinnlich zu erleben, noch mehr, ihn mit Arbeit zum persönlichen Werk zu gestalten, ist, wenn es richtig gemacht wird—wie überall gibt es auch hier Fehler durch Übertreiben oder sonstigen Fehleinsatz—eine der besten psychotherapeutischen Techniken, die wir uns vorstellen können."

10. The rhetorical structures of these postwar writings could form a study in itself. Companies that published popular gardening magazines often commissioned these books. The books typically would begin with a highly philosophical discussion of the first principles of landscape design

followed by the architect's design ideas and unreferenced photographs and ground plans for three or four gardens. These photographs were a sort of roman à clef, since the professional readers could play the game of guessing from which gardens the photographs came. The club of landscape architects was so small that everyone knew who had designed which lucrative projects. The photographs were always of well-financed projects that ordinary gardeners could rarely imitate.

11. Bertalanffy's first article on systems appeared as early as 1929. His first complete discussion, including the coining of the term *steady-state* (*Fliessgleichgewicht*), dates from the 1942 German edition of this work.

12. Ironically, Richard Neutra produced some of the most striking designs in the 1930s in southern California. Neutra was a Viennese-trained architect who moved to the United States in the early 1920s and worked with Frank Lloyd Wright. His designs integrated the house in the surrounding landscape even more fully that did Seifert's. Neutra, writing on his view of the site, said, "Anything that may serve the satisfying illusion of expanse is important. . . . Opening the enclosure around us can achieve the feeling of a much more expanding site" (1951:54). Neutra's antimodern naturism produced landscapes that favored native varieties and natural terrain. He placed his houses on the tops of hills to afford better views of unspoiled valleys. He saw this incorporation of nature as wholesome: "A return to natural wholesomeness—as much as we can reproduce it or recreate it—is more important than a romantic revival of superficial decoration, which is no longer convincing" (ibid.:60). Living in the United States insulated Neutra from the reactionary politics of landscape design during the prewar period. His designs applied the naive sensibilities of the Wandervogel and similar romantic naturist ideas to the desert hills of southern California, producing distinct landscapes of intense visual interest. Photographs of these houses were available to both designers and patrons in the postwar period, reinforcing the feeling for naturist sensibilities as separate from the extreme designs of the Autobahn and Siedlungskonzept during the Third Reich.

13. In the election of April 5, 1919, the Social Democrats won 100 seats in the 165-seat city council. The Christian Socialists won 50 seats, and three splinter parties won the rest (Brandstätter and Treffer 1986:404).

14. These figures, and the ones following, are based on a random survey of Viennese households in 1978 (Magistratsabteilung 66: 318–21).

15. "Eigentlich hatte ich in allen bisherigen Wohnungen grössere Probleme oder ein schwierigeres Verhältnis mit Nachbarn. Das ist logisch. Aber es war immer so. In den Gemeindehäusern hört man halt den Plattenspieler. In einem Gemeindehaus ist es halt das Stiegenhaus. In einem Haus empfindet das keiner als Teil des Lebensbereichs. Während hier gehört die Strasse zum Lebensbereich. Ich sag immer, das ist keine Strasse. Da gibt s auch keinen Durchzugsverkehr. Da ist eigentlich die Garage oder eben der Zugang zur Wohnung. Diese Strasse ist ein intimerer Raum als in einem Haus das Stiegenhaus" [Mitterhofer].

16. "Der soziale Raum reicht bis ins Haus hinein. Die private Sphäre reicht hinaus bis auf die Strasse. Hinter dem Haus, sieht man wie die private Sphäre in die Öffentlichkeit reicht. Es ist mir aufgefallen, dass ich die erste zwei, drei Wochen immer den Bauch eingezogen hab, wenn ich in der Badehose rausgegangen bin. Nachher hat sich das aufgehört, denn dann kannte ich den Bauch vom Nachbarn. Jeder kennt den Bauch des anderen und man erfährt sehr viel aus dem Privatleben des Nachbarn. Da kriegen Sie mit, wie der Nachbar mit seiner Frau spricht, und der Nachbar weiss, wenn du gestritten hast mit deiner Frau. Also, das ist schon sehr interessant. Erstens, weil dein Privatleben öffentlich ist, also auch, weil man sich dann bemüht, über diesen äusseren Druck, es is ja kein Druck, sondern über diese Beeinflussung, . . . es hat also einen sehr positiven Einfluss auf das Privatleben" [Mitterhofer].

17. "Ja, wir haben sehr lange gesucht, weil wir nicht in einem Innenstadtbezirk wohnen wollten, eher einen Garten haben wollten, womöglich eine eigenständige Wohneinheit. Haben da sehr heftig gesucht, ein halbes Jahr lang, uns vieles angeschaut und dass wir das hier bekommen haben, war wohl ein grosses Glück. Warum wir s bekommen haben, weiss ich nicht. Ich hab auch versucht, es herauszufinden, aber man hat es mir nicht gesagt, warum man sich entschlossen hat, das uns zu geben. Ich kann das nur vermuten. Also, ich war sehr hartnäckig. Ich habe diese Herrschaften alle sehr bestürmt. Ich war ja schon lange hier angemeldet, nur das heisst nichts. Das ist keine Garantie dafür, dass man s kriegt" [Mitterhofer].

18. There is always the potential that respondents lie to interviewers. To acknowledge that political meddling had taken place would be an admission of one's personal culpability in corruption. Ordinarily, I have found ways of discussing special treatment and patronage activities with Viennese in the past. There is a special vocabulary that permits people to discuss such things without admitting to corruption themselves. In all five interviews I kept returning to the issue of political meddling in recruitment from as many of these permissible angles as possible. I did so at both the local and the cooperative level. I am convinced that the presidents and chairmen with whom I spoke believe in their hearts that their recruitment activities have executed the values of their cooperatives and were not influenced by political favoritism. The extent to which there was a coincidence of interpretation between what was best for the community and what was best for the political linkages of the community to city hall remains a conscience-assuaging possibility. For a fuller discussion of the problems of recruiting cooperative families see Rotenberg (1992a).

19. The efforts to provide these special streets did not meet with automatic acceptance by the population. The projects also involved hidden costs. Maria Auböck, a landscape architect and keen observer of municipal green space policies, observed: "They tried Wohnstrassen, such as Wichtelgasse in Ottakring in 1978. These were too Mediterranean for the Viennese and they didn't use them. Now they are trying 'traffic-reduced' streets. These

would be with fewer cars and fewer people. In five years, the tree care costs on these will be extremely high, and the city will abandon them. Now, they are back to buying parklands" [personal communication].

20. Since these internal memos were not for publication, they are not available through ordinary archives. Given the strength of the evidence of back-peddling contained in this document, I want to explain why I consider it credible and use it here as prima facie evidence of the city's interpretation of its own declaration. My copy is a photocopy entitled "Bericht zur Grünlanddeklaration aus Sicht der Stadtstrukturplanung." A running head on the first page refers to it as "Beilage," an addendum to some other document. That other document was not attached, and I do not know what it was. A senior city planner gave it to me under the condition of maintaining his anonymity. Other city planners corroborated the existence of such memos circulating in other departments. Finally, the authors of the declaration admitted to me privately that they never expected the city to implement its provisions and that such memos would have to exist to reduce confusion in the planning departments. On inspection of the memo in my possession, these senior planners believed that the bureaucratic planning language and approach to details in the memo authenticated it.

21. This is not the place to explore the collective experience of the Viennese in the defeat of the Reich in World War II. I have mentioned these issues briefly in one short report (Rotenberg 1989) and will address them in more detail in a later study. For those who wish to learn more about the central themes involved in this experience, I recommend an insightful discourse analysis of contemporary anti-Semitism in the city developed by the Speech and Prejudice Project of the Institute of Linguistics of the University of Vienna (Cillia, Gruber, Mitten, Pelikan, Seifert, and Wodak 1988).

CHAPTER 10: GARDENS OF DISCOVERY

1. "Aber in meinem Garten gibt es nur Wiesen. Das ist etwas ganz Verwandtes. Ich hätte schon gern eher ein kreatives Durcheinander, gestaltete Unordnung. Das ist schon wichtig, denn mein Kind muss wissen, dass manchmal Sachen wachsen, die man nicht gesät hat. Keiner weiss, woher es kommt. Zum Beispiel gefällt mir, wie auch die Geschichte dieser Siedlung, lese ich ja im Laufe eines Jahres die Geschichte meines Gartens. Da wachsen ja Sachen, die sind unglaublich. Im Winter sieht man sie nicht, was ist das für ein bizarrer Busch? Und plötzlich im Frühjahr sieht man ein sonderbares japanisches Gewächs, das muss schon ewig lang hier wachsen, weil s so langsam wächst, oder eine sonderbare Geschichte. Und da bin ich keiner, der grundsätzlich alles rodet und neu macht. Da lass ich erst alles kommen und dann selektiere ich. Aber mir ist lieber ein bissl mehr Unkraut als zu wenig" [Mitterhofer].

2. "Wenn man so lebt wie wir, dann ist es ein Erholungsraum. Das heisst, es muss auch immer die Komponente, die Pflege des Gartens immer die zweitrangige sein. Also, ich werde nicht da arbeiten, wenn es mir Mühe be-

reitet. Wenn ich keine Zeit habe, keine Lust habe, dann wird ich das nicht machen. Also, die Arbeit muss lustvoll sein, sonst soll man s bleiben lassen. Es darf keine Pflicht daraus werden. Mein Naheverhältnis ist gross genug, dass ich das immer wieder mache, aber nur um es schöner zu haben als der Nachbar, das muss ich nicht. Dann Finger weg! Das ist kein Verhältnis. Natur ist Leben" [Mitterhofer].

3. "Naja, Das lebt. Da sind Regenwürmer und Igeln und Schmetterlinge und auch die Pflanzen sind ja eine Form von Lebewesen, das sind Zellen, die sich bewegen, sprechen zwar nicht, haben aber ein Bewusstsein, ist also Leben und das darf nichts mit Pflicht zu tun haben. Das muss immer freiwillig sein. Man muss immer Ruhe dazu haben, nur wenn man . . . es gibt ja so viele kleine Pflanzen, die sind so unterschiedlich. Und man muss sich das immer genau ansehen, bevor man s ausreisst. Unkraut . . . beim Rasenmähern da gibt s ja Schwammerln in der Wiese und die muss man ja sehn. Da kann man nicht so geschwind drüber. Ich mag diesen Terror nicht, der davon ausgeht, wenn man diesen Schöngartenwahn hat. Da gibt's ja Menschen, die stehen wirklich drei Stunden früher auf, um herumzuwühlen, und dann kommen s von der Arbeit nach Haus und wühlen schon wieder. Terrorisieren darf mich der Garten nicht. Ich terrorisiere ihn ja auch nicht" [Mitterhofer; all of these quotes are continuous in the transcript.]

4. As conceived by designers, the Biotop is the totality of the life space for animals and plants. Its direct translation in English is *biosphere*. When used in the context of a specific location, it can also be translated as *ecological community*. In actual practice, however, when Viennese gardeners refer to their Biotope they mean a pool of still water in the garden. The pool is left to its own devices, and over time, a living community develops within it. In Vienna, Biotope have been constructed in both public and private gardens since their value in ecological landscape was first discussed by Neuenschwander (1978, 1981).

5. "Ja, an etwas nicht ganz Gezähmtes. Ich hab eine Gartenvorstellung, die nicht mit Rasenmähern verbunden wird, also ich hab lieber ein bisserl Gestrüpp. Also insofern ist das eine Naturannäherung. Es war ein Herr da, auch von den Haus—Parteien, der wollte überhaupt alles planieren, alles gradmachen, alles ausreissen und Gras säen. Und alle Bäume rausschmeissen und neue pflanzen und da sind massiv die anderen gekommen und haben gesagt: Nein. Wir wollen hier nichts anders als die Wildnis haben, in der alles wuchert, es war, . . . also ziemlich verwunschen hat's schon ausgeschaut. . . . . Wollens aber eigentlich ein bisschen wild lassen, sodass man sitzen kann. Ich bin nicht gartentechnisch interessiert. Ich bin kein Gärtner, ich mach gern was im Garten, solange ich Lust hab. Aber nicht, dass ich jetzt jeden Tag etwas Bestimmtes machen muss und die anderen machen das auch nicht. Also, es ist so halb wild, es schaut recht nett aus; manchmal nicht. Also, man könnt mehr machen. Wenn wir fünf jeder fünfhundert Schilling gibt, kann man nichts machen. Nicht? Es stört mich nicht, wenn der Zweig bis zu mir hereinhängt, das ist mir egal. Das ist, also wir haben gesagt, wir möchten lieber Gras, also nicht in Form von Rasen, sondern Pflanzen, also so ver-

schiedene Gräser oder so was. Also, es muss nicht dieser gepflegte Rasen sein, wo alles ausgezupft wird, nicht?" [Lietsch].

6. "Wir merken dadurch, dass wir das Fallobst lassen, zum Beispiel sehr viel Vögel kommen und essen, picken, also Nahrung für Kleintiere ist also genug da. Und sichtlich reflektiert niemand auf die paar Zwetschken. Und wir lassen sie hängen, und das find ich also völlig richtig.... Wir haben nur heuer Rattenplage gehabt und da wurde also Rattengift gespritzt und darum haben wir uns diesen Sommer eigentlich nicht sehr viel aufgehalten, was mir auch leid getan hat" [Lietsch].

7. "Bei 'einheimisch' denken wir durchaus regionalpatriotisch. Für einen Bewohner des schweizerischen Mittellandes sind Pflanzen aus den Alpen oder dem Jura bereits nicht mehr einheimisch, und ein Gartenbesitzer in Köln sollte kein Pflanzenmaterial von der Nordseeküste oder dem Rheinischen Schiefergebirge mit nach Hause bringen. Das 'kleinkarierte Denken' geht sogar noch weiter: Wer auf Moränenschotter wohnt, holt sich keine Pflanzen vom nahen Kalkgebirge, selbst wenn die Distanz nur ein paar Kilometer beträgt. Das hat seine Gründe: Mit Ausnahme von Allerweltsarten wachsen die Pflanzen nicht zufällig an unterschiedlichen Standorten. Dieser sind nämlich durch ganz besondere Voraussetzungen wie Klima, Bodenbeschaffenheit, Hangneigung, Konkurrenz durch andere Arten bedingt. Darum kann hier nicht einfach eine Liste mit für den Naturgarten geeigneten Pflanzen folgen, denn jeder Naturgarten soll ja anders aussehen—nämlich angepasst an die örtlichen Verhältnisse."

8. "Die Ausprägungen der Gartengestaltung entstanden demnach immer als Folge der jeweiligen Lebensauffassungen. Unsere Forderungen an den Garten heute sind möglichst individuelles Gartenleben und Kontakt mit lebendiger Natur. Das Ergebnis soll ein Garten für den täglichen Gebrauch sein.... Das Finden einer überzeugenden Gesamtgestaltung für einen Garten, organisch aufeinander abgestimmt und optimal nutzbar mit dem Wohnhaus eng verbunden, ist anstrengende Gedankenarbeit.... Richtig ist immer, die Gartenplanung vom 'grossen' ins 'kleinen' zu entwickeln. Je einfacher und selbstverständlicher ein Garten wirkt, desto schwieriger war manchmal der Weg zu diesem Ergebnis."

9. "Zum Zweck des Gartens ist die Repräsentation geworden. Verschwunden ist die begeisterte Amateurgärtnerin mit dem Strohhut in einem zwar unübersichtlichen, aber mit Blüten und Früchten strotzenden Garten. Der Kampf mit dem Unkraut, der in diesen Gärten immer verloren wurde, ist für pure Zweckmässigkeit darangegeben worden. Auf der anderen Seite deuten viele Indizien darauf hin, dass Menschen nach alternativen Lebensreformen in eine 'heilen' Welt suchen. Viele verlassen die Stadt und gehen aufs Land. Das Leben im Freien ist wieder zu einem erstrebenswerten Abenteuer geworden. Der Garten mit seinen alten Aufgaben ist eine wichtige Einrichtung, um eine neue Beziehung zum Leben in und mit der Natur zu gewinnen. Seine ursprüngliche Aufgabe ist es, Kulturpflanzen zu sammeln. Nutzen ist nicht unbedingt identisch mit Geniessbarkeit; auch die Freude am lebendigen Grün, das Arbeiten mit dem 'Material Pflanze' gehören, als

Begegnung mit der Natur, zum Nutzen einer Pflanze. Wirkliche Sehnsucht nach der Natur führt von selbst zum nützlichen (natürlichen) Garten. Von solch einem Naturgarten zu einem künstlerisch gestalteten Garten ist es ein weiterer Schritt."

10. "Die Natürlichkeit einer Grosslandschaft ist vom Planer in einen Garten umzusetzen, wo die Natur zu einer Kunstlandschaft wird. Der Gestalter sieht die Natur aus seine Warte und bestimmt die Schwerpunkte. Jeder Landschaftstyp hat seine besonderen Schwerpunkte. Es sind diese besonderen Eigenschaften, die den Betrachter fesseln, die ihn dazu reizen, den Ort immer wieder aufzusuchen, die ihm bei Nennung spontan als Bild erscheinen. Dazu gehören die Struktur der Erdoberfläche, die Farbe des Materials sowie Farbe und Habitus der Pflanzen."

11. "The rustle of Nature's life is silenced in the stillness of thought" (Hegel 1970:7; cited in Pugh 1988). It could be argued that even in Kent's day, the appearance of a pristine nature was illusory. If so, it was an illusion maintained by the entire culture.

12. "Auch vor der Haustür, also in der täglichen städtischen Umwelt, hat man die letzten Reste der Natur durch Surrogate ersetzt, und unsere abgestumpftes Bewusstsein reagiert nicht mehr, wenn kostbare Brachflächen rigoros planiert und mit Cotoneaster verödet werden, wenn in klotzigen Betontrögen auf dem Strassenpflaster ein paar Pflanzen wie Tiere im Zoo ausgestellt werden. In den Balkonkästen blühen die Plastikgeranien, an unseren Strassen grünen die ersten Kunststoffbäume, und Duftsprays mit Waldgeruch ersetzen das Erleben des echten Waldes. Während hochgezüchtete Rosen ihren Geruch verlieren, perfektioniert man den Ersatz: In den Kaufhäusern duften parfümbestäubte Blumen aus Plastik."

13. Nohl's survey research is based on Bavarian urban populations. Viennese landscape critics accept this research as valid for Vienna as well. Whether they are justified or not is an issue that I cannot resolve. It is entirely possible for one survey's results to reflect the similarity in the priority of various factors in other cities (as intuited by sensitive critics) but to obscure differences in the order of magnitude between the factors. It is also possible for the sensitive critics to read into the survey from another city the desired outcomes for their own city. Until someone actually replicates Nohl's work in Vienna, both of these possibilities make this entire discussion tentative. My reason for discussing Nohl's findings in terms of the Viennese experience revolves around the role of aesthetics in ecological gardening within the landscape discourse.

References

Abel, Lothar. 1876. *Garten-Architektur*. Vienna: Lehmann und Wentzel.
———. 1878. *Die Gartenkunst in ihren Formen planimetrisch entwickelt*. Vienna: Carl Gerold's Sohn.
Allinger, Gustav. 1953. *Das Gartenheim*. Munich: Verlag F. Bruckmann.
Althöfer, Heinz. 1956. "Der Biedermeiergarten." Ph.D. dissertation, University of Munich.
Anonymous. 1781. *Über die Kleiderpracht im Prater*. Vienna.
———. 1826. *Allgemeine Deutsche Gartenzeitung* 9.
———. 1828. *Wiens öffentliche Gärten, Bäder, Theater mit Angabe der Eintrittsprise und der Sehenswerten Kunstausstellungen*. Vienna.
———. 1861. "Ein Park auf den Glacis." *Morgen Post* January 23, 2.
———. 1869. "Die öffentlichen Gärten Wiens." *Die Presse (Lokalanzeiger)* May 16, 1.
———. 1909. *Schlussbericht des Landesausschusses für das Erzherzogtum Österreich unter der Enns über die Errichtung der niederösterreichischen Landes-Heil- und Pflegeanstalten für Geistes- und Nervenkranke am Steinhof, Wien XIII*. Vienna.
———. 1912. "N. Oe. Landes-Heil- und Pflegeanstalten für Geistes- und Nervenkranke 'am Steinhof' in Wien, XIII." In *Die Irrenpflege in Österreich in Wort und Bild*. Halle: Carl Marhold.
———. 1914. *Kaiser Franz Joseph-Landes-Heil- und Pflegeanstalt in Mauer-Öhling*. Vienna: Verlag des niederösterreichischen Landesausschusses.

———. 1954. "Soziales Grün in Wien." *Der Aufbau* 24:10–11.
Applegate, Celia. 1990. *A Nation of Provincials: The German Idea of Heimat*. Berkeley: University of California Press.
Arbeiter-Zeitung. 1921. "Ein Fest der Arbeit: Der Eröffnung der Kleingartensiedlung Rosenhügel." *Arbeiter-Zeitung* 44 (February 14):6.
Auböck, Maria. 1975. *Die Gärten der Wiener*. Vienna: Jugend und Volk.
Auböck, Maria, G. Köhler, and P. Mutensky. 1972. *Schrebergärten in Wien*. Vienna: Authors' Collective.
Auböck, Maria, and Ernst Makovetz. 1975. *Historische Grundlagen der natürlichen Landschafts Wiens*. Vienna: Institut für Freiraum- und Erholungsplanung.
Auer, Alfred. 1974. *Wien und seine Gärten*. Vienna.
Avenarius, Ferdinand. 1899. "Piepenbrinks im Garten." *Kunstwerk* 12.
Bacherer, Gustav. 1843. *Schattenrisse und Querstriche aus den Reisepapieren des Michel Teut, ans Licht gestellt durch G. B.* Darmstadt.
Baltzarek, Franz. 1980. "Das territoriale und bevölkerungsmässige Wachstum der Grossstadt Wien im 17., 18., und 19. Jahrhundert." *Wiener Geschichtsblätter* 35(1): 1–29.
———. 1982. "Introduction." In *Grün in der Grossstadt: Geschichte und Zukunft europäischer Parkanlage unter besonderer Berücksichtigen Wiens*, edited by R. Schediwy and F. Baltzarek, 1–8. Vienna: Tusch.
Banik-Schweitzer, Renate. 1967. "Die Cottage-Anlage in Wien Währing." *Wiener Geschichtsblätter* 22:240–52.
———. 1968. "Der Türkenschanzpark. Ein Abriss seiner Entstehungsgeschichte." *Wiener Geschichtsblätter* 23:343–53.
Bellamy, Edward [1880]. 1960. *Looking Backward*. New York: Penguin.
Benjamin, Walter. 1977. *The Origin of German Tragic Drama*. London: Verso.
Berchtold, Klaus, ed. 1967. *Österreichische Parteiprogramme 1868–1966*. Vienna.
Berger, Franz. 1907. "Baubeschreibung der-n-Ö Landes-Heil- und Pflegeanstalten für Geistes- und Nervenkranke 'am Steinhof' in Wien XIII." *Psychiatr.- Neurologischen Wochenscrift* (October 8): 21–27.
Bermann, Moritz. 1881. *Maria Theresa und Josef II: In Ihrem Leben und Wirken*. Vienna.
Bernatzky, Aloys. 1960. *Von der mittelalterlichen Stadtbefestung zu den Wallgrünfächen von heute: Ein Beitrag zum Grünflächeproblem deutsche Städte*. Berlin: Patzer Verlag.
Bernd, H., J. Karasz, and B. Kleedorfer. 1988. *Über Höfe und Dache: Verborgenes Grün in der Stadt*. Endbericht. Vienna: Bundesministeriums für wirtschaftliche Angelegenheiten-Wohnbauforschung.
Bertalanffy, Ludwig von. 1948. *Theoretische Biologie*. Ann Arbor: University of Michigan Press.
Bobek, H., and E. Lichtenberger. 1978. *Wien: Bauliche Gestalt und Entwicklung seit der Mitte des 19 Jahrhunderts*. Vienna: Verlag Hermann Böhlaus Nachf.

Böckh, F. H. 1823. *Merkwürdigkeiten der Haupt- und Residenzstadt Wien und ihrer nächsten Umgebung*, Volume 2. Vienna.
Bolognese-Leuchtenmüller, Birgit. 1983. "Immer und von allem das Wohl der Arbeiter im Auge habend, scheute die Firma weder Kosten noch Mühe . . ." Zur Wohnsituation der Fabriksarbeiter in den österreichischen Industriegebieten vor dem Ersten Weltkrieg. In *Die Zukunft liegt in der Vergangenheit: Studien zum Siedlungswesen der Zwischenkriegszeit*, edited by Margit Altfahrt, Birgit Bolognese-Leuchtenmüller, Wolfgang Förster, Robert Hoffman, and Dieter Stiefel. Volume 12. *Studium zum Geschichte der Stadt Wien*, 37–60. Vienna: Franz Deuticke.
Botz, Gerhard. 1975. *Wohungspolitik und Judendeportation in Wien 1938 bis 1945: Zur Funktion des Antisemitismus als Ersatz nationalsozialistischer Sozialpolitik*. Vienna: Geyer-Edition.
Boyer, John W. 1981. *Political Radicalism in Late Imperial Vienna: Origins of the Christian Socialist Movement, 1848–1897*. Chicago: University of Chicago Press.
Brandstätter, Christian, and Günther Treffer. 1986. *Stadtchronik Wien: 2000 Jahren in Daten, Dokumenten und Bildern*. Vienna: Verlag Christian Brandstätter.
Brandstetter, Gertfried. 1981. "Anarchismus als Alternativbewegung: Zur soziologischen Bewertung des Anarchismus in der Ersten Republik am Beispiel der Siedlungsbewegung." In *Das Geistige Leben Wiens in der Zwischenkriegszeit*, edited by N. Leser, 34–45. Vienna: Österreicher Bundesverlag.
Breitenmoser, Urs, and Urs Schwarz. 1981. "Der Naturgarten." In *Grün in der Stadt*, edited by Andritzky and Spitzer, 224–29. Reinbek bei Hamburg: Rowoht.
Bronsart, H. von. 1923. "Objektive Philosophie." *Der Zwiespruch* 5(17):5.
Burckhardt, Lucius. 1981. "Gartenkunst wohin?". In *Grün in der Stadt*, edited by Andritzky and Spitzer, 256–64. Reinbek bei Hamburg: Rowoht.
Bürgerstein, A. 1907. *Die K. u. K. Gartenbaugesellschaft in Wien (1837–1907)*. Vienna.
Burrow, G. M. 1822. *Untersuchung über gewisse die Geisteszerrüttung betreffende Irrthümer und ihre Einflüsse auf die physischen, moralischen und bürgerlichen Verhältnisse des Menschen*. Leipzig.
Cassandra. 1926. "Der Wille des Proletariats zum Eigentum." *Schönere Zukunft* 1:900.
Cillia, Rudolf de, Helmut Gruber, Richard Mitten, Johanna Pelikan, Katharina Seifert, and Ruth Wodak. 1988. "'Wir sind alle unschuldige Täter! . . .' Antisemitismus im öffentlichen Diskus Österreichs seit 1986." Zwischenbericht. Projekt "Sprache und Vorurteil." Vienna: Philology Institute, University of Vienna.
Collins, George R., and Christiane Crasemann Collins. 1986. *Camillo Sitte: The Birth of Modern Urban Planning*. New York: Rizzoli.
d'Avigdor, Elim H. 1873. *Der Wienfluss und die Wohnungsnot. Ein Vorschlag*. Vienna.

References

Dumont, Henrietta. 1868. *The Floral Offering*. Young Lady's Parlor Library Series. Philadelphia: Theodore Bliss.

Eder, Ernst Gerhard. 1983. "Lobau-Indianer: Lebensäusserungen mit Prinzipieller Affinität zur Alternativbewegung. Historische Lern- und Orientierungsbeispiele für eine menschenwürdiger Gesellschaft." Master's thesis, Geisteswissenschaftlichen Fakultät, University of Vienna.

Eitelberger, R., and H. Ferstel. 1860. *Das bürgerliche Wohnhaus und das Wiener Zinshaus*. Vienna.

Engels, Friedrich [1887]. 1955. *On the Housing Question*. Moscow: Foreign Language Publishing House.

Ernst, Kurt, ed. 1975. *Aufsatzwettbewerb der Leopoldstädter Volks- und Hauptschulen, Schuljahr 1974/75. "Die Bedeutung der Grünanlagen in der Stadt."* Vienna: Bezirksvorstehung Leopoldstadt.

Erp-Houtepen, Anne van. 1986. "The Etymological Origin of the Garden." *Journal of Garden History* 6(3): 227–31.

Falke, Jakob von. 1884. *Der Garten, seine Kunst und Kunstgeschichte*. Berlin.

Fassbender, E. 1893. *Erläuterung zum Entwurf eines Generalregulierungsplans über das gesamte Gemeindegebiet von Wien*. Vienna.

Fellinger, Karl. 1972. "Referat." In *Der XVIII. Kongress der Grünen Internationale in Wien*. Vienna.

Fellner, Ferdinand. 1860. *Wie Soll Wien Bauen? Zur Beleuchtung des "Bürgerlichen Wohnhauses" des Herren Professor R. v. Eitelberger und Architekt Heinrich Ferstel, mit einigen Bemerkungen über die Wiener Baugesetze*. Vienna.

Filippi, Moriz. 1905. "Friedhöfe." In *Wien am Anfang des XX Jahrhunderts*, edited by the Österreichische Ingenieur und Architekten Verein, Volume 1, 361–64. Vienna: Gerlach und Wiedung.

Fischer, Alice. 1961. "An Analysis of the Writings of Alfred Lichwark as They Apply to the City and Civic Improvement." Master's thesis, Columbia University.

Fischer, Friedrich. 1971. *Die Grünflächenpolitik Wiens bis zum Ende des Ersten Weltkrieges*. Vienna: Springer Verlag.

Fischer, Hermann. 1929. *Mittelalterliche Pflanzenkunde*. Munich.

Förster, Wolfgang. 1983. "Bauen für eine bessere Welt? Von den Fruhsozialisten zur Kurzarbeitersiedlung." In *Die Zukunft liegt in der Vergangenheit*, Volume 12, 61–76. Vienna: Franz Deuticke.

Foucault, Michel. 1965. *Madness and Civilization*. New York: Random House.

———. 1980. "The Eye of Power." In *Power/Knowledge: Selected Interviews and Other Writings 1972–77*, edited by C. Gordon, 146–65. New York: Pantheon.

———. 1986. "Of Other Spaces." *Diacritics* (spring): 22–27.

Francé, Raoul Heinrich. 1908. "Das Gesetz des Waldes." *Der Wandervogel. Zeitschrift des Bundes für Jugendwanderungen "Alt-Wandervogel"* 3(7/8): 100–105.

———. 1923. *Die Entdeckung der Heimat*. Stuttgart.

Fuchs, E. 1909. *Illustrierte Sittengeschichte vom Mittelalter bis zur Gegenwart. Renaissance*. Munich.

Fuhrmann, F. 1766. *Historische Beschreibung und kurz gefasste Nachrichten von der Römisch, Kaiserl, und Königlichen Residenz-Stadt Wien und ihren Vorstädten.* Vienna.
Furttenbach, Joseph [1640]. 1988. *Architectura Recreationis.* Berlin: Reprint VEB Verlag für Bauwesen.
Gaheis, F. d. P. A. 1794. *Spazierfahrten in der Gegenden um Wien.* Vienna.
Gälzer, Ralph. 1987a. *Vergleich der Grünsysteme Europäische Grosstädte mit Jenem vom Wien.* Wissenschaftliche Studie im Auftrag der Magistratsabteilung 18—Stadtstrukturplanung. Beiträge zur Stadtforschung, Stadtentwicklung und Stadtgestaltung, Volume 17. Vienna: Magistrat der Stadt Wien, Geschäftsgruppe Planung und Stadtentwicklung.
———. 1987b. "Gedanken zur Gestaltqualität städtischer Grünräume." In *Gestaltete Lebensraum: Gedanken zur örtliche Raumplanung.* Festschrift für Friedrich Moser, edited by the Institut für Örtliche Raumplanung, Technische Universität/Vienna. Vienna: Picus Verlag.
Goebel, Ferdinand. 1909. "Soziale Briefe." *Der Wanderer* 2(2): 46–48.
Goody, Jack. 1993. *The Culture of Flowers.* Cambridge: Cambridge University Press.
Gottdeiner, Mark. 1985. *The Social Production of Urban Space.* Austin: University of Texas Press.
Gradmann, Eugen. 1910. *Heimatschutz und Landschaftspflege.* Stuttgart.
Greif, Franz. 1966. "Der Erwerbsgartenbau von Wien: Ein Beitrag zur Problematik der Landnutzung am Grosstadtrand." *Geographischer Jahresbericht aus Österreich* 31:1–29.
Gröning, Gert. 1984. "Gestaltung im Kleingarten." *Das Gartenamt* 33:755–60.
Gröning, Gert, and Joachim Wolschke-Bulmahn. 1986. *Natur in Bewegung: Zur Bedeutung Natur- und freiraumorientierter Bewegungen der erste Hälfte des 20. Jahrhunderts für die Entwicklung der Freiraumplanung. Die Liebe zur Landschaft.* Part 1. *Arbeiten zur sozialwissenschaftlich orientierten Freiraumplanung,* Volume 7. Munich: Minerva Publikation.
———. 1987a. *Der Drang nach Osten: Zur Entwicklung der Landespflege im Nationalsozialismus und während des Zweiten Weltkrieges in den "eingegliederten Ostgebeiten." Die Liebe zur Landschaft.* Part 3. *Arbeiten zur sozialwissenschaftlich orientierten Freiraumplanung,* Volume 9. Munich: Minerva Publikation.
———. 1987b. "Politics, Planning and the Protection of Nature: Political Abuse of Early Ecological Ideas in Germany, 1933–45." *Planning Perspectives* 2:137–48.
Gross-Hoffinger, Anton Johann [Hans Normann]. 1833. *Österreich wie es ist. Erste Teil: Wien wie es ist.* Leipzig: Eschrich.
Günther, Harri. 1985. *Peter Joseph Lenné: Gärten/Parke/Landschaften.* Stuttgart: Deutsche Verlags Anstalt.
Habekern. 1926. "Die Wiedergeburt." *Der Jugendbund im G.D.A.* 16(5): 90–91.
Habermas, Jürgen. 1979. *Communication kimthe Evolution of Society.* Boston: Beacon.

Habsburg, Kaiser Joseph von (II). 1766. "Proclamation on the Opening of the Prater." *Wienerisches Darium* (Wiener Zeitung, April 7).

Haiko, Peter, H. Leupold-Löwenthal, and M. Reissberger. 1981. "'Die Weisse Stadt'—Der Steinhof in Wien: Architektur als Reflex der Einstellung zur Geisteskrankheit." *Kritische Berichte* 9(6): 3–37.

Hajós, Géza. 1989. *Romantische Gärten der Aufklärung: Englische Landschaftskultur des 18. Jahrhunderts in und um Wien*. Vienna: Böhlau.

Hampel, C. 1902. *Die Deutsche Gartenkunst*. Leipzig.

Hannerz, Ulf. 1992. *Cultural Complexity: Studies in the Social Organization of Meaning*. New York: Columbia University Press.

Harbers, Guido. 1952. *Der Wohngarten: Seine Raum- und Bau-Elemente*. Munich: Verlag Georg D. W. Callway.

Harl, Otto. 1979. *Vindobona-Das römische Wien*. Vienna.

Harry. 1869. "Die öffentlichen Gärten Wiens." *Die Presse (Lokalanzeiger)* (May 16): 1–2.

Hassinger, Hugo. 1910. "Beiträge zur Siedlungs- und Verkehrsgeographie von Wien." In *Mitteilungen der K. u. K. Geographische Gesellschaft*, Volume 53. Vienna.

———. 1912. *Wiener Heimatschutz und Verkehrsfragen*. Vienna.

Häusler, Wolfgang. 1980. "Von der Manufaktur zum Manschinesturm. Industrielle Dynamik und sozialer Wandel im Raum Wien." In *Wien im Vormärz: Verein für Geschichte der Stadt Wien*, edited by Renate Banik-Schweitzer. Vienna: Jugend und Volk.

Hebenstreit, W. 1832. *Der Fremde in Wien und die Wiener in der Heimath*. Vienna.

Heicke, Karl. 1918. "Kleingartenbau und Siedlungswesen in ihrer Bedeutung für eine künftige deutsche Gartenkultur." *Gartenkunst* 31:64–70.

Hennebo, Dieter. 1962. *Geschichte der deutschen Gartenkunst*. Volume 1. *Der Garten in Mittelalter*. Hamburg: Brosclek.

———. 1965. *Geschichte der deutschen Gartenkunst*. Volume 2. *Der Deutscher Garten in Renaissance und Rokoko*. Hamburg: Brosclek.

———. 1970. *Geschichte des Stadtgrüns*. Volume 1. *Von Antike bis zur Zeit des Absolutismus*. Hannover: Patzer Verlag.

———. 1980. "Gartenkünstlerische Tendenzen in Deutschland um Mitte des 18. Jahrhunderts." In *Historische Gärten in Donauraum in Geschichte und Gegenwart*, edited by Maria Auböck. Seminar Bericht. Schriftenreihe des Instituts für Landschaftsplanung und Gartenkunst der Technischen Universität Wien, Volume 1, 15–41. Vienna: Institut für Landschaftsplanung und Gartenkunst.

Hertzka, Theodor. 1890. *Freiland: Ein Soziales Zukunftsbild*. Leipzig: Duncker and Humbolt.

Hirschfeld, C. C. L. 1779. *Theorie der Gartenkunst*, Volume 5. Leipzig.

Hoffmann, Alfred. 1970. *Geschichte des Stadtgrüns*. Volume 3. *Der Landschaftsgarten*. Hannover: Patzer Verlag.

Hoffmann, Robert. 1978. "Entproletarisierung durch Siedlung? Die

Siedlungs-bewegung in Österreich 1918 bis 1938." In *Bewegung und Klasse: Studien zur österreichischen Arbeitergeschichte*, edited by Gerhard Botz, H. Hautmann, H. Konrad, and J. Weidenholzer, 713–42. Vienna: Europaverlag.

———. 1983. "Zwischen Wohnreform und Agroromantik. Siedlungswesen und Siedlungsideologie in Österreich von der Jahrhundertwende bis zur Weltwirtschaftskrise." In *Die Zukunft liegt in der Vergangenheit*, Volume 12, 5–36. Vienna: Franz Deuticke.

Hösl, Wolfgang, and Gottfried Pirhofer. 1988. *Wohnen in Wien, 1848–1938: Studien zur Konstitution des Massenwohnens. Forschungen und Beiträge zur Wiener Stadtgeschichte*, Volume 19. Vienna: Franz Deuticke.

Howard, Ebenezer. 1898. *Tomorrow: A Peaceful Path to Real Reform*. London.

Hunt, John Dixon. 1986. *Garden and Grove: The Italian Landscape Garden in the English Imagination*. London: Dent.

———. 1990. "'Ut Pictura Poesis': The Garden and the Picturesque in England (1710–1750)." In *The Architecture of Western Gardens: A Design History from the Renaisssance to the Present Day*, edited by Monique Mosser and Georges Teyssot, 231–41. Cambridge, Mass.: MIT Press.

Hunt, John Dixon, ed. 1990. *The Dutch Garden in the Seventeenth Century*. Twelfth Dumbarton Oaks Colloquium on the History of Landscape. Dumbarton Oaks, Washington, D.C.: Trustees of Harvard University.

Jackson, J. B. 1980. *The Necessity for Ruins*. Amherst: University of Massachusetts Press.

Kampffmeyer, Hans. 1911. *Die Deutsche Gartenstadtbewegung*. Berlin.

———. 1926. *Siedlung und Kleingarten*. Vienna: Verlag von Julius Springer.

Kaut, Hubert. 1975. "Wiens Gärten im 19. Jahrhundert." In *Wien-Stadt im Grünen*, edited by Alfred Auer. Vienna: Jugend und Volk.

Keller, Fritz, ed. 1985. *Lobau-Die Nackteren von Wien*. Vienna: Junius.

Kisch, Wilhelm. 1883. *Die alten Strassen und Plätze von Wiens Vorstädten*. Vienna.

Klaar, Adelbert. 1971. *Der Siedlungsformen Wiens. Wiener Geschichtsbücher*, Volume 8. Vienna: Paul Zsolnay Verlag.

Klauner, F. 1941. "Das Möbel des Biedermeiers." Ph.D. dissertation, University of Vienna.

Klausch, Helmut. 1971. "Alfred Lichtwark und der Beginn der Modernen Gartenkunst." *Das Gartenamt* 3:99–104.

Koch, Hugo. 1914. *Gartenkunst im Städtebau*. Berlin.

Koch, Matthias. 1842. *Wien und der Wiener*. Karlsruhe.

Kolakowski, Leszek. 1990. *Modernity on Endless Trial*. Chicago: University of Chicago Press.

Kortz, Paul, ed. 1905. *Wien am Anfang des XX. Jahrhunderts*, Volume 2. Vienna.

Kratochwijle, Fritz. 1931. *Die städtische Gärten Wiens*. Vienna.

Küchelbecker, J. B. 1730. *Allerneueste Nachrichten vom römisch-kayserlichen Hofe nebst einer ausführlichen historischen Beschreibung der kayserlichen Re-*

sidenzstadt Wien, und der umliegenden Örter, theils aus Geschichten, theils aus eigener Erfahrung zusammengetragen, und mit sauberen Kupffern ans Licht gegeben. Vienna.

Kunisch, Johannes, 1985. "Bäuerliche Gartenanlagen im Wandel der Zeit." In *Beiträge zur Landschaftsgestaltung in Österreich*, edited by B. Asperger, P. Hafergut, R. Ivancsics, M. Kastner, J. Kunisch, S. Leberl, P. Mayerhofer, A. Muhar, S. Muhar, P. Reitinger, W. Saiko, F. Schanda, K. E. Schönthaler, B. Stöhr, and I. Wollansky. Festschrift für O. Univ. Prof. Dr. Friedrich Woess zur Vollendung seines siebziger Lebensjahres. Vienna: Institute für Landschaftsgestaltung und Gartenbau, Universität für Bodenkultur.

Kuper, Hilda. 1972. "The Language of Sites in the Politics of Space." *American Anthropologist* 74:411–24.

Langschwert, Gabriele. 1987. *Wir Leben in der Stadt. Wie Leben Wir?* Vienna: Compass Verlag.

Lears, Jackson. 1981. *No Place of Grace: Antimodernism and the Transformation of American Culture 1880–1920*. New York: Pantheon.

Lebisch, Franz. 1908. *Wiener Jungenstil Gärten*, edited by Werner J. Schweiger. Vienna: Edition Maioli.

Le Corbusier (Pierre Jeanneret). 1935. *Oeuvre Complète 1929–1934*. Zurich.

Lefebvre, Henri [1974]. 1991. *The Social Production of Space*. London: Basil Blackwell. [Original: *La production de l'espace*. Paris: Anthropos.]

Lemmer, Ludwig. 1927. "Der Pachtgarten in der städtische Planung." *Baupolitik* 2:21–25.

Lendholt, Werner. 1973. "Professor Dr. h. c. Heinrich Weipking zum Gedanken." *Das Gartenamt* 22(8):476.

Lenné, Peter Josef. 1826. "Über die Anlage eines Volksgarten bei die Stadt Magdeburg." In *Verhandlungen des Vereins zur Beförderung des Gartenhauses in der königlich Preußischen Staaten*, Volume 2, 160–69. Berlin: Rücker.

LeRouge. 1787. "Jardins anglo-chinois ou détails de nouveaux jardins à la mode," cited in Mosser, Monique. 1990. "Paradox in the Garden: A Brief Account of Fabriques." In *The Architecture of Western Gardens: A Design History from the Renaisssance to the Present Day*, edited by Monique Mosser and Georges Teyssot, 279. Cambridge, Mass.: MIT Press.

LeRoy, Louis G. 1978a. *Natur ausschalten—Natur einschalten*. Stuttgart: Klett-Cotta.

———. 1978b. Brennessel und Rosen. *werk + zeit* 4.

Levine, Lawrence W. 1988. *High Brow/Low Brow: The Emergence of Cultural Hierarchy in America*. Cambridge, Mass.: Harvard University Press.

Lichtenberger, E. 1977. *Die Wiener Altstadt: Von der mittelalterlichen Bürgerstadt zur City*. Vienna: Franz Deuticke.

Lichtwark, Alfred. 1883. "Die Kunst und die Hygienischen Ausstellung." *Die Gegenwart (Berlin)* (July–December): 110–21.

———. 1892. *Makartbouquet und Blumenstrauss*. Munich.

———. 1909. *Park und Gartenstudien: Die Probleme des Hamburger Stadtpark-Heidegarten*. Berlin: B. Cassirer.

Loidl, Hans J. 1981. "Landschaftsbildanalyse—Ästhetik in der Landschaftsgestaltung?" *Landschaft + Stadt* 13(1): 7–19.

Longinus. 1987. *On the Sublime*. Translated by James A. Arieti. Lewiston, N.Y.: Edwin Mellen.

Loudon, J. C. 1850. *An Encyclopedia of Gardening* (German editions in 1823, 1825, and 1826). London: Longman, Brown, Green, and Longman.

Lützow, K. von, and L. Tischler. 1874. *Wiener Neubauten*, 3 Volumes. Vienna.

Mäding, Erhard. 1942. *Landespflege. Die Gestaltung der Landschaft also Hoheitsrecht und Hoheitspflicht*. Berlin.

Magistratsabteilung 22. 1986. *Grünlanddeklaration*. Vienna: Magistrat der Stadt Wien.

Magistratsabteilung 66. 1980. *Statistisches Jahrbuch der Stadt Wien, 1979*. Vienna: Magistrat der Stadt Wien.

———. 1981. *Statistisches Jahrbuch der Stadt Wien, 1980*. Vienna: Magistrat der Stadt Wien.

———. 1983. *Statistisches Jahrbuch der Stadt Wien, 1982*. Vienna: Magistrat der Stadt Wien.

Marcuse, Peter. 1986. "A Useful Installment of Socialist Work: Housing in Red Vienna in the 1920s." In *Critical Perspectives on Housing*, edited by R. G. Bratt, C. Hartmann, and A. Meyerson, 558–85. Philadelphia: Temple University Press.

Marschalek, Manfred. 1985. "Der Traum der Dr. Schrebers: Die Bedeutung des Kleingartens im Wandel der Zeit." *Arbeiter-Zeitung* (August 2):31.

Marzell, H. 1951. "Fränkische Bauerngärten." *Garten und Landschaft* 61:6–20.

Masaidek, F. F. 1832. *Wien und die Wiener aus Spottvogelperspektiv*. Vienna.

Mathias, R., ed. 1985. *Wieneu: Innenhofbegrünung. Presse- und Informationsdienst der Stadt Wien*. Vienna: Druckhaus Vorwärts.

Mayreder, Karl. 1895. *Über Wiener Stadtregulierungsfragen*. Vienna.

Meiners, C. 1794. *Kleinere Länder- und Reisebeschreibungen*, Volume 1. Berlin.

Menzel, C. A. 1825. *Magazine von architektonischen Entwürfen zur Verschönerung der Gärten*. Berlin.

Meyer, Gustav. 1859. *Lehrbuch der schönen Gartenkunst*. Berlin.

Michelis, Marco De. 1990. "The Green Revolution: Leberecht Migge and the Reform of the Garden in Modernist Germany." In *The Architecture of Western Gardens: A Design History from the Renaisssance to the Present Day*, edited by Monique Mosser and Georges Teyssot, 409–20. Cambridge, Mass.: MIT Press.

Migge, Leberecht. 1913. *Die Gartenkultur des Zwanziger Jahrhunderts*. Jena.

Mollik, K., H. Reining, and R. Wurzer. 1980. *Planung und Verwirkung der Wiener Ringstrassezone*. Wiesbaden: Franz Steiner Verlag.

Morris, William. [1890] 1970. *News from Nowhere, or an Epoch of Rest*. London: Routledge and Kegan Paul.

Mossbäck, Max. 1905. "Öffentliche Gartenanlagen." In *Wien am Anfang des XX Jahrhunderts*, edited by the Österreichische Ingenieur und Architekten Verein, Volume 1, 349–60. Vienna: Gerlach und Wiedung.

Mosser, Monique. 1990. "Paradox in the Garden: A Brief Account of Fabriques." In *The Architecture of Western Gardens: A Design History from the Renaisssance to the Present Day*, edited by Monique Mosser and Georges Teyssot, 263–80. Cambridge, Mass.: MIT Press.

Mosser, Monique, and Georges Teyssot, eds. 1990. *The Architecture of Western Gardens: A Design History from the Renaisssance to the Present Day*. Cambridge, Mass.: MIT Press.

Motivenbericht. 1905. *Motivenbericht zum Generalprojekte eines Wald- und Wiesengürtel und einer Höhenstrasse für die K. u. K. Reichhaupt- und Residenzstadt Wien*. Vienna: Gerlach und Wiedlung.

Müller, Rudolf. 1912. "Die Kehrseite des Eigenhauses." In *Der Kampf. Sozialdemokratische Monatsschrift* 5 (January 1):170.

Muthesius, Hermann. 1904. "Das englische Haus." *Anlage und Aufbau*, Volume 2. Berlin.

———. 1907. *Landhaus und Garten*. Munich.

Nehring, Dorethee. 1990. "The Gardens of Josef Furttenbach the Elder." In *The Architecture of Western Gardens: A Design History from the Renaisssance to the Present Day*, edited by Monique Mosser and Georges Teyssot, 160–62. Cambridge, Mass.: MIT Press.

Neubauer, Erika. 1966. *Lustgärten des Barock*. Salzburg.

———. 1975. "Wie es in Wien Begann." In *Wien-Stadt im Grünen*, edited by Alfred Auer. Vienna: Jugend und Volk.

———. 1980. *Wiener Barockgärten in zeitgenössischen Bedeuten*. Dortmund: Harenberg.

Neubauer, E., and M. Auböck. 1980. *Barocke Gartenkunst in Wien: Eine Ausstellung im Burggarten Glashaus vom 15.5–30.5.1980*. Vienna: Komitee für Historische Gärten.

Neubert, Wilhelm. 1853. *Schlüssel zur Bildenden Gartenkunst: Eine Anleitung zur Anregung oder Verschönung von Gärten verschiedener Grösse für Gärtner und Privatliebhaber*. Stuttgart.

Neuenschwander, Eduard. 1978. "Figl und Möglichkeiten der Neuanlage natürlicher Biotope im Stadtmilieu." *Deutsche Bauzeitung* 10.

———. 1981. "Natürliche Biotop im Stadtmilieu." In *Grün in der Stadt*, edited by Andritzky u. Spitzer, 216–23. Reinbek bei Hamburg: Rowoht.

Neurath, Otto. 1923. *Österreichs Kleingärtner und Siedlerorganisation*. Vienna.

Neutra, Richard. 1951. *Mystery and Realities of the Site*. Scarsdale, N.Y.: Morgan and Morgan.

Nohl, Werner. 1974. "Ansätze zu einer unweltpsychologischen Freiraumforschung." *Landschaft + Stadt* 13.

———. 1977. *Motive zum Besuch städischer Freiräume*. Working Paper 1. München: Technische Universität München Weihenstephan, Lehrstuhl für Landscaftsarchitektur.

———. 1979. "Der Einfluss der Ortskenntnis auf das Freiraumerlebnis." *Das Gartenamt* 28(10): 638–46.

———. 1980. "Visuelle Stimulation des Raumes und Aufmerksamkeitsverhalten der Benutzer als Bausteine einer Freiraumästhetic." *Garten und Landschaft*. Part 1, 3:194–98; Part 2, 4:290–93; Part 3, 6:482–88.

———. 1982. "Das Naturschöne im Konzept der städtischen Freiraumplanung." *Das Gartenamt* 31(9): 525–32.

Novy, Klaus. 1981. "Die Pioniere vom Rosenhügel: Zur wirklichen Revolution des Arbeiterwohnens durch die Wiener Siedler." *Umbau* 4:43–60.

Novy, Klaus, and Wolfgang Förster. 1985. *Einfach Bauen: Genossenschaftliche Selbsthilfe nach der Jahrhundertwende. Katalog zu einer wachsenden Ausstellung*. Vienna: Verein für moderne Kommunalpolitik.

Oehler, J. 1807. *Panorama von Wien*. Vienna.

Pertl, Josef. 1939. "Dauerkleingärten im öffentlichen Grün." *Gartenkunst* 52: 233–35.

Petzold, E. 1861. *Die Landschaftsgärtnerei. Ein Handbuch für Gärtner, Architekten, Gutsbesitzer und Freunde der Gartenkunst. Nach Humphrey Reptons "The Landscape Garden."* Leipzig.

Pezzl, Johann. 1807. *Die Umgebungen Wiens*. Vienna.

———. 1823. *Neueste Beschreibung von Wien*. Vienna.

Pietznigg, Franz. 1833. *Mitteilungen aus Wien. Zeitgemälde des Neuesten Wissenwürdigstens*, Volume 2. Vienna.

Posch, Wilfried, 1981. *Die Wiener Gartenstadtbewegung: Reform Versuch zwischen ersten und zweiten Gründerzeit*. Vienna: Tusch-Urbanistica.

Pückler–Muskau, Hermann Fürst v. 1830. *Briefe eines Verstorbenen, Ein fragmentarisches Tagebuch aus England, Wales, Irland, Frankreich, geschrieben in den Jahren 1826/27, 1828, u. 1829*. Munich.

———. 1834. *Andeutungen über Landschaftsgärtnerei*. Stuttgart.

Pugh, Simon. 1988. *Garden-Nature-Language*. Manchester: Manchester University Press.

Rainer, Roland. 1982. *Gärten: Lebensräume, Sinnbilder, Kunstwerke*. Graz: Akademische Druck- u. Verlagsanstalt.

Rathaus Pressebüro. 1984. "Kleingartengesetz soll novelliert werden." *Rathauskorrespondenz* (press release) (July 20): 1640–41.

Rauch, Anton. 1950. *Der Ziergarten im Kleingarten: Planung, Bepflanzung und Wartung*. Vienna: Scholle Verlag.

Realis. 1846. *Der Prater*. Vienna.

Reil, J. C. 1803. *Rhapsodien über die Anwendung der psychischen Curmethode auf Geisteszerrüttungen*. Halle.

Repton, Humphrey [1816]. 1982. *Fragments on the Theory and Practise of Landscape Gardening*. New York: Garland.

Rogge, Mieze. 1919. "Von unserem Pilster." *Jung-Wandervogel* 9(2/3): 24–25.

Roller, C. F. W. 1831. *Die Irrenanstalt nach allen ihren Beziehungen*. Karlsruhe.

Rotenberg, Robert. 1989. "A Tale of Two Squares: The Progressive Response to Waldheim's Vienna." *Anthropology of East Europe Review* 1(1): 2–10.

———. 1992a. "Recruitment and the Reproduction of Community in Cooperative Garden Estates in Vienna, Austria." *Open House International* 17(2): 17–29.

———. 1992b. *Time and Order in Metropolitan Vienna: A Seizure of Schedules.* Smithsonian Series in Ethnographic Inquiry. Washington, D.C.: Smithsonian Institution Press.

———. 1993. "On the Salubrity of Sites." In *The Cultural Meaning of Urban Space*, edited by Robert Rotenberg and Gary McDonogh, 17–30. Amherst, Mass.: Bergin and Garvey.

Rudorff, Ernst. 1880. "Über das Verhältnis des modernen Lebens zur Natur." *Preussische Jahrbücher* 45(3): 261–76.

Rust, Franz. 1924. "R. Francé: Die Entdeckung der Heimat." *Der Wanderer* 19(5/6):165.

Rybszinski, Witold. 1986. *Home: A Short History of an Idea.* New York: Penguin.

Sack, Manfred. 1972. "Reglements für deutsche Gartenlauben." *Zeitmagazin* 33:14–17.

Sahlins, Marshall. 1976. *Culture and Practical Reason.* Chicago: University of Chicago Press.

Sartori, Franz. 1809. *Länder- und Völker-Merchwurdigkeiten des österreichischen Kaiserthums*, Part 1. Vienna.

Sax, Emil. 1869. *Die Wohnungszustände der arbeitenden Classen und ihre Reform.* Vienna.

Schediwy, Robert, and Franz Baltzarek. 1982. *Grün in der Grossstadt: Geschichte und Zukunft europäischer Parkanlage unter besonderer Berücksichtigen Wiens.* Vienna: Tusch.

Scheichl, F. 1885. *Ein Beitrag zur Geschichte des gemeinen Arbeitslohnes vom Jahre 1500 bis auf die Gegenwart.* Dritter Jahresbericht der Öffentlichen Handels-Akademie in Linz a. d. Donau. Linz.

Schellenburg, Carl, ed. 1947. *Lichtwark: Briefe an Max Liebermann.* Hamburg.

Scheu, Gustav. 1919. "Zur Wohungsreform." *Der Sozialdemokrat* (April): 10–13.

Schiegerl, Gertrud, and Armin Stiegler. 1985. "Die Gärten Alwin Seiferts." Master's thesis, Technische Universität München-Weihenstephan, Munich.

Schiller-Bütow, Hans. 1979. *Die Landschaft als Vorbild: Gestaltungsanregungen für Landschaftsgärten.* Hannover: Patzer Verlag.

Schimmer, J. A. 1874. *Die Bevölkerung von Wien und seiner Umgebung nach dem Beruf und der Beschäftigung.* Vienna.

Schmidt, Franz. 1975. "Der Schrebergarten als kulturelle Faktor: Ein Überblick über das Kleingartenwesen von seinen Anfängen bis in der heutige Zeit unter besonderer Berücksichtigung des Raumes Wien." Ph.D. dissertation, University of Vienna.

Schmitt, Peter. 1969. *Back to Nature: The Arcadian Myth in Urban America.* New York: Oxford University Press.

Schorske, Carl E. 1981. *Fin-de-Siècle Vienna.* New York: Vintage.

Schultz, A. 1892. *Deutsches Leben im 14. und 15. Jahrhundert*. Vienna.
Schultze-Naumburg, Paul. 1909. *Kulturarbeiten in Wort und Bild*. Volume 2. *Gärten*, 3rd Edition. Munich.
Schwarz, Urs. 1980. *Der Naturgarten. Mehr Platz für einheimische Pflanzen und Tiere*. Frankfurt am Main: Wolfgang Krüger.
Schweizer, J. 1956. *Kirchhof und Friedhof*. Linz.
Sckell, F. L. v. 1818. *Beiträge zur bildenden Gartenkunst für angehende Gartenkünstler und Liebhaber*, 2nd Edition, Volume 2. Munich.
Sedlmayr, H. 1948. *Verlust der Mitte*. Salzburg.
Seifert, Alwin. 1927. "Was Man von Gärten Wissen Muss." *Baumeister* 25: 37–53.
———. 1929. "Von bodenständiger Gartenkunst." *Gartenkunst* 42: special issue.
———. 1933. "Architekt und Gartengestaltung." *Baugilde* 15:847–49.
———. 1962. *Ein Leben für die Landschaft*. Düsseldorf: E. Diederichs.
Sheehan, James J. 1979. *German Liberalism in the Nineteenth Century*. Chicago: University of Chicago Press.
Siebeck, Rudolph. 1856. *Das Decameron oder 10 Darstellungen vorzüglichen Formen und Charakterverbindungen aus dem Gebiethe der Landschaftsgartenkunst*. Leipzig: Arnold.
Sieferle, Rolf Peter. 1984. *Fortschrittsfeinde? Opposition gegen Technik und Industrie von der Romantik bis zur Gegenwart*. Munich.
Siller, Franz, and Camillo Schneider. 1920. *Wiens Schrebergärten, Kleingarten, und Siedlungswesen*, Volume 1. Vienna.
Sitte, Camillo, and T. Goecke. 1900. "Grossstadt-Grün." *Der Lotse, Hamburgische Wochenschrift für deutsche Kultur* 1:139–46; 225–32. Translated in 1986 as "Greenery within the City." In *Camillo Sitte: The Birth of Modern Urban Planning*, edited by George R. Collins and Christiane Crasemann Collins, 303–29. New York: Rizzoli.
Spitzer, Klaus. 1981. "Ökologische Ästhetik: Ein Weg zu neuen Gestaltungsprinzipien." In *Grün in der Stadt*, edited by Andritzky and Spitzer, 265–78. Reinbek bei Hamburg: Rowoht.
Stadt Wien. 1872. *Wiener Kommunal Kalendar und Statistischen Jahrbuch für 1872*. Vienna.
Steinhaus, Hermann. 1940. *Die Arbeiten der Kleingärtner-Organisation im Kriege*. Frankfurt.
Stiefel, Dieter. 1983. "'Die Zukunft liegt in der Vergangenheit': Innenkolonisation und nährungswirtschaftliche Siedlung als atavistische Utopie der Zwischenkriegszeit." In *Die Zukunft liegt in der Vergangenheit*, Volume 12, 101–28. Vienna: Franz Deuticke.
Stifter, Adelbert. 1844. *Wien und die Wiener*. Pesth.
Stübben, Josef. 1907. *Der Stadtbau*, 2nd Edition. Stuttgart: Kröner.
Tanzer, Gerhardt. 1982. "Spazierengehen-Zum ungewöhnlichen Aufschwung einer gewöhnlicher Freizeitsform in Wien des ausgehendes 18. Jahrhunderts." *Beiträge zur historischen Sozialkunde* 12(2): 67–72.
Tenschert, Gerhardt. 1982. "Forscher, Warner, und Prophet. Über Raoul H.

Francé und sein Werk." Introduction to R. H. Francé, *Die Entdeckung der Heimat*, 7–21. Asendorf.

Uhl, Friedrich. 1861. "Der Wiener Stadtpark." *Die Presse (Lokalanzeiger)* (December 4): 1–4.

Wagner, Otto. 1911. *Die Grossstadt, eine Studie über diese*. Vienna: Anton Schroll u. Komp.

Wahmann, Birgit. 1990. "The Jugendstil Garden in Germany and Austria." In *The Architecture of Western Gardens: A Design History from the Renaissance to the Present Day*, edited by Monique Mosser and Georges Teyssot, 454–56. Cambridge, Mass.: MIT Press.

Walpole, Horace. 1798. "History of Modern Gardening." *The Works*, Volume 2, 517–45. London.

Weber, Alfred. 1960. *Kulturgeschichte als Kultursoziologie*. Munich.

Weber, Peter, Heidrun Feigelfeld, Maria Auböck, and Wolfgang Lehner. 1986. *Kleingarten Konzept für Wien*. Magistrat der Stadt Wien, MA18-Stadtstrukturplanung. Vienna: Institute für Stadtforschung.

Weidmann, F. C. 1824. *Die Rosenbaum'sche Gartenanlage*. Vienna: Strauss.

Weihsmann, H. 1985. *Das Rote Wien: Sozialdemokratische Architektur und Kommunalpolitik, 1919–1934*. Vienna: Promedia.

Weyr, Siegfried. 1969. *Wien, Zauber der Vorstadt*. Vienna.

Widemann, J. 1805. *Malerische Streifzüge durch die interresantesten Gegenden um Wien*. Vienna.

Wiepking-Jürgensmann, Heinrich Friedrich. 1941. "Raumordnung und Landschaftsgestaltung. Um die Erhaltung der schöpferischen Kräfte des deutschen Volkes." *Raumforschung und Raumordnung* 5(1): 17–23.

Williams, Raymond. 1973. *The Country and the City*. Oxford: Oxford University Press.

Wirth, Peter. 1984. *Hausgärten planen: Entwürfe und Beispiele*. Stuttgart: Verlag Eugen Ulmer.

Wolf, Eric. 1990. "Facing Power." *American Anthropologist* 92(3): 586–96.

Wolschke-Bulmahn, Joachim. 1990. *Auf der Suche nach Arkadien: Zu Landschaftsidealen und Formen der Naturaneignung in der Jugendbewegung und ihre Bedeutung für die Landespflege. Arbeiten zur sozialwissenschaftlich orientierten Freiraumplanung*, Volume 11. Munich: Minerva Publikation.

Zobel, Viktor. 1905. *Über Gärten und Gartengestaltung*. Munich.

Zohary, D., and P. Speigel-Roy. 1975. "Beginnings of Fruit Growing in the Old World." *Science* 187:319–27.

Permissions

Austrian National Library for permission to reproduce Müller's "Plan of the Princely Rasumowsky Pleasure Garden"; Gurk's four lithographic views of the Rosenbaum Park; Nagel's lithographic ground plan of the Wieden section of the city of Vienna; and the section of the Josephinische Landesaufnahme showing the central city.

Bruckmann Verlag for permission to reproduce Figures 11 and 12 (Architects W. Eggeling and Son) from Gustav Allinger's *Das Gartenheim* (1953).

Bavarian State Library for permission to reproduce Matthäus Merian's engraving of the Neugebäude of Maximilian in Kaiser Ebersdorf.

Magistrate of the city of Vienna (MA 18) for permission to reproduce the planning maps on green space from the Planungsatlas für Wien. 2. Lieferung.

Wilfred Posch for permission to reproduce his drawing of the plans of Ehmers and Renner for enlarging the city of Vienna.

Gemeinnütziger Siedlungs-Genossenschaft Altmannsdorf und Hetzendorf Registrierte Genossenschaft M.b.H. for permission to reproduce their archive photographs for Rosenhügel.

Permissions

Stiftung Schlösser und Gärten, Potsdam-Sanssouci, for permission to reproduce Lennés plan for Pfaueninsel.

Verlag Georg D. W. Callway for permission to reproduce Guido Harbers's photo of the garden of Roland Weber.

Edition Maioli zu Wien for permission to reproduce the Franz Lebisch postcard.

Index

Abel, Lothar, 122, 140, 156
absolutism, 4, 47, 66, 135
Albrecht II (Habsburg), 36
Allinger, Gustav, 259, 264
allotment gardens. *See* small gardens
Alsergrund, 58, 104
Althöfer, Franz, 95
Altstadt (Old City), 34, 86
Am Tivoli, 237
Arbeitergärten, 209–10
Arcadian, 201–2, 236
Arensbergpark, 179
Armengärten, 209–10
art nouveau style. *See* Jugendstil
Auböck, Maria, 328n. 3, 357–58n. 19
Augarten Palace, 27, 32, 47, 79, 80, 81, 84, 249
Augsburg, 112
Austrian People's Party. *See* Österreichische Volkspartei
Auwald, 29. *See also* Lobau
Avenarius Ferdinand, 195

Baltzarek, Franz, 125, 328n. 3
Banik-Schweitzer, Renate, 170
Bavaria, 263
Bellamy, Edward, 211
Belvedere Palace, 4, 47, 53, 58, 63, 83, 179
Berger, Franz, 183
Berlin, 152, 163, 176, 235, 351n. 10
Bertalanffy, Ludwig von, 262, 356n. 11
Besserlparks, 27
Beyer, Wilhelm, 57
Biedermeier, 89–90, 337n. 2, 340n. 21, 342n. 3
Biogarten, 292
biologism. *See* Biologismus
Biologismus, 194–95, 203, 262
Biotop, 70, 189, 296, 307, 312, 359n. 4

379

Blankenburg, 102
Bodenständigkeit, 191, 194, 196–97, 266, 299
Boos, Joseph, 122
Botz, Gerhard, 208
Bronsart, H. von, 203
Brown, Capability, 72, 118, 301, 334n. 8
Burgenland, 229
Busbecq, Olgier Chislain, 329n. 9

California, 8, 356n. 12
Castelli, I. F., 109, 341n. 10
Central Cemetery. *See* Zentralfriedhof
Charlemagne, 30, 51, 329n. 10
Chernobyl, 289
Chicago, 179
Christaller, Walter, 204, 348n. 11
Christian Socialist Party, 43, 151, 167, 178, 188, 205, 206, 236, 237, 239, 272, 347n. 6
classic revival style, 104, 108, 112, 336n. 14
Clusius, Carolus, 35
conservatism, 88, 193
cooperative garden settlement movement, 206, 221–23, 226–28, 236, 240, 272, 276–77
Corvinius, Matthias, 32
Cottageviertal, 173–76
customs wall. *See* Linien wall

Darmstadt, 195
d'Avigdor, Elim, 171, 172
Deutsche Volkspartei, 188, 238
Deutschwald, 272
Döbling, 100, 104, 129, 130, 175, 179
Donauinsel, 308
Dornbach, 129
Düsseldorf, 195, 263
Dutch style, 57, 332n. 15

Eitelberger, Edler von Edelberg, Rudolph, 168, 235

Engels, Frederich, 172–73
English Garden (Munich), 112, 120
English style, 57, 67–68, 71–75, 79, 117, 123, 137, 333n. 1
Enlightenment, the, 50, 68, 73, 76, 84–85, 95, 116, 144, 186, 284
environmentalism, 193, 289. *See also* Öko-welle
Erholungsgärten, 250–58
Ermers, Maximilian, 239–40, 350n. 10
Erp-Houtepen, Anne van, 328n. 5
Esterházy Palace, 249
Eugene of Savoy, Prince, 54, 332n. 16

fabrique(s), 75–76, 107
Falke, Jakob von, 124
Fassbinder, Eugen, 42, 142, 178
Faucher, Julius, 172
Favoriten, 41
Fellinger, Karl, 258
Fellner, Ferdinand, 152, 168–73, 235
Ferdinand I (Habsburg), 32, 33, 36
Ferdinand II (Habsburg), 35
Ferstel, Heinrich Freiherr von, 152, 168–73, 235
Fiebiger, Max, 243
Fischer, Friedrich, 133, 328n. 3
Förster, Ludwig, 131, 133
Foucault, Michel, 15–19, 184, 327n. 3
Francé, Raoul, 202–4, 291, 348nn. 8–10
Frankfurt, 233
Franz I (Habsburg), 57, 66, 83, 106
Franz Josef (Habsburg), 66
Freemasonry, 74
Freihof, 237
French style, 47, 57, 67–68, 137–38, 333n. 1
Friedrich I (Habsburg), 32
Friedrich III (Habsburg), 32
Fuhrmann, F., 73–74

functionalism, 154–56, 187, 193, 228, 235, 262, 285
fundamentalism, 193
Fünfhaus, 129
Furttenbach, Josef, 51–52, 112, 331n. 9

Gälzer, Ralph, 13, 25, 305
gardeners. *See* Gärtner
gardens of paradise. *See* Paradiesgärten
Gärtner, 222–25, 230, 236, 271, 273
Gegenden, 47, 87, 186, 320
Genet, Jean, 18
German Resettlement Policy. *See* Siedlungskonzept
Gesner, Conrad, 34
Geymüller family, 68, 76
Glacis, 34, 40–41, 80, 82, 84, 86, 106, 131–35, 139, 336n. 15
Goecke, T., 161
Goldemund, Heinrich, 153, 176–77, 179, 239
Goody, Jack, 341n. 24
Gradmann, Eugen, 202
Greater German People's Party. *See* Grossdeutsche Volkspartei
Greek antique style, 56, 76
Green Party of Austria. *See* Grünen, Die
Grillparzer, Franz, 109
Grinzing, 32, 94, 123, 129
Grohmann, J., 76, 118
Gröning, Gurt, 233, 346n. 1
Grossdeutsche Volkspartei, 206
Gruber, Franz Xaver, 106
Grünen, Die, 45, 289, 303
Grünkeile, 279–80, 282, 307
Grünverbindungen, 279–80
Grünzüge, 279–80, 307
Gumpendorf, 127, 339n. 18
Gurk, Joseph, 96
Gürtel, 36, 41, 166–67, 179

Habermas, Jürgen, 4
Hacking, 129

Haeckel, Ernst, 347n. 7
Hainburg, 87
Hajós, Géza, 78
Hamburg, 325, 344n. 3
Hannerz, Ulf, 5
Harbers, Guido, 263, 300
Hassinger, Hugo, 205
Hauschild, Ernst, 210
Hausdenken, 114–15, 144
Haussmann, Baron, 131
Heicke, Karl, 233–34, 301
Heiligenstadt, 100, 129, 179
Heiligenstädterpark, 179
Heimat, 198, 201–4, 266, 288, 346–47n. 3
Heldenplatz, 139
Hénard, Eugène, 179
Hennebo, Dieter, 50, 72, 327n. 2
Hermesweise, 237
Hernals, 127
Hertzka, Theodor, 211
Herzl, Theodor, 211
heterotopia, 15–21
Hetzendorf, 101, 340n. 19. *See also* Hohenberg
Heuberg, 242
Heurigen, 93–94, 338n. 11
Hietzing, 100, 101, 104, 129, 176, 339n. 19
Himmler, Heinrich, 204
Hirschfeld, C. C. L., 81, 335n. 12
Hoffmann, Robert, 118
Hohe Warte, 100
Hohenberg, Johann Ferdinand Hetzendorf von, 55, 83
homeopathy. *See* Naturheilkunde
House of Palms. *See* Palmenhaus
Howard, Ebenezer, 206, 235, 238, 239, 353n. 23
Huber, Viktor, 172
Hügel, Karl Freiherr von, 84, 100, 101 104, 106, 156, 165, 339n. 19
Hügelpark, 176
Hunt, J. D., 123
Hütteldorf, 129

Index

381

Imperial Garden Society, 84, 106, 165
Innerkolonisation, 353n. 24
Italian renaissance style, 47, 50–51, 333n. 1

Jacquin, Josef Nicholas Prince von, 122
Josefstadt, 58
Joseph II (Habsburg), 37, 38, 41, 66, 73, 75, 80–81, 87, 88, 334n. 9
Jugendbewegung, 198–99, 347n. 4
Jugendstil, 159, 195

Kaiser Ebersdorf, 112, 141
Kaiserberg, Geiler von, 50
Kaiserin Elizabeth memorial, 159–61
Kampffmeyer, Hans, 239, 241, 243
Karl Marx-Hof, 245, 354n. 29
Kaunitz-Rietberg, Wenzel Prince, 73
Kent, William, 71–72, 118, 302
Kisch, Wilhelm, 99
Klein, Franz, 239
Kleingarten. *See* small gardens
Knapp, Johann, 106
Koch, Julius, 239
Krebs, Heinrich, 239
Küchelbecker, Johann, 73–74
Kuglerpark, 179

Laaer Strasse, 237
Laarberg, 27
Lacy, Franz Moritz Graf von, 68, 75
Lainz, 129
Lainzer Tiergarten, 27, 79
Lanauer, Gustav, 237
landscape, improvement of. *See* Landschaftsverschönung
Landschaftsverschönung, 116
Landstrasse, 104, 179
Laxenburg Castle, 122
Lebensreform, 192, 194, 350n. 10

Lebisch, Franz, 159, 195, 234, 353n. 21
Le Corbusier, 244
Lefebvre, Henri, 17
Lehnert, Johannas, 152
Leipzig, 210
Lenné, Peter Josef, 112, 120–22, 131, 133, 176
Le Nôtre, 47, 53, 333n. 1
Leopold III (Babenberger), 329n. 3
Leopold IV (Babenberger), 31
Leopoldstadt, 1, 60, 104
Lerchenfeld, 58, 127
Le Rouge, 76
LeRoy, Louis, 197–98, 303
Letchworth, 245
Liberal Party of Austria, 43, 110, 135, 188
liberalism, 67, 116, 135, 136
Lichtenberger, Elisabeth, 328n. 3
Lichtwark, Alfred, 156–58, 179, 183, 192, 195, 223, 261, 344nn. 3, 6
life-style reform. *See* Lebensreform
Linien wall, 36, 37, 39, 41, 125
Lobau, 237–38
Lockerwiese, 237, 244, 245
London, 170
Longinus, 68
Loos, Adolph, 240–43, 350n. 10
Loudon, J. C., 122
Louis XIV (Bourbon), 47
Lower Austria, 60, 150–51, 205, 208–9, 229
Lueger, Karl, 43, 151, 188, 272
Lustgärten, 49, 50, 111, 112, 329–30n. 10
Lützow, Karl von, 171
Lux, J. A., 159

Machu Picchu, 328n. 4
Mäding, Erhard, 204
Magnus, Albertus, 329n. 10
Mannheim, 195
Marchfeld, 29, 329n. 7

Maria Theresa (Habsburg), 56, 66, 75, 82, 150
Mariabrunn, 237
Marx, Karl, 23
Mauer-Ohling, 181, 183
Maximilian I (Habsburg), 32, 36, 51, 112
Maximilian I of Mexico (Habsburg), 57
Maximilian II (Habsburg), 35, 36
Maxingpark, 57
May, Karl, 211
Mayer, Hugo, 241, 242
Mayreder, Karl, 152, 239
Meidling, 129
Menzel, C., 118
Metternich, Prince Klemens, 39, 67, 87, 88, 142
Meyer, Gustav, 122, 156, 195
Meyer, Konrad, 193, 204
Migge, Leberecht, 158, 183, 189, 192, 223, 232, 235, 261
Mödling, 205, 209
Morris, William, 211
Mosser, Monique, 6, 76
Müller, Rudolph, 238, 256
Munich, 112, 120, 197, 235, 263, 303
Muthesius, Hermann, 195

Napoleon I, Bonaparte, 83, 87
national socialism, 188, 193, 194
nativism. *See* Bodenständigkeit
naturalism, 50, 144, 185
naturalness, 185
Naturfreunde, 247
Naturgärten, 68
Naturheilkunde, 210
Neubauer, Erika, 53
Neubert, Wilhelm, 122
Neugebäude Palace, 36, 50, 56, 112
Neurath, Otto, 247
Neustadt, 34–37, 53, 86
Neustift, 32, 129
Neutra, Richard, 356n. 12

Neuwaldegg, 68, 69, 75, 129, 130
New Orleans, 179
New York, 176
Niederösterreich. *See* Lower Austria
Nohl, Werner, 303–5, 361n. 13
Nüll, Edward van der, 132, 133
Nussdorf, 32, 94
Nutzgärten, 219, 225

Oberlaa sanitarium, 27
Öffentlichkeit, 116
Ohmann, Josef, 159–60
Öko-welle, 289–92
organic gardening. *See* Biogarten
Österreichische Volkspartei (ÖVP), 271–72
Ottakring, 129, 357n. 19
Otto I (Babenberger), 30

Paine, Tom, 66
Palmenhaus, 57, 106
Pannonian Basin, 29
Paradiesgärten, 36, 49, 82, 123, 329n. 10
Paris, 131, 179
Penzing, 129
Perchtoldsdorf, 189
Persia, 17, 47
Pertl, Josef, 235, 301
Petzold, Ernst, 122, 156
Philippovich, Eugen, 239
Piccolomini, Aeneas Sylvius. *See* Pious II
pioneers. *See* Pioniere
Pioniere, 223–30, 273, 305, 350n. 5
Pious II, 34
pleasure gardens. *See* Lustgärten
Posch, Wilfried, 206
Pötzleinsdorf, 27, 68, 69, 104, 129, 130
Prater, 27, 32, 79, 80–82, 234
Pronay's Garden, 100, 104, 340n. 19
Pückler-Muskau, Hermann Fürst von, 112, 119–22, 124, 140

Index

383

Pugh, Simon, 145
Purkersdorf, 212

Rasumofsky, Andreas Duke, 75
Rathauspark, 131, 139–41, 245
Rauch, Anton, 259
reactionary thought, 189–90, 192–94, 196, 246, 353n. 20
recreational gardens. *See* Erholungsgärten
Reich, German Third, 44, 193, 198, 208, 216
Remy, Ludwig von, 83
Renner, Karl, 206
Repton, Humphrey, 112, 118–20, 328n. 6
republicanism, 39, 66–67, 89
Ringstrasse, 27, 40–42, 131–41, 162, 166, 179, 183
rococo style, 57, 94, 107, 123
romanticism, 111, 116, 179
Rome, 146
Rosenbaum, Joseph, 96, 100–101, 104, 106
Rosenbaum'sche Garten, 96–98, 109
Rosenhügel, 235, 242
Rosenthal, Konrad, 75, 76
Rossau, 35, 58
Rousseau, Jean-Jacques, 66, 75, 87, 334n. 9
Rudolf II (Habsburg), 36
Rudorff, Ernst, 202
Rupprecht, J. P., 98–99, 100–101, 104

Saint Augustine, 8
St. Gall, 7
St. Marx Friedhof, 141–42
St. Veit, 129
Sandleiten, 354n. 27
Sanssouci Palace, 120, 122, 176
Sax, Emil, 171–72
Schartelmüller, Karl, 245
Schediwy, Robert, 328n. 3
Scheu, Gustav, 239–41, 243

Schiller-Butow, Hans, 300–302
Schmelz, 236, 241, 245
Schmidt, Franz, 257
Schmuckplätze, 180–81, 185, 187
Schneider, Camillo, 219, 234
Schönbrunn Palace, 27, 32, 47, 55–57, 80, 106, 130
Schreber, Daniel Gottlieb Moritz, 195, 210, 214, 258
Schrebergärten, 209–14, 216, 219, 232, 271
Schultze-Naumburg, Paul, 124, 193, 342n. 4
Schumacher, Franz, 179
Schutte-Lihotzky, Greta, 350n. 10
Schwarz, Urs, 297–99, 300, 303
Schwechat, 209
Schweizergarten, 179, 189
Sckell, F. L., 112, 119–20
Sechshaus, 129
Seifert, Alwin, 191, 193, 196–97, 261–62
Seiller, Johann Kasper Freiherr, 180–81
Selleny, Josef, 135, 343n. 8
Sennholz, Gustav, 176
Settlements Bureau. *See* Siedlungsamt
settlers. *See* Siedler
Sezession, 159
Sheehan, James, 116
Sicardsburg, August Sicard von, 131, 133
Siebeck, Rudolph, 122–23, 135–39, 157, 164, 245
Siedler, 222–25, 228, 230, 236, 253, 270–71, 273, 276, 282, 288
Siedlungsamt, 240–41, 243–44
Siedlungskonzept, 194–95, 198, 204–5
Sievering, 32, 129
Siller, Franz, 219, 234
Simmel, Georg, 163
Simmering, 141, 152
Sitte, Camillo, 161–65, 180, 343n. 2, 353n. 27

Sitte, Siegfried, 239, 353n. 27
small gardens, 27, 209, 219. *See also* cooperative garden settlement movement
Social Democratic Party of Austria (SPÖ), 44, 194, 205, 211, 230, 236, 238, 242, 271–72
Spencer, Herbert, 347n. 7
Spiegelgrund, 237
Spitzer, Klaus, 302–3
Stache, Friedrich, 42, 131
Stadtpark, 131–39, 179, 343nn. 7, 8
Stammersdorf, 94
Steckhofen, Adrian van, 55
Steiner, Max, 238
Steinhof, 181–84, 185
Stifter, Adelbert, 336n. 16
Strahemberg Palace, 96
Strebersdorf, 94
Stübben, Josef, 42, 151–52, 165–66, 178, 180, 331n. 16
Suleiman I, 36
Sullivan, Louis, 155
Superbaublock, 222, 237, 243–45, 248
Swiss gardens, 332n.14

Teyssot, Georges, 6
Trehet, Jean, 55
Türkenschanzpark, 174–76, 179
Turkish siege(s), 34, 36, 38, 53, 54, 60, 112, 124

Umlauf, Josef, 204

Versailles Palace, 47, 53
Vienna Basin, 45, 206
Vienna Woods. *See* Wienerwald
Vindobona, 30, 328n. 4
Vogelers, Heinrich, 237
Volksgarten, 36, 82, 83–84, 86, 132, 136, 159, 340–41n. 23
Vormärz, 89, 103

Wagner, Otto, 42, 152, 161, 163–64, 178, 243, 331n. 16, 344–45n. 8, 345n. 13

Wagner, Richard, 164
Währing, 127, 173, 175
Wald- und Wiesen Gürtel, 152–53, 185, 223, 278, 279–83, 307
Walpole, Horace, 302
Wandervogel, 199–202, 212, 215, 247, 262
Wasserglacis, 82, 132–33, 135
Wasserwiese, 234
Weber, Alfred, 124
Weghuber, Alfred, 342n. 3
Weipking-Jürgensmann, Heinrich Friedrich, 193, 204
Weiskirchner, Richard, 239–40
Weissenböckstrasse, 237
Weissgrund, 58
Wertheimsteinpark, 179
Weyr, Siegfried, 171
Wieden, 36, 58, 96, 104, 339n. 18
Wien Sud, 328n. 1
Wiener Neustadt, 33, 44, 206
Wienerwald, 29, 32, 40, 58, 75, 96, 130, 149–52, 189, 212, 216, 219, 237, 266, 281, 329n. 7
Wienportal, 159–60
Wildgarten, 189, 291–92, 295, 308
Williams, Raymond, 116
Wirth, Peter, 299–300
Wodak, Ruth, 14
Wolf, Eric, 46
Wolschke-Bulmahn, Joachim, 346n. 1
Worpswede, 237
Wurstelprater, 80, 82

youth movement. *See* Jugendbewegung

Zentralfriedhof, 41, 141–44, 178, 181–82
Zentralstelle für Wohnungsreform in Österreich, 239–40
Ziergärten, 48, 68
Zobel, Victor, 195

LIBRARY OF CONGRESS CATALOGING-IN-PUBLICATION DATA

Rotenberg, Robert Louis, 1949–
    Landscape and power in Vienna / Robert Rotenberg.
    p.   cm.
    "Published in cooperation with the Center for American Places, Harrisonburg, Virginia"—T.p. verso.
    Includes bibliographical references (p.   ) and index.
    ISBN 0-8018-4961-6 (alk. paper)
    1. Landscape gardening—Austria—Vienna.   2. Gardens—Austria—Vienna—Design.   I. Title.
SB470.55.A9R68   1995
304.2'3—dc20   94-42624